UNITED NATIONS PEACEKEEPING IN AFRICA SINCE 1960

The Postwar World
General Editors: A.J. Nicholls and Martin S. Alexander

As distance puts events into perspective, and as evidence accumulates, it begins to
be possible to form an objective historical view of our recent past. *The Postwar World*
is an ambitious series providing a scholarly but readable account of the way our
world has been shaped in the crowded years since the Second World War. Some
volumes will deal with regions, or even single nations, others with important
themes; all will be written by expert historians drawing on the latest scholarship
as well as their own research and judgements. The series should be particularly
welcome to students, but it is designed also for the general reader with an interest
in contemporary history.

UNITED NATIONS PEACEKEEPING IN AFRICA SINCE 1960

NORRIE MACQUEEN

Longman

An imprint of **Pearson Education**

London · New York · Toronto · Sydney · Tokyo · Singapore · Hong Kong · Cape Town
New Delhi · Madrid · Paris · Amsterdam · Munich · Milan · Stockholm

PEARSON EDUCATION LIMITED

Head Office:
Edinburgh Gate
Harlow CM20 2JE
Tel: +44 (0)1279 623623
Fax: +44 (0)1279 431059

London Office:
128 Long Acre
London WC2E 9AN
Tel: +44 (0)20 7447 2000
Fax: +44 (0)20 7240 5771
Website: www.history-minds.com

First published in Great Britain in 2002

© Pearson Education 2002

The right of Norrie MacQueen to be identified as Author
of this Work has been asserted by him in accordance
with the Copyright, Designs and Patents Act 1988.

ISBN 0 582 38253 X

British Library Cataloguing in Publication Data
A CIP catalogue record for this book can be obtained from the British Library

Library of Congress Cataloging in Publication Data
A CIP catalogue record for this book can be obtained from the Library of Congress

Typeset in Baskerville MT 11/13pt by Graphicraft Limited, Hong Kong
Produced by Pearson Education Asia Pte Ltd.

Printed and bound in Great Britain by
CPI Antony Rowe, Chippenham and Eastbourne

Transferred to Digital Print on Demand 2009

The Publishers' policy is to use paper manufactured from sustainable forests.

EDITORIAL FOREWORD

The aim of this series is to describe and analyse the history of the world since 1945. History, like time, does not stand still. What seemed to many of us only recently to be 'current affairs' or the stuff of political speculation, has now become material for historians. The editors feel that it is time for a series of books which will offer the public judicious and scholarly, but at the same time readable, accounts of the way in which our present-day world has been shaped since the Second World War. The period which began in 1945 has witnessed political events and socio-economic developments of enormous significance for the human race, as important as anything which happened before Hitler's death or the bombing of Hiroshima. Ideologies have waxed and waned, the developed economies have boomed and bust, empires of various types have collapsed, new nations have emerged and sometimes themselves fallen into decline. While we can be thankful that no major armed conflict occurred between the so-called superpowers, there have been many other wars, and terrorism emerged as an international plague. Although the position of ethnic minorities improved in some countries, it worsened dramatically in others. As communist tyrannies relaxed their grip on many areas of the world, so half-forgotten national conflicts re-emerged. Nearly everywhere the status of women became an issue which politicians were unable to avoid. The same was true of the natural environment, apparent threats to which have been a recurrent source of international concern. These are only some of the developments we hope will be illuminated by this series as it unfolds.

The books in the series will not follow any set pattern; they will vary in length according to the needs of the subject. Some will deal with regions, or even single nations, and others with themes. Not all of them will begin in 1945, and the terminal date may vary; as with the length, the time-span chosen will be appropriate to the question under discussion. All the books, however, will be written by expert historians drawing on the latest research, as well as their own expertise and judgement. The series should be particularly welcome to students, but it is designed also for the general reader with an interest in contemporary history. We hope that the books will stimulate scholarly discussion and encourage specialists to look beyond their own particular interests to engage in wider controversies.

History, and especially the history of the recent past, is neither 'bunk' nor an intellectual form of stamp-collecting, but an indispensable part of an educated person's approach to life. If it is not written by historians it will be written by others of a less discriminating and more polemical disposition. The editors are confident that this series will help to ensure the victory of the historical approach, with consequential benefits for its readers.

A.J. Nicholls
Martin S. Alexander

CONTENTS

MAPS

ABBREVIATIONS AND ACRONYMS

AFDL	Alliance of Democratic Forces for the Liberation of the Congo (*Alliance des Forces Démocratiques pour la Libération du Congo*)
AFL	Armed Forces of Liberia
AFRC	Armed Forces Revolutionary Council [Sierra Leone]
ANC	African National Congress [South Africa] (or) Congolese National Army (*Armée Nationale Congolaise*)
APC	All-People's Congress [Sierra Leone]
BBTG	Broad-Based Transitional Government [Rwanda]
CAR	Central African Republic
CIA	Central Intelligence Agency [United States]
CIO	Central Intelligence Organization [Rhodesia]
CNN	Cable News Network
CSC	Supervision and Control Commission (*Comissão de Supervisão e Controle*) [Mozambique]
DPKO	Department of Peacekeeping Operations
DRC	Democratic Republic of Congo
DTA	Democratic Turnhalle Alliance [Namibia]
ECOMOG	Economic Community of West African States Military Observation Group
ECOWAS	Economic Community of West African States
ELF	Eritrean Liberation Front
EO	Executive Outcomes [commercial military organization]
EPLF	Eritrean People's Liberation Front
EPRDF	Ethiopian People's Revolutionary Democratic Front
FAA	Angolan Armed Forces (*Forças Armadas Angolanas*)
FAC	*Forces Armées Congolaise* [DRC]
FACA	Central African Armed Forces (*Forces Armées Centrafricaines*) [CAR]
FADM	Defence Forces of Mozambique (*Forças Armadas de Defesa de Moçambique*)
FNLA	National Front for the Liberation of Angola (*Frente Nacional de Libertação de Angola*)

Frelimo	Front for the Liberation of Mozambique (*Frente para a Libertação de Moçambique*)
Frolinat	Chad National Liberation Front (*Front de Libération Nationale Tchadien*)
GPA	General Peace Agreement [Mozambique]
GURN	Government of National Unity and Reconciliation (*Governo de Unidade e Reconciliação Nacional*) [Angola]
ICGL	International Contact Group for Liberia
ICJ	International Court of Justice
IGNU	Interim Government of National Unity [Liberia]
IMF	International Monetary Fund
INPFL	Independent National Patriotic Front of Liberia
JMC	Joint Military Commission [DRC]
MINURCA	United Nations Mission in the Central African Republic (*Mission des Nations Unies en République Centrafricaine*)
MINURSO	United Nations Mission for the Referendum in Western Sahara (*Mission des Nations Unies pour l'Organisation d'un Référendum au Sahara Occidental*)
MISAB	Inter-African Mission for the Supervision of the Bangui Accords (*Mission Interafricaine de Surveillance des Accords de Bangui*) [CAR]
MLC	Congo Liberation Movement (*Mouvement de Libération du Congo*) [DRC]
MONUA	United Nations Observation Mission in Angola (*Missão de Observação das Nações Unidas em Angola*)
MONUC	United Nations Organization Mission to the Congo (*Mission de la Organisation des Nations Unies au Congo*)
MPLA	Popular Movement for the Liberation of Angola (*Movimento Popular de Libertação de Angola*)
MRNDD	National Republican Movement for Democracy and Development (*Mouvement Républicain National pour la Démocratie et le Développement*) [Rwanda]
NGO	non-governmental organization
NIF	Neutral International Force [Rwanda]
NPFL	National Patriotic Front of Liberia
OAU	Organization of African Unity
ONUC	United Nations Operation in Congo (*Opération des Nations Unies au Congo*)
ONUMOZ	United Nations Operation in Mozambique (*Operação das Nações Unidas em Moçambique*)
PDD	(US) Presidential Decision Directive

Polisario	Popular Front for the Liberation of Saguia el Hamra and Rio de Oro (*Frente Popular para a Liberación de Saguia el-Hamra y Río de Oro*) [Western Sahara]
RCD	Congolese Rally for Democracy (*Rassemblement Congolais pour la Démocratie*) [DRC]
Renamo	Mozambican National Resistance Movement (*Resistência Nacional Moçambicana*)
RPF	Rwandan Patriotic Front
RUF	Revolutionary United Front [Sierra Leone]
SADC	Southern African Development Community
SADF	South African Defence Forces
SADR	Saharan Arab Democratic Republic [Western Sahara]
SAP	structural adjustment programme
SLA	Sierra Leone Army
SLPP	Sierra Leone People's Party
SMC	Standing Mediation Committee [Liberia]
SNA	Somali National Alliance
SWAPO	South West African People's Organization [Namibia]
TNC	Transitional National Council [Somalia]
ULIMO	United Liberation Movement of Liberia
UMOSOM (I-II)	United Nations Operation in Somalia
UNAMIR	United Nations Assistance Mission for Rwanda
UNAMSIL	United Nations Mission in Sierra Leone
UNASOG	United Nations Aouzou Strip Observer Group [Chad]
UNAVEM	United Nations Angola Verification Mission
UNCIVPOL	United Nations Civilian Police
UNEF	United Nations Emergency Force [Suez]
UNHCR	United Nations High Commission for Refugees
UNITA	National Union for the Total Independence of Angola (*União Nacional para a Independência Total de Angola*)
UNITAF	Unified Task Force [Somalia]
UNMEE	United Nations Mission in Ethiopia and Eritrea
UNOHAC	United Nations Office of Humanitarian Aid Co-ordination [Mozambique]
UNOMIL	United Nations Observer Mission in Liberia
UNOMSIL	United Nations Observer Mission in Sierra Leone
UNOMUR	United Nations Observer Mission Uganda-Rwanda
UNOSOM	United Nations Operation in Somalia
UNTAC	United Nations Transitional Authority in Cambodia
UNTAG	United Nations Transition Assistance Group [Namibia]
USC	United Somali Congress
ZANU	Zimbabwe African National Union

ACKNOWLEDGEMENTS

This book has turned out to be a more protracted project than originally envisaged. In large part this has been due to the nature of the subject. United Nations peacekeeping in Africa has proved to be a fast-moving target in recent years. While there is obviously no difficulty in fixing its beginnings in 1960 with the arrival of the first blue berets in the Congo, the peacekeeping endeavour in Africa remains a rapidly evolving and ever-continuing phenomenon. It offers no obvious point at which a concluding line might be drawn. Since work began on this book some three new operations have been established (in the Democratic Republic of Congo, Sierra Leone and on the border between Ethiopia and Eritrea) while three others have ended (in Angola, the Central African Republic and, again, in Sierra Leone). As a result, it often seemed that new issues were arising faster than existing ones could be written up in the ever-diminishing time available in the bureaucratic marshlands that have recently crept over British universities. The opportunity to impose some authorial will on what threatened to be a permanent work in progress came with a period of sabbatical leave. In a moderately sized department such as my own at Dundee, uncovered leave of this sort inevitably places extra burdens on already hard-pressed colleagues. I am very grateful indeed to them for their willingness to cover the spaces my absence created.

Over the period of writing, I – and certainly the finished book – benefited greatly from a number of seminars in which I was able to air some of the more conceptual and theoretical aspects of the work in hand. As well as at Dundee these took place in the Department of International Relations at the University of St Andrews, the social science research seminar at Aalborg University in Denmark and the biennial *Colóquio sobre África* at the Technical University of Lisbon. I am very grateful to the participants in these sessions for their various challenges and suggestions, many of which have been incorporated in the present text.

The general editors of the Longman Postwar World series, of which this work forms part, have been of immense help in bringing the book to publication in its present form. Martin Alexander and Tony Nicholls were afflicted with typescripts of the original draft just as they prepared for the Christmas break. With spectacular despatch both had produced extensive reports within weeks. Their observations, corrections and suggestions, which derived from the closest of readings of the text, were invaluable. I am extremely grateful to them.

Finally, thanks are due closer to home – in the most literal sense. The tolerance and equanimity (if often bemused and occasionally strained) of my wife Betsy and daughter Triona have been the foundation of the entire undertaking – as they have with all previous ones.

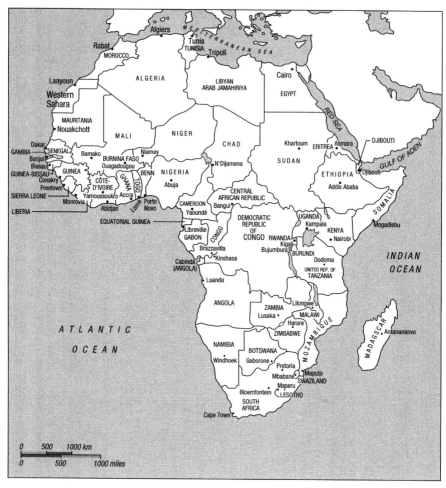

Africa

CHAPTER ONE

The Setting
The History, Politics and Law of United Nations Engagement with Africa

In his award-winning book of reportage from post-genocide Rwanda, *We Wish to Inform You That Tomorrow We Will be Killed with Our Families,* the American journalist Philip Gourevitch recalls a tense night on a remote road in an area infiltrated by anti-government guerrillas. A cry is heard from a nearby settlement and men from his convoy immediately dash off to investigate. Later, a soldier explains the reaction:

> [T]he whooping we heard was a conventional distress signal and . . .
> it carried an obligation. 'You hear it, you do it, too. And you come
> running . . . No choice. You must. If you ignored this crying you would
> have questions to answer. . . . We all come running, and the one that
> stays quiet, the one that stays home, must explain. Is he in league with
> the criminals? Is he a coward? And what would he expect when he cries?
> This is simple. This is normal. This is community.'[1]

Intended or not, this could be taken as a comment on the inadequate response on the part of the UN and the international 'community' it represented to the events of 1994 in that country. The 'Rwandan way' here described (and probably idealized) is a prescription for purposeful intervention as a response to threat, whether at the level of the village or of the international system. The UN's actual performance in Rwanda, coming in the wake of its intervention in Somalia and following the collapse of the peace process in Angola, represented for many another stage in the accumulating 'failure' of peace-keeping in Africa in the mid-1990s. It was a perception strengthened by events

---

1   Philip Gourevitch, *We Wish to Inform You That Tomorrow We Will be Killed with Our Families*
    (London: Picador, 1999), p. 34.

beyond Africa as well, in Bosnia and to an extent in Cambodia, where major UN undertakings had also struggled to live up to expectations.

In fact, this pessimistic assessment represented something of a reversal in the view hitherto. The performance of the UN in Africa prior to these tragedies was more successful than the pervasive sense of failure that spread from the mid-1990s might suggest. UN intervention had been crucial to the essentially peaceful achievement of Namibian independence in 1989–90. Although ultimately failing in its mandate to oversee a comprehensive resolution of Angola's decades-old civil war, the UN had been wholly successful in the specific task of managing the withdrawal of Cuban forces from the country in 1990 and 1991. The small observer mission in northern Chad – deployed just weeks before the Rwandan genocide began – contributed to a lasting solution to a previously intractable border problem with Libya. The record was far from uniformly bad, in other words.

These more successful interventions benefited from the diplomatic setting in which solutions were developed. All of them involved the management of clear-cut international agreements reached by well-established states, usually with diplomatic backing from beyond Africa. But this was not of itself a prerequisite for successful UN peacekeeping. Credit could also be claimed for the resolution of civil war and the management of democratic transformation in Mozambique in 1992 and 1993. The United Nations also left the Central African Republic (where it had been operating in a special relationship with other inter-governmental agencies) in a much better state than when it arrived, even if the transformation wrought was less striking and potentially less durable than those in Namibia and Mozambique.

What this shows is that perceptions of success and failure in an area as politically and diplomatically fraught as multilateral military intervention are inevitably volatile. They tend to be shaped disproportionately by the most recent impressions. The aim of this book is to present an overview of the United Nations' peacekeeping role and experience in Africa during the last four decades of the twentieth century and in this way provide an opportunity for a more distanced – and therefore more sustainable – judgement. It will pursue this primarily on the basis of a region-by-region, mission-by-mission analysis. But before we embark on that some broad conceptual and historical issues have to be explored. Firstly, we have to investigate the general evolution of the activity that has come to be described – sometimes very imprecisely – as 'peacekeeping' in the post-1945 period. Secondly, we must attempt to incorporate Africa's late colonial and post-colonial experience within broader international processes. These preliminaries are important to an understanding of some central questions. Why, for example, has the United Nations responded to African crises in the particular, sometimes inappropriate and inadequate, ways it has? What factors – of history, politics or international law – have constrained and limited these military interventions? On the other side, what has determined the character of the African crises that the UN has been called on to respond to? Why has the African state, both in its external behaviour and its internal dynamics, been so vulnerable to the violent conflicts that have brought multilateral intervention?

The elusive concept of 'peacekeeping'

The term 'peacekeeping' has come to be used to describe almost the entire range of activities that can be carried out by international military personnel. The variety of these 'peacekeeping' functions has probably found a broader application in Africa than in other parts of the world where UN military missions have been deployed. These activities have ranged from discreet observation and monitoring carried out with the lightest of touches to the enforcement of outcomes by large, combat-configured forces. Between these two extremes lies what might be called the 'classic' concept of peacekeeping based on the physical interposition of an external third force exerting moral rather than physical pressure between antagonists.

Initially, though, the military function of the United Nations was intended to take a quite different form. The roles of observation, interposition and monitoring that became the staple activities of UN military intervention from the mid-1950s onwards in fact had no place in the original conception of the UN's role which was worked out as the organization's Charter was formulated in the mid-1940s. At this stage the intention was that the United Nations would deploy military power as a forceful instrument in a global system of collective security. This vision was shared, with varying degrees of enthusiasm, by all five of the powers that became permanent members of the Security Council (the United States, the Soviet Union, Britain, France and China). At the centre of these plans was Chapter VII of the UN Charter. This covered 'Action with Respect to Threats to the Peace, Breaches of the Peace, and Acts of Aggression' and presented an extensive and precise series of commitments to be undertaken by all member states. These involved, at their most exacting, the placing of national military resources at the disposal of the Security Council once it had determined that an act of aggression or threat to international peace had taken place. The underlying aim of this ambitious approach to international security was to ensure that the United Nations would succeed where its predecessor, the League of Nations, had failed in the 1930s. One of the most notorious of these failures had in fact been in Africa when Ethiopia (then called Abyssinia) fell victim to the aggressive expansionism of fascist Italy in 1935 and 1936. The League's abandonment of Abyssinia was for many the defining moment in the decline of the organization as a significant force in international relations.

Article 39 of Chapter VII of the UN Charter made the Security Council responsible for deciding when a situation required collective security action and what form that action should take. The options available followed an escalating scale until, by article 42, the Council was empowered 'to restore international peace and security' using the 'air, sea or land forces of Members of the United Nations'. Article 43 then detailed the commitments of member states: the provision of forces and facilities to enforce Security Council decisions against 'aggressor' states. The blueprint suggested that the ensuing United Nations operations would be co-ordinated by a Military Staff Committee composed of the chiefs of staff of the five permanent members of the Security Council.

The high ambition of Chapter VII, however, was simply incompatible with the global bipolarity that soon characterized international relations in the post-1945 era. The division of the world between two competing blocs quickly overtook the international system after the UN's foundation and formed the structure within which the cold war was pursued. At the centre of the collective security system laid out in Chapter VII of the Charter was an assumption of co-operation and consensus among the five permanent members of the Security Council. With the United States and the Soviet Union constituting the two poles of the bipolar system, this emphasis on the big powers as a cohesive 'police force' regulating the behaviour of others was clearly misplaced. How could there be any prospect of viable collective security when the decisions of the Security Council, which was required to manage it, were subject to veto by its mutually hostile permanent members? In such a divided international system virtually all international crises would be seen through the opposed ideological lenses of the two sides. The objective identification of an 'aggressor' in any crisis, which was central to the collective security concept, would be impossible. The Charter itself offered no help in this. Although repeatedly making use of the term, it offered no definition of 'aggression' and so provided no legal compass. Similarly, the notion that the military staff of the permanent members could act as a unified command was nonsensical. It hardly needed the Korean War, fought out between the forces of east and west from 1950 to 1953, in which the UN played an ambiguous and ideologically partial role, to expose finally the emptiness of the original collective security ambition.[2] The United Nations, its blue flag co-opted

---

2   The Korean War was fought between North Korea (and eventually China) against a 'UN' collective security force that sought to defend South Korea against forced unification. In reality this 'UN' force was a western alliance dominated and led by the United States. Its 'UN' identity was possible only because the Soviet Union had been absent from a crucial Security Council meeting and therefore could not veto the proposal.

opportunistically by the west to legitimize its campaign, emerged from the affair with its authority and credibility somewhat compromised. While its standing in western perceptions was probably enhanced, the circumstances of the conflict and the 'international' response raised reasonable questions in the broader world about the organization's even-handedness.

It was clear by the early 1950s that if the UN was to have any meaningful security role in the cold war it would have to be in a form other than 'conventional' collective security. In fact some pointers towards such a role were already present. The UN had already been involved in 'military' operations in two parts of the post-colonial world. Military observer missions had been established in Palestine and Kashmir in 1948 and 1949 to super-vise peace agreements between Israel and its Arab neighbours and India and Pakistan, respectively. While not peacekeeping 'forces' as such, these opera-tions were based on methods of observation and interposition that were to become characteristic of the peacekeeping 'model' that later emerged. It was in 1956, though, that the first 'peacekeeping operation' as widely recognized was put in place. This was the United Nations Emergency Force (UNEF), which was deployed to separate the warring parties after the Anglo-French invasion of (and Israeli attack on) Egypt. As with Palestine and Kashmir, Suez was essentially a conflict rooted in problems of post-colonial adjustment. At this time, in the mid-1950s, the United Nations seemed well positioned to deal with such crises. In a world in which imperial ideologies were increas-ingly discredited at the western pole of the cold war as well as the eastern one, it was becoming evident that intervention by former imperial powers in post-colonial crises was unacceptable.[3] The Suez conflict drove this home when the United States made it clear to its European allies, Britain and France, that their behaviour was unhelpful to the western cause. Washington as much as Moscow was aware of the importance of manoeuvring for the favour of the new emerging 'Third World'. In such a situation the UN could provide a convenient neutral force in containing local conflicts and reducing their capacity to destabilize the already hostile relations between east and west.

Multilateral intervention by the UN thus came to be accepted by the superpowers as preferable in some situations to unilateral interference by politically or historically interested parties. Firstly, it offered a means of inoculating troubled new states against entanglement in the politics of the cold war. Secondly, it could contain local conflicts and prevent their spread to

---

3   Britain and France invaded Egypt after its nationalization of the Suez Canal (hitherto 'owned' by an Anglo-French company) in retaliation for western withdrawal from the funding of the ambitious and expensive Aswan Dam irrigation project. Israel had earlier been prompted to attack Egypt to provide a pretext for Anglo-French intervention.

the broader, possibly unstable, international regions in which they occurred. Thirdly, UN intervention could protect the sovereign independence of fragile emerging states. In this it served the interests of the more powerful states in the world by underpinning the basic architecture of the international system. The building blocks of this 'systemic' structure were territorial states. Peace-keeping, in other words, could shore-up the so-called 'Westphalian' system on which the prevailing conception of the political and diplomatic world was based.[4] This 'systemic self-interest' became an important – though often under-acknowledged – aspect of UN interventions, and has remained such into the twenty-first century. It has been a particularly significant part of the UN's interventions in Africa since the early 1960s, as we shall see. The issue acquired a greater urgency in the minds of western policy-makers after the terrorist attacks on the United States in September 2001. Subsequently the 'failed state' came to be seen as a problem not merely within its own borders and immediately around them but for the world as a whole. Without the rules and norms imposed by membership of the international system, and their acceptance by a responsible state, territories such as Afghanistan could all too easily, it seemed, become the geographical bases of global terrorist networks.

A key actor in the establishment of the Suez operation in 1956 and the subsequent elaboration of the peacekeeping concept was the second secretary-general of the United Nations, Dag Hammarskjöld of Sweden. Hammarskjöld indeed would later come to be seen, not altogether accurately, as the father of modern peacekeeping. His cerebral and introspective char-acter, along with the circumstances of his death in Africa while pursuing peace in the Congo, secured a particular posthumous image. He came to be celebrated as a heroic servant of peace determined to construct a distinct role for the United Nations as a force for conflict resolution that would replace the now defunct collective security function.

Crucially, Hammarskjöld understood the importance of political and institu-tional independence for the United Nations in the cold war. In pursuit of this independence he and his supporters in the UN secretariat and in key national delegations were both constrained and empowered by the absence of any established 'constitutional' basis for peacekeeping. No reference to the concept existed in the Charter. The original vision articulated in Chapter VII was for the UN to act as an enforcer of collective security, and this was not

---

4 The Treaty of Westphalia of 1648 followed the Thirty Years War in Europe. It laid down the principle of the territorial sovereignty of states (rather than religion or other affective relationships) as the basis of postwar international relations in Europe – and by extension those of the broader world as European power was projected through imperial expansion in the following centuries.

peacekeeping. Peacekeeping, as represented by UNEF and already suggested by the missions in Palestine and Kashmir, was about consent, neutral interposition and moral presence rather than enforcement. The nearest the Charter came to accommodating this idea was in Chapter VI dealing with the 'Pacific Settlement of Disputes'. Article 34 gave the Security Council authority to 'investigate' any situation of 'international friction', and article 36 charged it with recommending 'appropriate procedures or methods of adjustment'. But nowhere was there any explicit reference to the mechanisms of what would come to be known as peacekeeping. Later references to peacekeeping being grounded in 'article six-and-a-half' – poised between the 'Pacific Settlement of Disputes' and the enforcement actions dealt with in Chapter VII – might evoke its operational character, but were legally meaningless.

The absence of a clear constitutional base would lead in future years to many political difficulties with the peacekeeping project – in particular over its authorization and financing. But it also provided Hammarskjöld and his aides with a conceptual *tabula rasa* on which to build a new military role for the UN, one capable of accommodating the realities of bipolarity without relying on the moribund collective security mechanisms of Chapter VII. In 1958 Hammarskjöld produced a so-called 'Summary Study' derived from the political and military experience of UNEF in Suez. The intention of this was to identify 'certain basic principles and rules which would provide an adaptable framework for later operations which might be found necessary'.[5] The Summary Study was therefore a blueprint for peacekeeping. It consisted, perhaps inevitably, of a rather idealized set of prescriptions based on a fairly slim body of prior experience. Some of it had little relevance beyond Suez and, as we will see, many of the issues it raised and the precepts it advanced would be of limited application to later experience in Africa. Nevertheless, the principles outlined in the Summary Study were soon distilled into a general 'definition' of peacekeeping.

Peacekeeping, the Summary Study made clear, was not 'the type of force envisaged under Chapter VII of the Charter'. Consequently, there was no legal requirement for the protagonists in the conflict to accept intervention. These parties were generally characterized as 'host states' in Hammarskjöld's original conception, which saw the peacekeeping role as essentially one involving governments in conflict with other governments. While this was wholly appropriate to Suez (and later conflicts in the Middle East) it would have only very limited relevance to subsequent peacekeeping projects, especially in Africa, where conflicts were frequently in whole or in part 'intra-state'

---

5 The 'Summary Study' was issued as United Nations document A/3943, 9 October 1958.

rather than inter-state. What Hammarskjöld did not envisage and what has proved repeatedly to be a feature of UN interventions in Africa was a situation in which a designated 'state' in any meaningful sense simply did not exist. Had the Summary Study been constructed just two years later, the experience of the Congo, where the state was both politically contested and territorially fragmented, would no doubt have been incorporated in it. As it was, however, the Suez force, and the missions in Palestine and Kashmir before it, had been 'validated' by the clear consent of established, internationally recognized states. But in the African context this was frequently not available. 'Ownership' of the state was fiercely contested in Rwanda, Sierra Leone and Liberia in the 1990s just as it had been in the Congo in the 1960s. In Angola and Mozambique it was tenuous, while in Somalia the state had simply ceased to exist. But the principle of consent of the parties remained central to peacekeeping whether those parties were states or less formal entities. Where there were more or less responsible states involved, however, 'consent', in the terms of the Summary Study, should not be allowed to mutate into interference in the conduct of the operation. For this reason individual 'status of forces agreements' were to be reached between the UN and the state in which operations were to take place. Again, this was a principle often difficult to translate into effective practice in the African context.

In this matter of state–UN relations, the Summary Study proposed that a number of operational benchmarks that had been established by the Suez operation should henceforward be regarded as general principles. Here too there were to be resonances that were not always positive in Africa in the coming decades. One of these was the issue of freedom of movement for peacekeepers within the operational area. Although this would appear to be a minimum prerequisite for effective peacekeeping, the unrestricted movement of non-national armed forces in a state obviously went to the centre of the issue of sovereignty. While the right to freedom of movement might be readily enough agreed at the point at which an operation was established, changing circumstances locally and changing mandates from the Security Council in New York could quickly cast such agreements into doubt. The issue would first become critical for the UN in the course of the Congo operation. The division of the Congo state in the course of the UN presence there (through the secession of Katanga province) was the major cause of this. The local authorities in Katanga, intent on the creation of an independent, sovereign entity, initially resisted the presence of a UN force, which had been mandated to operate in 'the Congo' and not 'Katanga'. Later it would be a major problem for the UN in Angola, where widespread fighting frequently restricted its movement to a small part of the national territory. Later still, in Sierra Leone, UN forces were to prove unwilling or unable to assert their freedom of movement when challenged by local armed elements.

Another principle laid down by the Summary Study was that the UN must not exercise its authority in ways that could be perceived to compete with that of the host state. Yet, as we have seen, the character and status of the 'host state' in Africa was frequently problematic. In the Congo, for a considerable part of the term of the UN presence there, the peacekeeping force was the only real authority in the country, despite the clamour of competing factions to capture control of the notional state. But the original warning about the danger of attempting to assert 'political' authority remained relevant, even where there was no discernible local state in competition. The rhetoric of national sovereignty exerted a powerful hold over the political imagination in Africa even in the absence of local capacity to exercise it. Nowhere perhaps was this more evident than in Somalia in the early 1990s. The UN's attempt to substitute for the 'missing' state in the capital Mogadishu at this time was frequently regarded by the competing clan factions as a grave provocation. In Rwanda in 1994 the failure of the UN to oppose 'state' authority (deployed in pursuit of genocide) underlay what has subsequently come to be seen as one of the major failures of the entire peacekeeping endeavour.

According to Hammarskjöld's blueprint, not only should UN missions avoid competition with – or substitution for – local political structures, they must also refrain from action that might interfere with the internal politics of the host state. In truth, this was an issue of principle at the UN that went much further than any *ad hoc* set of rules for the conduct of peacekeeping. It was fundamental to the organization's identity and functions. If the Charter had nothing to say about the specifics of peacekeeping, it was certainly not silent on the principle of non-intervention, which was central to the very being of the United Nations. Whatever its ambitions in the area of collective security, the UN was ultimately an inter-governmental organization composed of sovereign states. It was not a putative world government. The big states would never countenance any interference in the exercise of their sovereign power either by other states on the Security Council (which were, potentially, their competitors), or by the small fry of the General Assembly. For their part those smaller states were determined that the United Nations should not become simply a vehicle by which the big states could project their power over everyone else. Many were suspicious of the degree of power concentrated in the Security Council and were insistent on a clear statement in the Charter about the 'untouchability' of domestic politics by the UN. Accordingly, article 2(7) of the Charter states that '[n]othing . . . shall authorize the United Nations to intervene in matters which are essentially within the domestic jurisdiction of any state or shall require the members to submit such matters to settlement under the . . . Charter.' Although the paragraph goes on to exclude Chapter VII-authorized enforcement from this, the exemption obviously did not apply to peacekeeping operations that had no precise legal base.

Once again, this was hardly a difficult issue for the Suez force, which merely interposed itself by agreement between the armies of hostile states in the desert. Subsequent operations would not be so easily fenced off from the political environment in which they had to operate. Again, it was in the Congo that the complexities bedevilling these broad codes of practice would first arise. They would do so again and again in the intra-state crises in Africa in which the UN was later called to intervene.

The Summary Study also offered prescriptions about the national composition of peacekeeping forces. The voluntarist principle applied here too. Contingents could only be requested by the secretary-general on behalf of the Security Council. They could not be demanded (as they could for enforcement action under the terms of Chapter VII). Hammarskjöld proposed that, as a general rule, peacekeepers should not come from the permanent members of the Security Council or from any other state that 'might be considered as possibly having a special interest in the situation which has called for the operation'. The Suez force had established this principle, being made up of contingents predominantly from what later came to be described as 'middle powers'. The term 'middle power' had two connotations during the cold war. Firstly it described military capacity. National contingents had to be capable of carrying out the mandate given to the operation by the UN. But the military strength of a contributor should not be such as to make the parties to a conflict nervous about its political intentions. Secondly – and of particular importance in the context of bipolarity – as far as possible, the force contributor should occupy the middle ground ideologically as well as militarily.[6]

The principle of 'middle power peacekeeping' guided UN practice throughout the cold war. However, it was eroded in some areas in the post-cold war period and the impact of this on African peacekeeping has been a mixed one. American involvement in Somalia in 1993 and 1994, for example, seemed to be fundamentally misjudged and proved counter-productive to the process of conflict resolution. The end of the cold war did not suddenly immunize the big powers from accusations of neo-colonialism, and the high-intensity tactics employed by the Americans in Mogadishu proved disastrous

---

6 In fact, relatively few peacekeepers were 'neutral' in the strict, international legal sense. Only Sweden and Finland in the initial composition of UNEF and Ireland and Austria in several later operations were actually 'neutral' constitutionally speaking. But other states, despite being formally aligned with international blocs, had a sufficiently respected international standing to permit their participation. In this way Canada, Denmark and Norway, although members of NATO, were acceptable in UNEF and several subsequent operations.

in this context. Judgements about the Security Council's authorization of the French Operation Turquoise in Rwanda in 1994, which ran alongside the established peacekeeping mission, would be more ambiguous. It is likely that the humanitarian zone established by the French saved lives. But France's motives for becoming involved in Rwanda in the way and at the stage it did were certainly questionable. However, the 'stiffening' effect of highly trained and well-equipped forces has been crucial in other situations where simple interposition has been inadequate to stabilize the situation. This was illustrated in Sierra Leone in 2000 when a demoralized and demotivated UN operation was given new impetus by the parallel presence of British forces.

As we have seen, the Summary Study acknowledged that peacekeeping was a wholly different activity from the UN's original collective security function. But this legal distinction raised questions about the circumstances under which a peacekeeping force could or should actually use 'force'. Peacekeeping, the Study asserted, 'could never include combat activity'. If it did the result could be to 'blur the distinction between [peacekeeping] operations . . . and combat operations, which would require a decision under Chapter VII of the Charter'. Here again, the Suez experience was an inadequate guide for those confronting the dilemmas that emerged round the issue in the future. The blurring of the border between mere interposition and enforcement became an ever-present problem for 'peacekeeping' operations from the Congo onwards. It was to be one of the most difficult and controversial aspects of UN military intervention. For one thing, it was a serious concern for contributing states anxious about the safety of their contingents and the circumstances and purposes of their deployment. But the use of force by UN personnel also went to the centre of the 'political interference' issue. Self-evidently, when force is used it is used *against* someone – and by extension their political interests. It was not even necessary that the use of force should be openly offensive in character to have this effect. Even what might appear to be the quite reasonable exercise of self-defence on the part of peacekeeping personnel could have an unintended political impact. The use of significant force by peacekeepers in the Congo and then in Somalia had more or less explicit political purposes, and provoked commensurate political reactions both in Africa and beyond. But there were also consequences flowing from situations where force was *not* used by peacekeepers. Had UN personnel been more robust in their own defence in the earliest phase of the Rwanda genocide in 1994, or in Sierra Leone in 2000, then the larger narrative in each crisis might have developed in significantly different ways. An evident reluctance to exercise force in one's own defence can easily be interpreted as a signal that it will not be used in the defence of others.

While over-strict adherence to some 'rules' of peacekeeping could be self-defeating, disregarding others could be disastrous. The model peacekeeping operation involved military intervention in an identified conflict. This did not, however, extend to the apportioning of blame by the UN. Identification of an 'aggressor' was intentionally excluded from the process. The peace-keeping role did not involve the enforcement of a pre-determined outcome. The nature and implementation of outcomes was the responsibility of the protagonists themselves. In the meantime the peacekeeping force (to whose presence the parties had agreed) would attempt to establish and maintain conditions that would facilitate this 'peacemaking'. Within this delicate landscape the 'naming and shaming' of one side as the 'aggressor' would be counter-productive. In Africa departure from this rule had perhaps its most disastrous consequences – for peacekeepers as well as those whose peace was supposedly being kept – in Somalia, where the United States selected an 'enemy' (the 'warlord' Mohammed Aideed) and proceeded to wage war against him. But judgements in these situations are necessarily fine. In other conflicts – such as those in Angola, Sierra Leone and even Western Sahara – the UN's adherence to the 'no blame' principle of peace-keeping has brought criticism when identifiable parties have patently acted in bad faith and evidently gone unpunished.

The appropriateness of Hammarskjöld's design to the realities of Africa's post-colonial politics was, then, tenuous. Virtually every problem that has confronted UN intervention in Africa can be traced to the gap between the peacekeeping 'model' and the political and operational realities of particular missions. This is not to say that operations on the 'traditional' inter-state, interpositionary pattern have not been successfully undertaken in Africa. The intervention in the Ethiopian–Eritrean conflict from 2000 was peace-keeping in the classic mould. So were the linked interventions overseeing the independence process in Namibia and the withdrawal of Cuban forces from Angola. Other UN operations that were intra-state rather than inter-state in character were still based on interposition and 'moral presence'. The settlement of the civil war in Mozambique was in this category (although the extent of the integrated humanitarian efforts of the UN in this operation was wholly unforeseen in the 1950s). The operations in Western Sahara and the Central African Republic were also fundamentally 'interpositionary' in character.

In many operations in Africa the distinction between interposition and enforcement has been much less clear, however. It may simply have been good luck rather than wise judgement that prevented some of these 'model' operations being complicated by dilemmas around enforcement. In other conflicts Security Council mandates that began with minimal military com-mitments have been adjusted to include reference to Chapter VII enforce-ment when circumstances – or attitudes in the Security Council – have changed.

Tellingly, perhaps, attempts to clarify the nature of UN military intervention for the post-cold war world seem to have found little favour with the permanent members of the Security Council who are responsible for the formulation of peacekeeping mandates. In his influential 1992 position paper on peacekeeping, *An Agenda for Peace*, the then secretary-general of the UN, Boutros Boutros-Ghali, proposed the creation of so-called 'peace enforcement units'.[7] *An Agenda for Peace* noted that the UN 'has sometimes been called upon to send forces to restore and maintain the cease-fire. This task can on occasion exceed the mission of peacekeeping forces and the expectations of peacekeeping force contributors.' Consequently, Boutros-Ghali recommended 'that the Security Council consider the utilization of peace-enforcement units in clearly defined circumstances. . . . They would have to be more heavily armed than peacekeeping forces and they would have to undergo extensive preparatory training.'[8] Such circumstances were familiar in Africa by the 1990s. It was perhaps not altogether fortuitous that it was Boutros-Ghali, the first UN secretary-general from the African continent (he was a former Egyptian foreign minister), who was first to initiate discussion of the problem at the level of the Security Council. In Angola, Mozambique, Rwanda and Sierra Leone the UN took responsibility for the management of processes in which government and rebel movements had agreed to submit their forces to programmes of reduction and integration as key parts of overall peace agreements. These would have been ideal circumstances for the deployment of such peace-enforcement units. But Boutros-Ghali's idea was not pursued by the Security Council. At least in part, perhaps, this was because of the political advantage seen by members of the Security Council in retaining maximum flexibility in formulating the mandates of each operation. At all events, 'peacekeeping' remains as amorphous a concept in Africa at the beginning of the twenty-first century as it had been in the middle of the twentieth.

The external state: Africa and the international system

By far the greater part of United Nations military involvement in sub-Saharan Africa has been in the post-cold war period. The phenomenon of

---

7 *An Agenda for Peace: Preventive Diplomacy, Peacemaking and Peacekeeping* was presented as a report to the Security Council. United Nations document S/22111, 17 July 1992. (It was subsequently published in pamphlet form.)
8 Ibid., paragraph 44.

'African peacekeeping' as understood at the turn of the twenty-first century is essentially one that began in the late 1980s and grew rapidly in the following decade. The UN's one prior peacekeeping venture in Africa pre-dated this by almost three decades. That operation had not been an unalloyed success. Between 1960 and 1964 the huge undertaking in the former Belgian Congo not only failed to achieve its immediate peacekeeping objectives, but had also helped to bring about the very cold war confrontation it had been established to prevent. Subsequently, the Congo (later Zaïre) had been left to suffer more than thirty years of misgovernment and corruption on a staggering scale.

Despite the pace of decolonization in sub-Saharan Africa in the 1960s and the problems associated with it, the Congo proved to be something of a one-off for the UN. No new peacekeeping commitments were undertaken in Africa by the organization until its involvement in the independence process in Namibia and the Cuban military withdrawal from Angola in 1989. In the meantime, the protracted domestic and international crises associated with the apartheid state in South Africa and the regional conflicts which emerged from white minority rule in Rhodesia were regularly aired at the UN, but no serious consideration was ever given to any 'peacekeeping' intervention. Over Rhodesia, the UN did go as far as legitimizing unilateral military action by Britain (in the form of a naval blockade of the Portuguese-controlled Mozambican ports that served the rebel colony). But when a multilateral force was eventually deployed in the territory during the transfer of power in 1980 it was the Commonwealth rather than the UN that provided it. Similarly, there was no dearth of discussion in both the General Assembly and Security Council of the liberation struggles in Portuguese Africa, but no feasible pro-posal for UN military intervention was ever put forward. Nor did the destruc-tive conflicts within independent Africa in the 1960s and 1970s (such as the war between Ethiopia and Somalia over the Ogaden, the Nigerian civil war and the Tanzanian intervention in Uganda) bring any peacekeeping intervention by the UN.

There were a number of reasons for this lack of involvement. As we have suggested, the experience of the Congo operation was on balance not a posi-tive one. Inevitably, this tended to blunt enthusiasm for further engagement on the part of potential force contributors. But beyond this, from the early 1960s up until the mid-1970s Africa was largely insulated from global ideo-logical competition. The continent was not in any major way part of the bipolar competition for spheres of influence that defined the cold war in the 1960s. The short sharp immersion in cold war confrontation that followed the UN's intervention in the Congo was something of an aberration in the broader African context. Although China, the Soviet Union and Cuba were all engaged with various African states and although they backed various anti-colonial guerrilla movements, this did not provoke significant conflict with the United States until the Angolan crisis of 1975. Washington was content to regard Africa as a diplomatic responsibility of its former colonial masters (and American allies) in Europe. This remained the position until the battlefront of the cold war expanded in the late 1970s and early 1980s to embrace significant areas of the continent. In the meantime, France most particularly but also Britain and Belgium had assumed in varying degrees continuing political and security responsibilities in many parts of their old empires. Simultaneously, United Nations peacekeeping as a global activity had 'retreated' in the later 1960s and 1970s back to the parts of the world it had originally engaged with (principally the Middle East).

In parallel with this broad international trend, though unconnected to it, was the fact that Africa remained relatively free of *internal* international conflicts for a considerable period after the early 1960s when the main drive of decolonization began. As we have noted, there had been fighting between Somalia and Ethiopia in 1963 and 1977 and an invasion of Uganda by Tanzania in 1978–79. But these were the exceptions to a general rule of uncontested international borders. This was a considerable record in a continent of more than forty states with often multiple international frontiers. In part this evident inter-state stability was a consequence of a self-denying ordinance by the Organization of African Unity (OAU) at the time of its foundation in 1963. Resisting the temptation to open up the Pandora's box of colonial frontiers, the OAU charter asserted the validity of national frontiers at the time of independence.[9] The new post-independence governments almost universally adhered to this principle. For one thing, the means available to these governments would rarely have been adequate to mount effective challenges to neighbouring states. But, more positively, the new governing classes recognized the importance of stable frontiers to the huge nation-building tasks that faced them, however imperfect the ethnic demarcation of these frontiers might be. Powerful external forces, in particular the former metropoles which had transferred sovereignty, strongly encouraged this. The maintenance of inherited borders was also important to the post-independence governments, many of which would have been stretched to construct new frameworks of territorial administration from scratch.[10] The effect of the UN's apparent retreat from African peacekeeping in the years following the Congo operation was therefore ameliorated by the fact that few of the continent's security problems were of an 'international' character.

---

9   Article III of the charter of the Organization of African Unity commits its members to respect for the territorial integrity of African states.

10   Christopher Clapham, *Africa in the International System* (Cambridge: Cambridge University Press, 1996), p. 35.

In the later 1970s the narrowing of the UN's world-wide peacekeeping role which was already under way accelerated, making it ever less likely that the UN would become involved in African conflicts, at least to the extent of deploying military forces. The underlying reason for the eclipse of UN peacekeeping was the crumbling of superpower détente. A decade or so of relative co-operation now gave way to what has been described as the 'second' cold war. For the ten years after the creation of the UN force for Lebanon in 1978 no new UN operation was established anywhere. The authorization of peacekeeping involves at least a minimal consensus in the Security Council, and this was simply not available at that time. The tempo of international peacekeeping had always depended on the superpowers' calculation of mutual self-interest. This determined the extent to which they were willing to 'franchise' crises from unilateral to multilateral management. The extent of UN peacekeeping initiatives at any one time had provided something of a barometer of superpower relations since the 1950s. In the newly tense late 1970s Africa moved from a position of relative isolation from cold war rivalry to become a major area of superpower competition – and therefore even further off-limits to the UN. External intervention in the civil war in Angola from 1975 (by South Africa and Cuba on the ground but backed by both superpowers) helped provoke and then sustain this reversion to bipolar conflict.

The situation was deeply paradoxical. Having previously been set apart from UN peacekeeping because of its remoteness from broader global tensions, Africa was now drawn more and more towards the epicentre of the cold war. And – because of rather than despite this new danger – UN intervention was now an even more distant prospect. There was insufficient common ground between the superpowers for them to agree to reduce the spread of the cold war through 'immunization' by the multilateralization of conflict management. The dormancy of the UN's military role in the 1980s, and the increased superpower unilateralism that underlay it, meant that the horrors of civil war and external destabilization in Angola and Mozambique grew inexorably in the absence of an effective multilateral response.

Further north, tensions mounted dangerously between the superpowers' 'clients' in the Horn of Africa. There, Ethiopia and Somalia settled into a regional confrontation, each confident in the support and encouragement of its bloc leader. Even western opposition to white minority rule in South Africa seemed to be increasingly qualified. The 'bigger picture' of the superpower competition now supplanted earlier, more ethically informed positions. Quite simply, the opportunities for multilateral intervention had disappeared as both Washington and Moscow came to regard all conflicts, regardless of how geographically peripheral or morally complex, as core national interests.

This situation changed dramatically with the Gorbachev thaw and the eventual collapse of the Soviet Union and its system of satellites in the late 1980s and early 1990s. The following decade saw around twenty significant new United Nations peacekeeping missions world-wide. Now, with the end of the cold war, Africa became a major focus in the rapid growth of this peacekeeping role.

At the global level the location as well as the extent of the new interventions was significant. Earlier UN operations from the 1950s to the 1970s reflected the geographical pattern of decolonization and its attendant problems. They tended to be established disproportionately in the Middle East and Asia with African intervention limited to the Congo operation. Now, a number of these new post-cold war commitments were in Europe (five in various parts of the former Yugoslavia alone) and others were in Central America and the Caribbean. But in the first dozen years of this 'new' peacekeeping, dated from 1988, eighteen operations were established across Africa. No longer 'excluded' from peacekeeping by the superpowers' perceptions of their national interests, Africa and its conflicts came to occupy a prime place in the 'new world order' multilateralism that followed the unexpectedly sudden end of the cold war.

The internal state: post-colonial trajectories in Africa

The peacekeeping endeavour is by definition a double-sided one. It is a process located in the relationship between the peacekeeper and those whose peace is being kept. Central to the latter side of this relationship in Africa has been the interior nature of the state there. The issue of the state in Africa lies somewhere in each of the conflicts in which the UN has been called to intervene, whatever their specific origins or outcome. In a number of instances the enfeeblement of the state in parts of Africa is a result of chronic structural weaknesses that derive from cultural inflexibilities and contradictions. In part too it has been a product of changes in the international political and economic environment brought about by the end of the cold war and the growth of what we have come to refer to as globalization. Generally, the crisis of the African state is a complex combination of both sets of factors.

We have already noted how the new political classes to which power was transferred in Africa at the time of decolonization were content to accept the existing colonial borders as the frontiers of their new independent states. It was regarded as a given both in Africa and beyond that the (essentially western) notion of the nation-state would drive both domestic politics and international relations. For their part, the former imperial powers simply assumed that this final act of imperialism, so to speak, was part of an inevitable process. Both effective governance and the efficient management of international relations were seen as inseparable from territorial statehood. In most African countries the new rulers had been encultured by the assumptions – and usually the educational systems – of the imperial metropole. (This was so even in states like Angola and Mozambique that had come into being only after bitter and protracted wars of liberation.) They were, therefore, predisposed to follow the models of political and diplomatic behaviour that had been held up to them by their imperial 'sponsors'.

Yet in some cases the capacity of the new regimes to establish and sustain effective sovereignty throughout the state territory was questionable from the outset. At its most basic, effective sovereignty must demonstrate two capabilities. Firstly, effective physical control must be extended over the territory of the state to guarantee its security from outside threat and to create and sustain an appropriate environment for social and economic activity. Secondly, there must be an administrative system capable of exercising fiscal control and of delivering basic services throughout the state. One of the most dramatic illustrations of state failure in terms of these criteria led to the UN's first peacekeeping effort in Africa when the successor state to the Belgian Congo virtually disintegrated within weeks of its establishment in 1960.

The Congo was not initially seen as a typical case, however. For one thing, the circumstances of its decolonization were peculiar. Belgium had withdrawn from the Congo with irresponsible speed having done virtually nothing to prepare the vast territory for independence. Moreover, during the 1960s there was a considerable fund of genuine international goodwill towards the new states of Africa. The great majority of new states did not follow the Congo into immediate chaos, and pessimism about their prospects tended to be dismissed as imperialist nostalgia. Both Britain and France, in contrast to Belgium, exerted great political energy in managing their own processes of decolonization. They also put considerable effort into establishing and nurturing a complex of post-imperial links (whether in the form of regular 'Francophone' summits and the African franc zone or the institution of the Commonwealth). However loudly these continuing ties might have been denounced as instruments of neo-colonialism by African nationalists, eastern bloc propagandists and western radicals, they did contribute to a general framework of state stability in the immediate post-independence period. Additionally, the global economy into which the majority of new African states emerged in the 1960s was relatively benign and the economic capabilities of the new regimes were not put under immediate test.

This favourable diplomatic and economic climate would not persist, however, and the underlying weakness of many African states was gradually exposed. By the beginning of the 1970s it was clear that 'development' was not happening in most of sub-Saharan Africa. Marxists and other critics of neo-colonialism elaborated 'dependency' theories to explain this failure of post-independence 'take-off' in terms of the mechanisms of the world capitalist system. But glaring failures of political leadership and economic management in Africa itself could not be ignored. The pressures of the international economic system certainly had a major role in Africa's mounting post-colonial economic crisis, not least the recurrent oil price escalations of the 1970s. But while the desperate instabilities in the oil market at this time were damaging to all non-oil producers (and particularly those in the Third World), the efforts of leaders in many parts of Africa to manage the resulting crises seemed particularly inadequate.

At the same time, the general sympathy with which western governments had followed the establishment of the new post-colonial states became increasingly qualified. The failure of economic development became associated with perceptions of corruption, human rights abuses and regime instability to a point where even the most sympathetic of Africa's western friends were hard put to defend the continent's political leadership in the 1970s and 1980s. With the beginning of the end of the cold war at the end of the 1980s, political and economic understanding for the problems faced by African states dwindled even further. At the political level, the end of bipolarity meant that African countries no longer had any significant diplomatic leverage to exert. There were no longer two blocs that could be played against each other. On the economic plane, the victory of the west became by extension a victory for capitalism and market-oriented economics. The imposition of so-called 'structural adjustment programmes' (SAPs) by the International Monetary Fund (IMF), which had become a feature of the 1980s, was now pressed with new vigour. The purpose of SAPs was to reconfigure national economies to enable them to perform in a rapidly globalizing, market-driven international economic environment. Their effect was to remove from the state the capacity to distribute economic resources, whether through industrial and agricultural subsidies or public sector employment. The result was even greater political and economic instability, and the further enfeeblement of the state. The decline of the African state, whatever its longer-term causes, therefore accelerated in the 1990s. By 1997 the World Bank (itself an agent of state decline through its lending policies) noted that in parts of Africa, 'typically, the reach and effectiveness of the state have withered away, and perforce the state has in effect withdrawn . . . even from areas that are its legitimate function. An institutional vacuum of considerable importance has emerged in many parts of Sub-Saharan Africa.'[11]

Moving back from the specific impact of the end of the cold war, it is possible to place this multi-layered dysfunction of the African state in a broad theoretical perspective. In the 1980s the debate about the 'failure' of the Third World had moved on from the sometimes sweeping simplicities of dependency theory, which saw the ills of the underdeveloped South as essentially imposed by the developed North. While the critique of exploitative neo-colonialism remained vigorous, 'endogenous' – that is to say, domestic – factors began to receive much more attention. In the African context this led a number of writers to explore the failure of what has been described as 'neo-patrimonial' forms of government.[12]

Put briefly, this view sees the crisis of the state in Africa as due in whole or in part to the fact that the state itself is an artefact of colonialism. As such, it is at odds with the underlying local political cultures that structures of government must reflect if they are to be successful. The pre-colonial political order in sub-Saharan Africa, it is argued, was essentially 'patrimonial'. That is to say, it was based primarily on patron–client relationships between rulers and ruled. The resources made available by the possession and exercise of political power would be disbursed by those who governed to those – or some of those – who were governed as the price of continuing support and loyalty. It was, in essence, a type of 'social contract', though it would usually be differentially applied on ethnic, religious or regional bases. The relationships of interdependence that emerged from this arrangement frequently formed the basis of sophisticated forms of political organization, and their effective manipulation demanded considerable political skill. This system ended with imperial conquest and the ensuing imposition of a colonial state. Elements of traditional patrimonialism were maintained in some places as a means of supervised colonial control in the form of 'indirect rule' (for example by the British in west Africa and the Belgians in central Africa) but it no longer constituted the dominant form of government.

With the coming of independence, the imperial powers created constitutional arrangements for the post-colonial state. These were usually based on metropolitan political structures. The new national leaders were as content to accept these structures as they were the ex-colonial frontiers within which

---

11   *1997 World Development Report* (Washington, DC: World Bank, 1998).

12   Among the best expositions of the various dimensions of neo-patrimonialism are:
Jean-François Bayart, *The State in Africa: the Politics of the Belly* (London: Longman, 1993);
Michael Bratton and Nicholas van de Walle, *Democratic Experiments in Africa* (Cambridge: Cambridge University Press, 1997); Patrick Chabal and Jean-Pascal Daloz, *Africa Works: Disorder as Political Instrument* (Oxford: James Currey, 1999).

they would operate. Embracing these elements of continuity was a reasonable price for the transfer of power. They also provided a familiar and apparently workable political environment in themselves. But ultimately the inherited state structures proved inappropriate to the underlying political culture, which remained enduringly patrimonial. Inevitably, this cultural undercurrent soon welled to the surface of political activity. One symptom of this was the appearance of one-party states throughout independent Africa, which supplanted the pluralist constitutional arrangements agreed at independence. One-party states were justified by those who ran and benefited from them (and by more than a few well-intentioned outsiders as well) as a pragmatic and efficient response to the tasks of nation-building and development. Political opposition, which was a central part of the constitutional structures inherited from the departing imperial power, was an expensive luxury, it was argued. Such 'alien' pluralism squandered scarce human resources by excluding a whole section of the political class from the 'national project'. Similarly, the argument ran, imported notions of the constitutional separation of powers between legislature, judiciary and executive were divisive and an impediment to the sense of national unity essential for the pursuit of development. But the reality was that the adoption of one-party systems was less about finding the best route to economic progress and modernity than about finding a way to bring the new state into alignment with the still-prevailing patrimonial political culture. It is at this point that traditional patrimonialism becomes 'neo-patrimonialism', because while the original social and cultural driving forces persist, they are now focused on control of the resources of the 'modern' state.

Difficulties deriving from the basic contradiction between the demands of patrimonial politics and the political architecture of modern statehood soon began to accumulate. In the mainly benevolent diplomatic and economic circumstances of the 1960s, the impact of these contradictions was cushioned. Scrutiny, whether from within or beyond the state, of how resources were being managed and distributed could to some extent be avoided or diverted by those in power. But the turbulence that characterized the world economy in the 1970s quickly had an impact on the fundamentally weak economies of sub-Saharan Africa. Although the primary problems (like the oil crises) came from the outside, their impact was aggravated by local mismanagement. This mismanagement derived only in part from inexperience in government. It was also a function of the nepotism and corruption associated with neo-patrimonialism. The result for African economies was protracted crisis. The resources available to the state (or 'patron') for disbursement to its 'clients' (the favoured sections of the population) were now sharply reduced. The most affected African regimes responded in one, or more often both, of two ways. Firstly, they increased borrowing in the international money markets to maintain their disposable resource base. The result, inevitably, was a deepening cycle of indebtedness and even greater long-term economic chaos. Secondly, they resorted to the organized coercion of the increasingly embittered sections of their citizenry that were either excluded from patronage or resentful at its new meagreness. This coercion was facilitated by the one-party system in the short term. But in the longer term it focused increased attention on the questionable legitimacy of such states. Finally, coercion also contributed to the cycle of economic decline as increasingly scarce resources were devoted to non-productive military and security sectors of national economies. In this way the conditions rapidly developed for both intra-state and, in certain circumstances, inter-state conflict, which local resources were wholly insufficient to resolve. External intervention therefore became the only option, and as African regional arrangements were rarely appropriate or capable of performing this function, the obvious recourse was to the United Nations.

We have already seen how the end of the cold war accelerated the decline of the patrimonial state by reducing its powers of patronage through the now largely uncontested forces of economic globalization. Now, by a historical irony, the 'victory' of liberal capitalism on a world scale actually intensified competition for control of the state. The west now had no need to sustain dictatorial regimes as bulwarks against Soviet influence and the Soviets were no longer in a position to sustain their own dictatorial clients. Pressure on the one-party state 'norm' now mounted throughout Africa as internal and external clamour for political liberalization and 'good governance' intensified. But despite early optimism, often expressed in the rhetoric of 'African renaissance', there was little change in the international economic dependency of the state and its vulnerability to patrimonial factionalism. Economic and political reform as a route away from political violence and instability proved a chimera. In short, the processes of 'democratization' did not appear to provide a solution to the kind of problems which eventually demanded a peacekeeping response from the UN.

This is, of course, only a broad theoretical narrative. It is not relevant to the experience of all African states. We must not lose sight of the fact that UN peacekeeping has been undertaken in less than a quarter of the states of Africa. Moreover, problems emerging from the vicissitudes of the neo-patrimonial state have not been at the centre of all of these interventions. The UN operations in Namibia and Western Sahara, for example, had no direct origins in the crisis of the post-colonial state. In these cases UN intervention came at the beginning rather than at the end of a process. The issue in these territories was state formation after 'decolonization' rather than the failure or collapse of an established state. But in many cases peacekeeping has been seen as a remedy to problems thrown up by states at critical points in their post-colonial trajectory. The crises in Liberia, Sierra Leone, the Central African Republic, Rwanda and the Democratic Republic of

Congo (DRC), while very different in their respective origins and in the ways in which conflict was manifested, can all be traced in part at least to failed neo-patrimonial systems. In all of them major crises resulted when the legitimacy of the state was contested by elements excluded from its patrimony. In the Congo in the 1960s and later in Somalia in the 1990s violence emerged from multi-sided contests for control of the state by aspirant 'patrons' mobilizing their 'clients', whether ethnic or regional, in attempts to exclude competitors. The cases of Angola and Mozambique are more problematic. The circumstances of their original statehood (under revolutionary regimes emerging from protracted liberation wars) do not fit easily into the process as outlined above. In both cases violent destabilization of the state by outside interests played a central part in their difficulties. At least in part, however, both conflicts derived from the failure of the regimes formed after independence to deliver adequately on their early promises and to make headway with inter-regional, pan-ethnic 'nation-building' projects. The model of the transient neo-patrimonial state as the ground on which UN peacekeeping takes place is hedged about with necessary qualifications. But it remains a persuasive explanation of a significant proportion of Africa's post-colonial conflicts.

System and state in collision: order in African international relations

Interlocked with the internal dynamics operating within the African state were a number of processes at the level of the international system that were also conducive towards conflict. Although the 'stateness' (defined in terms of capacity to perform the basic functions of the state) of many African polities was dwindling in the 1980s and 1990s, it was unthinkable within the international system as a whole that 'states' should cease to exist in Africa. As suggested earlier, this would threaten the integrity of the broader state system on which international relations had been based for the past four hundred years. Initially, of course, this 'Westphalian' concept applied only to those countries in the global north and west that formed the new state system of the seventeenth and eighteenth centuries. But as this system expanded over the coming centuries its 'rules' shaped the character of modern international relations. One of the major vectors of this expansion was, of course, the process of colonization and subsequent decolonization. The new states of Africa were presented with the status of 'sub-system' in this international system in the same package as their new, imported constitutions at the time of decolonization.

In time several African states whose membership of the international system had been a result of this process were apparently disintegrating from within. In a system made up of state sub-systems these potential 'blank spaces' posed an implicit threat to the integrity of the whole. By the mid-1990s Somalia, Liberia and Sierra Leone had become little more than war-afflicted geographical expressions. The statehood of Mozambique and Angola was fiercely contested and that of many other countries was tenuous. In truth, of course, these entities had for some time been what Robert Jackson has characterized as 'quasi-states'.[13] That is to say, their statehood was based on a tacit acceptance by the key actors in the international system that they should be publicly acknowledged and treated as states despite serious questions over their level of 'stateness' in terms of their behaviour and capacities. This illusion was necessary for the continued 'integrity' of the broader international system. But for the range of reasons we have discussed, the illusion could not easily be sustained by the 1990s, and a number of African states slipped below even the very loose qualification threshold for statehood required of them hitherto.

A further difficulty at this time was that the relatively stable web of international frontiers between Africa states – which had originally been a saving feature of the immediate post-independence period – began to break down. It is something of an anti-colonial cliché that African borders were arrived at simply by the arbitrary drawing of lines on maps. In reality imperial borders (and therefore post-imperial frontiers) were usually delimited on the basis of at least some geographical rationality. Given natural settlement patterns, this often involved a certain ethnic rationality as well. Nevertheless, disjunction between ethnicity and nationality is a fact of African political life. Paradoxically, the very weakness of the African state in the exercise of control over its territory had its positive side. Borders were often ethnically permeable by default as the resources to control them were simply not available to governments. This permitted an element of freedom of 'international' movement that served important local social and economic purposes. But in certain regions cross-border activity eventually became less innocent. Control of the post-colonial state was increasingly contested by armed force in the 1980s and 1990s. As part of this, guerrilla groups – taking their cue from the older generation of African freedom fighters who had begun their struggles against white minority rule and Portuguese imperialism in the 1960s – sought rear bases in neighbouring states. Often, a symbiotic relationship existed or developed between the guerrillas and their host, in which each would use the other in pursuit of their respective political and economic agendas. The borders between Angola and Zaïre, between South Africa

---

13   R.H. Jackson, *Quasi-States: Sovereignty, International Relations and the Third World* (Cambridge: Cambridge University Press, 1993).

and Mozambique, between Liberia and Sierra Leone, between Uganda and Rwanda, and between Western Sahara and Algeria were the scenes of this sort of activity.

Frequently, the interests involved would be economic as well as political (it was often difficult to disentangle the two). As the 'modern' sector of African economies in the form of processing and manufacturing failed to develop, increasing attention was focused on sources of natural wealth. This was particularly the case in respect of resources that were of high value and small bulk, and that were physically easy to exploit and transport. Diamonds were the most obvious example of this. The informal plundering of these resources both motivated and financed guerrilla activity. It also deepened the involvement of neighbouring states in internal conflicts as leaders exploited political weakness across their borders in pursuit of easy riches. The inter-related conflicts in Liberia and Sierra Leone provide the most obvious examples of this, but it was an element too in the Angolan war and later in the Democratic Republic of Congo, where the trade in so-called 'blood diamonds' became a major factor in the conflicts. In this way, from a situation in the 1960s and 1970s in which state-versus-state cross-border conflict was virtually unknown in Africa, it had become by the mid-1990s a common characteristic of conflicts in the continent.

The evident departure of whole regions of Africa from the 'rules and norms' of state behaviour raises questions even about the persistence of neo-patrimonialism as a description of the political process. However much at odds with contemporary western notions of how states should govern, neo-patrimonialism nevertheless still regards the state as a central instrument of power. It is, in a sense, a 'commodity' in its own right, providing access to resources via formal political power. Recently, however, writers like William Reno have suggested that 'rule' in parts of Africa is better characterized as 'warlordism'. In this model rulers (who have generally come to power through a more effective deployment of violence than their rivals) have no particular interest in the control of the state as a means of enrichment. Cutting out the middleman, so to speak, their exploitation of natural resources is direct rather than 'legitimized' through the trappings of state power. They are mainly interested not in the comprehensive control of a 'country', but only in the control of resources. Control of the state is primarily a strategy of denial – a means of pre-empting competition rather than a good in itself. The 'foreign policy' of the warlord state is limited to commercial agreements, usually with private companies and individuals.[14] The warlord phenomenon has not, of course, been a characteristic of Africa as a whole. (It is even

---

14   William Reno, *Warlord Politics and African States* (London: Lynne Rienner, 1998).

arguable whether the phenomenon as here described was a feature of the Somali conflict, where the term 'warlord' was frequently used to describe the local protagonists.) But 'economic warlordism' has been a factor in a number of UN interventions, most obviously perhaps in west Africa, where the missions in Liberia and Sierra Leone confronted special difficulties in locating any 'state' capable of acting as an interlocutor.

The inability – or, if we accept the warlordism thesis, the unwillingness – of some African states to reverse the deterioration of their internal and external security capacity in the 1980s and 1990s was compounded by the simultaneous retreat of external forces of stabilization from the continent. The end of what might be described in broad terms as the 'imperial presence' in Africa had various facets. In the most narrow sense it involved the withdrawal of the colonial powers – Britain, France, Belgium, Portugal and Spain – from their formal imperial responsibilities. But there are two further senses in which the imperial presence, more broadly defined, has been withdrawn. Firstly, the phenomenon also embraces the more gradual retreat of the one-time imperial states from political and security relationships they established with their former colonies in the early post-independence years. Secondly, the term can also be extended to the 'presence' of external hegemons other than the colonial state. The most obvious examples of this would be the cold war superpowers. In other words, the withdrawal of the 'imperial presence' refers to the end of, for example, *Pax Americana* in Somalia as much as the more obvious *Pax Britannica* and *Pax Franca* of Anglophone and Francophone Africa respectively. The effect of this general retreat was not merely to leave existing African problems disregarded by powerful states that might formerly have been involved in seeking a solution. Beyond this, conflicts could now break out in situations that might previously have been suppressed or resolved by external intervention before reaching a flash-point. In this sense, Africa in the 1990s had some similarities with central and eastern Europe after the collapse of *Pax Sovietica*, when the removal of externally imposed 'discipline' allowed tensions to grow into major domestic and international crises.

There were various reasons for the withdrawal from Africa of the political and security presence of outside states. Just as formal imperialism eventually became too politically, diplomatically and financially 'expensive' for the European metropoles, so eventually did their post-imperial engagement. Clearly, this process varied between the European states involved. The African focus of British foreign policy was reduced sharply from the later 1960s as part of a broader post-imperial contraction of foreign and defence policy. Subsequently, the only pressing piece of unfinished business calling for direct British engagement was the 'sore thumb' of Rhodesia/Zimbabwe, which was eventually resolved in 1980–81. France, in contrast, retained a strong set of security ties with Francophone Africa that were only slowly loosened in the

1990s. The smaller imperial powers had established only very limited post-colonial relationships. Belgium, with its relatively sparse resources and with the experience of domestic and diplomatic crisis surrounding its withdrawal from central Africa in the early 1960s, retained limited links with its former colonies. Portugal, too, had meagre domestic resources and experienced particular difficulty in re-engaging with Africa after independence. Its decol-onization came at the end of long and bitter wars, and the new states that emerged identified with the Soviet rather than the western bloc in the years after independence. For Spain, Africa had never had the prominence in the national consciousness that it did in Portugal. Madrid's withdrawal from Western Sahara and Equatorial Guinea in the mid-1970s was done with barely a backward glance.

The withdrawal of superpower influence was more rapid and complete than that of the former imperial metropoles. The active engagement of the cold war superpowers with Africa had been relatively short-lived. An early interest in independent Africa on the part of the Kennedy administration in the early 1960s did not really survive the trauma of the Congo crisis. Later US administrations appeared unwilling to bear the contradictions that would beset an active African policy. While strategic interests seemed to require that Washington pursue good relations with the strongest anti-communist forces in Africa like South Africa and Portugal, the domestic consequences of high-profile relations with these racist regimes would have been grave. As long as the Soviet Union was willing to co-operate in avoiding direct cold war confrontation in Africa, then the United States was happy to maintain a low diplomatic profile. And, in fact, beyond some inevitable rhetoric of revolutionary solidarity, Moscow seemed as ready as Washington to fence Africa off from the cold war after the Congo experience.

The ideological and military battle for control of the Angolan state after Portugal's withdrawal in 1975, however, changed everything. Soviet support for the Marxist forces in Angola, along with the presence of thousands of Cuban troops despatched to prevent their defeat, was met by escalating American backing for their supposedly pro-western enemies. As we have remarked, the Angolan crisis was both a cause and an early symptom of the unravelling of superpower détente in the later 1970s. Subsequently, the United States was less coy about pursuing its perceived strategic interests in Africa. Concerns over the balance of naval power in the South Atlantic region drove continuing American involvement in Angola and contributed to Washington's 'constructive engagement' with South Africa during the presidency of Ronald Reagan. Meanwhile, there were similar geo-strategic concerns over the Indian Ocean and the Arabian Gulf that led the United States and the Soviet Union to back more extensively and more openly their local clients there — respectively Somalia and Ethiopia. When this strategic rivalry came to an abrupt end at the close of the 1980s with the passing of the cold war, the principal basis of the superpower presence in Africa simply dissolved. With it went their 'imperial presence'. Initially, of course, this was regarded as a force for peace in Africa. The Angolan war and the tensions in the Horn region were seen by many foreign observers as products of superpower involvement. The reality was more complex, however. The underlying local causes of conflict remained – but they were now no longer regulated and ameliorated by powerful outside patrons.[15]

The withdrawal of the 'imperial' presence was not total, either on the part of the old colonial powers or by the former superpowers. But the instruments they began to deploy in the post-cold war period shifted from the unilateral to the multilateral. While individual states showed a decreasing interest in direct involvement, Africa and its problems could not be abandoned. For one thing, as we have seen, there was the integrity of the state-based Westphalian international system to be considered. Beyond this, though, genuine humanitarian concerns played a part in policy formulation. The consciences of western policy-makers were sharpened by an increasingly informed public opinion in the 1990s. This was heightened by the so-called 'CNN effect' – the instant transmission of images of destruction and destitution from African trouble spots directly into western homes. Now, just as economic relationships with the former colonies could be conducted in the post-imperial age through metropolitan-based trans-national companies, so the United Nations was seen to offer a similar service in the security and humanitarian areas. The Security Council – still dominated by former imperial powers and cold war superpowers – now began to commit the UN to the resolution of African crises.

A typology of UN peacekeeping in Africa

Typically, the interventions that followed from this new multilateralism could be placed in one of four categories. Firstly, there were problems either that had been caused by state disintegration or that threatened to bring about state disintegration. Long before, the UN's first peacekeeping foray into Africa belonged essentially in this category. While intervention in the Congo

---

15   The respective arguments of those taking an optimistic and pessimistic view of the impact of the end of the cold war on Africa are discussed by Keith Sommerville, 'Africa after the cold war: frozen out or frozen in time?', in Louise Fawcett and Yezid Sayigh (eds), *The Third World After the Cold War: Community and Change* (Oxford: Oxford University Press, 2000), pp. 134–5.

from 1960 to 1964 came originally in response to a plea from the post-independence government, the new state imploded soon after the arrival of the first UN troops. Factional conflict at the centre and secession at the periphery changed utterly the nature of the relatively limited crisis in which the Security Council had originally agreed to intervene. In the later period a similar crisis of statehood underlay the UN's involvement in Somalia between 1992 and 1995. Here, the withdrawal of the imperial presence that helped precipitate the crisis was not that of the historical colonial powers but of the United States, which had been the dominating external presence in the late 1970s and 1980s. The end of the cold war meant the end of American interest in bolstering its client regime in Somalia. The consequence was a 'collapsed' state and an explosion of inter-clan violence as competing warlords fought among themselves for dominance.

Secondly, the UN undertook missions in which its main role was to accompany, monitor and legitimize interventions by regional multilateral forces. The crisis in Liberia followed the collapse in 1980 of a long-standing – though corrupt and inequitable – patrimonial system and the failure of its successor regime adequately to replace it. Liberia had been an 'independent' state since the mid-nineteenth century, and the nature and extent of any 'imperial presence' there is not easily discerned, though a long-term special relationship, transcending the cold war, had been maintained with the United States. The initial multilateral response to the crisis was a regional one by the Economic Community of West African States (ECOWAS), but the UN was drawn in to 'supervise' this intervention. The same role was carried out initially by the UN in Liberia's northern neighbour, Sierra Leone. There, after a lengthy period of apparent stability following independence, military coups and guerrilla activity, much of it encouraged from outside, brought violent chaos throughout the country in the 1990s. Eventually, the UN's role in Sierra Leone underwent a fundamental change when it took over the primary peace-keeping role in 1999. In the Central African Republic the United Nations was involved from 1998 to 2000 in a stabilization operation following a series of military mutinies. This UN intervention replaced an earlier regional intervention by Francophone African states in which France itself had a prominent role. Following a decision by Paris to withdraw from the effective leadership of this operation, a United Nations command structure was put in place. However, the composition of the force remained largely – as previously – predominantly French-speaking African. Its 'imprimatur', however, was provided by the UN.

The third type of United Nations mission were those mandated to manage the implementation of peace agreements that had been reached to end internal conflicts within African states. In Angola, following its successful management of the withdrawal of Cuban forces between 1989 and 1991, the UN was drawn into the supervision of a more fundamental effort to end the civil war that had been in progress – with extensive external involvement – since before the country's independence in 1975. For eight years from 1991 successive efforts were made by the UN to implement peace plans that had been agreed by the parties. These agreements were based on what would become a familiar template for other interventions of this type in Africa. This involved the integration of rebel forces into a new political process and the simultaneous demobilization and disarmament of fighters. Although this process ultimately failed in Angola, the UN was more successful in implementing it in the other large Portuguese-speaking territory of southern Africa, Mozambique. Here, between 1992 and 1994 a similarly long-standing, foreign-nurtured civil war was successfully resolved through the transformation of the main rebel force into a political party and an accompanying mechanism by which former fighters were demobilized and reintegrated into post-conflict society.

Just as the UN intervention in Mozambique was drawing to a close in 1994, however, a similar process collapsed into horrific chaos in Rwanda. For obvious reasons, the UN involvement in Rwanda has become associated with the genocide of 1994 and the evident failure of the international community to act decisively either to prevent it or to stop it after it had begun. In fact, the original mandate of the United Nations in Rwanda had been to supervise and provide security for the implementation of a peace agreement between the government and rebel forces. It was the refusal of elements in and around the Rwandan government to accept the terms of this agreement that un-leashed the genocide. Thereafter the UN force, mandated originally for an essentially supervisory role, found itself powerless to intervene.

From 1999 the United Nations grappled with a similar role in the wake of an unsatisfactory internal 'settlement' in Rwanda's neighbour in central Africa, the Democratic Republic of Congo. Formerly Zaïre and originally the Congo, site of the first UN operation in Africa, the crisis here bore superficial similarities to that of the early 1960s, although the respective international environments in which the two episodes were played out were wholly different. In the later period a supposedly 'legitimate' regime that had been established after a complex and violent transition had proved incapable of exerting effective control over the state. The international dimension came from the involvement of neighbouring African states in pursuit of their own security and economic agendas. In particular, the origins and evolution of the crisis in the DRC cannot be separated from the circumstances of the Rwandan genocide and its aftermath. Reflecting this, the UN's later role was to help implement an essentially pan-African settlement.

Finally, the UN has also undertaken in various parts of Africa the activity that most closely fits the 'classic' peacekeeping role: the oversight of international agreements affecting the international relations of established states. The decolonization process in Namibia was one of the most complex to be confronted in sub-Saharan Africa. The agreement of the parties to the creation of an independent Namibia came only after a protracted guerrilla war and intense diplomatic pressure against the *de facto* colonial power, South Africa. However, in the circumstances of southern Africa in the 1980s, South Africa was clearly not acceptable either regionally or internationally as a manager for the process. Moreover, there were international interests around the independence of Namibia that went far beyond southern Africa. The continued presence of tens of thousands of Cuban troops in neighbouring Angola was a major issue for the United States. Their presence was justified by the Angolan government and Cuba itself as a necessary counter to repeated South African invasions of Angola through Namibia. Namibian independence and Cuban withdrawal from Angola, therefore, became inextricably linked. The United Nations, which had a special responsibility for Namibia dating back to the peace settlement after the First World War, was the obvious body to manage the overall process.

In the former Spanish territory of Western Sahara a UN mission was deployed in 1991, fifteen years after 'decolonization'. The settlement of 1976, which divided the territory between its neighbours, Morocco and Mauritania, was fiercely resisted by indigenous forces and a protracted guerrilla war ensued. As in the case of Namibia, regional international relations were deeply affected by the situation, with a three-way competition developing between the two inheritor states and a third powerful neighbour, Algeria, which supported the guerrillas in the territory. With the removal of the broader global resonances from the conflict at the end of the cold war (Morocco and Algeria having been, broadly speaking, pro-west and pro-Soviet respectively), UN involvement seemed an obvious recourse. We can also include in this category of intervention the UN presence in northern Chad in 1994, which supervised an agreed withdrawal of occupying Libyan forces. Miniature in scale, the Chad operation was a textbook success for military observation. The most recent operation in this category is the interpositionary force deployed by the UN between Ethiopia and Eritrea in 2000. This followed a massively destructive war between these two neighbouring countries in the Horn of Africa, which had previously maintained a close and co-operative relationship. The disintegration of this relationship caused particular dismay in the broader international community as both states, in their internal politics and international relations, had been widely admired.

By its nature, intervention in continuing political conflicts is an inherently fluid phenomenon, and the reduction of UN interventions in Africa to these four divisions can only be approximate. Some missions could arguably occupy more than one category. As we have remarked, this was certainly the case in

Sierra Leone. UN involvement there began as oversight of a regional peace-keeping effort, but in its later incarnation was designed to manage a peace settlement. There is also uncertainty over the categorization of the mission in the Central African Republic which was a 'United Nations' operation, but one composed mostly of contingents from an earlier, regional intervention and which was also involved in the implementation of an internal peace agreement. The primary purpose of involvement in Rwanda was to oversee a peace settlement, but the UN's presence in the region also had an inter-national dimension in its monitoring of the Rwandan–Ugandan border. In the Congo and Somalia the UN's role was primarily to shore up states (though not particular regimes) threatening to collapse. But in both cases there was at different times also an element of agreement implementation in the UN mandates. The general categorization remains valid as a way of placing UN operations in Africa in broad political contexts. But the ambi-guities we have just pointed up suggest that it does not provide an entirely satisfactory structure for the detailed anatomization of UN peacekeeping in Africa.

Partly for this reason, the exploration that follows will be organized region-ally rather than conceptually. This approach also permits the primary geo-graphical structure to be overlaid with an element of historical progression through the ordering of the regions examined. More importantly, though, a regional approach enables us to make the necessary connections between what might be quite separate missions in their character and aims but which are linked either by their cross-border implications or by regional particularities.

We will begin by exploring the history of peacekeeping in central Africa, in particular what has come to be called the 'Great Lakes' region. This part of the continent saw the UN's first African engagement in the Congo and later those in Rwanda, the DRC and, further to the north, the Central African Republic. We then move to southern Africa, where we begin with the United Nations' second African operation after the Congo, which was in Namibia, as well as the linked Cuban withdrawal from Angola, the subsequent pro-tracted engagement with Angola's internal chaos, and the more successful intervention in Mozambique. We will look next at the Horn of Africa in the north-east, where the UN was involved in Somalia and, most recently, between Ethiopia and Eritrea. Moving to west Africa, we will examine the separate but linked conflicts in Liberia and Sierra Leone. Finally, we will consider two operations of very different scale and outcome in what can be described as 'trans-Saharan' Africa: those in Western Sahara and northern Chad. As a conclusion we will return to some general questions about the performance of the UN in Africa as a whole, the extent of its contribution to conflict resolution and its prospects for the future.

CHAPTER TWO

Patrolling the Ethnic Frontier
Central Africa

United Nations involvement with central Africa began with the operation in the Congo in 1960, its first peacekeeping venture in Africa. UN military engagement with that country continued, though in a new form, forty years later. In the intervening period the Congo had undergone two name changes, several more changes of regime and an unending ebb and flow of political and inter-ethnic violence. Between the first and second engagements with the Congo the UN had also been involved in other parts of the region, most dramatically Rwanda. The interconnections between the Rwandan genocide of 1994 and the subsequent war, rebellion and foreign intervention in the Congo were such as to make the second crisis virtually a continuation of the first – though the unresolved issues of the 1960s also loomed large in the Congo in the late 1990s.

Further to the north in the central African region, away from the ethnic, political and diplomatic crucible of the 'Great Lakes', United Nations forces were involved in another crisis of the 1990s, in the Central African Republic. Here UN intervention was in different ways more complex and more simple than that in the Congo and Rwanda. It was more complex in the terms of the international context of the UN peacekeeping operation – which could be described as a continuation of regional intervention by other means. It was more straightforward than the involvements further to the south in that it was largely free of the constantly shifting dynamics of these crises and more tightly delimited in its functions and objectives. These four UN interventions in central Africa between them illustrate almost all of the characteristic difficulties and challenges, political and operational, that have confronted peacekeeping in the continent. The problems thrown up by neo-patrimonial forms of government were close to the heart of each crisis. The conflicts which drew UN intervention were between groups competing for control of the state and its resources, a competition that brought the state itself to the point of disintegration. The ethnic basis of these competing interests, and the discontinuity between ethnicity and nationality, were also particularly marked in the violence that afflicted the Great Lakes area, and gave these crises a clear international dimension. This was not merely regional. Broader rivalries that were present in other parts of Africa were particularly evident. These took different forms – from the east–west rivalry that attached itself to the first Congo crisis (which took place at the height of the cold war) to the Anglophone–Francophone divide that was at least an element in Rwanda and in the later Congo conflict. On the ground these political subtexts hugely complicated the task of the peacekeepers. Security Council mandates for the operations changed (in the Congo) or failed to change (in Rwanda) to meet shifting circumstances, re-ordered priorities and competing diplomatic objectives. At the centre of these shifting operational demands lay the dichotomy between interposition and enforcement, that is to say, between 'peacekeeping' narrowly defined and the type of 'collective security' action that was envisaged by Chapter VII of the UN Charter. It was not clear that the passage of four decades between the first and the latest engagement by the United Nations had seen any significant change in these general conditions in the region – but the UN itself had certainly acquired a new and necessary institutional caution over the period.

Beginnings: the Congo, 1960–64

The United Nations operation in the Congo – known as 'ONUC', an acronym of its French initials, *Opération des Nations Unies au Congo* – began in July 1960. The last elements of the force were withdrawn almost four years later in June 1964. It was by far the largest undertaking attempted by the UN up to that time with almost 20,000 troops from twenty-eight contributing states deployed at its height. Although larger operations would be undertaken in the post-cold war period (in Somalia and, further afield, in Cambodia and Bosnia), the 250 fatalities suffered by the UN in the Congo remained by far the highest casualty figure in any peacekeeping operation.

The Congo crisis was in many ways a model subject for UN peacekeeping in the early 1960s. It was pre-eminently a crisis of post-imperialism, just as the UN's previous interventions in the late 1940s and 1950s had been. The location of these earlier operations – Palestine, Kashmir and Suez (along with a short-lived observer mission in Lebanon in 1958) – reflected the historical geography of decolonization. Now, in the new decade, the geographical focus was shifting to sub-Saharan Africa, and in Dag Hammarskjöld's view, UN

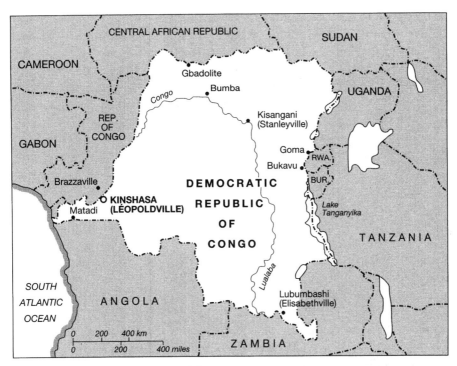

Congo – Democratic Republic of Congo

attention ought properly to shift with it. The danger of the Congo crisis being sucked into the broader cold war conflict was at least as great as it had been in the earlier interventions, and 'immunization' by peacekeeping seemed both appropriate and urgent.

Eventually, though, it was to be the Congo that first exposed the limits of 'peacekeeping' as defined by the experience of Suez and then elaborated and articulated by Hammarskjöld in the Summary Study. As a peacekeeping venture the Congo threw up a range of exceptions to the 'rule-book'. For one thing, the crisis in the Congo was only an 'international' problem by implication and potential. In essence it was a crisis of the internal state. This of course made UN intervention highly questionable under the terms of the Charter. The nature of the Congo emergency also made the principle of 'host-state consent' largely irrelevant when the identity, even the existence, of the 'host state' was frequently problematic. Perhaps most significantly, the Congo operation would starkly demonstrate the difficulty of separating the strategy of 'interposition' from that of 'enforcement'. The Congo intervention therefore posed a variety of challenges to the vision of peacekeeping as an alternative to the collective security enforcement that had been deemed unworkable in a bipolar system. Finally, the Congo experience illustrated the danger that UN intervention, far from fencing-off local conflicts from the larger global contest, could actually become an element in that contest, encouraging the very embroilment it was designed to prevent.

Occupying an area of 2.3 million square kilometres (only exceeded in Africa by Sudan), the ex-Belgian Congo embraced about 250 separate ethnic groups populating the basin of the great Congo river. The Congo had borders with nine other African territories at the time of its independence in 1960, which between them represented the residual interests of all the main European imperial powers. To the west was Congo-Brazzaville, which, along with the Central African Republic to the north, had until their own independence (also in 1960) formed French Equatorial Africa. To the north too was Sudan, independent since 1956. South of the Congo was the huge Portuguese territory of Angola. In the east, around Africa's Great Lakes, was a complex of colonies and quasi-colonies. Belgium itself still administered the United Nations Trust Territories of Rwanda and Burundi. Uganda remained a British colony until 1962, and Tanganyika, another British territory, was due to become independent in 1961. East of Tanganyika and to the south of the Congo was the British Federation of Rhodesia and Nyasaland, which was administered with a high degree of autonomy by its white settler minority.[1] In short, the Congo lay at the centre of an immensely complex web of late-colonial and post-colonial relationships.

The background to the crisis

The Congo's own colonial history had been a complicated one. It had also, in a number of respects, been a particularly disgraceful one. The area's first European contacts had been with the Portuguese, who, at the end of the fifteenth century, were ranging the coasts of Africa in pursuit of new sea-routes and way-stations for the trade with Asia. Subsequently the local rulers of the Kongo kingdom around the mouth of the river joined with the Portuguese in the new Atlantic slave trade. By the eighteenth century, however, Portuguese influence diminished. As European interest in Africa intensified in the later nineteenth century the Belgian king, Léopold II, saw in the Congo an opportunity for personal enrichment. Under the guise of a 'civilizing mission', he asserted his control over large areas of the territory. The reality was far from civilized. Léopold set about the systematic plundering of the so-called Congo Free State's natural resources (principally

---

1   In 1964 Tanganyika joined with the Indian Ocean island of Zanzibar to become Tanzania. The Federation of Rhodesia and Nyasaland was made up of modern-day Zambia (Northern Rhodesia), Zimbabwe (Southern Rhodesia) and Malawi (Nyasaland).

rubber and ivory) through the brutal exploitation of forced labour. By the first years of the twentieth century international outrage at Léopold's methods forced the hand of the Belgian government and in 1898 the state took over the territory from the personal control of the king, establishing the 'Belgian Congo'.[2] While the conditions of the local population improved under the rule of the Belgian state, Belgium's colonial attitudes were paternalistic in the extreme. There was considerable economic development in the territory, especially in the south-eastern province of Katanga, which had great and relatively easily accessible mineral wealth, in particular cobalt and copper. Katanga quickly became urbanized and its mining towns as well as the provincial capital, Elisabethville, developed as centres of European settlement.[3] Little effort was made to develop the human resources of the Congo. By the end of the Second World War the territory was little better prepared for self-government, let alone independence, than it had been half a century earlier. Recognition of its responsibilities in this regard came to Belgium only in the later 1950s, at which point there were no more than a handful of Congolese with a university-level education and none with any significant political or administrative experience.

Whatever the long-term intentions of Brussels, the Congo could not be insulated from the rapid growth of nationalism throughout Africa. In January 1959 anti-colonial rioting broke out in the capital, Léopoldville (renamed Kinshasa after independence). In the wake of this a multiplicity of new political parties sprang into being and began to agitate for independence. Belgium now made a belated effort to retrieve the situation by offering a graduated process towards independence by way of increasing autonomy. But the nationalist genie was now out of the bottle and casting its spell across the country. Evidently unwilling to confront this, Brussels abandoned its gradualist approach and simply announced that the Congo would become fully independent on 30 June 1960.

Prominent among the nationalist politicians who emerged to fill the leadership vacuum were two contrasting personalities. Joseph Kasavubu was as close to a 'veteran' nationalist politician as the foreshortened political history of the Congo could claim. A former Catholic seminarian, he had been prominent in the limited local government that Belgium had opened to the native population in the 1950s. A Bakongo – from the large ethnic group that dominated the Léopoldville area and much of the southern part of the

---

2 For an excellent account of the Congo Free State under Léopold see Neal Ascherson, *The King Incorporated: Leopold the Second and the Congo* (London: Granta, 1999).
3 Katanga produced about 60 per cent of the world's cobalt and 10 per cent of its copper. It also supplied the American atomic bomb programme with its uranium during the Second World War.

Congo – Kasavubu was relatively downbeat and reticent in his political style. Patrice Lumumba, on the other hand, was a politician of a more recent stamp. Initially better regarded by the Belgians as they rapidly prepared to withdraw than older-style nationalists like Kasavubu, by the time independence arrived Lumumba had undergone something of a self-reinvention as a radical pan-African. With a power base in Orientale province in the east of the country away from the national capital, his strong anti-tribalist stance was at least in part due to the fact that, unlike Kasavubu, his own ethnic base was relatively weak in the national context. In contrast to Kasavubu too, Lumumba commanded considerable rhetorical skill. Following the success of their respective groupings in the Congo's pre-independence elections in May 1960, Kasavubu became the national president and Lumumba prime minister following the final transfer of power.[4]

In addition to these two national leaders, a third political personality was to play a crucial part in the crisis leading to UN intervention. Moise Tshombe, one of a handful of successful African businessmen in the Congo, had become leader of the provincial government in Katanga after independence. His administration of the mineral-rich province with its large white population relied heavily on expatriate, mainly Belgian, advisers. Katanga was of vital economic importance to the new state as its exports constituted about 80 per cent of the Congo's trade revenues. The relationship between these three men determined the chaotic dynamics of Congolese politics that the UN struggled to come to terms with in the first months of its presence in the country.

A sense of the pace and depth of the crisis that overtook the new state can be gained from a simple chronology of events over the first two weeks of independence. Almost immediately after the declaration of independence on 30 June 1960, public order was threatened by the violent reaction of parties and ethnic groups that felt themselves to have been excluded from the new post-colonial settlement. On 4 July the first of a series of military mutinies broke out in Léopoldville. The 25,000-strong paramilitary *Force Publique* of the colonial period was in the process of being transformed into the army of the new state – the *Armée Nationale Congolaise* (ANC). The transformation, however, was accompanied by great discontent on the part of the rank and file. African soldiers were still under the orders of about 1000 Belgian officers, a situation that may have been practically necessary but that nevertheless jarred with African expectations of independence. Within days the mutinies and the generalized disorder that accompanied them had spread to other parts of the Congo. Europeans now became the targets of the rebel

---

4 Kasavubu led the Bakongo Alliance (Abako) and Lumumba the Congolese National Movement (*Movement Nationale Congolaise*).

soldiers and the mobs that followed them. Murder and rape became wide-spread and a white exodus from the country began.

By 8 July the disorder had reached Katanga. Here the violence was firmly resisted by Tshombe's administration in Elisabethville, which immediately appealed for Belgian military intervention to restore order. Brussels acted the next day when troops garrisoned in the Congo by the terms of the independence agreement were deployed to protect foreign residents. They were quickly reinforced by other troops who were rushed into the country. Within a few days there were about 10,000 Belgian soldiers in the territory, a far greater number than had been posted there during colonial rule. As the situation stabilized in Katanga while the rest of the Congo remained in chaos, the Elisabethville administration made a fateful decision. On 11 July, with the encouragement of his foreign advisers, Tshombe declared the independence of Katanga from the Congo and refused the leaders of the central government admission to the territory.

On the day that the first Belgian soldiers were deployed, Lumumba had approached UN under-secretary-general Ralph Bunche (an African-American who was in the Congo to assess development needs) with a request for UN help in training the ANC. He did not at that stage ask for a peacekeeping force. The day following Katanga's declaration of independence, however, Kasavubu and Lumumba formally requested United Nations intervention. The initial request was couched in terms that emphasized the supposed 'international' dimension to the crisis. The problem according to the Congolese leaders was 'Belgian aggression' rather than internal collapse. 'The essential purpose of the requested military aid', according to their telegram to Hammarskjöld, 'was to protect the national territory of the Congo against the present external aggression which is a threat to international peace.'[5]

The United Nations intervenes

The assault on the new state by Belgium, in the view of the Léopoldville government, lay not only in its military intervention, but also in the allegedly orchestrated secession of Katanga. In this view, Belgium and other European 'imperialists' had subverted the structures of the new state in order to safe-guard their neo-colonial commercial and industrial interests. At the heart of the conspiracy, in the eyes of the central government, was the Belgian concession company the *Union Minière du Haute Katanga*, which had dominated mineral extraction in the province. Formally, though, it was the uninvited presence of Belgian forces that constituted the 'international' dimension to

---

5   United Nations document S/4382, 12 July 1960.

the crisis, which could be used to justify UN intervention. The issue was brought to the Security Council by the secretary-general himself. To do this Hammarskjöld invoked for the first time in the UN's history a power of personal initiative given to the secretary-general under article 99 of the Charter.[6] He initially sought Security Council authorization for an operation that would permit Belgian forces to be withdrawn from the Congo in much the same way as UNEF had earlier allowed Britain and France to leave Suez without too great a loss of face. The UN presence would then help train and prepare the ANC for its role as national army (thus also meeting the terms of Lumumba's original approach to Ralph Bunche).

While article 99 permitted the secretary-general to initiate discussion in the Council, it did not extend to the presentation of resolutions. To work round this, Tunisia, which was currently one of the non-permanent members of the Security Council, produced a draft that included the main outlines of the response Hammarskjöld sought. The resolution called on Belgium 'to withdraw its troops from the territory of the Republic of the Congo', though it did not explicitly condemn their original deployment. It went on to authorize Hammarskjöld 'to take the necessary steps, in consultation with the Government of the Congo, to provide the Government with such military assistance as may be necessary until, through the efforts of the Congolese Government with the technical assistance of the United Nations, the national security forces may be able, in the opinion of the Government, to meet fully their tasks.'[7] It was envisaged, therefore, that the Léopoldville government, which had first sought UN assistance, would have a key role in determining the nature and duration of that assistance. Host state consent, a key element in the peacekeeping concept, was thus made explicit in the initial mandate.

On 14 July the Security Council authorized the establishment of ONUC. The United States strongly backed the initiative. While the Soviet delegation had some misgivings about ceding such a potentially large degree of authority to the secretary-general, it was anxious not to be seen as obstructive by the African states in the UN who wanted immediate action.[8] The commitment to intervention was not, even at the height of the cold war, a matter for superpower argument – for the moment. Dissent in the Security Council, so far as there was any, lay along an older fault-line. There was still, evidently, an 'imperial' tendency as well as western and eastern ones. Britain and France

---

6   Article 99 of the Charter states that the 'Secretary-General may bring to the attention of the Security Council any matter which in his opinion may threaten the maintenance of international peace and security'. It was designed to give the secretary-general a personal 'political' role not available to his predecessors in the League of Nations.

7   United Nations document S/RES/143, 14 July 1960.

8   Joseph P. Lash, *Dag Hammarskjold: a Biography* (London: Cassell, 1962), p. 229.

registered their sympathy for the Belgian position by abstaining. So far, so good, it seemed, to the extent that peacekeeping in the image of the Summary Study was concerned.[9] But in reality the commitment was crowded with hostages to fortune. For one thing, it was predicated on the continued existence of a unified and legitimate central government to act as interlocutor and partner. It also assumed that the disorder which preceded the Belgian intervention would end once Belgian forces had withdrawn. Similarly, the secession of Katanga was assumed to be a temporary gesture that would end with the disorder in the Congo as a whole.

The first UN troops began to arrive in the Congo on 16 June – a much faster deployment than would be typical of later African peacekeeping operations. While the United States and other big powers were to help with transport and logistics, the main body of the force was to be drawn (initially at any rate) from African states. As there were still only a limited number of independent states south of the Sahara, this included a large number of north African troops. In addition, European sensitivities were to be allayed with contributions from two western 'middle powers', Sweden and Ireland (both of which were formally neutral states). The first contingent in place was from Ghana. Although independent since 1957, Ghana still had a preponderance of British officers in its army and this was reflected in the composition of the initial contingent. Within two weeks ONUC was 8400-strong and now also included contingents from Tunisia, Morocco, Ethiopia, Guinea and Liberia. Aside from the obvious desirability of using African personnel to deal with African problems, it has been suggested that Hammarskjöld had another motive, By co-opting those African armies with the capacity to intervene into the UN's multilateral effort, he made them unavailable for unilateral involvement on behalf of the various Congo factions.[10]

Almost immediately the potential contradictions in the UN's role in the Congo became evident. To what extent was ONUC to act in a direct policing role rather than simply a training one in the absence of any local forces competent to restore order? The resolution establishing the operation suggested that both tasks would be undertaken, but if ONUC was to impose order, on whose orders and with what tactics would it do so? Was the UN force to be effectively an executive arm of the central government while the ANC was trained properly to carry out its national security functions? The mandate was ambiguous over this, emphasizing the importance of

---

9   Arthur Lee Burns and Nina Heathcote, *Peacekeeping by UN Forces from Suez to the Congo* (London: Pall Mall, 1963), p. 25.

10 Keith Kyle, 'The UN in the Congo', Initiative on Conflict Resolution and Ethnicity (INCORE) occasional paper. Found at www.incore.ulst.ac.uk/home/publication/occasional/kyle.html.

'consultations' with the government but not specifying lines of command. Most crucially in this respect, how was ONUC to respond to the secession of Katanga? On the one hand, the UN had intervened at the request of a government whose legitimacy over the entire territory of the Congo it had itself acknowledged. If ONUC was to act in support of this government in restoring order, then the fragmentation of the state was surely a major threat to that order. Whatever the wording of the Security Council resolution, the terms of article 2(7) of the Charter (and the less formal strictures in Hammarskjöld's Summary Study) were perfectly clear about the unacceptability of interference in the internal politics of sovereign states. Amidst these concerns the original reason for UN involvement in the crisis – the contested presence of Belgian troops – seemed increasingly unimportant. In reality the Belgian intervention was a symptom and not a cause of the Congo's myriad ills. The Suez crisis, it was soon clear, belonged to a different, simpler political world and provided no useful compass for the direction the UN should follow in the Congo.

For Hammarskjöld, however, the Congo was, initially at any rate, a challenge to be embraced with almost missionary enthusiasm. It was an issue that went to the heart of the great tectonic shifts in mid-twentieth-century international relations. While political attention had, understandably, been focused on the ideological polarity that characterized the international system of the time, the cold war was ultimately a transitory phenomenon. The transformations in international relations being wrought by decolonization and the huge expansion in the state system that followed were in reality more permanent and more fundamental. Inescapably, though, global bipolarity provided a complicating and at times dangerous background to the evolution of this larger process. For the cerebral Hammarskjöld, whose vision of the United Nations and its purposes was nothing if not a broad historical one, the organization's role in the Congo was both important in itself and as an emblem of the UN's part in the long-term scheme of things. The interventions in Palestine and Suez had been symptomatic of this in the context of the late 1940s and 1950s when the territorial organization of the Middle East and the impact of Arab nationalism was the major post-imperial challenge. Already in 1960 it seemed clear that it would be Africa that would demand particular attention in the new decade.

This larger view provided the real 'international' dimension to the Congo crisis in Hammarskjöld's view, and not the scant and rather laboured rationalizations around the reappearance of Belgian troops on Congolese territory. It was a perspective that was at odds with the shorter-term concerns of the Congo prime minister, who had sought to enlist the UN as an ally in an essentially local problem. Lumumba had asked for UN involvement as a means of bolstering the Congo state (and his leadership of it) in the face of a specific threat. This fundamental dissonance between the views of Hammarskjöld and Lumumba – and their respective supporters in the wider world – would quickly push the Congo operation into confusion and controversy. Moreover, while there seemed no immediate danger in July 1960 that the Congo crisis would be dragged in to cold war politics, this unusual superpower consensus was not to survive for long.

To some extent, the conflicting visions of Lumumba and Hammarskjöld over the UN's proper role in the Congo were academic. It was unlikely that the UN would have had the capacity to achieve Lumumba's objectives even if it had been willing to do so. Belgium showed no enthusiasm for withdrawing its forces and handing the situation over to ONUC until stability had been achieved. The ambivalence of Britain and France, both permanent members of the Security Council with the power of veto over its decisions, was already evident from their abstention in the vote establishing ONUC. They would certainly have opposed any direct action on the part of the UN against Belgian forces. Although more enthusiastic about UN intervention, the United States would not have compromised its relations with Belgium, a NATO ally, by supporting action against it. Belgian compliance with the original call for its withdrawal in the establishing resolution, therefore, was to be gained by creating sufficient stability in the Congo to permit the repatriation of its forces. Part of this would clearly involve the subduing, and in some areas the disarming, of the ANC, whose violence had provoked the Belgian intervention. Lumumba's perception of the crisis essentially placed this cause and effect in reverse. In his view Belgian interference, whether direct, in the form of military intervention, or indirect, in its continued officering of the Congolese military, had caused the disorder.

In the event, after the deployment of ONUC the Belgians gradually reduced their force numbers. By the second week in September 1960 Belgian forces had either returned to the bases they had previously occupied by agreement or had been withdrawn from the country altogether. The big exception was Katanga, where the Belgian military presence was maintained. Inevitably, this continued European involvement became associated with the province's secession, which was proving more enduring than many originally thought it would.[11] The question of Katanga was now at the crux of the UN's dilemma in the Congo. Was Katangese secession, as Hammarskjöld felt, an internal problem in which ONUC must as far as possible remain uninvolved and towards the resolution of which the UN had no adequate resources to deploy? Or was it, as in Lumumba's view, a fundamental source

---

11 Something in excess of 200 Belgian military personnel remained in Katanga after the withdrawal from other parts of the Congo. Alan James, *The Politics of Peacekeeping* (London: Chatto & Windus, 1969), p. 357.

of the national crisis that the UN had been mandated to help resolve? The secession was being rapidly consolidated in the first weeks of ONUC's presence in the Congo, and was sustained by a wide spectrum of support in many western governments. With a well-trained and equipped paramilitary *'gendarmerie'* (in reality a small army) under Belgian officers and encouraged by locally based western diplomats, Katanga's defiance of the central government continued effectively unchallenged by ONUC throughout the remainder of 1960.

For Lumumba and his supporters the UN had simply reneged on the original terms on which its assistance had been sought and offered. Beyond the Congo this perception of ONUC as an instrument of 'imperialism' was also increasing among Third World states and was, moreover, beginning to strike a new threatening chord in Moscow. On 9 August the Security Council determined that the presence of ONUC personnel in Katanga was essential to the overall operation, while at the same time affirming that the UN would 'not be a party to or in any way influence the outcome of any internal conflict, constitutional or otherwise'.[12] Three days later Hammarskjöld, with some personal courage, ignored Tshombe's threats of resistance and himself flew into Elisabethville with two companies of Swedish troops.[13] But this proved to be little more than a token presence. Real military and police power in Katanga remained with the *gendarmerie*, its Belgian officers and a growing number of foreign mercenaries. The secession therefore continued largely unaffected by the symbolic deployment of ONUC troops. If anything, Katanga was strengthened by the implicit legitimization of an apparently tolerant UN presence.

The September crisis: Léopoldville and New York

In the meantime, in the absence of forceful action by the UN, Lumumba – utilizing Soviet-supplied transport and equipment – began to mobilize his own forces. In doing so he merely added to the Congo's overall instability and his own separation from the main flow of central government politics, which remained largely supportive of ONUC. The situation deteriorated dramatically for both the UN and Lumumba at the beginning of September when the central government imploded. The long-standing and barely suppressed tensions between Kasavubu and Lumumba had led to a situation in which each attempted to dismiss the other. At this stage the conflict between

---

12 United Nations document S/RES/146, 9 August 1960.
13 Anthony Verrier, *International Peacekeeping: United Nations Forces in a Troubled World* (Harmondsworth: Penguin, 1981), p. 57.

the two men was both personal and ideological. Both in their different ways were ambitious politicians with their own autocratic tendencies, forced to share national power in an ambiguous constitutional relationship. This would have been a difficult situation to sustain even without the gathering chaos that was destroying the fabric of Congolese statehood. Fatally, the breach was now cast in ideological terms that could be (and quickly were) drawn out beyond the Congo into the broader cold war contest. Lumumba became the revolutionary, pro-Soviet prophet of Afro-Asian liberation. Kasavubu, on the other hand, became the pragmatic and helpful friend of the west. ONUC was caught in the middle of a squabble which was rapidly mutating into an international crisis. The principle of UN non-intervention in domestic affairs was now meaningless. For better or worse the UN had now become a major, if not *the* major, actor in the Congo's politics.

To find itself in the forefront of Congo politics at this time would have been bad enough even without the complication of the unresolved constitutional wrangle in Léopoldville. But with Kasavubu and Lumumba continuing to insist that each was the legitimate leader of the Congo state, any action of commission or omission by the UN would inevitably be perceived as partial. At this point certain crucial decisions were taken by the UN that would shape the organization's relations with both the Congo factions and their international patrons throughout the following calamitous year. Hammarskjöld's representative in Léopoldville at this time was Andrew Cordier. Although a member of the UN secretariat and therefore an international civil servant, Cordier was an American national. This inevitably became an issue in the various reactions to the steps that he now took. UN troops were ordered to close all airfields in the country and to shut down the capital's radio station. Ostensibly these were prudent moves designed to prevent the movement of factional forces and the dissemination of inflammatory propaganda, but the overall effect was to favour Kasavubu at the expense of Lumumba. By grounding air traffic the UN prevented the transfer to the capital of forces loyal to the prime minister from his power base in Stanleyville (now Kisangani), the capital of Orientale province. By closing the radio station Lumumba was denied his only means of mass communication. The Léopoldville area was predominantly Bakongo in ethnic composition, which obviously favoured Kasavubu, who was also able to broadcast from the capital of the 'friendly' former French Congo, Brazzaville, just across the Congo river from Léopoldville.[14]

It is impossible to come to any firm judgement about whether these steps on the part of the UN in Léopoldville were intentionally partisan. But the

---

14   Brian Urquhart, *Hammarskjold* (London: Bodley Head, 1973), p. 96.

inescapable fact was that not only Cordier but virtually all senior UN figures in the Congo at this stage were westerners.[15] The military force commander was a Swedish general, Carl von Horn (replaced in December 1960 by General Sean McKeown from Ireland). The officer in charge of political operations was another Swede, Sture Linnér. He had been chosen personally by Hammarskjöld and was widely seen as the real locus of UN power in the Congo. Similarly, the emerging group of advisers around Hammarskjöld in New York – the so-called 'Congo Club' – also consisted mainly of officials from western states. This simply reflected the political culture of the whole peacekeeping project. In its origins and assumptions it was fundamentally 'liberal' and pluralist – and therefore 'western'. Even the neutral European force contributors to ONUC, Ireland and Sweden, were 'neutral' only in the formal sense that neither was a member of NATO (and, additionally, had no embarrassing imperial history). In all other respects they, in common with most other 'middle-power' peacekeepers of the cold war years, were of the west. It was perhaps inevitable that, even with the best will in the world, there would always be a risk that those responsible for the direction of peacekeeping in the field would bring, however unwittingly, their own cultural and ideological assumptions to their operational decisions.

It was certainly possible that Lumumba's increasingly violent anti-ONUC and pro-Soviet rhetoric had some impact on local UN decision-making, at whatever level of consciousness. Ideologically speaking, the concept of impartial peacekeeping had no place in Soviet views of international relations. Peacekeeping as an idea was just about acceptable to the Soviet view of things to the extent that it was explicitly not about enforcement. In Suez the peacekeeping effort was sweetened for Moscow by the political embarrassment it brought to the western alliance. Initially at any rate the Congo intervention could have been expected to follow the same pattern. It was supposed to 'sort out' the consequences of neo-colonial mischief – with Belgium being cast as culprit just as Britain and France had been in Suez. But as the Congo crisis deepened and the prospect of a simple interposition operation receded, the politics of the cold war began to impinge and the Soviet leader, Nikita Khrushchev, took an increasingly critical stance on the day-to-day direction of ONUC.

Cordier was replaced as Hammarskjöld's special representative soon after the events of early September. While this was reported as a routine rotation of duties, the fact that Cordier's replacement was an Indian national, Rajeshwar Dayal, was seen as significant in that it put a key post in the

15   Evan Luard, *A History of the United Nations: Vol. II. The Age of Decolonization, 1955–65* (London: Macmillan, 1989), p. 248.

hands of an official from a leading state of the Afro-Asian bloc.[16] This was not enough to assuage the growing resentment of the Soviet Union at the direction of the operation, however. The Soviet representative in the Security Council began a campaign of denunciation of ONUC's supposed failure to confront the forces of 'imperialism' in the Congo. This impression of a UN administration conspiring to frustrate legitimate African nationalist aspirations (personified in the Congo by the increasingly mythologized and self-mythologizing Lumumba) had some resonance within the Afro-Asian member states in the UN.

In the meantime, the stand-off between Kasavubu and Lumumba in Léopoldville continued. In mid-September Lumumba won important support from parliament, which endorsed his continuing authority. But this was followed immediately by what was in effect a military *putsch* carried out by Colonel Joseph Mobutu. A few months previously Mobutu had been a non-commissioned officer in the ANC. He had then been rapidly promoted amidst the chaos of the mutinies to become the chief-of-staff of the army. His stated purpose for intervening was to break the Lumumba–Kasavubu impasse. Accordingly, the government was suspended and day-to-day powers handed over to a 'college of commissioners' composed of supposedly non-political administrators. Kasavubu, either by persuasion or by complicity, seemed ready to accept this and appointed a new 'prime minister', the malleable Joseph Ileo. For his part, Lumumba sought to rally the ANC to his support against this new political axis. When this failed, his personal position in Léopoldville became extremely vulnerable and he was placed under UN protection.

The Security Council was fundamentally divided on developments in Léopoldville, which were now being cast in explicitly cold war terms. As a result it found it impossible quickly to agree a new strategic direction for ONUC. When the Soviet Union vetoed a proposed resolution, the discussion of the issue passed to the General Assembly.[17] The Assembly opened its Emergency Special Session on 17 September 1960. More confident of support in the General Assembly, which had a large Afro-Asian representation, than in the Security Council, the Soviet Union now launched a frontal assault on Hammarskjöld and his handling of the crisis. In some respects he was vulnerable to such an attack. He personally had brought the issue to the

---

16   George Abi-Saab, *The United Nations Operation in the Congo, 1960–1964* (Oxford: Oxford University Press, 1978), pp. 77–8.

17   N.D. White, *Keeping the Peace: the United Nations and the Maintenance of International Peace and Security* (2nd edn, Manchester: Manchester University Press, 1997), pp. 255–6. The General Assembly was brought into the issue at this stage through the so-called 'uniting for peace' process, which had been adopted during the Korean War to evade inevitable Soviet dissent in the Security Council.

Security Council through the exercise of his prerogative under article 99. He had proposed the nature of the UN's response and persuaded the Security Council to back his plan. Therefore, whatever the limits of his personal control over the politics of either the UN or the Congo, he was the obvious culprit for whichever factions, Congolese or international, felt themselves to have lost out as a result of ONUC's action or inaction.

On 23 September Khrushchev himself addressed the General Assembly. Hammarskjöld, in failing to support Lumumba and tolerating the continued secession of Katanga, was, he claimed, 'following the colonialists' line, opposing the lawful government of the Congo and the Congolese people and supporting the renegades who, under the guise of fighting for the independence of the republic of the Congo, are actually continuing the policy of the colonialists'. He then widened the attack from the specific question of the Congo to the whole issue of peacekeeping operations and, ultimately, the structure of the United Nations itself. If peacekeeping forces were

> to be used . . . to suppress liberation movements, it will naturally be difficult to reach agreement on their establishment, since there will be no guarantee that they will not be used for reactionary purposes that are alien to the interests of peace. Provision must be made to ensure that no state falls into the predicament in which the Republic of the Congo now finds itself.

Therefore, the Soviet government had 'come to a definite conclusion on this matter. . . . Conditions have clearly matured to the point where the post of Secretary-General, who alone directs the staff and alone interprets and executes the decisions of the Security Council and the sessions of the General Assembly, should be abolished.' Instead there should be a triumvirate (or 'troika') composed of representatives of the three groups of states that dominated the international system of the time: western, communist and Afro-Asian. This would ensure that neither of the cold war blocs could exploit the power of the office. Such a reform would ensure a truly internationalized United Nations.[18] The result would be to abandon the concept of the neutral international civil servant owing loyalty to the UN as an institution rather than to any state. The troika system would, in short, have formalized global bipolarity and incorporated the cold war as a permanent feature of the UN's architecture.

There was, in the event, little support for the troika plan.[19] The Soviet proposal seemed to be based on the assumption that the non-aligned Afro-Asian states in the General Assembly had been so outraged at ONUC's

---

18 United Nations document A/PV.869, 23 September 1960.
19 Luard, *A History of the United Nations: Vol. II*, p. 206.

actions in the Congo that their support would be automatic. In fact the response of the Afro-Asians to events in the Congo was more nuanced and showed an appreciation of the complexity of the issue that Moscow appeared unable – or more likely unwilling – to share. There was also a more general distaste for the 'politicization' of the UN secretariat proposed in the troika plan. Even delegations that would normally have been counted reliable supporters of the Soviet Union at this time, like Cuba, Egypt and Indonesia, seemed almost embarrassed by the proposals.[20] Realizing that he was pursuing a lost cause, Khrushchev quietly dropped his plan.[21]

Yet it was unarguable that there were some serious issues to be explored around the management of ONUC. It was a matter of fact that the senior and most politically sensitive levels of the UN secretariat were dominated by western officials, and not only in relation to decision-making for the Congo. The Soviet bloc remained greatly under-represented in the UN's bureaucracy. It was also now evident that peacekeeping, which was designed to prevent cold war involvement in peripheral areas of bipolar competition, could actually become the focus of such involvement. As one writer put it, the UN 'did not . . . keep the cold war out of the Congo. On the contrary, it further politicized the crisis and ensured that the cold war would be fought in that chaotic arena.'[22] With the Congo, cold war competition had come, paradoxically, to pose a threat to the idea of peacekeeping – an activity that had itself developed to neutralize that competition. The Congo operation illustrated something that was not applicable to the Suez operation: that dangerous situations could deteriorate not just despite but actually because of UN intervention.

The death of Lumumba and the February 1961 resolution

In Léopoldville Mobutu's 'college of commissioners' had been installed at the end of September with the full support of Kasavubu. Lumumba continued to contest the arrangement and fight against his own political marginalization. However, he was obviously constrained by his lack of freedom of movement and his continued dependence on ONUC protection. A UN Conciliation Commission was established by the General Assembly at the beginning of November with the aim of bringing the factions together, but it was not

---

20 Urquhart, *Hammarskjold*, p. 461.
21 Nikita Khrushchev (ed. Strobe Talbott), *Khrushchev Remembers: the Last Testament* (London: André Deutsch, 1974), pp. 483–4.
22 E.W. Lefever, *Crisis in the Congo: a United Nations Force in Action* (Washington, DC: Brookings Institute, 1965), p. 207.

successful. The main international manifestation of Lumumba's continuing power struggle with the Kasavubu–Mobutu faction was a dispute over which of them should be recognized as the representative of the Congolese state at the United Nations. This was obviously an issue of much greater significance than simply the identity of a General Assembly delegation. In the absence of any other available criteria, a seat at the UN was effectively a stamp of legitimacy. The state would 'belong' to the faction recognized in New York. It was not to be Lumumba's. In November 1960 the General Assembly (which was the competent organ in the matter) finally accepted the credentials of the Kasavubu delegation.[23]

Hammarskjöld himself was unhappy with the General Assembly vote. He had hoped that the UN-organized conciliation process might still have succeeded in getting an accommodation between the factions.[24] His concerns about the UN's taking of political sides in this way were well founded. The decision to accept the credentials of the anti-Lumumba faction triggered a sequence of events in the Congo that would make Hammarskjöld's position and that of ONUC on the ground even more difficult. After the victory of his rivals in New York, Lumumba slipped away from the protection of ONUC in Léopoldville with the aim of returning to his political base in Stanleyville and there mobilizing sufficient military support to confront Mobutu's ANC. It was an ill-planned and badly executed venture, however, and he was quickly captured by soldiers loyal to Mobutu. Anger at ONUC's failure to protect Lumumba beyond Léopoldville was expressed from within the operation itself and several African contributors now threatened to withdraw their contingents from the force. Worse, with Lumumba out of the way, Mobutu, with Belgian connivance, was mobilizing his forces on Katanga's northern borders against those still loyal to the ex-prime minister.[25] Hammarskjöld's protests at this were ignored in Brussels. Then, in an act of brutal pragmatism, Mobutu arranged to have the imprisoned Lumumba transferred to Katanga. He was murdered shortly after he arrived on 17 January 1961, an outcome that had probably been pre-arranged between Mobutu and Tshombe.

The consequences for ONUC of Lumumba's death were immediate. As we have seen, the UN's failure to protect him from capture in the first place was deeply resented by many in the Afro-Asian world. Now, its failure to prevent his transfer to Katanga and subsequent murder seemed to suggest

---

23   United Nations document A/1498, 22 November 1960.
24   Luard, *A History of the United Nations: Vol. II*, p. 257.
25   Belgium agreed to permit the movement of Mobutu's forces through the territory of Ruanda-Urundi (present-day Rwanda and Burundi), which, although administered by Brussels, was in legal fact a United Nations Trust Territory. Ibid., pp. 259–60.

something more than just incompetence and negligence. Although no direct claim of UN complicity in Lumumba's fate was ever made, there were persistent suspicions of the involvement of western states, in particular the United States, which increasingly saw Lumumba as a Soviet dupe. It emerged in the mid-1970s that the American Central Intelligence Agency (CIA) had prepared plans for his assassination just prior to his capture by Mobutu. Later, credible claims were made that the White House itself had approved this project in the last days of the Eisenhower administration. [26] It is likely though that Washington achieved its ends without the need for any direct involvement. There were other foreign interests in play as well. Much later an investigation by the Belgian parliament suggested that Brussels was directly implicated in the affair.[27] Whoever was or was not involved behind the scenes of the murder, the impression among a growing number of states – and not all of them Afro-Asian or Soviet satellites – was that the UN was in real danger of becoming compromised by western policy objectives in the Congo. Egypt, Guinea, Mali and Morocco now withdrew their troops from ONUC, greatly weakening its 'African' character. They were followed by Indonesia and Yugoslavia, two powerful members of the emerging non-aligned grouping that had sent contingents to the Congo when the scale of the operation outstripped the capacities of African contributors. More ominously, Egypt and Guinea now formally recognized an 'alternative' Congo government established in Stanleyville by Lumumba's deputy, Antoine Gizenga. The threat of a major international split on the very identity of the Congo state now loomed. It was only held off by a newly acquired caution on the part of the Soviet Union. For the moment Moscow contented itself with renewed demands for the replacement of Hammarskjöld.

In the aftermath of Lumumba's death, and amidst the political confusion that underlay it, the United Nations sought to retrieve the situation by authorizing a new, more robust mandate for ONUC. In February 1961 the Security Council agreed a resolution effectively giving ONUC the power to impose peace in the Congo by military means. The border between 'peacekeeping' and enforcement, uncertain from the beginning of the UN's intervention, had now more or less dissolved. The new mandate represented an early example of a phenomenon that was to become familiar in military interventions three decades later when it would be described as 'mission creep'. The February resolution authorized ONUC to 'take all appropriate measures to prevent the occurrence of civil war in the Congo'. This could involve 'the use of force . . . in the last resort'. The Security Council also

---

26   See, for example, Richard Crockatt, *The Fifty Years War: the United States and the Soviet Union in World Politics 1941–1991* (London: Routledge, 1994), p. 198.

27   For the recent theories of external involvement see *The Guardian*, 10 August 2000.

called 'for the immediate withdrawal and evacuation . . . of all Belgian and other foreign military and paramilitary personnel and political advisers not under the United Nations Command, and mercenaries'. Finally, 'an immediate and impartial investigation' was to be undertaken into Lumumba's murder.[28] The resolution was passed with nine in favour and none against but with the Soviet Union and France, for their own quite different reasons, abstaining. In Moscow's view the resolution did not go far enough in denouncing western 'imperialism', while for Paris it went too far. In the wake of the resolution the UN retrieved at least some of its credibility as an actor in the crisis. A change of administration in Washington that came just at this time also eased the cold war tensions growing around the crisis. With John F. Kennedy in the White House, American policy appeared much more sensitive to African concerns than it did during the Eisenhower presidency.

Whatever the international consequences of Lumumba's murder, in the short term it served its intended purpose as far as most of his internal political opponents were concerned. Although a 'Lumumbist' regime still controlled Stanleyville and large parts of Orientale province, and though factional violence continued in Kasai and Kivu provinces in the east, the permanent removal of Lumumba strengthened the position of Mobutu, Kasavubu and Ileo. Their regime was now reasonably well consolidated in Léopoldville. Paradoxically, though, this did not augur well for Katanga. As long as Lumumba was a political threat, Léopoldville and Elisabethville had a common enemy to unite against. Now the Léopoldville regime became aware of the long-term economic consequences of the continued secession of Katanga. Soon the central government moved behind international efforts to extinguish Katangan 'independence'.

In the meantime ONUC had its troubles in the rest of the Congo. Sporadic conflicts continued between its contingents and the still armed and dangerous factions of the ANC and other armed groups. These resulted in considerable losses from a number of contingents, including the Sudanese, Ghanaians and Irish. This continuing disorder served the propaganda purposes of the Katangese well. While the rest of the country had been struggling through the successive crises of army mutiny, foreign intervention and violent political factionalism, 'independent' Katanga could present itself (and be presented by its foreign sponsors) as an island of stability and tranquillity.[29] Despite being equipped with a more effective mandate after February 1961, and although the great majority of UN members were hostile to Katanga, it was never clear whether ONUC was specifically authorized to end its secession

---

28 United Nations document S/RES/161, 21 February 1961.
29 Alan James, *Peacekeeping in International Politics* (London: Macmillan, 1990), p. 298.

by force. Could such a course of action reasonably be interpreted as 'preventing civil war'? The Security Council itself could not agree on this, and it is likely that the ambiguity was to some degree intentional: the price of getting a resolution through the Council at all. The question of the resolution's significance in relation to Katanga was never resolved. Attempts by the General Assembly to pressure the Council into adopting a more vigorous and transparent approach were unavailing.[30] Within this continuing ambiguity lay the seeds of the UN's next major crisis in the Congo.

The secretary-general himself seemed to have little enthusiasm for what might be described as the 'maximalist' interpretation of the February resolution regarding Katanga. For Hammarskjöld the new mandate threatened too great a departure from his original peacekeeping model. At the same time, the more muscular rhetoric of the resolution had restored some prestige to the UN and relieved it (and him) of much of the pressure from the non-aligned states, which had been present at varying levels of intensity since September 1960. Moreover, both Moscow and Washington, after the change of administration there, were now publicly committed to a unified Congo. But this improved international context could not in itself create the conditions necessary for Suez-style interpositionary peacekeeping. The internal situation in the Congo remained highly volatile. There was, in short, no peace for ONUC to keep and the UN's position remained complex and dangerous. Throughout the first half of 1961 the Katangese regime continued to defy all UN attempts to negotiate its reintegration into the Congo. Its *gendarmerie*, stiffened by a steady supply of white mercenaries despite Security Council prohibitions, appeared to give it the military capacity to do so with impunity. Meanwhile, Tshombe and his European advisers could simply ignore or obfuscate UN attempts to broker a settlement.

Crisis in Katanga and the death of Hammarskjöld

In June 1961 Hammarskjöld had appointed as his representative in Katanga a diplomat seconded from the Irish UN delegation, Conor Cruise O'Brien. O'Brien's appointment had been in line with the secretary-general's continuing efforts to balance the competing sensitivities of those who felt most comfortable with 'European' personnel and those who were suspicious of 'pro-western' officials. The only western states to contribute contingents, it will be recalled, were neutral Sweden and Ireland (which had also provided ONUC's first two force commanders). O'Brien was of a particularly

---

30 In April the General Assembly had voted 61 to 5 with 33 (mainly western) abstentions that foreign personnel should 'be completely withdrawn and evacuated' from Katanga.

independent stamp, however, and soon became frustrated and angry at the combination of arrogance and evasiveness that characterized the *galère* of Europeans and white Africans that formed the backbone of the Katangan administration and its armed forces. Meanwhile, ethnic tensions began to mount around the Katangan situation in the first half of 1961. Tshombe himself was a Lunda, who were an ethnic group with a sophisticated tradition of political organization pre-dating the imperial incursion. Their traditional rivals in the Katanga region were the Baluba, who historically had been more adaptive to the colonial state. The Baluba, who had originally been ambivalent about secession, now felt increasingly menaced by the Elisabethville regime and called for reunification with Léopoldville. This stance put them under even greater threat in Katanga, and they now looked to the UN for protection. In addition to the political crisis caused by secession was now added a humanitarian emergency as large-scale refugee movements began. By the middle of 1961, therefore, tension in and around Katanga had grown dramatically.

The central government, now with a more forceful prime minister in the person of Cyrille Adoula, had become determinedly anti-secession. It issued an order 'expelling' mercenaries and other foreign personnel from Katanga, and requested UN assistance to implement it. In Elisabethville at the end of August 1961 O'Brien used this appeal, in tandem with a liberal interpretation of the February resolution, to order UN forces to arrest and deport foreign military personnel. Although initially quite successful in detaining the targeted individuals, the operation lost momentum when the UN accepted Tshombe's undertaking that he would now co-operate with ONUC. The UN then agreed that the consular corps in Elisabethville should administer the expulsions. In doing so it was effectively asking the ringmasters to shut down their own circus. Whatever threat O'Brien's initial moves had posed to Katanga, it was now wholly dissipated.

Unsurprisingly, follow-up talks between Tshombe and O'Brien achieved little. In mid-September, therefore, O'Brien, with the support of the UN headquarters in Léopoldville, ordered a second, more forceful operation against the mercenaries. Once again, the operation seemed initially to be successful, and in the first flush of this apparent triumph O'Brien overstepped himself by announcing nothing less than the ending of Katanga's secession. While Tshombe's supporters in western Europe had been constrained by the February resolution from criticizing specific action against the mercenaries, this rashly political statement provided them with an opportunity to rush onto the moral high ground. Not even the most maximalist interpretation of the February resolution could be stretched to cover the extinction of Katangese secession by military force. The western members of the Security Council expressed anger at not having been consulted about this apparent new objective. Simultaneously, elements of the western press, with the encour-agement of Katanga's skilful propaganda machine, launched a ferocious attack on O'Brien in particular and the UN in general.

There now began, for the first time in the peacekeeping experience, a process that would become familiar in subsequent operations – most notably perhaps that in neighbouring Rwanda in 1994: a self-exculpating wrangle over orders, responsibilities and their interpretation. O'Brien, with some support from UN officials in Léopoldville, claimed that Hammarskjöld had given prior approval to the operation. Certainly, O'Brien had worked closely with the UN special representative in Léopoldville, the Tunisian diplomat Mahmoud Khiary, who had succeeded Rajeshwar Dayal the previous May. The secretary-general, through his aides in New York, insisted, on the con-trary, that the entire adventure had been conceived and organized locally without his approval. Less clear was the view of events taken by Sture Linnér, Hammarskjöld's grey eminence in Léopoldville. Whatever the real sequence of events and chain of responsibility, in the face of the hostile reaction from important states in the west, and with Hammarskjöld himself seemingly disowning it, the operation in Katanga petered out, its initial gains squandered as they had been in the previous action.[31]

The emergency was deeply unwelcome for Hammarskjöld, who had struggled through the crises of the previous September and January, and who had hoped to have put such diplomatic upsets behind him. The angry reaction among western states was particularly disheartening as many of them over the previous months had been more supportive of the UN's efforts than hitherto.[32] Hammarskjöld now flew to the Congo in an attempt to rescue the situation. After consultations in Léopoldville he set about easing the now dangerously high tensions in Katanga by arranging a face-to-face meeting with Tshombe. This had to be held in neighbouring Northern Rhodesia as Tshombe had fled there at the start of ONUC's sweep when he discovered that the UN held a central government arrest warrant for him. On the evening of 17 September 1961 Hammarskjöld and everyone aboard his aircraft were killed when it crashed on its approach to the airstrip in Ndola, the agreed venue

---

31 In December 1961 O'Brien resigned his posts with both the UN secretariat and the Irish diplomatic service. An elegant and persuasive writer, he put his side of the story in articles in *The Observer* on 10 and 17 December 1961 which were then expanded into his book *To Katanga and Back* (London: Hutchinson, 1962). The most effective representation of Hammarskjöld's position was provided by his subordinate in the secretariat, Brian Urquhart, in his 1973 biography *Hammarskjold*, pp. 545–89.

32 Some sense of the stress and isolation besetting Hammarskjöld can be gleaned from the terse, dejected verse he wrote at the time and which was collected and published after his death. See Dag Hammarskjöld (trans. Leif Sjöberg and W.H. Auden), *Markings* (London: Faber & Faber, 1964).

for the meeting. Inevitably, numerous conspiracy theories emerged after the event claiming that the plane crash was not accidental and that Hammarskjöld had been assassinated. Admittedly, there was no dearth of possible culprits from across the spectrum of violently held views on the Congo. But no firm evidence for this has ever been produced and it is probable that his death was simply a tragic accident.

Hammarskjöld's death did not bring any immediate change to the character of the UN operation in the Congo, but its consequences, in terms of the change in actors and the reassessment of political possibilities, were profound. He was succeeded as secretary-general (initially in an acting capacity and then on a substantive basis) by the Burmese diplomat U Thant. He was the UN's first non-European secretary-general and his Afro-Asian identity was to prove significant. Although, as we have seen, the cold war dimension to the conflict had declined with changing attitudes and personnel in Moscow and Washington, there remained other international divisions, sharply illustrated in Katanga in the weeks before Hammarskjöld's death. Loosely speaking, the division now was once again that hinted at right at the beginning of the UN's involvement in the Congo: between the European 'imperialists' (Belgium, Britain and France), on the pro-Katanga side, and the Afro-Asian world, on the other. The United States, although angered at the lack of consultation over ONUC's military operations in Katanga in August and September, was now somewhat separated from its European allies on this 'colonial' issue – as it had been over the Suez affair in 1956. The resulting configuration within the UN, which brought together the two superpowers, the Afro-Asian bloc and the new secretary-general, suggested that, despite the September débâcle, Katanga would not remain an independent entity for much longer.

The November resolution and the end of Katangese secession

In November 1961, two months after Hammarskjöld's death and the immediate crisis around it, the Security Council passed a new resolution on the Congo. This was the strongest anti-Katanga statement so far and both Britain and France abstained in the vote, though they did not risk using their vetoes against American wishes. The Council denounced 'the secessionist activities illegally carried out by the provincial administration of Katanga, with the aid of external resources and manned by foreign mercenaries [and] the armed action against United Nations forces and personnel in pursuit of such activities', and insisted that they must end immediately. The secretary-general was authorized 'to take vigorous action, including the use of the requisite measure of force', to detain and deport foreign political and military personnel in Katanga. Finally, the resolution declared that 'all secessionist activities against the Republic of the Congo are contrary to . . . Security Council decisions and [must] cease forthwith.'[33] Any residual doubts around the 'internal' character of the secession and the legality of the UN taking a position on it were now dispelled. Interventionism and enforcement were to be the guiding principles of the UN involvement in Katanga.

The UN's mission in the Congo was now moving towards its dénouement, though its conclusion in both Katanga and the Congo as a whole did not come quickly. A year of feverish but unavailing negotiations now took place. Repeated proposals were put to Tshombe and repeatedly rejected by him, usually after long-drawn prevarication. By now, though, the increasingly threadbare international coalition that had supported the secession was unravelling. Even Belgium began to put pressure for compromise on Katanga. The United States was becoming increasingly stern in its demands for movement, with threats of comprehensive sanctions against the province.

The secession ended finally with a political whimper rather than a bang. The behaviour of the gangs of foreign mercenaries (who had long-since replaced Belgian regulars in Katanga) became increasingly thuggish towards UN personnel as they misread the political stand-off as conferring immunity. Then, just before Christmas 1962, UN positions in Elisabethville came under fire. After four days of forbearance, the predominantly Indian forces on the ground responded under the terms of the November 1961 resolution. Within thirty-six hours the UN had taken control of Elisabethville. Katanga's small 'air force', which had been an irritant to UN forces and a source of terror to parts of the civilian population who opposed Tshombe's regime, was destroyed on the ground.[34] Two weeks later, on 14 January 1963, Tshombe announced the end of Katanga's secession and his unconditional acceptance of U Thant's plan for reunification. Although ONUC remained in being for another eighteen months, its mandate, to all intents and purposes, had now been fulfilled.

From the Congo to Zaïre . . . to the Congo

When the UN left the Congo in June 1964 its formal mandate had been accomplished, though at a high cost in both lives and resources. The Congo state was unified under an ostensibly stable central government. Ethnic and regional conflicts, though still very much present, did not for the moment

---

33   United Nations document S/RES/169, 24 November 1961.
34   Michael Harbottle, *The Blue Berets* (London: Leo Cooper, 1975), pp. 69–70.

threaten the integrity of the state. Yet the rapidly shifting – sometimes circular – winds of politics in the new Congo were a source of mystery to many observers. Following the capitulation of Katanga, prime minister Adoula, with the encouragement of the United Nations, formed a new national parliament that included Katangan representatives and also gave a voice to the loose grouping of former supporters of Patrice Lumumba.

A few months later, though, in September 1963, Adoula dissolved parliament and the leading Lumumbists left the capital and dispersed in the mountains of eastern Congo, Lumumba's original power base. By August 1964, a few months after the final departure of ONUC, the Lumumbists once more controlled Stanleyville. Challenged by central government forces, which were now in their turn backed by white mercenaries, the rebels seized European hostages. In a further tangling of earlier affinities Belgian paratroops were now dropped by American aircraft to retake the town and return it to central government control. The cast members of the Congo's continuing drama remained largely unchanged, but their roles and their relationships one to another rarely stayed constant for very long. The rebels dispersed back into the mountains and continued a desultory series of actions against the central government's army. Among the leaders of this long-drawn-out and half-hearted guerrilla war was Laurent-Desiré Kabila, who would occupy centre-stage at the time of the UN's next major engagement with the country.

In the meantime the personalities who crowded Congolese politics continued to conduct their changing relationships and roles with bewildering speed. Cyrille Adoula stood down as prime minister of the central government to be replaced by his former enemy, Moise Tshombe. The Katangan leader had remained active in national politics since the collapse of his fiefdom in 1963, and at the beginning of 1965 he managed to win a reasonably free and fair parliamentary election at the head of a loose coalition of parties and interests. Joseph Kasavubu, who had worked quietly and shrewdly to retain the presidency throughout the upheavals of 1964 and 1965, now moved quickly to depose Tshombe, about whose political motives he remained deeply suspicious. A few months later he in turn was displaced by Joseph Mobutu, who had remained at the head of the army and maintained an ominous presence close to the centre of power in Léopoldville. Within a year of his seizure of power in December 1965 Mobutu had established himself as president and dictator. Renaming himself 'Mobutu Sese Seko' in 1972 and his state 'Zaïre' the previous year, he would remain in power until 1997. Sustained by powerful friends in the west as a bulwark against any potential communist threat in central Africa, he presided over the wholesale plundering of state resources with impunity. During the long dark years of his misrule in Zaïre he accumulated a personal fortune estimated at US$4 billion, while the national economy collapsed and even the most basic government services with it. Eventually, no longer a western 'asset' in a post-cold war world, Mobutu's shambolic kleptocracy became an embarrassment to his former foreign friends, who now abandoned him. Although managing to hang on for longer than many thought possible, he eventually fell from power. In 1997, gravely ill and with few friends either at home or abroad, Mobutu finally succumbed to an alliance of Congolese and regional forces nominally led by Kabila but energized by extensive support from the Rwandan army.

The nature of Kabila's victory and the regional setting within which it was achieved in 1997 did not auger well for any rapid improvement in the lot of the Congolese people or for the greater stability of the Congolese state. Kabila's democratic credentials were far from impressive and he had few evident political skills. Worse, perhaps, the shortcomings of the new regime in the renamed 'Democratic Republic of Congo' would inevitably have an impact on the entire Great Lakes region of central Africa.[35] The size and position of the Congo, as well as the contingent circumstances of Kabila's victory over Mobutu (which we will look at in more detail in due course), made this inevitable.

In the broad development of the peacekeeping project the UN's first engagement in Africa would become somewhat 'stranded' as an artefact of African and global circumstances that belonged essentially to the early 1960s. A quarter of a century was to elapse between the departure of the last UN soldier from the Congo and the arrival of the next in Namibia, by which time the African and the global political environments were fundamentally altered. Yet the Congo experience, by dint of its pioneering character, was in many respects a prototype for future UN interventions in sub-Saharan Africa. The basic dynamics of the Congo crisis, local and international, would not be replicated, but they bore similarities to those in various parts of Africa where UN peacekeepers were deployed in later years. The UN in the Congo confronted a fragile central state beset by internal division, ethnic tensions and secessionist pressures. All or some of these were the defining circumstances of later interventions. The pace of local events was such that the initial grounds for intervention were quickly superseded by new imperatives – just as they were much later in two of the Congo's neighbours, Angola and Rwanda. Rapidly changing conflict dynamics in the Congo led to shifting, often ambiguous, operational mandates – a situation seen again in Somalia in the early 1990s. As we will see, Somalia and Rwanda also confronted the UN with problems around the command and control of national peace-keeping contingents whose home states sought to pursue their own political interests – problems that first emerged in the Congo. Whatever the claims

---

35   One of Kabila's first acts was to restore the country's pre-Mobutu name, 'Zaïre' having been a confection of the dictator himself.

made about the emergence of a 'new peacekeeping' in the 1990s characterized by 'multi-functionalism', the first such mission (embracing armed security, humanitarian relief activities and political reconstruction) took place in the Congo.

Spectators to genocide: Rwanda, 1993–96

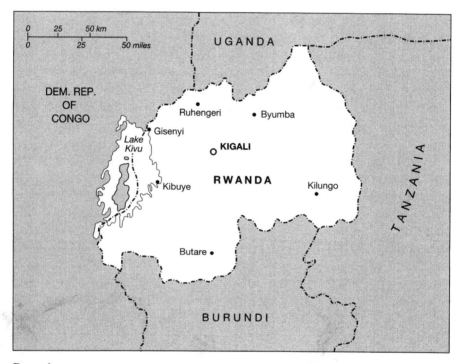

Rwanda

Thirty-five years separated the departure of the last United Nations soldier from the Congo and the arrival of the first in the renamed Democratic Republic of the Congo. Before this second intervention, and deeply entangled with it, was another crisis and another UN peacekeeping venture in the region. The UN's involvement in Rwanda between 1993 and 1996 was one of the most controversial of any undertaken by the organization in Africa. As in the Congo in the early 1960s, the UN's actions and inactions became an issue in international relations far beyond central Africa.

Located virtually at the geographical centre of sub-Saharan Africa, Rwanda was at the hub of the complex of ethnic and international conflicts that afflicted central Africa in the 1990s and into the new century. Rwanda's northern and eastern neighbours are the one-time British colonies of Uganda and Tanzania respectively. To the south and west are the former Belgian territories of Burundi and the Democratic Republic of Congo. Rwanda thus lies at the nexus between Anglophone and Francophone central Africa. More significantly in terms of its stability and security, however, Rwanda has also been a cockpit in the inter-ethnic strife that has been a long-term feature of the region. Nowhere else in Africa, perhaps, has the discontinuity between ethnic identity and national borders caused such protracted violence and misery. As we have just seen, United Nations involvement in the region dated back to its first peacekeeping operation in Africa. Since the early 1990s UN involvement of one type or another (though not always in the form of peace-keeping interventions) has extended to the DRC, the Uganda–Rwanda border, Burundi and the Central African Republic.

It was within the borders of Rwanda itself, however, that the United Nations faced perhaps its most serious crisis of credibility. The sheer scale of the death toll during the genocide of 1994 and the perceived failure of the UN to take any significant steps to prevent it came to dwarf the more protracted shortcomings of the peacekeeping endeavours in Angola and in Somalia. In a period of a few weeks about one in ten of Rwanda's entire population of eight million died in a single murderous spasm. The blame for the inadequacy of the world's response to the events of 1994 is not so easily apportioned as some have supposed. A tangle of historical, political, diplomatic and cultural factors overlay the tragedy. Generations-old tensions and sus-picions along with a failure of leadership and inadequate peacemaking processes formed the local bases of conflict. At the international level the inconsistent and uncertain policies of powerful external players ensured the grim outcome of events. The United Nations as an institutional actor also proved gravely wanting, though not perhaps to the criminal degree that other actors, for their own reasons of self-exculpation, have conspired to suggest.

The background: history, ethnicity and frontiers

The origins of Rwanda's contemporary ethnic division date from the fifteenth century. Around that time the territory was subject to an inflow – part migra-tion, part conquest – from the north-east, probably from the Horn of Africa. The new arrivals – the Tutsi – eventually dominated the local Hutu people economically and politically. Although always a minority of the population (never more than about 10 per cent), the Tutsi established their own monarch-ical system and subsequent relations between the two peoples were based on the feudal overlordship of the Tutsi over the Hutu 'peasantry'. This social structure proved remarkably enduring in a continent where elsewhere such non-regional ethnic divisions tended to become permeable over time. In neighbouring Burundi, for example, a similar structure of relations between Hutu and Tutsi was more flexible, with a greater degree of inter-marriage and a less absolute system of monarchical rule. In Rwanda, though, the system remained rigid. The social structure of both Rwanda and Burundi was exploited by the region's German colonizers when they arrived in the 1880s. Like the British in west Africa the Germans were quick to appreciate the financial and administrative advantages of what became known as 'indirect rule'. A further layer was thus grafted on to the feudal relationship between Tutsi and Hutu, with Germany becoming the ultimate 'overlord'.

This situation was little changed after the First World War when Germany was stripped of its empire. Rwanda and Burundi were passed to Belgium (the imperial power in neighbouring Congo) as League of Nations 'mandates', and subsequently became the Territory of Ruanda-Urundi. Belgium was happy to maintain, indeed further formalize, the system of indirect rule established by Germany. This arrangement and the relationships on which it was based took on an added significance as the era of decolonization approached. Under the Belgians the Tutsi became the colonial elite, favoured in terms of education and jobs in the administration. The Tutsi thus assumed, reasonably enough, that they were being groomed for government and would be the beneficiaries of the transfer of power at independence. In the meantime, however, the Hutu were not immune from the democratic spirit that was part of the general nationalist wave passing over Africa in the later 1950s. 'Independence', Hutu activists argued, would have little meaning if it amounted to no more than the removal of the uppermost layer of political domination leaving the rest of an exploitative structure intact. Tensions exploded in 1959 in widespread anti-Tutsi violence. This led eventually to the flight of the traditional monarch (the '*mwami*') along with some 200,000 of his fellow Tutsi. In pre-independence elections held in September 1961 both the end of the monarchy and the new ascendancy of the Hutu were confirmed. It was the Hutu majority, therefore, rather than the Tutsi elite, that took power in the Rwandan capital Kigali after independence in July 1962 (a date agreed between Brussels and the United Nations Trusteeship Council, which had assumed responsibility for the old League mandates in 1945[36]). The new state was ruled by the Hutu-dominated Democratic Republican Movement under the presidency of Grégoire Kayibanda.

The stability of Rwandan politics in the immediate post-independence period was only apparent. There was deep and continuing inter-ethnic

---

36 The nature and purposes of the Trusteeship system and the responsibilities of the Trusteeship Council that was established to manage it were laid down in Chapters XII and XIII of the UN Charter.

tension. The Hutu remained suspicious of the intentions of the Tutsi, who had been disempowered after centuries of dominance. For their part, the Tutsi were unwilling to accept the new role of second-class citizens in the emerging state. Tensions spilled over into violence in 1963, as they had in 1959. The occasion of this outbreak was an 'invasion' by a small group of Tutsi who had been plotting from exile in neighbouring Uganda. The military challenge posed by this group was minimal but in the prevailing atmosphere the outcome was the widespread and indiscriminate killing of Tutsi across the country. The following decade was punctuated by periodic outbursts of such violence. Inter-ethnic tension was meanwhile exacerbated by the inflow to Rwanda of Hutu refugees from Burundi. Rwanda and Burundi had become independent simultaneously in 1962, but in contrast to Rwanda, where pre-independence violence had reversed the historical balance of power, the new state in Burundi took the form of a constitutional monarchy under the hereditary Tutsi '*mwami*'. The ruling minority lived in permanent fear of a Hutu uprising on the Rwandan model, and opted for repression rather than accommodation. The result was a population movement of Hutu, often political activists, bearing tales of brutality and discrimination into the ethnic 'homeland' of Rwanda. Inevitably, this caused a racking up of tension.

Intra- as well as inter-ethnic conflicts added a further complication to Rwandan politics in the late 1960s and early 1970s. The Hutu in Rwanda did not constitute a wholly cohesive political force. There was also a regional dimension to Rwandan politics. In 1973 – amidst the heightened tensions of anti-Hutu pogroms in Burundi – the then defence minister, General Juvénal Habyarimana, who was a 'northern' Hutu, moved against the 'southern' President Kayibanda, who had been in power since independence. Habyarimana's control of the army ensured the success of his coup. After a period of dictatorial rule, he sought a degree of legitimacy by placing himself at the head of a new political party that became the National Republican Movement for Democracy and Development (*Mouvement Républicain National pour la Démocratie et le Développement* – MRNDD).

Habyarimana and the MRNDD remained in control into the 1990s, but his 'Hutu-power' regime faced a mounting challenge by exiled Tutsi forces. The Uganda-based exiles who had first launched themselves inconsequentially against the Hutu regime in 1963 had now evolved into a formidable fighting force. They had done so with the patronage of Yoweri Museveni, the Ugandan president, who had come to power in 1986 after the long years of chaos and misrule under Idi Amin and Milton Obote. Moreover, the Rwandan Patriotic Front (RPF), as the main exile movement was now called, was not an exclusively 'Tutsi' movement; the ever more extreme Hutu 'nationalism' of the Habyarimana regime had driven a significant number of moderate Hutu into the ranks of the opposition. Significantly, after its years of exile and planning in Uganda the RPF had developed into an essentially 'Anglophone' movement (in both linguistic and regional political terms). It confronted a Francophone regime in Rwanda where the Belgians had bequeathed French as the *lingua franca* and where France worked assiduously to extend its diplomatic and military influence over Habyarimana and his government during their years in power.[37]

This broad diplomatic cleavage was exposed in the early 1990s when the RPF was for the first time politically and militarily strong enough to threaten the existence of the Hutu regime in Rwanda. In October 1990 the rebels launched a co-ordinated and sustained attack from its bases in Uganda. French and Belgian military aid was rushed to Habyarimana to prop up his government. At the same time a first 'peacekeeping' intervention was attempted under the auspices of the Organization of Africa Unity when a multinational force composed of units from Burundi, Uganda and Zaïre was deployed to encourage 'reconciliation'. Given the political implications of this mixed Francophone–Anglophone contributor base (and the general indiscipline of the forces involved), this was a vain hope.[38] The OAU subsequently deployed a second observer group with a less politically inept composition, but it was largely ineffectual. Only continuing arms shipments from Egypt and South Africa (underwritten by France) and the periodic deployment of French paratroops guaranteed the continuation of the Hutu regime and the exclusion of RPF forces from Kigali.[39]

The Arusha settlement and the establishment of UNAMIR

The war between the RPF and the Kigali regime continued throughout 1991 and 1992 despite continued efforts by various mediators to broker an effective cease-fire and organize definitive peace talks. At the beginning of 1993 pressure from the OAU and the Tanzanian government – coinciding with a new offensive by the RPF – persuaded Habyarimana to come to the negotiating table at Arusha in northern Tanzania. Developments were now being followed by the UN Security Council which added its weight to the momentum towards a settlement by sending a so-called 'goodwill mission' to the region and adopting a resolution calling for comprehensive negotiations.[40]

---

37 For a detailed and insightful account of the RPF's origins and development see Gérard Prunier, 'The Rwandan Patriotic Front', in Christopher Clapham (ed.), *African Guerrillas* (Oxford: James Currey, 1998), pp. 119–33.

38 Eric G. Berman and Katie E. Sams, *Peacekeeping in Africa: Capabilities and Culpabilities* (Geneva: United Nations Institute for Disarmament Research, 2000), pp. 58–9.

39 William Shawcross, *Deliver Us from Evil: Warlords and Peacekeepers in a World of Endless Conflict* (London: Bloomsbury, 2000), p. 106.

40 UN document S/RES/812, 12 March 1993.

Henceforward Boutros Boutros-Ghali, the UN secretary-general, was officially represented at the Arusha talks by the leader of the goodwill mission.
Crucially, though, this UN presence was in the capacity of observer rather
than participant. Therefore, the supposedly final agreement that was eventually reached at Arusha in August 1993 had no significant input from the
United Nations, though it assigned the organization a key role in its implementation.[41] This arrangement was ominously similar to that of the Bicesse
agreement on Angola in 1991 which led to the failed electoral process and
return to war the following year (see below pp. 125–7). In both cases a peace
process agreed by the protagonists under considerable external pressure
committed the United Nations to a central role in the form of the provision
of an observation and peacekeeping presence without the organization itself
having shaped that role or even having assessed its feasibility. The centre-
piece of the agreement for Rwanda was the creation of a so-called 'Broad-
Based Transitional Government' (BBTG) made up of representatives of the
Kigali regime, other more moderate Hutu then in opposition and the RPF.
Simultaneously, the opposing military forces would undergo the process (by
now familiar from a range of other African peace agreements) of disarmament and cantonment followed either by demobilization or by integration in
a new national army. Finally, there would be elections for a new Rwandan
government organized by the BBTG before the end of 1995.

The Rwandan parties had in fact acted in advance of the final agreement
when they wrote to Boutros-Ghali in June 1993 requesting the creation of a
'Neutral International Force' (NIF).[42] This would, with the OAU's blessing
(and no doubt to its hearty relief), subsume the existing pan-African monitoring group. The mandate proposed for the NIF by the Rwandan parties
was detailed and comprehensive. It was also over-ambitious and impractical.
This should have been clear to anyone with even a rudimentary grasp of
the politics of UN peacekeeping at a time when its resources were at full
stretch. Undeterred, however, the proposal from Arusha was that the force
should assist in maintaining public order and safeguard the distribution
of humanitarian aid. In addition, the NIF should search for illegally held
weapons, disarm civilians, confront armed bands and undertake de-mining
operations. It was to be responsible for the disarmament and concentration
of the opposing forces. All of this was in addition to its central function as
monitor and guarantor of the general peace process.

Prior to any significant discussion of this proposed commitment in New
York, the UN had authorized a parallel military operation in the region as

---

41   A lucid and concise analysis of the Arusha process is provided by Christopher Clapham,
     'Rwanda: the perils of peacemaking', *Journal of Peace Research* 35(2), 1998, pp. 84–6.
42   UN document S/25951, 14 June 1993.

a contribution to the peace process. At the end of June 1993 the Security Council established the Observer Mission Uganda–Rwanda (UNOMUR) to monitor movements on the border between the two countries and to verify that the transit of arms and supplies to the RPF had ceased in line with under-takings made to facilitate the Arusha process.[43] Although the new operation followed days after the letter to the UN from Arusha requesting the NIF, its provenance was older. It had emerged from a joint approach to the Security Council by both Rwanda and Uganda after an upsurge in fighting in February 1993 that had threatened the negotiations then just beginning at Arusha. A group of eighty-one military observers from eight countries was eventually deployed, wholly on the Ugandan side of the border. UNOMUR remained in place for fifteen months, being withdrawn only after the victory of the RPF in Rwanda rendered its mandate irrelevant. While the observer mission was soon overshadowed by the horror of the genocide, it served an important function as a confidence-building presence in the final stages of the Arusha process.

The substantive mission proposed by the parties was clearly much more problematic. Already aware of some of the potential dangers on the ground from various reports produced by UN agencies and non-governmental organizations (NGOs) over the previous years, the secretary-general, prior to taking the Arusha request to the Security Council, sent a reconnaissance mission to Rwanda in the second half of August. This was led by the Canadian brigadier-general Romeo Dallaire, who was chief observer with UNOMUR at the time. Meantime, in mid-September, while the report of this mission was still awaited, Boutros-Ghali met a joint government–RPF delegation that sought to drive home the initial appeal from the peace con-ference by emphasizing the dangers in delaying the deployment of the pro-posed UN force. Maintaining their evident disregard for the realities and possibilities of peacekeeping at this time, the delegation urged the immediate despatch of more than 4200 troops. The secretary-general responded with a lesson in the facts of UN life at this time, indicating the virtual impossibility of getting such a force approved, let alone deployed quickly amidst the com-peting demands and dangers of Somalia, Bosnia and elsewhere. Peacekeeping activities were indeed at a post-cold war peak. About 70,000 military per-sonnel from seventy countries were engaged in seventeen operations world-wide. The costs of these operations was running at about US$3 billion annu-ally, much of which the UN was required to borrow in default of prompt payment from certain key members, most notably the United States. But although the secretary-general's message to the parties was an important

---

43   UN document S/RES/846, 22 June 1993.

one, it would have been better delivered at an earlier stage in the process. Effectively, the Arusha agreement had been built round a superstructure of external management that now looked unlikely to be available.

In the last week of October, with the report from the reconnaissance mission now presented, Boutros-Ghali took a request for the operation to the Security Council. His proposal was for a force strength of 2548 troops – just over half the personnel originally sought by the parties. Even this reduced force would be deployed gradually, he proposed, and should be tied to the achievement of key stages of the Arusha agreement. The first phase, which would last until the formation of the BBTG, would have a maximum strength of 1400 at its completion. The force would be concentrated in Kigali and in an interpositionary role in a demilitarized zone between the opposing armies. Military observers would be assigned to each side, and UNOMUR, already deployed on the Ugandan side of the border, would be subsumed into the new operation. The proposed mandate was much narrower than that originally requested from Arusha. The UN force would be responsible for the security of cantonment centres, the supervision of policing and the recovery of arms from the two sides.[44] This United Nations Assistance Mission for Rwanda (UNAMIR) was approved by the Security Council on 5 October 1993.[45]

The Security Council's approval of the Rwandan mission came just two days after the deaths of eighteen American special forces troops in the UN operation in Somalia (see below pp. 215–16). This event fundamentally changed American – and therefore Security Council – perceptions of the peacekeeping role in Africa, and was to shape in a quite fateful way the UN's role and conduct in Rwanda. Its impact was felt from the beginning when the Security Council narrowed even further the mandate for UNAMIR proposed by the secretary-general. According to the enabling resolution the UN force was not to be involved in the recovery of arms. It had been in pursuit of armed elements that the American losses had been incurred in Somalia. In Rwanda the UN would merely contribute to the security of designated areas already established as 'weapons-secure' by the Rwandan parties themselves. This formulation would take on great significance in the light of coming events.

Two weeks after the Security Council authorized the venture, Brigadier-General Dallaire, now transferred from UNOMUR to command the larger force, arrived in Kigali with a small advance party. In the immediate aftermath of the killings in Somalia, and against the broader background of the ever-growing demands for peacekeepers, the secretary-general did not have

---

44   UN document S/26488, 24 September 1993.
45   UN document S/RES/872, 5 October 1993.

an easy task in recruiting national contingents. Eventually the force was built round sub-battalion units from Belgium, Ghana and Bangladesh. The latter two contingents, attracted by the revenue-raising opportunities of UN service as much as by instincts of global 'citizenship', were woefully under-equipped for the task in hand, and this brought another complicated round of hat-passing by the UN.

Simultaneously, the secretary-general named Jacques-Roger Booh Booh, one-time foreign minister of Cameroon, as his special representative. Booh Booh had been appointed, according to Boutros-Ghali's later account, both because of his knowledge of the region and as part of a policy to bring more Africans into key positions in the UN.[46] Whatever Booh Booh's particular skills, however, both the military and political arms of the UN intervention were soon starkly aware of the fundamental fragility of the Arusha agreement. As in the case of Angola, signing a comprehensive peace agreement under the spotlight of regional and international attention was one thing; carrying it through in the face of opposition from entrenched elements who saw in it the demise of their own political power was another. Such limited optimism that had attended the Arusha signing rapidly evaporated in the acrid air of increasing violence on the ground.

There had, in reality, been little enthusiasm for the agreement on the part of Habyarimana himself or his government's negotiators. And there was outright and fierce opposition from other Hutu elements in and around the volatile coalition of interests that dominated the Kigali regime. For the militants Arusha was a sell-out that would bring a reversion to domination by the Tutsi and the subordination of the Hutu which had characterized both pre-colonial and colonial Rwanda. Now these elements expressed their own insecurities and nurtured those of others by ratcheting up the level of violence against Tutsi and moderate Hutu. Moreover, at the end of October 1993 the ever-present tension in Rwanda had been sharply heightened by the assassination of the Hutu president of Burundi, Melchoir Ndadye (who had been in office only since August after being elected in June), by members of the Tutsi-dominated army. Despite the fact that Ndadye was succeeded by another Hutu, Cyprien Ntaryamira, the murder was used by militant Rwandan Hutu as proof of the dangers of putting Tutsi in positions of power – which, of course, was a central purpose of the Arusha agreement.

The response of the United Nations to the growing threat to the peace settlement was to attempt to build a momentum towards implementation and thus minimize any 'drift' that could be exploited by those set on

---

46   Boutros Boutros-Ghali, *Unvanquished: a US–UN Saga* (New York: Random House, 1999), p. 130.

sabotaging the agreement. The most appropriate time for such momentum-building would, of course, have been immediately after UN involvement was mooted but the delays in reaching agreement about the size and purpose of UNAMIR had prevented this. They had in fact contributed to the very flux that had now to be addressed. In December a meeting was held under the chairmanship of Booh Booh at which the parties re-dedicated themselves to the Arusha process and agreed to drive it on. The concrete effect of this, however, was limited to the implementation of some straightforward 'structural' components of the agreement. Nothing was done to put in place the underlying political mechanisms that were essential to the long-term success of the project. In short, UN pressure brought a focus on form rather than substance. In the last days of 1993 an RPF detachment moved into Rwanda as agreed at Arusha, for example, but there was little prospect of effective liaison, let alone co-operation, with the Hutu government army. Similarly, in the first week of January 1994 Habyarimana was installed as president in the Broad-Based Transitional Government, but there was little sign that the government itself, or the legislature that was supposed to underpin it, was actually being constructed, and inter-ethnic and inter-factional violence continued unabated. Redoubled pressure from the Security Council for the rapid implementation of the peace agreement had no evident impact.[47]

The one position on the overall process shared by Hutu and Tutsi activists alike – though based on fundamentally different premises – was an underlying mistrust of UNAMIR. In the case of the Hutu this mistrust was of the UN's basic objectives; for the Tutsi it was of the UN's capacity. On one side UNAMIR was perceived as the agent of political extinction and on the other as an inadequate source of protection. Within this dangerous and unpromising environment General Dallaire sought to shape a meaningful security role for the new force. In November 1993, shortly after his arrival in Kigali, he had formulated a set of proposed rules of engagement aimed at clarifying the force's day-to-day mandate. In this he sought agreement from the Department of Peacekeeping Operations (DPKO) at UN headquarters that UNAMIR should be authorized to use force to prevent violence against civilians. He received no response from New York and the extent of the force's operational range therefore remained unresolved. In the meantime, however, UNAMIR developed what was in the circumstances a reasonably effective intelligence network. From this there emerged in January 1994 information from what Dallaire described in an urgent

---

47 For example, a resolution at the beginning of January 'stress[ed.] that continued support for UNAMIR will depend upon the full and prompt implementation by the parties of the Arusha agreement'. UN document S/RES/893, 6 January 1994.

telegram to New York as 'a very, very important government politician'. This source (later identified as the prime minister designate in the BBTG, Faustin Twagiramungu) had indicated that a concerted plan was taking shape among Hutu extremists to eliminate opposition politicians, both Tutsi and moderate Hutu. Additionally, according to the report, a crisis was to be triggered for the UN by the calculated killing of Belgian troops serving with UNAMIR. The forces that would undertake these actions would be drawn from elements of the army but, more significantly, from the informal Hutu 'militias' that had growing since the Arusha agreement – the so-called 'Interahamwe'. These forces would be armed from a substantial cache concealed within Kigali.

Dallaire now sought, firstly, physical protection for his informants and, secondly, permission to pre-empt this conspiracy by deploying UNAMIR to enforce the 'weapons-secure area' that had supposedly been established in Kigali. Again, he received no clear response from the DPKO in New York (at this time under the direction of under-secretary-general Kofi Annan, later to be Boutros-Ghali's successor). As we have noted, the responsibility for the creation and maintenance of the weapons-secure area was considered to lie with the Rwandan parties themselves, the UN having a purely 'supervisory' role. This interpretation of the situation in January 1994 meant that the DPKO ruled out any decisive action by UNAMIR on the matter as lying beyond its mandate. Instead Dallaire and Booh Booh were instructed to inform the American, Belgian and French ambassadors in Kigali of the situation. They were also to make clear to Habyarimana what was going on and that the UN was aware of it.[48]

This was perhaps the last opportunity available to UNAMIR to divert the direction of events in Rwanda then flowing towards genocide. An effective response, though, would have required robust enforcement action of the type urged by Dallaire. Having rejected this, the UN was left as a largely passive witness to the continued decline of the political and security situation in the country over the first months of 1994. In his report on Rwanda to the Security Council at the end of March Boutros-Ghali made no attempt to under-state the problems facing the peace process and the UN intervention, though he recommended a further extension of UNAMIR's mandate for six months.[49] Now extremely wary, the Security Council agreed to an extension of little more than half this duration, with the threat of review during this period if progress was not made in the peace process.[50]

48   Philip Gourevitch, *We Wish to Inform You That Tomorrow We Will be Killed with Our Families* (London: Picador, 1999), pp. 104–6; Shawcross, *Deliver Us from Evil*, pp. 109–11.
49   UN document S/1994/360, 30 March 1994.
50   UN document S/RES/909, 5 April 1994.

The killings begin

On the evening of 6 April 1994 the two Hutu presidents of Rwanda and Burundi, Juvénal Habyarimana and Cyprien Ntaryamira, flew back together from a session of talks on the Arusha agreement held in Dar-es-Salam in Tanzania. At about 8.30 p.m., as their aircraft approached Kigali, it was shot down, killing everyone on board. Responsibility for the attack has never been conclusively located, but the finger of suspicion has been pointed most firmly at Hutu extremists disenchanted with Habyarimana's leadership and determined finally to destroy the peace process.[51] This was certainly the effect of the action. Almost immediately, elements of the army (led by the Presidential Guard) and gangs of Interahamwe had set up roadblocks in and around the capital and the first of what would eventually be about 800,000 deaths had taken place.

The first indications of the political motivation behind the killings came with the apparently pre-planned murders of those moderate Hutu politicians who had been working for the implementation of the Arusha settlement. Prominent among these was Rwanda's acting prime minister, Agathe Uwilingiyimana. In response to a request for UN protection a detachment of ten Belgian troops was sent to her residence. There, however, the Belgians found themselves outnumbered and surrounded by elements of the Presidential Guard, who disarmed them and took them prisoner. In the meantime Uwilingiyimana escaped with her family and sought refuge at a UN volunteer compound. She was later found and shot by Hutu soldiers there early on 7 April. Uwilingiyimana was merely among the first in a mounting toll of more moderate Hutus from the government, civil service and judiciary. The primary target of the killings, however, was nothing less than the Tutsi population of Rwanda in its entirety. The extremists in the army and Interahamwe were using massacre as an instrument of demographic engineering in their attempt to shape the entire people of Rwanda in their own political image. The outrageous scale of the undertaking soon became clear in towns and villages throughout the country.

The abducted Belgian UN soldiers had in the meantime been killed by their captors at an army base. The consequences of these ten deaths amidst the mounting thousands of Rwandan victims proved fatal for the UN operation. On 12 April, five days after the killing of the UN troops, Boutros-Ghali met the Belgian foreign minister, Mark Eyskens, in Bonn. Eyskens

---

51 In the view of the UN secretary-general of the time a 'plausible interpretation was that the two presidents had been killed by Hutu extremists who were opposed to the concessions the two Hutu presidents had been making to the Tutsis in Rwanda and Burundi'. Boutros-Ghali, *Unvanquished*, p. 131.

informed the secretary-general that the Belgian contingent was to be withdrawn immediately and urged that the UNAMIR operation as a whole should
be abandoned. He proposed this course of action on the grounds that the
intervention had proved a failure. It is likely, however, that his main motive
was to 'sanitize' Belgium's withdrawal by presenting it as something other than
a unilateral act. Boutros-Ghali rejected the idea of total abandonment and
attempted to persuade the Belgians to change their mind. At the least, he
suggested, they should leave behind their heavier weapons and equipment
with the residue of UNAMIR in order to soften the impact of the withdrawal of the most effective troops in the operation and leave the other two
under-equipped contingents with some reasonable *matériel*. This they declined
to do. In Boutros-Ghali's view the Belgian government had been 'afflicted
with the "American syndrome"' as displayed in Somalia – a tendency to
opt for escape at the first sign of serious trouble.[52]

The international politics of genocide

This anti-American jibe from Boutros-Ghali came at the end of a protracted wrangle over the UN's role in the Rwandan genocide that saw him
in repeated conflict with the United States in the Security Council. Eventually, in 1996, the issue, along with other differences, would contribute to
Washington's determination to block his second term in office, which was
customary for secretaries-general. In his own account of the issue the former
secretary-general was particularly scathing about the role of the then US
representative on the Security Council, Madeleine Albright. Boutros-Ghali's
narrative was no doubt in part to do with personal score settling and in part
an exercise in self-exculpation over events in Rwanda. While obviously a
key actor in events, Washington did not bear total blame for the UN's inadequacies in the crisis. There was, rather, a general, embarrassed shrugging-
off of responsibility at the level of the international system as a whole. As we
have seen, Belgium was not content merely to withdraw its contingent after
the killing of its troops at the beginning of April; it also sought to engineer the
end of the entire UN intervention. It continued to canvass support among
Security Council members for this after Boutros-Ghali had explicitly rejected
the suggestion. Later, America may have led the move for only a minimal
response by the Security Council, but it had willing followers motivated by
interests other than a mere wish not to depart from the American position.
And beyond the Security Council, there could be no certainty that a more
robust response would have elicited the necessary support from the broader

---

52   Ibid., p. 132.

UN in terms of troop contributions and other resources. Difficulties in this regard, it will be recalled, afflicted the original establishment of UNAMIR long before the situation had plunged into the abyss of violence after April 1994. But it is certainly the case that Washington's post-Somalia trauma had a major impact on the 'permitted' response of the UN to events in Rwanda, however easily a coalition of the like-minded could be marshalled in its support.

The first open difference between the secretary-general and the United States came in the aftermath of the Belgian withdrawal and amidst reports of widening genocide. Boutros-Ghali insisted in the Security Council that the Belgians had to be replaced with an equally effective and well-equipped force. With the Belgians gone the UN force consisted of a scant 1500 infantry troops mostly concentrated in the Kigali area. It would have been incapable at its current strength of making any significant impact on the situation regardless of the scope and limits of its mandate. Failing this reinforcement, the arguments deployed by the Belgians for total withdrawal would become self-fulfilling. A useless presence was, arguably, worse than no presence at all. There was, in fact, a 'legal' case to be made for withdrawal of UNAMIR in that the chaos that had now descended on Rwanda had effectively ended the Arusha process. As the whole purpose of UNAMIR had been to assist in the management of this process, it was now without a raison d'être and, arguably, should be pulled out. But to western governments subject to public opinion shaped by graphic reports of the genocide this could not be a favoured option. Such an abandonment was not, in other words, feasible in either humanitarian or 'political' terms. This was made clear when Boutros-Ghali, in order (according to his own account) to underline his own arguments for the replacement of the Belgians, ordered Booh Booh and Dallaire to prepare contingency plans for a full withdrawal of UNAMIR. The proposal was rejected by the Americans. Yet when the secretary-general then proposed an enlarged force with an enforcement mandate he received no support.[53] Security Council members, others as much as the United States, were faced with a delicate set of considerations, both domestic and international, in formulating their response to the crisis in Rwanda. The outcome was not necessarily consistent or effective policy.[54]

On 20 April, following a period of intense consultation between the DPKO in New York and Booh Booh and Dallaire in Kigali, the secretary-general presented the Security Council with three options for the future

---

53   Ibid., pp. 132–3.
54   For a forensic – and highly critical – narrative of the interior politics of the Secretariat and Security Council at this time see Linda Melvern, *A People Betrayed: the Role of the West in Rwanda's Genocide* (London: Zed, 2000).

of the UN operation. Firstly, UNAMIR could be massively reinforced and given an extensive enforcement mandate under Chapter VII of the Charter. Secondly, it could be reduced to a small mission about 270-strong under Dallaire and restricted to a mediation role. Thirdly, the operation could be ended and all forces withdrawn.[55] It was soon clear that there was no support in the Council for the 'maximalist' first option. Opposition to it was much wider than just the American delegation. The British representative, Sir David Hannay, pointed to the recent experience in Somalia as a warning against attempts to enforce outcomes in complex internal problems in Africa. But, in common with the other permanent members, he also rejected total withdrawal as offensive to public opinion in the context of the continuing killings.[56] The vote in the Council favoured the second option. Henceforward a reduced UNAMIR was to act as an intermediary between government forces and the RPF, and attempt to broker a cease-fire. It was also to assist where possible in the humanitarian aid effort and to monitor and report on the overall situation.

The Council's resolution did leave one door open to the secretary-general. It undertook to consider any further recommendations he might 'make concerning the force level and mandate of UNAMIR in the light of developments'.[57] Boutros-Ghali grasped this opportunity just a week later when he wrote to the Security Council pointing to the ever-deteriorating situation throughout the country. There was now a full-scale 'conventional' conflict between the RPF (which had abandoned its 'Arusha' cease-fire once the massacres began) and the Hutu army around the capital. At the same time the organized slaughter of the Tutsi population and Hutu moderates was accelerating throughout the country, with as many as 200,000 people having been killed in the three-week period since the shooting down of the presidential plane. The secretary-general now asked the Security Council to consider once again 'forceful action' to end the chaos. He ended with an admonition about the implications of an effective response: '[s]uch action would require a commitment of human and material resources on a scale which Member States have so far proved reluctant to contemplate.'[58]

The Council did not respond immediately to what was in effect a plea from Boutros-Ghali to reverse its decision of 21 April, when it had opted for a reduced force and diminished mandate, and adopt the maximalist option instead. Initially it issued a statement through its president that reiterated general pieties without making any clear response to the proposal that had

---

55   UN document S/1994/470, 20 April 1994.
56   Shawcross, *Deliver Us from Evil*, p. 117.
57   UN document S/RES/912, 21 April 1994.
58   UN document S/1994/518, 29 April 1994.

been put to it. Perhaps reflecting its own collective indecision, it temporized by stating 'its intention to consider urgently the letter of the Secretary-General . . . and further recommendations that [he] might provide'.[59] No time-frame for this was indicated, however.

Prominent in the tangled roots of the Council's irresolution was the quasi-legal issue of the concept of 'genocide'. In 1946, a year after the end of the Second World War, when the experience of the Nazi holocaust was still shocking and immediate, 'genocide' had been designated a crime under international law. Two years later the General Assembly of the United Nations had adopted its own Genocide Convention. This required its signatories to 'undertake to prevent and punish . . . acts committed with intent to destroy, in whole or in part, a national, ethnical, racial or religious group'.[60] All the major powers had been enthusiastic signatories of the Convention; in 1948 any other course would have been unthinkable. Now, though, forty-six years later, some unpredicted pigeons had come home to roost. To acknowledge – for example in a resolution or official report – that what was happening in Rwanda was indeed 'genocide' would commit the members of the Security Council to robust enforcement action to 'prevent and punish' such behaviour. The United States was especially anxious to side-step what one writer described dryly as 'the g-word'.[61] This concern with linguistic usage was shared in varying degrees by other permanent members of the Security Council, but it became a particular preoccupation for Washington in its determination to avoid embroilment in enforcement action. For one thing, the American political tradition is notably 'legalistic', as befits the world's first successful constitutional republic, and formal obligations therefore occupied a more prominent place in political calculations than they might in other, less formalistic states. For another, the term 'genocide' had a particular resonance for influential groupings in American society and politics, particularly the so-called 'Jewish lobby'. There was therefore a concern to prevent any build-up of opinion that might push towards action but that would not be sustained if costs mounted. The experience of Somalia merely underlined this perceived danger.

Legal and historical concerns over the semantics of the Rwanda horror were just one symptom of American agitation with the peacekeeping project at this time. On 3 May President Clinton signed Presidential Decision Directive (PDD) 25: 'Policy on Reforming Multilateral Peace Operations'.

---

59   UN document S/PRST/1994/21, 30 April 1994.
60   UN document A/RES/260A, 9 December 1948.
61   Gourevitch, *We Wish to Inform You That Tomorrow We Will be Killed with Our Families*, p. 152. Gourevitch describes in some detail of the lengths to which official American spokespersons sought to avoid uttering the word 'genocide' in relation to Rwanda (pp. 151–4).

This was a statement of executive thinking that placed strict limits on American support for future peacekeeping operations. The seeds of PDD 25 had been sown in the alleys of South Mogadishu in October 1993, but it was nurtured into blossom by the perceived diplomatic and legal threats now posed in Rwanda. Henceforward not only American participation in, but also American support for, UN peacekeeping was to be subject to a rigorous checklist of criteria. The national interests of the United States would now be a factor in any decision. If American forces were to be deployed, command and control structures would have to be acceptable to Washington. The aims and object-ives of any proposed operation would have to be clearly enunciated and 'achievable' in terms of the mandate agreed, and there would have to be an effective 'exit strategy'. Prior evidence would be required that proper financial and other resources would be available to see an operation through to com-pletion.[62] Although PDD 25 was presented as an American contribution to the improvement of UN peacekeeping activities, it was evident that it rep-resented a significant retreat from the multilateralism that had characterized Washington's post-cold war foreign policy hitherto in both the Bush and Clinton administrations.[63]

On 11 May, following up on his as yet unanswered proposal for an expanded force, Boutros-Ghali submitted a so-called 'non-paper' (that is, one not designated as an official document) to the Security Council. The pur-pose was to present a possible mandate for a revamped operation. After consulting with Dallaire and Booh Booh, who in turn had sought the views of what remained of a government in Kigali and the RPF, the secretary-general argued for a force of 5500. Its primary function would be to pro-vide protection for, and ensure aid deliveries to, the now massive population (perhaps up to two million-strong) of internal refugees. It would also secure Rwanda's borders to prevent its conflicts spilling over into neighbouring countries. After initial discussions with members of the Security Council Boutros-Ghali issued a formal report containing the recommendations of the 'non-paper'.[64]

At this point, according to the secretary-general, the United States attempted to impose the terms of PDD 25 on the Security Council as a whole. It did so with some initial success, he claimed: 'The behaviour of the

---

62 The terms of PDD 25 and an official commentary on it by the US State Department can be found in Michael G. MacKinnon, *The Evolution of UN Peacekeeping Policy under Clinton: a Fairweather Friend?* (London: Frank Cass, 1999), Annex I, pp. 125–39.

63 See Mats Berdal, 'Peacekeeping in Africa, 1990–1996: the role of the United States, France and Britain', in Oliver Furley and Roy May (eds), *Peacekeeping in Africa* (Aldershot: Ashgate, 1998), pp. 55–7.

64 UN document S/1994/565, 13 May 1994.

Security Council was shocking: it meekly followed the United States' lead in denying the reality of genocide.'[65] However, the Council – the individual members of which were still under great domestic pressures to take action – was now prepared to accept the thrust of Boutros-Ghali's proposal. The new operation – effectively 'UNAMIR II' – was agreed by the Council on 17 May. The force was now authorized to 'contribute to the security and protection of displaced persons, refugees and civilians at risk in Rwanda'. Although ostensibly unexceptional as a mandate in other circumstances, in Rwanda this was in effect an order to stop the genocide by force. In addition UNAMIR II was to provide security for the UN's humanitarian relief activities. Beyond the mandate for the re-formed peacekeeping operation, the Council also imposed an obligatory arms embargo on all sides in Rwanda under Chapter VII of the Charter.[66]

At this point, disputes and debates about the culpability for the UN's failure to act decisively and in a timely manner became somewhat academic. Boutros-Ghali later accused the Americans of continued obstruction on the basis of PDD 25, specifically in attempting to restrict the initial size of the new operation.[67] But the reality was that there was no prospect of attracting sufficient contingents to get anywhere near target numbers, restricted or otherwise. The complexities and dangers of the situation meant that few governments were willing to commit contingents. Unsurprisingly, public opinion in many western countries, while pressing for 'something to be done', was much less enthusiastic about the prospect of their own soldiers doing the something. Despite repeated public requests by the secretary-general and the Security Council, resources were simply not forthcoming.[68] By the end of July, more than two months after authorization for UNAMIR II had been given by the Security Council, only about 550 troops – one tenth of the total proposed force – had been found. Kofi Annan later reported that his approaches to a hundred different governments (about half the total membership of the UN) with requests for contingents in his capacity as under-secretary for peacekeeping affairs met with virtually no success.[69] In this sense the United States was exercising itself rather unnecessarily to delay not the inevitable but the impossible.

---

65 Boutros-Ghali, *Unvanquished*, p. 135.
66 UN document S/RES/918, 17 May 1994.
67 Boutros-Ghali, *Unvanquished*, p. 136. It was Boutros-Ghali's suspicion that Madeleine Albright's orders on this came directly from the White House.
68 For example, UN document S/RES/925, 8 June 1994 asked for prompt support 'for rapid deployment of additional UNAMIR forces'.
69 Shawcross, *Deliver Us from Evil*, p. 117.

The UN sidelined: Operation Turquoise and the victory of the RPF

This reluctance on the part of the UN membership as a whole to respond in any effective material way to the crisis created the conditions for one of the more controversial aspects among the many of the organization's involvement in Rwanda. On 19 June the secretary-general wrote to the Security Council pointing to the general inadequacy of the resources available to UNAMIR II. In the letter he referred to a proposal from the French delegation that France could lead its own (Francophone) 'multinational' force 'to assure the security and protection of displaced persons and civilians at risk in Rwanda', which he urged the Council to consider.[70] The proposed French intervention would be of a character that would later enter the language of peacekeeping as 'a coalition of the willing': not a formal UN mission but one politically legitimized and legally indemnified by the Security Council.[71] Specifically and controversially, France sought authorization under the (enforcement) terms of Chapter VII of the UN Charter. The proposal was fraught with diplomatic and political difficulties.

The Security Council discussed the issue over three days from 20 to 23 June. At the end of this protracted debate the Council adopted a French draft resolution. The context of the proposed force was carefully delineated in this. Individual member states would 'co-operate with the Secretary-General in order to achieve the objectives of the United Nations in Rwanda through the establishment of a temporary operation under national command and control aimed at contributing, in an impartial way, to the security and protection of displaced persons, refugees and civilians at risk in Rwanda'. The operation was authorized for a two-month period, at the end of which it was hoped UNAMIR II would be at sufficient strength to take over. Costs for what became knows as 'Operation Turquoise', it was to be clearly understood, would be met by those participating in it – effectively France.[72] When the vote was taken one permanent member, China, abstained. So did four of the ten non-permanent members, including Nigeria, which, as the leading Anglophone state of west Africa, was particularly sensitive about French policies in the continent.[73] While at one level abstentions do not point to especially fierce opposition, any dissent in peacekeeping resolutions in the Security Council was highly unusual, at least in the post-cold war years.

---

70   UN document S/1994/728, 19 June 1994.
71   Perhaps the most prominent later example of this was the Australian-led intervention in East Timor in 1999 in the chaos surrounding the supposed Indonesian 'withdrawal' from the territory.
72   UN document S/RES/929, 22 June 1994.
73   The other abstaining members were Brazil, New Zealand and Pakistan.

Despite the evident conflicts and tensions surrounding the UN's presence in Rwanda during the genocide, no other resolution on the issue was other than unanimous. But ultimately both the secretary-general and the other permanent members were happy to accept the French offer whatever its terms and implications. Imperfect as the arrangement undoubtedly was, it allowed the Security Council to persuade itself and others that it was actually 'doing something'. It also provided a means of covering the apparent failure of the UNAMIR II venture before it had had the chance to begin.

Despite the cosmetic layer of multilateralism applied to the venture, Operation Turquoise was essentially a unilateral undertaking on the part of France. (Philip Gourevitch later described it as simply a French 'military expedition . . . with some rented Senegalese troops along for the ride to create an aura of multilateralism'.[74]) As we have seen, the Anglophone–Francophone dimension to the conflict in Rwanda was real and important. Inevitably, France, by its previous policies and actions, was associated with Hutu interests. Never reticent to pursue its own perceived interests in Africa, France was regarded with the deepest suspicion by the RPF. By this stage in the fighting the RPF was within striking distance of total victory in Rwanda as the Hutu army disintegrated and fled. Now the Security Council had authorized the deployment of a considerable body of French troops and equipped them with Chapter VII enforcement powers. Coming after the months of slaughter into which the UN failed to make any significant intervention, the RPF understandably saw Operation Turquoise as adding gratuitous insult to grave injury.[75]

Preoccupied with its final assault on Hutu power, however, the RPF avoided direct conflict with the French. Operation Turquoise, which was composed of 2500 mainly French troops, was launched the day following Security Council authorization. Its main function was the creation and control of a 'humanitarian protection zone' in the south-west of the country that extended over about one fifth of the national territory. It was designed to offer a safe haven for refugees fleeing the genocide – or, as the RPF pointed out bitterly, for those who had committed the genocide fleeing justice.

Representing the UN on the ground, Dallaire was strongly opposed to the French intervention. It presented the already beleaguered UN force with a plethora of problems. There would now be two separate military interventions in the country, and UNAMIR would be required to expend scarce resources and energies in maintaining a system of liaison. Moreover, the new force

---

74 Gourevitch, *We Wish to Inform You That Tomorrow We Will be Killed with Our Families*, p. 155.
75 The French role in Rwanda, before during and after Operation Turquoise, is explored in some detail by Gérard Prunier in his two books, *The Rwanda Crisis, 1954–94* (London: Hurst & Co., 1995) and *Rwanda in Zaïre: From Genocide to Continental War* (London: Hurst & Co., 2000).

was equipped with enforcement powers under Chapter VII, powers hitherto denied the 'real' UN force. The 'quasi-UN' character of the Francophone force would inevitably compromise the position of UNAMIR with the RPF, in whose territory it was now operating and with which its relationship was already delicate after UN inaction during the worst of the genocide. Specifically, the presence of Operation Turquoise would require the precautionary withdrawal of Francophone elements already serving in UNAMIR (from Congo-Brazzaville, Senegal and Togo), further weakening its very limited resources.

In the rapidly shifting circumstances of Rwanda at this time the impact of Operation Turquoise was not great. The worst of the genocide was over by the time the French arrived, largely because the RPF (by then composed of about 20,000 well-equipped and organized fighters) had become the dominant force in the country. The Hutu army, so far as it could be said still to exist, had been driven out of areas where Tutsi might still have been at risk. The French withdrew at the end of July, little more than half-way through the two-month mandate given by the Security Council.

By the time of the French withdrawal the remnants of the old Hutu regime had fled, mostly to Zaïre. Many high-ranking 'génocidaires' had undoubtedly done so by way of the French 'protection zone'. The huge concentration of Hutu refugees, innocent and guilty, that was building on the Zaïrean side of the border in mid-1994 would soon be the catalyst of profound and enduring cycles of conflict and change throughout the entire Great Lakes region. Most affected by this would be Zaïre itself (to which we will return in the next section). For now, however, Rwanda's immediate horror was beginning to pass. On 14 July the Security Council, alarmed at the humanitarian and political ramifications of the scale of the refugee outflow (which was growing inexorably towards a total of about 1.3 million people), called for an immediate end to the fighting.[76] On 18 July 1994 the RPF declared a cease-fire, though not in response to the Security Council, long since discredited in its view. Quite simply, the RPF no longer had an enemy to fight in Rwanda. The following day a government of national unity was formed with a moderate Hutu, Pasteur Bizimungu, as president and the Tutsi commander of the RPF, Paul Kagame, as vice-president.

Peacekeeping after the genocide

Despite the end of the genocide and the conclusion of the civil war, UNAMIR II remained in Rwanda until March 1996. Its tasks in this

---

76   UN document S/PRST/1994/34, 14 July 1994.

remaining period were increasingly concerned with the huge humanitarian problems that had been produced by the convulsions of April to July 1994. Although many of these problems were now regional rather than national (as a result of the outflow of Hutu refugees), they still had major domestic impacts. To meet these problems UNAMIR II had to expand its geographical spread throughout the country as a whole from its previous concentration in the Kigali area. The new situation benefited from the fact that by October 1994 – when the main dangers and uncertainties had passed – recruitment problems had eased and the force was finally approaching its planned level of 5500 authorized the previous May.[77]

The return of refugees from Zaïre, agreed by the new Rwanda government and the UN alike to be a major priority, was complicated by a number of factors. For one thing, the reception awaiting returnees in an utterly changed, RPF-controlled Rwanda was uncertain. Those innocent of participation or complicity in the genocide shared much of the fear of the guilty. But there were more insidious – and in the longer term more dangerous – issues complicating the repatriation of refugees. Fleeing before what had become a lightning advance by the RPF in the later stages of the fighting, large number of Hutu soldiers and Interahamwe militia who had joined the exodus of refugees had established themselves in the anarchy of the Zaïrean camps. They now sought to exploit their position in their continuing struggle against the new regime in Rwanda. They imposed their 'rule' over the camps, swelling their own numbers by recruitment from among the refugees and preventing the return of those disposed to take their chances back in Rwanda. The UN meanwhile sought to encourage the return of refugees as a means of normalizing conditions in Rwanda and stabilizing the situation in the Great Lakes region as a whole. UNAMIR II had a major role in providing the transport and logistics as well as some assurance of personal security to those who managed to break free of their own fears and the pressure of the extremists in the Zaïrean camps.

It had a similar role among the tens of thousands of internally displaced persons in camps inside Rwanda established originally within the French protection zone of Operation Turquoise. Events surrounding the dissolution of one such camp by the RPF could have brought the new regime in Kigali and UNAMIR into serious conflict. The circumstances of the Kibeho affair and the fact that the conflict they threatened was avoided illustrated the nature of the post-genocide relationship between the peacekeepers and the 'host state' (as it could now properly be described). In April 1995 the RPF sought to shut down the Kibeho camp by force in order to speed the return

---

77   UN document S/1994/1133, 6 October 1994.

of the refugees to their villages and flush out and arrest any *génocidaires* concealed within it. The camp provided refuge to about 80,000 Hutu in all, however, and the operation was fraught with dangers. Despite the presence of a Zambian battalion at the scene, UNAMIR did not intervene when, in confused circumstances, RPF forces opened fire on apparently fleeing refugees. The Zambians, heavily outnumbered by about 2000 Rwandan troops, were unsuccessful in their attempts to negotiate with RPF commanders. Accounts of the death toll at Kibeho varied widely, but probably at least 4000 people were either shot, trampled in the ensuing panic or killed by local villagers.[78] Although tragic, the events at Kibeho had some positive consequences for RPF–UNAMIR relations. The killings came at the end of a period of heightened tension in Rwanda as Interahamwe based in the Zaïrean camps mounted increasingly destructive cross-border raids. In the first months of 1995 the resulting nervousness and suspicion of the RPF had led to a sharp deterioration in relations with UNAMIR. Government security forces became more aggressive and anti-UN feeling, which had been dormant for some time, came out into the open. Kibeho indicated that UNAMIR's capacity and appetite for direct intervention in the RPF's 'normalization' drive were in reality strictly limited, whatever the terms of its mandate from the Security Council. While this would have been of scant comfort to the Kibeho Hutu and in other circumstances would have raised serious concerns about the capacity and commitment of UN forces, it contributed to a working understanding between the UN force and its 'host'.

At the beginning of June 1995 Boutros-Ghali proposed that the functions of UNAMIR should be fundamentally revised in a way that would allow a sharp reduction in its strength. Its mandate up to that point had been unchanged since May 1994 when the Security Council had finally agreed, belatedly and ineffectually, to deploy a strengthened UNAMIR to stop the genocide. Now, the secretary-general argued, UNAMIR should be engaged in 'confidence-building' efforts designed to assure returning refugees of their safety. This would involve a reduction in the force to 2330 troops with an additional 300 military observers and civilian police. At the same time, he reported that the Rwandan government had sought an even narrower mandate, focused on the security of humanitarian relief supplies and protection of UN installations. The UN force level proposed by Kigali for this was 1800 for a period of six months (effectively until the end of 1995), after which UNAMIR should be totally withdrawn.[79] The Security Council, faced by both an issue of host-state consent and a cost-cutting opportunity, opted

---

78 Oliver Furley, 'Rwanda and Burundi: peacekeeping amidst massacres', in Furley and May (eds), *Peacekeeping in Africa*, pp. 250–1.

79 UN document S/1995/457, 4 June 1995.

for the more limited plan of the Rwandan government.[80] The new reduced force level was reached at the end of October 1995. The mandate of the mission was in fact extended by agreement with the Rwandan government in December 1995 when its immediate withdrawal proved impracticable,[81] but in March 1996 the UN's painful and fateful peacekeeping engagement with Rwanda was completed.

Consequences and lessons: the 1999 Independent Inquiry report

The impact of the Rwandan genocide on the institutional consciousness – and conscience – of the United Nations was considerable. The failure of the organization to prevent or even significantly ameliorate the protracted massacre of so many people, despite having committed itself to the management of a peace process in the country and having a 'force' *in situ*, struck at the heart of the entire peacekeeping project. That the fundamental failings were not institutional as much as national became somewhat lost in the *post facto* recriminations. These 'national' shortcomings were those both of the permanent members of the Security Council, who sought to avoid decisive engagement, and of the broader membership of the General Assembly, who declined to provide the forces and resources required for decisive action. But the United Nations as an institution is 'configured' for public self-criticism in a way that the states that comprise its membership are not.

In May 1999 Kofi Annan, now UN secretary-general, established an 'Independent Inquiry into the Actions of the United Nations during the 1994 Genocide in Rwanda'. The members of the tribunal were Ingvar Carlsson, the ex-Swedish prime minister, Han Sung-Joo, a former foreign minister of South Korea, and Rufus Kupolati, a retired Nigerian general. The enquiry was given access to all relevant UN documentation and carried out an extensive programme of interviews with participants in the events. Its report was produced in December 1999. Its general conclusion spread the blame widely:

> [T]he response of the United Nations before and during the 1994 genocide in Rwanda failed in a number of fundamental respects. The responsibility for the failings of the United Nations to prevent and stop the genocide in Rwanda lies with a number of different actors, in particular the

---

80   UN document S/RES/997, 9 June 1995.
81   UN document S/RES/1029, 12 December 1995.

Secretary-General, the Secretariat, the Security Council, UNAMIR and the broader membership of the United Nations.[82]

Even before the genocide began, the report noted, UNAMIR had not been 'planned, dimensioned, deployed or instructed in a way which provided for a proactive and assertive role in dealing with a peace process in serious trouble'. This observation touched on the broad problem we have already identified – the 'co-option' of the UN into the implementation of agreements and processes that it had no part in formulating. Sheer relief at the signing of the Arusha agreement had distracted attention from its extreme fragility. As a result, there 'was no fall-back, no contingency planning for the eventuality that the peace process did not succeed'. In reality, of course, there were (probably insurmountable) political difficulties in resourcing such a 'plan B' in circumstances where even the minimal requirements for the creation of the 'inadequate' UNAMIR were barely achievable. In this regard the report referred specifically to 'the aftermath of Somalia' and criticized the Security Council for the hesitance this seemed to have engendered. The failure of the secretariat (and specifically Kofi Annan and the DPKO) to follow up General Dallaire's January 1994 telegram warning of militant Hutu plans violently to disrupt the peace process was a particular cause of regret. When the genocide began there was, according to the Report, too much UN attention focused on reaching a cease-fire between the RPF and the Hutu government forces rather than on the moral outrage of the spreading genocide. And, in the confusion of the first phase of the killings, a problem inherent in multilateral peacekeeping came to the fore: conflict of loyalties at the level of national contingents when caught between the orders of the peacekeeping organization and the divergent directions of their home governments. Belgium in particular was criticized for undermining the authority of Dallaire and UNAMIR headquarters by issuing its own instructions to its troops in Rwanda.[83]

In sum, the inquiry concluded,

[w]hile the presence of United Nations peacekeepers in Rwanda may have begun as a traditional peacekeeping operation to monitor the implementation of an existing peace agreement, the onslaught of the genocide should have led decision-makers in the United Nations – from the Secretary-General and the Security Council to Secretariat officials and the leadership of UNAMIR – to realize that the original mandate, and

---

82   *The Report of the Independent Inquiry into the Actions of the United Nations during the 1994 Genocide in Rwanda* (December 1999). Found at http://www.un.org/News/ossg/rwanda_report.htm.

83   This problem had recently been noted in Somalia, where the behaviour of Italy – like Belgium in Rwanda, the former colonial power – had been criticized. See below pp. 214–15.

indeed the neutral mediating role of the United Nations, was no longer adequate, and required a different, more assertive response, combined with the means necessary to take such action.

This criticism was misdirected. The evidence was clearly that the different elements within the UN system itself did recognize the inadequacy of the original mandate after the genocide began. The problem lay in persuading the member states at both Security Council and General Assembly level to do anything about it. The report offered no concrete suggestions as to how these political and diplomatic circumstances could have been altered to permit an effective response.

Boutros-Ghali was in no doubt about the proper allocation of blame. Unsurprisingly, in view of his later experience, he laid most of it at the door of the United States. Had the massive deployment he had called for at the end of April 1994 been quickly approved by the Security Council many thousand lives could have been saved, he argued, blaming the American delegates in New York and their political masters in Washington for preventing this. But the inescapable fact was that American policy was supported by the other permanent members of the Security Council, all of which voted consistently and as one with the US delegation. Nor was there any reason to believe that, even with Washington fully committed, other members of the UN would have been any more enthusiastic about providing the manpower for such a deployment. As Boutros-Ghali himself acknowledged, rather contradicting his own case in doing so, in private discussions with national delegations '[m]any of them cited PDD 25, but this seemed to me merely a convenient cover for their own reluctance to get involved.'[84]

Horrific as the extent of the genocide in Rwanda was, its ending proved to be merely the beginning of a sequence of events that would build up to a protracted conflict drawing in all states of the Great Lakes region (and eventually several from beyond). The massive outflow of refugees from Rwanda and the attempts of Hutu militants to use the regional anarchy this created to sustain their struggle against the new RPF regime quickly exposed fundamental and long-standing instabilities in neighbouring states. As we have seen, Zaïre, the largest and most ill-governed state in the region, was the main recipient of the refugees and of the Interahamwe extremists who had intertwined themselves among them. Soon the attention of the UN would once again focus on the huge territory and convoluted politics of the country that first brought its peacekeepers to Africa three and a half decades earlier.

---

84 Boutros-Ghali, *Unvanquished*, p. 140.

Back to the Congo, 1999–

We left the Congo at the end of our exploration of the UN's first intervention there with the victory of Laurent Desiré Kabila's coalition – with the crucial backing of Rwanda – over the ailing Mobutu. The new regime took power amidst almost universal goodwill both in Africa and beyond. The Democratic Republic of Congo, it was fervently hoped, would rise phoenix-like from the corrupt ashes of Zaïre. The end of the cold war was a profoundly important factor in Mobutu's fall. In the new structure of the international system African clients were no longer necessary in the strategic calculation of the major powers, especially ones as utterly discredited as Mobutu. But the demise of the Mobutu regime was facilitated by other, more local international conditions as well. The entire Great Lakes area of central Africa had been in a state of political and ethnic turmoil since the Rwandan cataclysm of 1994. As we have just seen, in July 1994, following the victory of the Rwandan Patriotic Front over the authors of the genocide, there was a massive outflow of Hutu refugees into makeshift camps in eastern Zaïre. These, while serviced and supplied by a huge United Nations humanitarian effort, fell under the control of Hutu militants. In their scheme of things the camps provided an ideal base for rebuilding Hutu power and, more immediately, for cross-border attacks against the new regime in Rwanda.

In this febrile climate the internal fabric of the Zaïrean state, already thin, began to tear apart. With the ethnic and political frontiers in the region bearing only the most approximate relationship to each other, it was not long before the racial conflicts that underlay the Rwandan genocide emerged inside the border of Zaïre. By the middle of 1996 indigenous Zaïrean Tutsi – the Banyamulenge – in the vicinity of the camps had become targets for attack by the Rwandan Hutu extremists. In the anarchic conditions of the time and place these Interahamwe elements found little difficulty in inciting undisciplined Zaïrean troops and local non-Tutsi Zaïreans to join in their violence with the promise of pillage. Eventually, with some training and weapons – and some direct help – from the new Rwandan regime's army, the Banyamulenge were able to turn on their persecutors. In this way, the dynamics of the now largely spent internal Rwandan conflict began to seep across the formal but ethnically permeable borders of the region.

This importation of ethnic violence was a potent, catalytic new element in the long-unstable formula of Zaïrean politics. By the mid-1990s conditions in Mobutu's fiefdom were absolutely set for just such a local upheaval to grow and spread. The conflicts in and around the refugee camps of eastern Zaïre soon became absorbed into already existing opposition pressures aimed at generating rebellion against the Kinshasa regime. During the second half of 1996 the different dissident strands gradually came together, forming the Alliance of Democratic Forces for the Liberation of the Congo (*Alliance des Forces Démocratiques pour la Libération du Congo* – AFDL). The 'natural' leader of the new movement was Kabila, who by this time had become as close to an 'elder statesman' of rebellion as the Congo could offer. It was not a highly competitive field, in truth. Neighbouring states, historically wary of the giant Zaïre and hostile to Mobutu for his periodic interference in their affairs, now took the opportunity to settle scores. For example, in a strange historical twist the Angolan government transported a special group from within their own army – the 'Katangan Tigers' – across the border in support of Kabila. The Tigers were in fact the descendants of the old Katangan *gendarmerie*, who, after their defeat by UN forces in 1963, had sought sanctuary in (then Portuguese) northern Angola. Uganda too intervened directly on the side of the rebels. But it was above all Rwanda, with its provision of well-equipped and battle-hardened troops, that ultimately decided the conflict. Determined to end once and for all the threat from the Hutu extremists whom the Kinshasa regime was now actively nurturing on its western border, the RPF government in Kigali committed its forces to the overthrow of Mobutu by launching a full-scale invasion of eastern Zaïre in October 1996.

With this wide range of local and international support Kabila's movement proved unstoppable by the now friendless Mobutu. Kisangani, previously Stanleyville, Lumumba's power base in the early 1960s and a long-standing centre of anti-regime opposition, fell to the AFDL in March 1997. Lubumbashi (once Elisabethville, capital of break-away Katanga during the first UN intervention) was taken by the rebels in April. The following month the AFDL forces had taken Kinshasa. Already terminally ill, Mobutu fled to Morocco, where he died four months later. His disorganized and demoralized army simply disintegrated and scattered.

The collapse of the post-Mobutu alliance

From the beginning of the new regime in Kinshasa there were doubts about both Kabila's political capacities and his commitment to seeing a genuine transition to democracy in the Congo. His opposition to the Mobutu regime had been distinguished by its duration rather than its effectiveness.[85] In fairness, the expectations of the new regime aroused both in the Congo and among its neighbours were often unrealistic. The long-term devastation

---

85 The Cuban revolutionary Che Guevara, who travelled to the Congo in 1965 to encourage the revolutionary effort in the east, painted a devastating picture of Kabila's incompetence and cupidity. Ernesto Guevara, *The African Dream: the Diaries of the Revolutionary War in the Congo* (London: Harvill, 2000).

of the country's resources and the comprehensive demoralization and degradation of its people wrought by three decades of Mobutuism would not be reversed overnight. Yet Kabila showed little energy for the long hard road to national reconstruction. The wholesale corruption at all levels of public life that had defined the Mobutu years was hardly challenged. Under pressure, Kabila, like his predecessor, sought respite by exploiting ethnic tensions and international rivalries. Moreover, the victorious AFDL had always been a loose alliance of different ethnic and international interests, and not a cohesive movement with an agreed post-revolutionary programme. It was also, just a year after its victory, a collection of still well-armed, battle-ready factions, some with a primary loyalty to states other than the DRC.

When growing tensions spilled into armed conflict at the beginning of August 1998, therefore, it was soon evident that a major war was in prospect. The trigger for the outbreak had been Kabila's dismissal in July of the Rwandan commander of the Congolese army (*Forces Armées Congolaise* – FAC) in an attempt to lessen his dependence on the foreign states that had sponsored the later stages of his insurgency. Rwanda and Uganda were immediately concerned that their presence in the DRC – which they regarded as strategically essential in their respective conflicts against dissident guerrilla movements – was now threatened. Rwanda in particular had been concerned that Kabila had proved either unable or unwilling to extinguish fully the Hutu extremists still active on its borders. Consequently, both of these one-time patrons of the Kinshasa regime now mobilized their client factions in the AFDL against the FAC in the east of the Congo, and intervened directly with their own regular forces. On his side, Kabila sought the help of other regional states. This he received with varying degrees of enthusiasm from Zimbabwe, Angola and Namibia, fellow members of the Southern African Development Community (SADC). The intervention of Angola in particular was probably crucial in preventing a lightning rebel victory in the first weeks of the conflict. Otherwise reliant on his own incompetent FAC (now deprived of its Rwandan 'backbone'), Kabila remained in control of the capital only after a frantic ground and air defence by the Angolans. Subsequently, help for Kabila in men or arms also came from Libya, Chad and Sudan and soon the region was engaged in what the US secretary of state, Madeleine Albright, would describe in the UN Security Council as Africa's 'first world war'.[86]

The conflict soon settled down to a bloody stalemate. The balance of the two forces and their foreign supporters was such that neither side could gain a decisive upper hand during the following year. In the meantime hundreds

---

86   UN press release SC/6789, 24 January 2000.

of thousands of people (mostly civilians) had died and about a million had been made refugees, either internally or externally. As in other African conflicts of the 1990s from Angola to Liberia, ideological issues, so far as they ever had any importance, were soon overshadowed by the pursuit of spoils in the form of portable and exploitable resources. In the DRC as elsewhere diamonds became both an engine and an objective of the conflict and were sought as a prize by both the indigenous and the foreign forces involved in the war.

The Security Council made regular statements of concern but left the peacemaking initiative with the regional agencies concerned, the Organization of African Unity and the SADC (though the credibility of the latter was compromised by the intervention of some of its leading members on the side of Kabila). The crisis and its timing were sensitive for the secretariat and the Security Council. The situation in the Congo was immensely complex from a peacekeeping perspective. There was clearly no peace to keep, therefore an interpositionary force would have been irrelevant at that time. Even an enforcement action would have presented the Security Council with a major conundrum as to what should be enforced – though there was anyway not the remotest possibility of such a mission being authorized. The UN was still in something of a post-Somalia, post-Rwanda trough. These two operations had proved in their different ways quite spectacular failures for UN military intervention in Africa in the mid-1990s. The large-scale intervention in Somalia had, despite the deployment of massive resources, been unable to stabilize the situation and reinstall a viable state. And, as we have seen, the Security Council's failure to respond effectively to the Rwanda genocide was deeply influenced by the Somalia débâcle, and reflected the new wariness towards intervention in 'internal' conflicts. The UN's 'under-involvement' in Rwanda had proved as damaging in its own way as its 'over-involvement' in Somalia. Despite these unpromising antecedents, in April 1999 the Security Council expressed its 'readiness to consider the active involvement of the United Nations, in co-ordination with the Organization of African Unity . . . to assist in the implementation of an effective cease-fire agreement and an agreed process for political settlement of the issue'.[87] This was evidently a signal to the African mediators that peacekeeping resources would be available if they could produce an appropriate framework.

The Lusaka agreement and the continuing conflict

Three months later such a framework was produced, complete with a detailed proposal for UN military involvement. It came out of a sequence of

---

87   UN document S/RES/1234, 9 April 1999.

meetings between the states involved in the conflict held in the Zambian capital, Lusaka. The Lusaka agreement involved an immediate cease-fire, followed by a comprehensive peace process to return the Congo to stability. It was signed on 10 July 1999 by the heads of state of the main international actors in the DRC: Kabila himself and the presidents of Angola, Namibia and Zimbabwe, on one side, and those of Rwanda and Uganda, on the other. The main internal rebel groups, the Congolese Rally for Democracy (*Rassemblement Congolais pour la Démocratie* – RCD) and the Congo Liberation Movement (*Mouvement de Libération du Congo* – MLC), initially declined to sign as they had not been formally represented at Lusaka, though they associated themselves with the process shortly afterwards.

Taking the Security Council at its word (as given in the April resolution), the Lusaka signatories proposed that the UN should provide a military presence to help implement key parts of the agreement.[88] This would work in co-operation with a Joint Military Commission (JMC) to be established between the signatories and the OAU. The JMC would carry out a process of demobilization, disarmament and reintegration of combatants. This scheme of demilitarization was already familiar from a range of African peacekeeping operations – including, ominously, that in Rwanda, where it had proved catastrophically unsuccessful in 1993 and 1994. The UN would also monitor the observation of a cease-fire, disarm civilians, schedule and supervise the withdrawal of foreign forces and provide humanitarian assistance. The agreement envisaged the provision by the UN of 'peace enforcement units' on the pattern originally proposed by Boutros Boutros-Ghali in *An Agenda for Peace* in 1992.[89] These would, it was proposed, confront any armed elements that failed to comply with the peace process.

The UN had previously been required to undertake inappropriate roles in the implementation of unsatisfactory peace agreements into the formulation of which it had no input. Perhaps the most notorious cases of this were Angola in 1991–92 and, of course, Rwanda in 1993–94. But in the case of the DRC, secretary-general Kofi Annan had, early in the search for an agreement, appointed a special envoy to the process – the Senegalese diplomat Moustaphe Niasse. Therefore, although not a principal mover of the Lusaka process, the UN was more than a mere observer as it had been in Arusha when the ill-starred Rwanda agreement was worked out. Here it was, in the language of the time, a 'stakeholder'. Consequently, the secretary-general's response to the Lusaka proposals was rapid and positive. Just five days after the signing of the agreement he produced a paper setting out the

---

88　The text of the Lusaka agreement was issued in UN document S/1999/815, 23 July 1999.
89　*An Agenda for Peace: Preventive Diplomacy, Peacemaking and Peacekeeping* (New York: United Nations, 1992), paragraph 44. See above p. 13.

UN role proposed by the Lusaka signatories and making specific recommendations to the Security Council.[90] Anxious that the implications of any UN involvement should be fully understood, Annan was candid about the commitment. In order to be effective any peacekeeping operation, '[w]hatever its mandate, will have to be large and expensive. It would require the deployment of several thousands of international troops and civilian personnel. It will face tremendous difficulties and will be beset by risks.' Initially, he sought immediate authorization for a group of ninety military liaison officers to work both inside the DRC and in the capitals of other countries involved in the conflict. As well as assisting the JMC, these observers would act as an intelligence source for the secretary-general. A second stage would involve the deployment of a corps of 500 military observers to monitor the cease-fire. The final part of a three-phase process would be the introduction to the DRC of a force of several thousand peacekeepers. The overall operation would be called the United Nations Organization Mission to the Congo (*Mission de la Organisation des Nations Unies au Congo* – MONUC). Three weeks later the Security Council unanimously accepted the general plan and agreed to the immediate despatch of the liaison officers, who left for their various locations in mid-September.[91]

While the Lusaka agreement held reasonably well as far as Congolese and foreign regular forces were concerned, fighting continued between various armed factions. In this delicate environment, moreover, the deployment of the MONUC liaison officers in the DRC itself was being obstructed by Kabila. Annan nevertheless pressed ahead, and in mid-November appointed the Tunisian diplomat Kamel Morjane as his special representative in the country. But by the beginning of 2000 the cease-fire had all but disintegrated. The interventionist armies as well as the rebel factions were now fully re-engaged in the fighting. A five-day special Security Council session at the end of January, which brought the main actors together in New York to recommit themselves to the Lusaka process, failed to produce any improvement. Yet despite the apparent unravelling of the Lusaka process, at the end of February the Security Council agreed to move on to the second phase of Annan's original plan, approving the dispatch of up to 500 military observers to be stationed within the DRC.[92] The general situation did not, however, improve, and at the beginning of May a disastrous new element entered the already complex equation of conflict when Rwandan and Ugandan forces, hitherto allies against Kabila, turned on each other in Kisangani. Bursts of fierce fighting continued between the two forces, each of which backed a

---

90   UN document S/1999/790, 15 July 1999.
91   UN document S/RES/1258, 6 August 1999.
92   UN document S/RES/1291, 24 February 2000.

different faction in the increasingly fractious rebel alliance. The fighting resulted in hundreds of civilian deaths over the following months.

This outbreak coincided with a visit to the Congo by a Security Council delegation led by the United States permanent representative, Richard Holbrooke (who had succeeded Madeleine Albright after her appointment as secretary of state). The mission was designed to reinvigorate the peace process, both locally in the Congo itself and at the regional diplomatic level.[93] It produced little movement at either location, however. Despite undertakings given to the delegation by Paul Kagame (now president of Rwanda) and Yoweri Museveni of Uganda respectively, their forces continued to fight each other. The status of forces agreement between the Kabila government and MONUC, which was signed in the presence of the delegation, was not properly observed by the Kinshasa government. The freedom of movement throughout the country essential to their proper functioning was denied to MONUC observers as it had earlier been to the liaison officers. As a result, by June 2000 only 200 of the authorized 500 military observers had been deployed.[94]

By the first anniversary of the Lusaka agreement (and the second of the civil war itself) the prospects for the peace process and therefore for the UN's peacekeeping role within it were extremely poor. In his report to the Security Council on the situation in the DRC and the work of MONUC presented in June 2000, Annan was deeply pessimistic.[95] Fighting continued between Rwandan and Ugandan forces in Orientale province, while Kabila's forces were in action against armed groups across the centre and east of the country. Additionally, it had become clear that the government was determined to pull MONUC into its own political manoeuvres when its Kinshasa headquarters were attacked in obviously orchestrated hostile demonstrations. It seemed that MONUC was being set up as a convenient alibi for the Kinshasa regime's own political and military incapacities.[96] In short, the position of MONUC was beginning to show striking similarities to that of ONUC forty years previously. Beyond these gathering political dangers, the physical environment for the conduct of a full-scale peacekeeping mission was actually worse than it had been in the early 1960s. The huge problems of the Congo's

---

93 The official report of the delegation was issued as UN document S/2000/416, 11 May 2000.

94 In total 224 observers were serving in MONUC from thirty-three contributing states. Some twenty of these were based in neighbouring states as liaison officers.

95 UN document S/2000/566, 12 June 2000.

96 Following protests from the Security Council the DRC's UN representative disingenuously excused the riots as the result of 'profound outrage because of the inactivity and the inability of the United Nations forces to prevent the fighting [in Kisangani]'. UN press release SC/6876, 15 June 2000.

degraded infrastructure (poor at the time of independence, routinely bad under Mobutu and dreadful after three years of war) would vastly exacerbate the logistical problems of peacekeeping.

In these circumstances any move to Annan's proposed third phase – the deployment of a 5500-strong peacekeeping force – would be fraught with political and practical difficulties. Few potential contributors would be willing to risk their forces in such a situation, which was if anything even more uncertain than that in the country four decades earlier. Ruefully, the secretary-general acknowledged this difficulty, noting that only in 'response to repeated requests, a few troop contributing countries have offered to provide the infantry battalions' necessary for a minimal force. Agreements in principle had been reached for battalions from Morocco, Pakistan and Senegal. The fourth contingent was proving difficult to find, though Nigeria and South Africa were regarded as both appropriate and feasible contributors. However, following the recent crisis around the equipment, training and capacity of the UN Mission in Sierra Leone (see below pp. 191–3), Annan had ordered a 'full review and reassessment' of the troops levels and other requirements before a larger force could be deployed in Congo, and elements of the proposed contingents had not passed muster.[97]

Throughout the second half of 2000 the UN's role on the ground was essentially suspended. The war-within-the-war between Rwandan and Ugandan forces around Kisangani provided a glimpse of the problems likely to be faced by any large-scale intervention before an effective cease-fire was in place and the overall peace process underway. MONUC's efforts to broker a truce between the two armies was brushed aside and the UN was denied a presence in the area until 'permitted' by the Rwandan force, which eventually won the day.[98] Eventually MONUC mediation helped secure an agreement from both parties for the maintenance of a 100-kilometre 'separation zone' between the two armies. A new consciousness of mutual self-interest in the aftermath of their bloodletting led both sides to observe this arrangement. The Security Council had been left to express its impotent 'outrage' at the behaviour of the two foreign armies and to make inevitably hollow demands for the withdrawal of all such outside forces.[99] None of this could encourage optimism about the outcome of a large-scale UN deployment in the Congo as a whole.

Meanwhile, at the level of the primary conflict, regional diplomatic pressure was mounting on Kabila, who was increasingly perceived (even by those neighbours supporting his government) as the main obstacle to the

---

97   UN document S/2000/566, 12 June 2000.
98   BBC World Service (Africa) report, 21 July 2000.
99   UN document S/RES/1304, 16 June 2000.

implementation of the Lusaka agreement.[100] These efforts were unavailing. Far from embracing the peace process, Kabila seemed intent on obstructing it, regardless of the interests of his own regime. He continued to refuse the necessary permission for the deployment of MONUC military observers in government-held territory and declined to co-operate with the mediator appointed by the UN, the former president of Botswana, Ketumile Masiri. By this stage in the war it was calculated that in the eastern half of the country alone (scene of the most intense battles), 1.7 million people had died, 200,000 directly in the fighting and the rest as a result of disease and starvation directly attributable to conflict.[101] By the end of 2000 the prospects for the Congo looked utterly bleak. Neither the internal factions nor the external interventionists had the political or military capacity to force the conflict to any sort of conclusion, and leadership of what passed for the Congo state was non-existent. But now a wholly unexpected element was about to be injected into the situation.

From Kabila to Kabila: a new opportunity for peacekeeping?

On 16 January 2001 the increasingly isolated Kabila was assassinated by one of his own bodyguards in Kinshasa. The motive for the killing remained unclear, but it did not appear to be a direct act in the ongoing war.[102] Kabila was succeeded, with a minimum of consultation, by his son, Joseph. The 31-year-old new president was a largely unknown quantity. He had occupied a commanding rank in the army of the DRC, but amidst the ubiquitous nepotism of the Kinshasa regime this was no indication of his abilities. Nevertheless, Joseph's quieter, less flamboyant style raised early hopes that he would not maintain his father's intransigence towards attempts to jump-start the moribund Lusaka agreement. With a Tutsi wife, moreover, there seemed to be some grounds to hope that he was reasonably placed to forge a new relationship with the strongest of the regime's foreign enemies, Rwanda. Within the UN the change of leadership, along with a distinct lull in the fighting in eastern Congo, were seen as providing an opportunity to reinvigorate MONUC's role.

---

100 BBC World Service (Africa) reports, 16 August 2000; 18 August 2000.
101 *The Sunday Herald* (Scotland), 20 August 2000.
102 Kabila's death may have been the result of a conspiracy among his closest associates rather than the act of an individual. No post-mortem or any forensic tests were carried out after the killing, and several members of Kabila's inner circle were later arrested. *Africa Confidential* 42(2), 26 January 2001; 42(7), 6 April 2001.

In February, with the first signs that the general cease-fire central to the Lusaka agreement was actually taking hold, the secretary-general proposed to the Security Council a revised plan of deployment for MONUC. Expressing 'grounds for cautious hope' in the new climate, he urged a more modest – but in the circumstances more feasible – format for MONUC than the large 'peace-guaranteeing' force originally envisaged. The current complement of 200 military observers would be increased to 550. In addition there would be a force of about 2300 troops (1900 infantry and 400 river-based). These would not be operational peacekeepers as such, but a security detachment for the protection of UN installations and property. In total, therefore, the operation would consist of about 3000 military personnel, but with neither the authority nor the capacity to act in an enforcement role. The deployment of this reformulated MONUC would be contingent on a meaningful cease-fire and disengagement between opposing forces.[103] The new plan was endorsed by the Security Council which repeated with increased emphasis its earlier demands for the complete withdrawal of foreign forces from the DRC.[104] Although the extent of his real power in the byzantine politics of the Kinshasa regime remained unclear, the western powers and the United Nations had embraced the new president as the best hope for progress on the Lusaka process.[105] He was, in truth, the only one available.

By mid-2001 MONUC had been expanded in line with Annan's revised plan to about 2500 military personnel. These were drawn from forty-four states, with the principal troop contributions coming from three African Francophones – Morocco, Senegal and Tunisia – and from Uruguay. The complement of military observers and liaison officers attached to the various factions and foreign forces had risen to 500 as planned. The remaining troops formed the UN's own security force – or 'infantry guard units', as they were styled. Disengagement between the major forces was now underway, though violence among smaller groups and generalized disorder continued in parts of the country, particularly in the ever-rebellious east. Despite several statements of intent, the intervention forces of neighbouring states remained in the Congo. Indeed, their presence had expanded with the arrival of a force from Burundi, which had become, like Rwanda, subject to violent incursions from Congo-based Hutu extremists intent on exploiting its own potentially explosive ethnic relationships. But compared with the picture only six months previously at the end of 2000, the situation had improved markedly.

---

103   UN document S/2001/128, 12 February 2001.
104   UN document S/RES/1341, 22 February 2001.
105   *Africa Confidential* 42(6), 23 March 2001.

In his report to the Security Council in June 2001, Annan gave voice to a 'cautious optimism about the immediate future of the Lusaka peace process'. But he had deep forebodings about the region as a whole, and particularly over the deteriorating situation in Burundi.[106] Like a fire-ship passing through a fleet, the ethnic and political tensions at the heart of the Great Lakes region had ignited Rwanda before crashing against Zaïre/the DRC. It was now, evidently, drifting towards the dry timbers of Burundi. It was probably beyond the capacity of any external force to manage this generalized firestorm once it was underway. The United Nations, however, had little option but to make the attempt, regardless of how well- or ill-equipped it was for the task. The inescapable truth was that no other actor, whether state or international organization, was either willing or able to do so. Prodded into action by member states anxious to be seen to address the interconnected crises of the region but with insufficient national political will to mobilize the necessary resources, UN peacekeeping served in the 1990s and beyond much the same function in the region's problems as it had in the early 1960s. That was to be either scapegoat for or tribune of the 'international community' as events and diplomatic preferences dictated.

Taking over: the Central African Republic, 1998–2000

The Central African Republic (CAR) borders the Democratic Republic of the Congo in the north along the Oubangi River. Although not involved directly in the interlinked conflicts of its southern neighbours in the 1990s and beyond, it was touched, both economically and politically, by these events. The southern Yakoma people of the CAR form a considerable population in the northern Congo as well. More generally, the Republic was also very much a state of the central African region in terms of its own crises of inter-ethnic, patrimonial politics, crises that, as in Rwanda and the DRC, brought UN intervention.

The United Nations Mission in the Central African Republic – 'MINURCA' (an acronym of the operation's French title, *Mission des Nations Unies en République Centrafricaine*) – was deployed from April 1998 until February 2000. The operation was in part a legitimizing exercise like those in Liberia and Sierra Leone which were designed to give an added dimension of international authority to a peacekeeping force established by 'regional' states. UN involvement in the CAR was eventually, however, of a more

---

106   UN document S/2001/572, 8 June 2001.

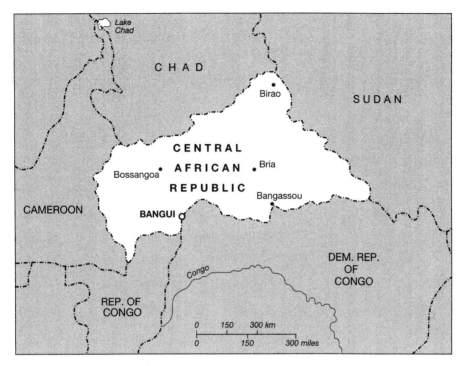

The Central African Republic

substantial character as the original terms of the crisis altered. The Security Council had first become involved through its 'authorization' of an otherwise autonomous Francophone force that had been deployed in the CAR originally at the beginning of 1997. This intervention was in response to a series of destabilizing army mutinies that followed a period of uncertain 'democratization' in the former French colony. Even as a 'UN' force MINURCA remained a predominantly Francophone operation in composition, but it was 'leavened' by other national contingents and a non-Francophone African head of mission. The mission was wound up at the beginning of 2000 after a three months 'margin of safety' following national elections in November 1999 which would, it was hoped, provide a solution to the country's long-standing political fragility.

The background

Appropriately named, the Central African Republic lies at the geographical hub of sub-Saharan Africa, bordered by Chad, Sudan, the Democratic Republic of Congo and Cameroon respectively, to north, east, south and west. For its considerable area it has a relatively sparse population, 3.3

million. About half of the population lives in and around the capital, Bangui, which became the main location of the UN's peacekeeping efforts. Although potentially rich in minerals and timber the CAR's resources remain under-exploited because of its poor infrastructure and the difficulty of its terrain. The area was first annexed by France in the 1880s at the height of the European scramble for Africa. Over the previous century its geographical location had forced it into a pivotal place in the Arab and European slave trades. Pre-colonial structures of 'government' were consequently tenuous and population movements frequent. Ubangi-Shari, as the French named it, was incorporated in French Equatorial Africa in 1910. Long-term European settlement was limited, however. The territory's main contribution to the empire was to provide concession companies with opportunities – often exploited with considerable brutality – for the export of cash crops and timber. From the end of the Second World War, in common with the other parts of French sub-Saharan Africa, the territory underwent a process of increasing autonomy until it became fully independent as the Central African Republic in 1960.

The Republic's first president, David Dacko, held office until January 1966, when he was overthrown by the army commander Colonel Jean Bédel Bokassa. Bokassa's lurid misrule was to last almost fourteen years. His corrupt and brutal autocracy degenerated into black comedy when, in 1977, he became monarch of the newly named Central African Empire at a spec-tacularly expensive 'coronation'. Bokassa's position remained secure as long as France maintained a stance of benevolent inactivity. In 1979, however, widespread demonstrations by schoolchildren and students provoked ever more gross acts of repression by the regime, and Paris finally acted to remove Bokassa. In September of that year French troops were deployed, ostensibly to protect the expatriate community but in effect to depose Bokassa and orche-strate the return of David Dacko to the presidency. Dacko sought, and apparently won, a popular mandate in elections in what was once again the Central African Republic in 1981. The legitimacy of his victory was con-tested, however, and amidst general political confusion he was replaced by the army commander General André Kolingba, who held the presidency for the following twelve years.

Democratization, instability and the MISAB interlude

In September 1993, after some false starts, a generally free and fair election saw Ange-Félix Patassé elected to the presidency. It was not Patassé's first taste of power. He had in fact been part of the group of conspirators around Bokassa that had ousted Dacko in 1966, and he had been prime minister for a time in Bokassa's regime. Electoral legitimacy was not sufficient to secure Patassé in the presidency and he was soon beset by the continuous rhythm of challenges that had become almost a defining characteristic of CAR politics by the 1990s. In May 1996 elements of the army garrison in Bangui mutinied over conditions and unpaid wages. These were issues that drew a sympathetic response throughout the country's large public sector. Central to the demands of the mutineers and their supporters was the resignation of Patassé.

There was an ethnic dimension to the affair as well. The rebel soldiers were predominantly from the southern Yakoma people and as such looked to the former president, André Kolingba, as their patron.[107] (Patassé's ethnic base was among the Sara of the north.) Once again, French troops stationed in the capital proved decisive, though the revolt was only suppressed after considerable loss of life and widespread destruction. Nor did the French intervention provide a permanent solution. Further mutinies broke out (with further French interventions) a few months later and again at the beginning of 1997, when fighting was particularly intense.

France became increasingly worried at the lack of any apparent solution to the problem and over the extent of its own commitment. It was also uncomfortable with its enforced alliance with the unpredictable Patassé. Consequently, it attempted to extricate itself from the front-line of the conflict by recourse to wider diplomacy. The issue had been discussed at the Franco-African summit (the regular expression of continuing French association with Africa) held in Burkina Faso in December 1996. There the presidents of Burkina Faso, Chad, Gabon and Mali were asked to broker a settlement to the crisis. The result of the intensive negotiations that followed was the Bangui Accords of January 1997. By the terms of these the mutineers, in return for laying down their arms, would be amnestied and offered the chance of reintegration into the armed forces.[108] Patassé, whose faith in his own enfeebled security forces was limited, sought and secured an agreement from the four mediating states for the establishment of a peacekeeping force to monitor the implementation of the agreement.[109] Accordingly, at the beginning of February 1997 the Inter-African Mission for the Supervision of the Bangui Accords (*Mission Interafricaine de Surveillance des Accords de Bangui* – MISAB) was deployed in the capital. It consisted initially of 800 troops from the four mediators and was later reinforced by other Francophone

---

107 *Africa Confidential* 38(20), 10 October 1997.

108 The full text of the Bangui Accords is to be found in UN document S/1997/561, Appendices III–VI, 4 July 1997.

109 A year after the Bangui Accords a UN report noted that the 'national security apparatus of the Central African Republic [has] been severely weakened . . . its command structure has disintegrated as a result of the mutinies, and it lacks vehicles, communication equipment and other essential assets.' UN document S/1998/61, 23 January 1998.

contingents from Togo and Senegal. Extensive logistical support, without which the mission could not have operated, was supplied by France.

The Security Council became involved six months later when both Patassé and President Omar Bongo of Gabon, who had assumed overall responsibility for MISAB, wrote to the Security Council seeking formal UN 'authorization' for the force.[110] Their motives were twofold. Firstly, the Bangui Accords notwithstanding, the crisis was far from resolved, and tensions between pro-government forces and MISAB on one side, and the still armed and dangerous mutineers on the other, remained high. The approach to the Security Council followed a series of particularly violent clashes involving MISAB in June 1997. The climate of insecurity that had developed along with the protracted politico-military wrangles had bred a general disorder in the country with banditry and lawlessness becoming endemic. Consequently, greater international attention and support was sought. Secondly, the continuing stand-off between the antagonists constantly threatened to spill over into another round of serious fighting and it was therefore important that the 'legitimacy' of the international force should be fully established. The Security Council was willing to help and found a legal justification for doing so by identifying the situation in the CAR as 'a threat to international peace and security in the region'. This enabled the Council to invoke Chapter VII of the Charter to 'authorize the Member States participating in MISAB and the States providing logistical support to ensure the security and freedom of movement of their personnel'.[111] The Council took care to emphasize that this new relationship would not extend to any commitment of financial or other resources, however, and as a price for this authorization MISAB would be required to report to the Security Council at two-week intervals. This condition reflected the concern of the British delegate in the Security Council that the UN 'must have a clear sense of the Mission's tasks in order to effectively monitor their implementation'.[112] Whatever conditions were applied, the Security Council had clearly accepted a formal role in the CAR. It was one that would soon be considerably more onerous.

The UN 'takes over' – the establishment of MINURCA

Pursuing its strategy of self-extrication, in September 1997 France began actively to plan its withdrawal from the CAR and from the MISAB operation. Relations between Paris and Patassé had never been cordial. Seeking to have

---

110   Letter to Security Council from Patassé – UN document S/1997/561, 4 July 1997; letter from Bongo – UN Document S/1997/543, 7 July 1997.
111   UN document S/RES/1125, 6 August 1997.
112   Security Council press release S/6407, 6 August 1997.

his political cake and eat it, Patassé continued to denounce French 'imperialism' in the country even as French troops were on the streets of Bangui preserving his regime.[113] Now, France decided, its entire 1400-strong contingent was to be repatriated by April 1998. This would leave MISAB without either essential logistical support or the often crucial operational backup that French troops had provided. While genuine progress had been made since MISAB had been deployed, the implementation of the Bangui Accords had not been completed. Although there was widespread agreement in the CAR and beyond that MISAB had been a success, particularly in the recovery of weaponry, the peace process remained delicate and unlikely to survive the precipitate withdrawal of the international force. The hard reality was that, however widely drawn the international participation in MISAB, it depended almost entirely on French resources.[114]

Unsurprisingly, Patassé returned to the United Nations, seeking to draw it further into his country's difficulties to fill the space to be vacated by France. In a letter to secretary-general Kofi Annan in January 1998 he argued that it was 'essential . . . that the United Nations ensure that a credible peacekeeping force is maintained in the country', and asked him to take the matter to the Security Council as a matter of urgency. Annan supported the essence of Patassé's argument and asked the Council to accept in principle the idea of a UN 'stabilization' force. He did so in the awareness that the present contributors to MISAB (other than France) appeared willing to maintain their commitment under a new UN structure.[115] On this basis the Security Council agreed at the end of March 1998 to the establishment of a United Nations force – MINURCA – to take over from the now depleted MISAB operation.[116] The unique circumstance of having units already deployed meant that the new force could become operational in mid-April, less than three weeks after its authorization. Kofi Annan also appointed a special representative, Oluyemi Adeniji from Nigeria, to 'parallel' the force commander, who remained a Francophone African, Brigadier General Barthélémy Ratanga from Gabon. The force was authorized to reach a maximum of 1350 troops with an additional small civilian police component. The exclusively Francophone composition of MISAB was widened in MINURCA to include Canadian, Egyptian and Portuguese participants.[117] Its mandate as

---

113 *Africa Confidential* 38(20), 10 October 1998.

114 Berman and Sams, *Peacekeeping in Africa*, p. 226.

115 UN document S/1998/61, 23 January 1998. Patassé's letter to Annan of 12 January 1998 is included as an annex to this document.

116 UN document S/RES/1159, 27 March 1998.

117 The composition remained predominantly Francophone African, however, with contingents from Benin, Burkina Faso, Cameroon, Chad, Côte d'Ivoire, Gabon, Mali, Senegal, Togo and Tunisia.

set out by the Security Council was principally to provide security in and around the capital, Bangui, the location of the main trouble over the previous two years. MINURCA was also to play a supervisory role in the process of disarmament of formerly dissident troops and, in the longer term, provide administrative support in the electoral process that was designed to resolve the political uncertainty that underlay the mutinies.

The unusual speed of its deployment apart, MINURCA experienced and demonstrated a range of difficulties that were common to the peacekeeping process in the 1990s. Prominent among these were the tight financial limitations within which it had to operate. Among several reasons for France's anxiety to withdraw were the financial burden it had been forced to assume and the evident disinclination of other western states to bear any significant share of this.[118] The Security Council, while willing to take over certain operational and administrative responsibilities from MISAB, was wary of the economic implications. MINURCA therefore was fundamentally under-resourced, and this had consequences for its performance and, more broadly, for the peace-building process. The crucial legislative elections that MINURCA had been mandated to assist with were delayed, in part because of its under-manning. To meet this problem, elements of the national army, the *Forces Armées Centrafricaines* (FACA), were recruited to bolster the UN's numbers.[119] The co-option of host-state forces by a UN peacekeeping mission was highly unusual and potentially dangerous, but in the CAR it provided a practical solution to a specific problem. The poll, which eventually took place in November and December 1998, was generally well conducted and passed off without serious incident, at least in part because of the temporarily augmented UN force.

The UN force was effective in its continuing responsibility for security in the Bangui area. The situation beyond the capital – and therefore outwith MINURCA's mandate – remained unsettled, however. The mission assumed responsibility for the storage and disposal of the great quantity of weapons retrieved by MISAB from the dissident soldiers. Throughout 1999 MINURCA remained as a security backstop as the state undertook a process of constitutional and economic reconstruction, and FACA gradually reacquired responsibility for national security. Specifically, MINURCA had a major role in the management of presidential elections held in September 1999, from which Félix Patassé emerged with a renewed democratic mandate. The following month the Security Council, encouraged by the apparent

---

118 France provided all transport to and from the CAR for MISAB troops, supplied them with weapons, fuel and equipment, and paid personal allowances to them. See Berman and Sams, *Peacekeeping in Africa*, p. 226.

119 Ibid., p. 228.

advances towards stability and normalization, voted for a final extension of MINURCA's mandate until mid-February 2000.[120] The mission was drawn-down on schedule, having completed a generally successful peacekeeping operation.

In reality, the apparently straightforward course and outcome of MINURCA was due to an accretion of special local circumstances and, therefore, of limited value as a model for the broader peacekeeping project in Africa. The ease with which initial contingents were 'recruited' and the consequent rapid deployment of the force was due simply to the fact that the rump of the MISAB participants agreed to continue under an altered command structure when the UN 'took over'. With this local, operationally 'acclimatized' core force in place, it was relatively easy to persuade other, non-African, states to provide contingents in order to 'globalize' the Francophone force. The impact of the limited budget assigned by the Security Council to the operation was reduced both by the restricted geographical range of MINURCA's mandate (the Bangui area) and by the fact that no serious – and expensive – crises afflicted the course of the operation.[121] The absence of such crises was itself an indication of the relative 'manageability' of the situation, due in large part to the presence of a regime under Patassé that, although under pressure, was nevertheless widely perceived as legitimate, both domestically and abroad. This in turn enabled the regime to deploy its own reasonably effective armed forces in support of the international force at crucial junctures.

MINURCA did not provide a permanent solution to the web of social, economic and ethnic problems that afflicted the Central African Republic. In June 2001, sixteen months after the UN withdrawal, the Patassé regime was shaken by a further, and unexpected, coup attempt led by General Kolingba. The army divided on this occasion as in the earlier mutinies that had first led to international intervention. Kolingba was able to mobilize sections of the army still dominated by his fellow Yakoma. Other sections of the military, however, notably the Presidential Guard, which had been restructured and retrained by MINURCA, remained loyal to the elected regime.[122] Narrowly escaping with his life, Patassé faced down the coup with a rapidly deployed force of Libyan troops. The UN's satisfaction with the outcome of the mission suddenly seemed misplaced. Inevitably, the withdrawal of MINURCA came to be seen as premature, and driven by financial pressure rather than operational judgements. In reality, though,

---

120   UN document S/RES/1271, 22 October 1999.
121   The entire MINURCA operation cost $33.3 million – which was notably cheap by the standards of peacekeeping of the time.
122   BBC World Service (Africa) report, 5 June 2001.

the underlying causes of the June 2001 coup were probably beyond the terms of the mandate and the operational capacity of MINURCA to solve. Ultimately, governments must govern, and cannot expect to do so above a permanent safety net of peacekeepers. Despite the obvious lessons of 1997 Patassé had allowed arrears of payments across the public sector to mount again. And, despite the urgings of Kolingba himself (with French support), he had failed to engage with the difficult, but in the CAR not insurmountable, problems of regional and ethnic relations.[123] It is unclear what a continued MINURCA presence in an evidently stabilized environment could have achieved in the absence of effective governance on the part of the regime.

Whatever the longer-term fate of the Patassé regime after the departure of MINURCA, the period of the UN's presence exhibited some character-istics that were hardly typical of its interventions elsewhere in the continent. Despite this, though, some elements of the MINURCA experience did point up potentially broader lessons. The construction of a peacekeeping intervention around a core of regional contingents – under UN command rather than that of a local organization – in some respects echoed the original plans put in place for ONUC in the Congo in 1960, before events there span out of control. In the context of later interventions of this type the MINURCA experience stood up well against those in Liberia and Sierra Leone. In these operations the lead role of a regional force led to inter-organizational conflict and diminished operational efficiency (see below chapter 4). The incorporation within the UN operation of such reliable local forces as may be available (though only after careful assessment of this reliability) and its extent might be another pointer from MINURCA. The problems in the CAR subsequent to UN withdrawal should not detract from what was, in almost all particulars, a success. (It is unclear whether the general under-reporting of the UN's efforts there in the wider world was despite or because of this.) This is not an assessment easily extended to the other UN interventions in the central African region.

---

123 France's urging of an agenda of inter-ethnic conciliation led Patassé to denounce
     supposed French complicity in the June 2001 coup attempt. BBC World Service (Africa)
     report, 18 June 2001.

CHAPTER THREE

Managing Delayed Decolonization
Southern Africa

The United Nations first became involved in peacekeeping in southern Africa at the end of the 1980s when it took on a major role in the linked processes of the South African 'decolonization' of Namibia and the withdrawal of Cuban troops from Angola. This was only the second UN peacekeeping venture in Africa, although almost two decades had passed since the operation in the Congo. The intervening period had seen the peacekeeping project as a whole, firstly, become focused on key areas of 'détente management' (principally the Middle East) and then fall fallow altogether as global bipolarity deepened once again into cold war. Coming just as that cold war was resolving itself, the Namibian venture was to be the first in a sequence of UN engagements in southern Africa over the following decade. Subsequently, major operations were established in Angola and Mozambique where they were supposed to manage peace settlements designed to end long-fought civil wars and to supervise associated processes of democratic change.

At the centre of all of these UN interventions lay the problem of white minority rule in the regional giant, South Africa. The problems of Namibia, Angola and Mozambique were all to some degree a function of the increasingly desperate struggle for self-preservation by the beleaguered apartheid state. The broader brush of cold war rivalries touched all three conflicts as well. Additionally, the Angolan and Mozambican conflicts had distinct indigenous elements. Local ethnic, regional and economic dimensions, in the case of Angola at any rate, proved to be much more intractable than many outsiders, including would-be peacemakers, had initially appreciated.

The effect of the southern African peacekeeping experience as a whole was to highlight the limitations of the United Nations as an agent of conflict resolution. This may seem paradoxical in a region where it had what could be described as a two-to-one success rate. But the United Nations only in small part created the necessary conditions for the 'successes'. It could facilitate and then exploit favourable circumstances in Namibia and Mozambique, but it did little to create them. In contrast, no matter what resources and ingenuity the United Nations might lavish on Angola at various points in its engagement there, until the internal dynamics of the conflict permitted it, peacekeeping could not succeed.

Linked withdrawal:
Namibia and Angola, 1988–91

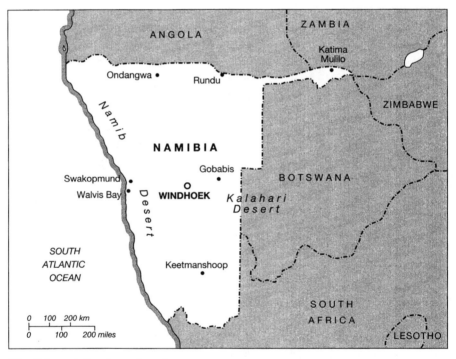

Namibia and Southern Angola

The United Nations intervention in Namibia and Angola at the end of the 1980s took the form of two linked operations, one a military observer mission and the other a large-scale, multifunctional undertaking of a type that would become increasingly common in Africa and elsewhere in the post-cold war period. Although unconnected operationally, they were tightly linked politically. The United Nations Angola Verification Mission (UNAVEM) was charged with supervising the withdrawal of Cuban forces, firstly from Angola's southern border with Namibia and then from the country as a whole. Simultaneously, the United Nations Transition Assistance Group (UNTAG) was established to manage the process leading to Namibia's independence from South Africa.

The success of this combined venture underlined an essential truth of the peacekeeping process. That is, that a combination of involvement by leading external powers exercising leverage over local state actors and a fundamental, self-interested commitment on the part of all involved to a pre-agreed outcome will virtually guarantee success. The Namibia–Angola settlement was not the first illustration of this truth. It had already been evident in the UN's first full-scale peacekeeping operation in Suez from 1956. It was a first for sub-Saharan Africa, however, and a welcome corrective after the confusion and complexity of the UN's experience in the Congo. Its very success, though, stored up some future difficulties for the UN, leading as it did to a certain over-optimism about the potential of peacekeeping solutions in other African situations. This was perhaps most obvious (and most understandable) in relation to the continuing problem of the civil war in Angola, which had been underway since the country's independence in 1975. The characteristics that we have identified as conducive towards success in the initial undertaking there were simply not present in this deeper-rooted 'local' conflict. But at the time the almost textbook outcome to the missions of UNAVEM and UNTAG fitted with a wider international optimism grounded in the end of the cold war and a culture of democratic change.

From South West Africa to Namibia

Namibia is a largely desert territory with a long western coastline on the Atlantic and eastern borders with Botswana and Zambia. It has, however, been its southern and northern borders, with South Africa and Angola, respectively, that have had the greatest and most destructive impact in its recent history. Despite its considerable area, Namibia has a population of only 1.6 million, most of which is dependent on traditional agriculture (though the country also has considerable mineral wealth, including precious metals and diamonds). Its international significance in the later twentieth century was strategic rather than economic in that it provided a buffer between South Africa and the independent states of black Africa. This role increased hugely in importance for the South African government in Pretoria after 1975 when Angola became independent of Portugal under a Marxist government. The obvious dangers in this for the white government of South Africa were underlined by the fact that independent Angola became host to a huge Cuban military presence. This reached some 50,000 soldiers at its peak in the 1980s as the Angolan regime fought for its survival against its internal – but foreign-backed – enemies.

Namibia had first become an element in international politics after it was colonized by Germany in 1884. German South West Africa, as it was known, was originally perceived by Britain as a low-level strategic threat to its inter-ests further to the south. In 1915, during the First World War, pro-British South African forces occupied the territory, and under the Treaty of Versailles after the war Germany was obliged to renounce all claims to it. In 1920 responsibility for South West Africa (though not 'sovereignty') was passed to South Africa under the new League of Nations 'mandate' system (just as Rwanda had passed to Belgian administration). The mandate arrange-ment laid down the principle that the colonial possessions of the defeated states were not 'spoils of war' with which the victors could reward them-selves. Rather, they were a devolved responsibility, usually passed to a state with a contiguous imperial frontier that would be expected to prepare the territory for eventual independence.[1] After the demise of the League of Nations the UN took over the mandates and incorporated them into a 'Trusteeship' system, which placed even greater emphasis on preparation for statehood.

In 1946 South Africa was formally requested by the UN to accept this revised Trusteeship agreement for South West Africa. Pretoria declined, and appeared to be set on the ever closer incorporation of the territory into South Africa itself. After the election of the hard-line Nationalist Party government in 1948 (which set the scene for the introduction of apartheid in South Africa) South Africa even stopped the submission of the required annual reports on South West Africa to the UN. Despite periodic discussions between South Africa and the UN during the 1960s the issue remained unresolved. The rapidly increasing representation in the United Nations of newly decolonized states at this time, though, brought the issue further and further up the agenda. The denial of self-determination to South West Africa (now increasingly given the 'non-colonial' name Namibia) was doubly offensive to these new states. Firstly, South Africa's presence in the territory was legal only as far as Trusteeship obligations were met. Clearly this was not happening, and South Africa was consequently in serious breach of international law. Secondly, South Africa's attempts to extend the apartheid system to Namibia turned mere illegality into a moral outrage.

---

1   Other parts of Germany's African empire that were mandated were Tanganyika (to Britain); Togoland and Cameroon (to Britain and France); and, of course, Rwanda and Burundi (to Belgium).

Although early attempts to have South Africa's behaviour formally declared illegal foundered on technicalities, it was clear by the mid-1960s that the issue could not be evaded indefinitely.[2] Nor, in a rapidly changing UN, could South Africa's dependence on the tacit support (or at least the benign inactivity) of the west be relied on for long. Even if the western powers exercised their veto in the Security Council to prevent a full-scale confrontation on the issue in the meantime, the General Assembly could not be constrained in the same way, and there was a growing stream of Assembly resolutions condemning South Africa. Moreover, the situation in Namibia itself was changing dramatically in the later 1960s as the forces of nationalism in the form of the South West African People's Organization (SWAPO) turned to armed struggle in pursuit of independence. Pretoria now had to confront guerrilla warfare as well as growing international isolation.

In 1970 the Security Council, no longer able to resist the mounting pressure from the General Assembly, adopted a resolution formally terminating the South African mandate and declaring the continued occupation of Namibia illegal.[3] The following year the International Court of Justice (ICJ) affirmed the Security Council position in an Advisory Opinion that South Africa's presence in Namibia was illegal and it should withdraw immediately. The ICJ also ruled that all states, whether UN members or not, were obliged to recognize this illegality and refrain from any action that might support it.[4] The battle lines between South Africa and the broad international system seemed to have been drawn. Pretoria's response was to temporize with a disingenuous offer to bring Namibia to 'independence' as a 'homeland'. This was the widely discredited model already being applied in some of the more remote and less economically productive areas of South Africa itself that had been handed over to 'African' puppet administrations closely controlled by the central state. The Security Council rejected this out of hand at the end of 1972, reaffirming the right of the Namibian people to self-determination.[5] A year later it voted to end formal discussions with Pretoria on the issue.[6]

---

2 In 1966 the International Court of Justice voted by eight to seven to dismiss on a technicality a claim brought by Ethiopia and Liberia that South Africa's actions in Namibia were in breach of the UN Charter. Found at http://www.icj-cij.org/icjwww/idecisions/isummaries/ilsaesasummary660718.htm.

3 UN document S/RES/276, 30 January 1970. Britain and France abstained in the vote.

4 'Legal Consequences for States of the Continued Presence of South Africa in Namibia (South West Africa) Notwithstanding Security Council Resolution 276 (1970), International Court of Justice Advisory Opinion, 21 June 1971. Found at http://www.icj-cij.org/icjwww/idecisions/isummaries/inamsummary710261.htm.

5 UN document S/RES/323, 6 December 1972.

6 UN document S/RES/342, 11 December 1973.

The independence of Angola and the western 'Contact Group'

In 1975 the regional setting in which the Namibian wrangle had been played out changed radically. Following the military coup in Lisbon in April 1974 negotiations with the nationalist movements in all of Portugal's African colonies quickly produced independence settlements. The agreement with Angola was the last of these. Its delay was partly due to Angola's special political and economic place in Portugal's empire but mainly it was a consequence of the division of the nationalist movement there into three mutually antagonistic groupings. This internal division threatened major consequences both for independent Angola and for its neighbours. Long before Angola's independence was even in prospect these strategic interests had brought the South African army across the border from Namibia. During the thirteen years of spasmodic guerrilla war against the Portuguese in Angola, South African military personnel had a significant though clandestine presence in the south of the country in support of the colonial forces. Now, on the eve of independence, South African involvement increased dramatically.

As it became clear that Portugal was wholly incapable of controlling events in Angola in the months leading up to its withdrawal in November 1975, the South African Defence Forces (SADF) attempted what was designed to be a decisive intervention. It moved against the Marxist Popular Movement for the Liberation of Angola (*Movimento Popular de Libertação de Angola* – MPLA). By the middle of 1975 the MPLA held the Angolan capital, Luanda, and it looked increasingly likely that it would be the beneficiary of the formal transfer of power when it came and that its leader, Agostinho Neto, would be recognized as Angola's head of state. An SADF column advanced north from the Namibian border accompanied by the forces of another of the Angolan movements, the supposedly pro-western National Union for the Total Independence of Angola (*União Nacional para a Independência Total de Angola* – UNITA) led by Jonas Savimbi.[7] The South Africans eventually reached a point about 200 kilometres south of Luanda.[8] At this point another foreign intervention – by a rapidly deployed force from Cuba – saved the situation for the MPLA. Cuban and Angolan forces eventually drove the South Africans back across the Namibian border at the beginning of 1976, by which time the MPLA had established itself as the government in Luanda.

Over the following years frequent South African incursions from Namibia – often in considerable force – were justified as 'hot pursuit' operations against

---

7 Fred Bridgland, *Jonas Savimbi, a Key to Africa* (Edinburgh: Mainstream, 1986), p. 146.
8 On the South African invasion of 1975 see Robin Hallet, 'The South African intervention in Angola, 1975–76', *African Affairs* 77(308), 1978, pp. 347–86.

SWAPO, which now maintained extensive bases in southern Angola under MPLA and Cuban protection. UNITA became a major beneficiary of these attacks in the capacity of South African proxy in the region. Eventually, the respective justifications for the MPLA regime's support for SWAPO and South Africa's interventions in southern Angola became circular. Luanda explained both its backing for the Namibian guerrillas and the continued presence of Cuban forces in Angola on the basis that this reduced South Africa's capacity for intervention in Angola. For its part, Pretoria claimed that its intervention was designed as a counter to the MPLA's support for SWAPO and a challenge to the presence of foreign communist forces in southern Africa.

The 'linkage' between the Namibian and Angolan situations was thus firmly established by the South African and Angolan regimes themselves from 1975. But it would be some time before the Security Council would acknowledge it. In the meantime, South Africa's continued occupation of Namibia – and its use of the territory to launch attacks against southern Angola – remained the focus of UN condemnation. In June 1975 a Security Council resolution declaring South Africa's presence in Namibia a threat to international peace and security under the terms of Chapter VII of the Charter had failed because of a British, French and American veto.[9]

Three months later, as its intervention in Angola deepened in the run-up to Portugal's departure, South Africa set about preparing a plan by which it would retain control of a supposedly 'independent' Namibia. The so-called Turnhalle conference held in the Namibian capital Windhoek in September 1975 proposed the establishment of a non-SWAPO, pro-Pretoria administration made up of 'friendly' parties. The western powers took fright at this, and efforts to build momentum towards genuine independence now gained pace.[10] The five western states in the Security Council at this point – Canada, France, Britain, the United States and West Germany – formed themselves into what became known as the 'Contact Group'. This set itself the task of finding a solution to a problem that was threatening to develop into a major embarrassment for the west.

A number of factors facilitated the work of the Contact Group. Firstly, there was the obvious pressure that its members could exert individually and collectively on Pretoria. Secondly, as it got down to work, signs were emerging of some self-questioning within the South African regime about military over-stretch and the viability of maintaining its position in the territory. This was

---

9   UN document S/11713, 6 June 1975.
10 Virginia Page Fortna, 'United Nations Transition Assistance Group', in William Durch (ed.), *The Evolution of UN Peacekeeping: Case Studies and Comparative Analysis* (New York: St Martin's Press, 1993), p. 354.

driven particularly by mounting (white) casualties in the war against SWAPO, but the conflict was also expensive, costing the South Africans about US$1 million a day to pursue. Thirdly, western stock was relatively high in Africa at this time, with the liberal Carter administration in Washington and left-of-centre governments elsewhere. Finally, détente still prevailed in superpower relations, and though a number of crises (including that in Angola itself) were putting increasing pressure on this understanding, there was less sus-picion of western motives than might have been the case a few years later.

At the beginning of 1978 the Contact Group, working in tandem with the UN secretary-general, Kurt Waldheim, produced its plan for a settlement. This involved a phased move to independence based on an externally mod-erated electoral process in the territory.[11] A few months later, in September 1978, Security Council resolution 435 authorized the formation of a United Nations 'transition assistance group' to support the work of the secretary-general's special representative (at this time Martti Ahtisaari, who would later become prime minister of Finland).[12] This was to be the basis of a major multifunctional peacekeeping operation for which planning began immediately.

It would not become a reality for more than a decade. Many of the cir-cumstances that had originally bolstered the efforts of the Contact Group were soon to change. The arrival of Ronald Reagan in the White House at the beginning of 1981 had a considerable impact on events. Pretoria, aware that the new administration in Washington did not share the same liberal instincts in international relations as its predecessor, now saw renewed advantages in intransigence. This position seemed to be vindicated as Wash-ington's new policy of 'constructive engagement' with South Africa replaced Carter's position of implicit hostility. More broadly, the deterioration of the relationship between the superpowers and the supplanting of détente with a 'second' cold war compromised western leadership of the settlement process in the eyes of non-aligned states in Africa and beyond. Finally, as American support for UNITA's continuing war against the MPLA regime in Angola became more extensive and overt, the Cuban presence expanded to meet the threat.[13] In these changing circumstances the Contact Group could not sustain either the momentum of the processes it had sought to put in train or its

---

11   The plan was first mooted in a letter from the Contact Group to the secretary-general –
     UN document S/12636, 10 April 1978. It was later embodied in UN document
     S/RES/431, 27 July 1978.
12   UN document S/RES/435, 29 September 1978.
13   A crucial development in US support for UNITA came in 1985 when the Reagan
     administration repealed the so-called 'Clark amendment' of 1976, which had prohibited
     American aid to the warring parties in Angola. See George Wright, *The Destruction of a Nation: United States Policy Towards Angola since 1945* (London: Pluto Press, 1997), pp. 118–23.

own internal cohesion. The Reagan administration – along with that of Margaret Thatcher in Britain – showed a greater 'understanding' of South Africa, and this put Washington and London at odds with the other members of the group. By the early 1980s, therefore, the Contact Group's involvement in the issue had effectively ended.

Towards agreement

Paradoxically, the effective transfer of the initiative on Namibia from the Contact Group to the United States – with Britain in a supporting role – probably helped to accelerate the move towards a settlement. South Africa, hitherto suspicious of the 'liberal' assumptions of the larger Contact Group, could now do business with right-leaning governments that it perceived as less hostile to its interests. Chester Crocker, the American deputy secretary of state with responsibility for Africa, was able to package up a settlement on Namibia with his policy of 'constructive engagement' with South Africa.[14] During the early 1980s the Security Council as a whole followed the American-led initiative. The Council had some misgivings, most particularly over South African insistence on the linkage between an independence settlement for Namibia and Cuban withdrawal from Angola. But Pretoria, with the United States appearing ambivalent on the issue, pushed this linkage with increasing insistence, and it seemed as though this might have to be the price of any solution.[15]

Other factors were also coming to bear on the situation. In 1985 Mikhail Gorbachev became Soviet president and the entire texture of east–west relations began to alter with the beginning of the end of the cold war. The rigid framework of superpower bipolarity within which the complex of issues around Namibia and Angola had been played out now changed fundamentally. On one side South Africa could no longer use 'communist expansionism' as a bogey to unsettle the west, and on the other Cuba and the Angolan regime its troops were supporting could no longer depend on the Soviet Union to underwrite their position. In the meantime, the war in Angola, and the parts played on opposite sides of it by both South Africa and Cuba, seemed to have become bogged down into a bloody stalemate. The static nature of the military confrontation was revealed at the end of 1987 and the beginning of 1988 when a hugely destructive battle was fought between the two sides

---

14   For his own account of developments at this time see Chester Crocker, *High Noon in South Africa: Making Peace in a Rough Neighborhood* (New York: Norton, 1993).

15   Anthony Parsons, *From Cold War to Hot Peace: UN Interventions 1975–1995* (Harmondsworth: Penguin, 1995), p. 118.

around the strategically important air-base at Cuito-Cuanavale in south-central Angola. Here the Angolans and Cubans on one side and the South Africans on the other had fought themselves to a standstill without significantly changing the balance of advantage in the war.[16] The ever-mounting casualty toll was bringing increasing domestic pressure to bear on the Pretoria government to produce an exit strategy for Namibia.

These factors had come together by the middle of 1988 to make an independence settlement based on linkage with Angola both achievable for South Africa and, at the same time, the best that it could expect to achieve. On 22 December 1988 a final agreement was signed in Geneva, though it had already been substantially agreed at a sequence of negotiations at various venues in Africa and Europe conducted in secret over the previous year. In this process South Africa, Cuba and Angola had been driven on by the United States and the Soviet Union, both of which were now determined to achieve a final conclusion to the linked issues of Namibian independence and Cuban withdrawal from Angola. The first concrete sign that the process was bearing fruit came with an interim cease-fire agreement between South Africa, Angola and Cuba at the end of August 1988 with which SWAPO's leader, Sam Nujoma, immediately associated himself. Javier Pérez de Cuéllar, the UN secretary-general (who had succeeded Kurt Waldheim in 1982), followed this the next month by a visit to South Africa. Strictly speaking there were two separate agreements: a bilateral one between Angola and Cuba covering the withdrawal of the latter's forces; and a tripartite one between Angola, Cuba and South Africa that effectively activated, from April 1989, the process outlined in Security Council resolution 435 more than a decade previously. The United Nations Transition Assistance Group was now to become a military reality.

A new Security Council resolution in the middle of January 1989 affirmed the UN's commitment. But it also called for a reduction in the costs – and therefore the scope – of the operation originally envisaged.[17] This cost-cutting was at the insistence of the five permanent members who would bear the main financial burden of UNTAG. It was opposed by the other Security Council members and accepted only with reluctance by the secretary-general. Instead of the 7500 troops envisaged in 1978, a force of 4650 would be deployed on 1 April 1989. This was to consist of three infantry battalions with headquarters, support staff and a military observer group. The reduced scale of the operation would, it was estimated, bring the cost of a one-year operation down to $416 million – which would still be equivalent to about half of

---

16   On the diplomatic impact of Cuito-Cuanavale see G.R. Berridge, 'Diplomacy and the Angola–Namibia accords', *International Affairs* 65(3), 1989, p. 465.

17   UN document S/RES/629, 16 January 1989.

the UN's regular annual budget at the time.[18] The smaller operation was justified on the basis that the Geneva agreement greatly lessened the danger of conflict on the Namibian–Angolan border – a preoccupation of the original planners in 1978. Against this, however, it was argued that the South African military and police presence in Namibia had increased considerably since 1978. It was one of UNTAG's central tasks to monitor the behaviour of these forces during the transition period. As both the intentions and the discipline of these forces, in particular the notorious Koevoet anti-insurgency unit, were uncertain, it was argued that the UN should ensure that it had sufficient 'dissuasive' force on the ground. Unsurprisingly, however, the wishes of the permanent members prevailed and UNTAG began its mission as a significantly less formidable force than first envisaged.

UNTAG deployed

Among those concerned with the reduced size of the operation was the force commander, the experienced Indian peacekeeper Lt. Gen. Dewan Prem Chand. In his view the multifunctional character of the operation required at least the 7500 personnel originally envisaged. UNTAG's initial responsibilities involved not merely monitoring the cease-fire throughout Namibia; they also covered the supervision of the agreed stand-down by the South African forces in the territory and the concentration of SWAPO fighters in agreed locations. Simultaneously, the UN had to shoulder the general policing and security responsibilities removed from the South Africans, including the prevention of cross-border infiltration. The force commander's concerns were shared by both SWAPO and the Organization of African Unity, which feared that the dilution of the UN's presence in the territory would enable South Africa to backtrack on the December agreement. The Security Council was unmoved, however, and at the end of February 1989 Prem Chand arrived in Windhoek with the advance party of the 4650 troops authorized. Twenty-one states in all contributed to the force, with the main burden being borne by infantry battalions from Bangladesh, Finland, Kenya, Malaysia, Togo, Venezuela and Yugoslavia.

Within weeks the depletion of the force's overall numbers and the relatively slow pace of its deployment were to contribute to a major crisis that momentarily threatened the entire transition process and the UN's role in it. The formal start of this had been fixed for 1 April 1989, when the interim cease-fire declared the previous August was to become permanent. At this precise moment a force of over 1500 SWAPO guerrillas crossed over into

---

18   Alan James, *Peacekeeping in International Politics* (London: Macmillan, 1990), p. 264.

Namibia from southern Angola in apparent defiance of the agreement. Martti Ahtisaari, who had remained the special representative of the secretary-general since UNTAG had first been mooted in 1978, was now confronted with a truly awful dilemma. Only about 1000 UNTAG personnel were in Namibia at this time and even these had not been fully deployed.[19] The residual South African administration in Windhoek pressed for action against the incursion and asked for permission to field SADF personnel in the absence of sufficient UNTAG forces. A long and difficult meeting between the South African foreign minister, R.F. Botha, and the South African Administrator-General of Namibia, Louis Piennar, on one side, and General Prem Chand and Martti Ahtisaari, on the other, ended with the UN giving permission for South African forces to confront the SWAPO infiltrators. When the resulting series of unequal engagements finished about 300 SWAPO fighters had been killed.

It was never clear why SWAPO had undertaken the incursion in the first place. It may have been a deliberate attempt to alter the balance of forces on the ground now that there were to be fewer UN troops to counter the South Africans. Or it may have been a genuine misunderstanding of the terms of the agreement.[20] In support of this latter interpretation is the fact that SWAPO had not been fully party to the negotiations leading to the December 1988 settlement plan, the precise terms of which only became public well after the event.[21] Certainly, the provisions of the original proposal of 1978, which had been built around resolution 435, had included the assembly of SWAPO guerrillas inside Namibia prior to their cantonment by UNTAG. Whatever the real explanation of the affair, however, the balance of opinion within the General Assembly saw SWAPO as the victim of the affair. There were angry protests over the UN's apparent complicity with the forces of the apartheid regime. The worst fears of those who had warned against the reduction in UNTAG's original planned strength appeared to have been justified.

In the event, the crisis passed, and no similar situation was to arise during the rest of the operation. But it was an inauspicious start to what was the UN's first new peacekeeping venture in Africa since the Congo operation and the first anywhere for a decade.[22] A tense month of recrimination and negotiation followed the April fighting, bringing United States and Soviet missions to Namibia to help get the transition process back on track.

---

19 Ibid., pp. 265–6.
20 See Page Fortna, 'United Nations Transition Assistance Group in Namibia', pp. 369–70.
21 The terms of the Geneva Protocol were revealed by South Africa on 5 April while the fighting continued in the north of Namibia.
22 The disintegration of superpower détente and the onset of the 'second cold war' at the end of the 1970s saw an end to peacekeeping initiatives by the Security Council after the establishment of the Interim Force in Lebanon (UNIFIL) in 1978.

At the beginning of June agreement was reached for the return of more than 40,000 refugees and political exiles to Namibia before the independence elections. These were to take place between 7 and 11 November. The election campaign itself was not without incident and controversy. While UNTAG provided adequate security, it was not capable of preventing continuing covert actions by South African agents. In mid-September a senior white member of SWAPO, Anton Lubowski, was assassinated in Windhoek. Suspicion settled on the SADF rather than freelance anti-independence elements. Lubowski, a former army officer himself, had become something of an icon for the increasing number of young South African whites resisting conscription and service in Namibia. There was concern too over the intimidatory behaviour of elements of the counter-insurgency Koevoet unit, who were widely believed still to be operational even after their supposed confinement to base areas as part of the transition agreement. Pretoria was also a generous patron of the main anti-independence party in the election campaign – which provided the principal opposition to SWAPO – the Democratic Turnhalle Alliance (DTA). The DTA and other smaller anti-SWAPO parties benefited from some US$35 million in funding from Pretoria.[23] In this regard, however, SWAPO itself could hardly complain about a lack of external support for its own election campaign. Resources flowed in from governments and other supporters throughout Africa and beyond.

One source of potentially serious conflict in the process was the status of Walvis Bay. This was Namibia's only deep-water port, which lay 400 kilometres west of Windhoek. The status of Walvis Bay was historically complex. It had been annexed by Britain in 1878 and incorporated in the Cape Province six years later – just as Germany was colonizing the territory surrounding it. It therefore remained a British – and then a South African – enclave until the First World War. Later, when South Africa took over South West Africa on the basis of the League of Nations mandate, it was logical that it should transfer Walvis Bay to the territory's new administration. When it began the long process of negotiation with the UN in the 1970s over Namibian independence, Pretoria put down its marker for continued control of the enclave by transferring its administration back to the Cape Province. Walvis Bay therefore remained South African sovereign territory during the transition process. Pretoria rebuffed SWAPO claims to a right to a presence in the enclave during the election campaign. Under quiet pressure from the UN, SWAPO eventually accepted that Walvis Bay was off-limits in the short term, and the danger of a major threat of conflict was removed from the electoral process.

---

23 Page Fortna, 'United Nations Transition Assistance Group', p. 370.

The Walvis Bay issue illustrated a larger truth about the management of events in Namibia at this time. Both SWAPO and South Africa had their political perimeter lines beyond which they would not wander for fear of jeopardizing their core objectives. For SWAPO the issue of Walvis Bay could await resolution after the main prize of national independence had been secured. On its side, South Africa set limits on both its use of clandestine violence and its financial intervention in the electoral campaign. Ultimately Pretoria as much as SWAPO was committed to a settlement in Namibia as the key aim, and both remained closely focused on it. This – along with the strength of the joint US–Soviet commitment to the process – assured the success of the United Nations operation despite the tensions and occasional violence of the electoral campaign.

In line with its multifunctional mandate, UNTAG took responsibility for an extensive voter education programme throughout the territory. It was unclear how necessary this actually was. Informed participation would undoubtedly have been high in any case in what had, over recent years, become a highly politicized population. In the event there was a 97 per cent turnout of registered voters. SWAPO took 57.32 per cent of the vote and the DTA 28.55 per cent. This gave them 41 and 21 seats respectively in the 72-seat Constituent Assembly, the remaining 10 seats being taken by five smaller groupings. In 1990, on the eve of independence, the Assembly approved a new national constitution and converted itself into the National Assembly. Independence was declared on 21 March 1990 under the presidency of SWAPO's Sam Nujoma.

Post-independence relations with Pretoria, which in the normal course of things could have been dangerously conflictual, were immeasurably eased by the momentous events of the early 1990s in South Africa. The release of Nelson Mandela from prison and with it the beginning of South Africa's transition to multiracial democracy came just weeks before Namibia's independence. The long-established and close links between the African National Congress (ANC) and SWAPO during their shared years of resistance provided a sound basis for the development of a good relationship between the neighbouring states. The eclipse of the apartheid regime in Pretoria contributed to the virtual rout of the DTA in the first post-independence elections in Namibia which were held in 1994. The Walvis Bay issue was resolved amicably with the creation of a Joint Administration Authority in 1992 and the complete transfer of sovereignty to Namibia at the beginning of 1994.

The linkage: Angola

The August 1988 agreement that had established a *de facto* cease-fire in Namibia and opened the way to the Geneva protocols the following December was at least as significant for Angola as it was for Namibia. Although the agreement was to be a historic point on the road to Namibian independence, its initial impact was much greater to the north. Central to the Angolan component of the overall settlement was, on the South African side, the withdrawal of SADF elements from southern Angola and an end to incursions in the future. On the other side, Cuba and Angola agreed to the withdrawal of Cuban forces to a point at least fifty kilometres from the Namibian border. Although the Angolan rebel movement UNITA did not follow SWAPO in associating itself with the cease-fire, the mutual disengagement of national forces set the scene for a permanent removal of 'foreign' elements from the conflict.

In truth, it was a linkage willingly enough accepted by Cuba and, if less enthusiastically, by Angola as well. Cuba was not only a small country but also one in permanent economic crisis, for which the maintenance of 50,000 troops in Angola had always been a huge burden. Then, with the beginning of the end of the cold war, the continued material and political support of the Soviet Union for the Angolan intervention could no longer be relied upon. Beyond economic considerations, the steady toll of casualties inevitably tested the Cuban people's genuine sense of solidarity with the MPLA regime in Angola. For Cuba as much as South Africa the protracted, bloody and indecisive battle of Cuito-Cuanavale in 1987–88 carried a sombre message about the likely future of involvement in Angola. Withdrawal as part of a process that had at its centre the liberation of Namibia and that would mean the end of South African attacks on Angola could reasonably be portrayed as a victory. It was in any event as close to one as Cuba was likely to get.[24] For the MPLA regime in Luanda the loss of their Cuban allies would in normal circumstances have been a fatal blow. But the government saw the removal of the SADF from the Angolan equation as sounding the death knell for UNITA. The rebels, it believed, would be incapable of sustaining their war in the absence of this external support. This was, as events would show, a catastrophic misjudgement, but it seemed a reasonable assessment of the situation at the time. The withdrawal of Cuban forces should, the Luanda regime assumed, bring an end to both the external aggression and internal insurgency that they were there to confront in the first place.

Angola and Cuba approached the United Nations with a request for the establishment of an observer operation to be established within Angola just five days before the signing of the Geneva protocols in December 1988. This operation would, assuming the successful completion of the Geneva negotiations on Namibia, monitor the total withdrawal of Cuban forces. Pérez de

---

24 On the Cuban position in the aftermath of the Battle of Cuito-Cuanavale see Karl Maier, *Angola: Promises and Lies* (Rivonia: William Waterman, 1996), pp. 32–3.

Cuéllar quickly complied, and the Security Council met on 20 December to discuss the issue.[25] The outcome was the creation of UNAVEM, which was mandated for a maximum period of thirty-one months. This allowed for its presence in Angola until one month after the completion date for troop withdrawals indicated by Angola and Cuba (the end of July 1991). UNAVEM would become operational immediately on the signing of the Geneva agreement.[26]

Never consisting of more than seventy unarmed military observers with some civilian support, UNAVEM was a virtually model UN operation. The first substantial Cuban departures were monitored a week after the deployment of the advance party of observers. Subsequently, UNAVEM verified the expatriation of the Cubans by sea and air from Luanda, as well as from the southern ports of Namibe and Lobito. The withdrawal of a large Cuban force was also verified from the Angolan coastal enclave of Cabinda between Zaïre and Congo-Brazzaville.[27] So smooth was the process that it was completed before the end of May 1991, more than a month ahead of the original schedule the Angolans and Cubans had set themselves. Much of the practical side of the operation as well as its timetable had in fact already been discussed and agreed by Cuba and South Africa prior to the Geneva protocols.[28] At a total cost over its two-and-a-half year duration of $16.5 million, it appeared a distinctly economical means of dealing with what had been for a considerable time during the previous fifteen years a running sore in east–west relations.

The ease and speed with which UNAVEM achieved its objectives should not disguise the fact that, coming as it did after the relaxation of cold war tensions, its success was to be expected. In effect the UN 'witnessed' rather than 'effected' the process of withdrawal, which was handled with high efficiency by, for the most part, the Cuban military. Crucially, the significant actors in the larger political process were sovereign states (Angola and Cuba, but also, of course, South Africa, the United States and the Soviet Union). To this extent it was a product of high diplomacy rather than local conflict resolution. There was, in short, a peace to keep and it was one that was firmly

---

25 The letters of request from Angola and Cuba were issued respectively as UN documents S/20336 and S/20337, 17 December 1988. The secretary-general then quickly produced a report for the Security Council urging its compliance – UN Document S/20338, 17 December 1988.

26 UN document S/RES/626, 20 December 1988.

27 Despite its small size UNAVEM drew on a wide range of participants. Observers were provided by Algeria, Argentina, Brazil, Congo-Brazzaville, Czechoslovakia, India, Jordan, Norway, Spain and Yugoslavia. The chief observer (mission commander) was Brigadier-General Péricles Ferreira Gomes of Brazil.

28 Virginia Page Fortna, 'The United Nations Angola Verification Mission I', in Durch (ed.), *The Evolution of UN Peacekeeping*, p. 381.

managed by forces and interests other than the UN. As we have seen, at the non-state level, UNITA in Angola, unlike SWAPO in Namibia, had not associated itself with the Geneva protocols. It had, to a degree, been excluded from the process as its involvement would have been fiercely contested by the Angolan government and would anyway have tended to muddy the purely 'international' nature of the settlement being pursued.[29] It would, however, have been politically suicidal for UNITA to have actively obstructed the process. Had it done so it would have jeopardized any residual support it had hopes of retaining from the United States which had been its patron throughout its war against the MPLA. It would also have left it facing the daunting prospect of an independent Namibia under a government friendly to the MPLA along with the continued presence of Cuban forces in Angola. The danger of precisely this outcome was brought home to UNITA when the Cubans briefly suspended their withdrawal after an attack (possibly authorized by Savimbi himself) in January 1990.[30]

In his final report to the Security Council on UNAVEM Pérez de Cuéllar noted that its 'success . . . demonstrates what can be achieved by a United Nations peacekeeping operation when it receives the full co-operation of the parties concerned'.[31] The observation could equally have been made for its larger 'sister' operation, UNTAG in Namibia. But in highlighting this self-evident truth, the secretary-general was in a sense acknowledging that 'classical' peacekeeping on the model of Hammarskjöld's post-Suez 'Summary Study' (see above pp. 7–11) had become worthy of remark rather than an assumed norm. Both UNTAG and UNAVEM succeeded because the basic elements of 'host-state consent' and prior commitment by the parties to the maintenance of a peace they had already established were fully present. In this setting the purpose of a UN presence is clearly prescribed and fairly easily carried through – even where its role is complex and multifunctional as it was in Namibia.

These conditions had certainly not always been present after the Suez operation. They had been markedly absent, for example, in the Congo. As the complexities of post-cold war international relations called into being an increasing number of UN interventions they were quickly to become the exception rather than the rule in the 'peacekeeping' experience, in Africa as elsewhere. Ironically, however, the easy 'success' of UNAVEM was now to prove seductive to the secretary-general and the Security Council, who sought to maintain its apparent momentum. In the same resolution that marked

29   G.R. Berridge, *Return to the UN: UN Diplomacy in Regional Conflicts* (London: Macmillan 1990), p. 77.
30   Ibid., p. 384.
31   UN document S/22627, 20 May 1991.

the completion of UNAVEM I, UNAVEM II was authorized. This was supposed to be the vehicle for the resolution of Angola's internal conflict, that between the MPLA government and UNITA. As we will now see, the experience of UNAVEM II and its successors would highlight even more sharply the 'remarkableness' of the original UN intervention.

Failure in Angola, 1991–99

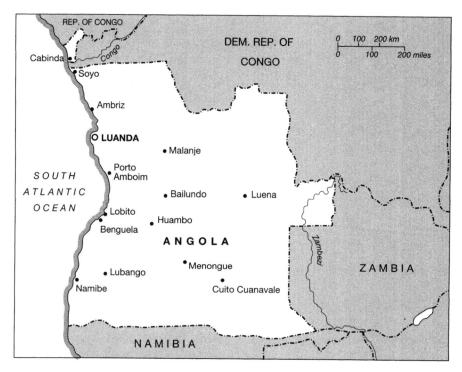

Angola

The success of UNAVEM in supervising the withdrawal of Cuban forces from Angola was not, as we have just seen, particularly remarkable when viewed in its broad diplomatic context. The problem it dealt with was essentially one created by the imposition of international competition on a domestic political conflict. When the international actors concerned resolved to end this involvement they were able to use the essentially 'technical' services of the United Nations to help them do so. The process was driven by powerful, non-African states, most notably the United States and the Soviet Union. The success of UNAVEM, though, tended to strengthen the view that the fundamental problem of Angola's civil war was itself sustained by these outside forces. This belief, common among even informed observers, saw the civil war as a cold war conflict that, now that global bipolarity was consigned to history, should be easily enough resolved with appropriate external encouragement. The reality, however, was less straightforward. Certainly the massive external input of military aid and diplomatic support had been hugely important in sustaining the civil war, particularly in its earlier stages after the independence of Angola in 1975. But this disguised the fact that the conflict had its own, specifically Angolan, dynamics that were much deeper than the 'cold war artefact' theory allowed.

The origins of the Angolan civil war

The Angolan conflict had its roots in the war of liberation against the Portuguese, which began in 1961 and which continued at varying levels of intensity until independence in 1975. Originally there were two main anti-Portuguese movements, which began their guerrilla wars more or less simultaneously. One of these was the MPLA, which, beyond its Marxist ideology, also had a racial and ethnic dimension to its support. Its main power base lay among the African urban industrial workers and professional class of the capital, Luanda. In ethnic terms it drew support from the Mbundu people of the Luanda area and from the considerable population of mixed-race (*mestiço*) city-dwellers. It also had the support of a small but significant section of Angola's white population, a form of anti-colonial solidarity uncommon beyond Portuguese Africa. The other 'liberation movement', which launched its separate guerrilla campaign against the Portuguese in 1961, was not in fact UNITA but the Union of the Peoples of Angola which soon renamed itself the National Front for the Liberation of Angola (*Frente Nacional de Libertação de Angola* – FNLA). The FNLA was first and foremost a movement of northern Angola, supported primarily by the Bakongo people whose traditional lands straddled the border with southern Congo/Zaïre. Enjoying the backing of Mobutu's regime in Kinshasa, it had no clear ideological identity beyond a kind of Bakongo micro-nationalism. However, the mere fact of its rivalry with the Marxist MPLA was sufficient for it to attract western support, even during the war against Portugal.

After it began its uprising in northern Angola the FNLA attempted to claim a 'national' identity by broadening its ethnic support to embrace the Ovimbundu people of Angola's central highlands. As part of this process the charismatic Ovimbundu Jonas Savimbi rose to a prominent position in the FNLA leadership. In 1966, however, frustrated at the continued Bakongo domination of the movement (and calculating that this would permanently exclude him from the top post), Savimbi broke away to form UNITA.[32]

UNITA was by far the smallest and least effective of the three anti-Portuguese movements during the colonial war but it survived until the eve of independence in 1975 when it formed an anti-MPLA alliance with the FNLA. This did not last, however. Exploiting its control of the capital after the Portuguese withdrawal, and backed by Cuban troops (the withdrawal of whose successors was monitored by UNAVEM as part of the Namibian settlement), the MPLA formed Angola's post-independence regime. Following this political and military defeat the FNLA quickly disintegrated. This left Savimbi and UNITA to confront the MPLA in a continuing civil war.

The breakdown of superpower détente in the later 1970s quickly brought the internationalization of the Angolan conflict. The subsequent determination of each superpower to keep close 'control' of local conflicts in which it perceived itself to have an interest meant that UN peacekeeping became virtually dormant as a means of 'firewalling' such crises. Therefore, a conflict that might if left alone petered out or ended with a local accommodation was fed and encouraged by external powers in pursuit of their own ideological and strategic interests. The Soviet Union and, most directly, Cuba provided ever-increasing aid to the MPLA regime, while South Africa and, less directly, the United States sustained UNITA.

This complex intertwining of indigenous and external elements in the civil war seemed not to be fully understood by the external actors when, in post-cold war mode, they decided to 'end' the crisis in the early 1990s. Immersed in the rhetoric of the 'new world order', the United States and the Soviet Union (later Russia) underestimated the Angolan as opposed to the cold war dynamics that sustained the conflict. As a result they sought to build on the momentum of UNAVEM in what they assumed would be a relatively straightforward 'imposition' of peace. They were joined in their efforts by Portugal, the former colonial power, whose chaotic decolonization of Angola in November 1975 had contributed to the ensuing civil war.[33] Lisbon now sought to develop a new special relationship with its former territories in Africa, and its participation in the resolution of the Angolan civil war would have provided an impressive launch for this. These three countries now brought pressure on the MPLA regime and its UNITA

---

32   For a detailed exploration of the ethnic and regional bases of the Angolan conflict see Franz-Wilhelm Heimer, *The Decolonization Conflict in Angola: An Essay in Political Sociology* (Geneva: Institut Universitaire de Hautes Études Internationales, 1979).

33   On Portugal's role at this time see Moses Venâncio, 'Portuguese mediation on the Angolan Conflict in 1990–1', in Stephen Chan and Vivian Jabri (eds), *Mediation in Southern Africa* (London: Macmillan, 1993), pp. 100–15.

enemies to enter into peace negotiations over which they would preside as 'Observer States'.

The Bicesse agreement and the establishment of UNAVEM II

The two sides were brought together at the resort of Bicesse north of Lisbon in May 1991. The agreement driven through by the Observer States involved a soon-to-be familiar process in African conflict resolution in the 1990s. It involved three basic stages. Firstly, rebel forces would be demobilized following a cease-fire. They would then be disarmed and concentrated ('cantoned') by a neutral intervention force. Finally, elements of the former rebel forces would be integrated in a new national force created after the democratic election of a post-conflict government. In Angola UNITA forces were to be either discharged or incorporated into the national army while preparations for parliamentary and presidential elections were underway. In these elections UNITA, acting as a political party, would run against the MPLA and whatever other parties might emerge during the process. Its leader, Jonas Savimbi, would contest the presidency against the incumbent, the MPLA's José Eduardo dos Santos (who had succeeded Angola's first MPLA president, Agostinho Neto, after his death in 1979).[34] Post-UNAVEM optimism, encouraged by the relative ease with which the Bicesse agreement seemed to be reached, and the apparent effectiveness of the cease-fire that immediately followed it, distracted attention from a necessary exploration of potential difficulties. The Observer States assumed that once the agreement was signed the United Nations would simply arrive to manage its implementation. But the UN as an institution had not been invited to participate in the Bicesse negotiations or in the formulation of the agreement. It would therefore be required to work with a process whose shortcomings quickly became obvious to those required to supervise it, in both its military and political aspects.

Formal UN involvement began with secretary-general Javier Pérez de Cuéllar's final report on UNAVEM in May 1991. This recorded the success of that operation and then went on to recommend the establishment of a second United Nations Angola Verification Mission to supervise the implementation of the Bicesse agreement, which had been signed earlier in the month.[35] The Security Council, two of whose permanent members had been the key Observer States at Bicesse, adopted the proposal unanimously and

---

34 The Bicesse agreement was issued as UN document S/22609, 17 May 1991.
35 UN document S/22627, 20 May 1991.

authorized the new operation. Its mandate was to extend for an initial period of seventeen months.[36] The Brazilian (and therefore Portuguese-speaking) brigadier general Péricles Ferreira Gomes, who had been chief military observer of UNAVEM I, continued in charge of the new undertaking. In this way the UN became tied to an inherently unsatisfactory process.

There were four basic and major flaws in the '*Acordos de Paz*' (peace accords), as the Bicesse agreement came to be known. Firstly, it made no structural connection between the military and political processes. It merely assumed that demobilization would take place in good faith while the electoral process advanced on parallel but unconnected lines. There was, therefore, no means by which the UN could insist on demobilization and disarmament as preconditions for political movement. Secondly, the political process itself was required to unfold within a very tight time-frame. The elections that were to complete the process were fixed for September–November 1992, barely fifteen months after UNAVEM II was to begin its work. After sixteen years of bitter uninterrupted civil war, with large armies equipped with abundant, sophisticated weaponry still confronting each other with uncertain confidence in the peace process, this was not a realistic timetable. Thirdly, the elections were designed to produce a victory for one of the protagonists, who would then form the post-civil war regime. This winner-takes-all approach, while reasonable in a well-embedded pluralist political culture, was dangerous in an environment in which just this sort of zero-sum outcome had been pursued by means of massive violence since the foundation of the state. Finally, UNAVEM II was grossly under-resourced for the management of such a process. UNAVEM I had held out to the UN and its major financial contributors the tantalizing possibility of peacekeeping on the cheap. It fell to UNAVEM II to prove this a mirage. At its maximum strength in the middle of the electoral process in October 1992, UNAVEM II had only 350 military observers and 126 civilian police in the field.

Despite these inadequate resources at the disposal of UNAVEM II, the electoral process was in fact completed within the timetable set for it. In February 1992 Boutros Boutros-Ghali, who succeeded Pérez de Cuéllar as UN secretary-general the previous month, had appointed the widely experienced British international civil servant, Margaret Anstee, as his special representative and chief of mission for UNAVEM II. While she conducted continuous shuttle diplomacy between the MPLA government in Luanda and Savimbi at his headquarters at Bailundo in the Ovimbundu-populated *planalto* of central Angola, her Electoral Division engaged in a herculean task of preparation. Five million voters were registered. At the end of September

---

36   UN document S/RES/696, 30 May 1991.

the elections for the 220-seat legislature (National Assembly) were held with a turnout of 91 per cent. The MPLA took 129 seats and UNITA 70. In the first round of the presidential contest dos Santos took 49.57 per cent of the vote against Savimbi's 40.07 per cent.[37] At this point the basic purpose of the Bicesse process had, in principle, been achieved. Following the completion of the presidential poll civil war should have been supplanted by parliamentary democracy. For an instant UNAVEM II appeared to have prevailed against two of its basic flaws. It had succeeded in preparing for and administering the elections within an extremely tight time-frame and it had done so with minimal resources. The illusion was not to last, however. The pace at which the elections had been organized had aggravated another of UNAVEM's problems: the failure to map political movement to military demobilization. Now, the win-all, lose-all outcome at the end of that political movement meant that the defeated party faced the temptation of using its still battle-ready forces to wreck the entire process. It was a temptation that the ego-driven Savimbi was unable to resist, and the small UN presence could do nothing to prevent a return to war.[38]

There followed a number of months in which Boutros-Ghali sought to reinstate the cease-fire and rescue the Bicesse process. A recognition that this was no more than wishful thinking was delayed by UNITA's continuing insistence that it was still committed to seeking an accommodation within the terms of the *Acordos de Paz*, despite the daily evidence on the ground. By the beginning of 1993, however, it had become clear that Bicesse was dead. Accordingly, the secretary-general recommended to the Security Council that the mandate of UNAVEM II be fundamentally altered. There was little point in maintaining military observers in scattered outposts throughout the country where their presence was meaningless in the context of the war and where their own lives were at risk. Instead, he recommended the concentration of UN resources, such as they were, in Luanda. The Security Council agreed, and a resolution changing the terms of the mandate was passed at the end of January 1993. The same motion called for an immediate cease-fire and a re-dedication to the principles of the *Acordos de Paz*. This it had to do, but in reality, there was little expectation of any notice being taken of Security Council exhortations at this stage.[39]

---

37 The electoral process and its results are analysed by Anthony W. Pereira, 'The neglected tragedy: the return to war in Angola, 1992–3', *Journal of Modern African Studies* 32(1) 1994, pp. 1–28.

38 Margaret Anstee herself has written by far the most comprehensive and detailed account of the UN's efforts in Angola at this time, *Orphan of the Cold War: The Inside Story of the Collapse of the Angola Peace Process, 1992–93* (London: Macmillan, 1996).

39 UN document S/RES/804, 29 January 1993.

The Lusaka process and UNAVEM III

Although UNITA gave no real indication that it was interested in a return to negotiations at this time, its position was far from strong either in Angola or on the wider diplomatic front. Exploiting the element of surprise, it had some initial military success in the resumed civil war. But the Luanda government's forces eventually began to make ground again, driving UNITA out of positions it had seized in its mini-*blitzkrieg* in November and December 1992. Moreover, by returning to war Savimbi had rejected an electoral process that had been certified by the Security Council as 'free and fair'.[40] This inevitably cost UNITA much of the sympathy it had once enjoyed among right-wing governments and conservative pressure groups in the west. It could no longer rely on even the clandestine support of the United States, and with the end of apartheid the position of South Africa had changed fundamentally.

The electoral victory of the MPLA, although sabotaged, nevertheless gave it a political legitimacy it had lacked since it took power in Luanda in 1975 as the Portuguese abandoned the country in the first phase of the civil war. The attention of the Security Council now turned to sanctions against UNITA. These were applied after a number of false starts in September 1993. Their main targets were UNITA's arms and fuel supplies.[41] UNITA had considerable stockpiles of weapons and other material inside Angola and it could still rely on the support of its long-standing regional ally, Mobutu's Zaïre. It could also access 'informal' sources of supply through the exploitation of those natural resources of Angola that fell into its hands (in particular diamonds). But its long-term prospects in the continuing war were not good. It was, therefore, vulnerable to continuing UN efforts to re-establish a peace process.

At the same time as UNAVEM II's mandate was being truncated by the Security Council at the beginning of 1993, Margaret Anstee had succeeded in arranging talks between the two sides in Addis Ababa in Ethiopia. These were followed by another round a few months later in the Côte d'Ivoire capital, Abidjan. Anstee herself was convinced that these latter negotiations, which lasted for six weeks in April and May 1993, had come tantalizingly close to producing an agreement. To her frustration, however, the UN was unwilling at that time to pursue the idea of the large peacekeeping presence that UNITA sought as the price of its co-operation.[42] There were ample grounds

---

40   UN document S/RES/785, 30 October 1992.
41   UN document S/RES/864, 15 September 1993. All states were now required to refrain from the supply of arms and oil 'other than through named points of entry on a list to be supplied by the Government of Angola'.
42   Margaret Anstee, 'Angola: a tragedy not to be forgotten', *The World Today* 52(7), July 1996, p. 190.

for suspicion of UNITA's motives. It may well have foreseen the UN's response and made the condition to give the impression of co-operation in the confidence that nothing would develop. Alternatively, it may genuinely have sought a large UN presence, but as a means of formalizing its own recent advances and preventing the now regrouped and effective MPLA forces from moving against it. In Anstee's view, however, the real reason for the UN's reluctance was a fading of interest on the part of the big powers after the failure of what they had originally assumed to be an easy piece of conflict 'engineering'. As she put it, '[T]he countries most closely concerned with Angola genuinely wanted peace to be restored, but they wanted a "quick fix", particularly the two superpowers. Their priorities had shifted to other matters.'[43]

In June 1993 Anstee was replaced as special representative of the secretary-general by Alioune Blondin Beye, a former Malian foreign minister, who managed to convene a further round of talks between the Luanda government and UNITA in Lusaka, the Zambia capital, the following October. These took place exactly a year after the resumption of fighting and a month after the application of Security Council sanctions against UNITA. Here, in contrast to the Bicesse process, the UN did have a central role. Blondin Beye chaired the negotiations, controlling the agenda and maintaining a veto over proposed settlement terms. Meanwhile, pressure was maintained on UNITA with the threat of further sanctions. In December the Security Council agreed to suspend the application of new measures (including a ban on foreign travel by the UNITA leadership) only for as long as UNITA continued to negotiate in good faith at Lusaka.[44]

The accretion of pressures on UNITA, military, political and diplomatic, seemed to succeed when Savimbi agreed in principle that the outcome of the 1992 elections was valid. By the beginning of 1994 the Lusaka talks had turned to the nature of post-settlement government. The principle on which discussion took place was now one of power-sharing rather than head-to-head contest for total victory. The depth of Savimbi's commitment, however, remained uncertain, even among his own lieutenants. The talks were not accompanied by any sort of truce on the battlefield. The war continued as, it seemed, each side sought to achieve the most favourable disposition on the ground in advance of any settlement. Security Council pressure was maintained throughout the talks, however. Influence was also brought to bear by the three Bicesse Observer States and by Nelson Mandela, who became president of South Africa in May 1994.[45]

---

43   Anstee, *Orphan of the Cold War*, p. 533.
44   UN document S/RES/890, 15 December 1993.
45   See Wright, *The Destruction of a Nation*, p. 188.

Finally, on 31 October 1994, an agreement was reached. Three weeks later the so-called 'Lusaka Protocol' was formally signed by the MPLA foreign minister, Venâncio de Moura, and the secretary-general of UNITA, Eugénio Manuvakola, after which a cease-fire came into effect. Jonas Savimbi, who had originally been expected to sign with President dos Santos, had not turned up in the Zambian capital, claiming concerns for his security. It was a worrying and, in retrospect, telling absence.

The starting point of the Lusaka Protocol was an acknowledgement of the continuing validity of the Bicesse agreement. It underlined the legitimacy of the 1992 elections, which had been an integral part of the *Acordos de Paz*.[46] The detail of the Protocol was concerned with the linked issues of military demobilization and disarmament, on one hand, and the implementation of the political settlement, on the other. The integration of the military and the political processes was to be facilitated by a key departure from Bicesse, however. In line with the principle agreed at Lusaka, political reconciliation was to be achieved by a joint commitment to a power-sharing arrangement rather than the creation of an MPLA government, as a strict implementation of the 1992 election result would have required. Instead there was to be a government of unity and national reconciliation (*Governo de Unidade e Reconciliação Nacional* – GURN). The seventy UNITA deputies elected to the legislature in the 1992 poll were to take their seats. The presidential election (which dos Santos had narrowly failed to win outright in the first round when Savimbi returned to war) was to be completed. UNITA was to have four ministries and would provide deputy ministers in seven departments under MPLA ministers. It would also have the governorships of three provinces (though significantly not that of its central highland power base, Huambo).

The role of the United Nations in the new process was spelled out with a precision and detail absent from the *Acordos de Paz* in 1991. Both UNITA and the MPLA set out their 'clear wish that the United Nations . . . should play an enlarged and reinforced role' from that following the Bicesse agreement.[47] Blondin Beye would chair the key 'Joint Commission' of government and UNITA nominees and representatives of the three Observer States, which would meet in Luanda as a kind of supreme arbiter of the process. The UN was also to be responsible for the 'supervision, control and verification' of the cease-fire as well as the concentration, disarming and demobilization of UNITA forces.

Despite the precision of the agreement and its detailed prescription of roles and responsibilities, its prospects were not viewed with great optimism. The

---

46   The text of the Lusaka Protocol was issued as UN document S/1994/1441,
      22 December 1994.
47   Ibid., Annex 8.

experience of 1991–92 had fundamentally reshaped attitudes in the United Nations and among other interested parties. Beyond the failure of the earlier process, pessimism was also fed by the intensity of the fighting between UNITA and the MPLA right up to the point of the cease-fire required by the Protocol and by the high level of violations afterwards. Peace prospects are always greater when a formal cessation of hostilities supplants a *de facto* truce already produced by the dynamics of the conflict. There was an apprehension that military leaders on both sides saw the peace agreement as at best a respite for regrouping and rearming preparatory to a resumption of fighting. On the MPLA side in particular there was a sense that UNITA was beginning to crumble as a fighting force and was close to final defeat. Additionally, after the rejection of the election result in 1991, there were considerable doubts on the government side about the extent of UNITA's commitment to a political settlement. Within UNITA there was a view that the end of fighting would be the death knell for the organization, which would be left with even fewer political prospects than in 1991. Characteristically, Savimbi's own views remained opaque, as he issued contradictory statements on the Lusaka process over the months after the signing of the Protocol.[48]

UNAVEM III deployed

In this highly uncertain climate the Security Council had to consider the precise shape and extent of its new peacekeeping role in Angola. Its response was to commit the UN to a far-reaching and generous involvement. 'UNAVEM III' was approved by a resolution at the beginning of February 1995. In contrast to the niggardly resources assigned to UNAVEM II, the new operation was to have an authorized maximum strength of 7000 infantry troops as well as 350 military and 260 police observers. The assumption was that its mission would be completed by February 1997, when all the terms of the Lusaka Protocol should have been implemented. The full deployment of the force would, however, take place only when the secretary-general judged conditions to be appropriate.[49]

The continuing hostility and suspicion that had surrounded the signing of the Protocol in November 1994 persisted, despite the cease-fire finally taking general hold at the beginning of 1995. There was a guarded tone to the secretary-general's first progress report to the Security Council on UNAVEM III at the beginning of March. It was, Boutros-Ghali insisted, 'essential that more concrete signs of co-operation and goodwill be provided by both parties'

---

48   *The Financial Times*, 13 February 1995; *The Economist*, 18–24 February 1995.
49   UN document S/RES/976, 8 February 1995.

before the full deployment of the force.[50] In the meantime the UN continued its attempts to arrange the direct meeting between dos Santos and Savimbi that had not taken place as scheduled at the Lusaka signing. Both leaders assured the secretary-general of their commitment to the peace process, but Savimbi offered no concrete undertaking to move the process on through further negotiation. In Boutros-Ghali's view it was 'becoming increasingly necessary to assist the parties in overcoming their mutual distrust'. To this end he decided that at least the preparations for the full deployment of the peacekeeping force should continue despite the absence of tangible progress between the parties.[51]

The withholding of full deployment was the only effective lever the UN had at this time and it clearly had to be used with care. It had fallen to the UN to drive the peace process forward. This had not been foreseen as an appropriate or necessary task at Lusaka, where it was assumed the Angolan parties themselves would provide the momentum. In the circumstances, though, Boutros-Ghali had little option but to accept the responsibility, and continuing with preparations for full deployment was, he judged, the best means available 'to create additional impetus'.[52] And, of course, the entire process could in principle be suspended at any stage. The MPLA and UNITA were made aware of this in Boutros-Ghali's next report which came in early April 1995. His threat followed intelligence reports of new troop movements and the continued acquisition of weapons by UNITA despite the Security Council sanctions and the undertakings made at Lusaka.[53] With so much already invested by the UN in the process, however, it is doubtful that either party in the conflict gave his warning much credence.

A face-to-face meeting between Savimbi and dos Santos did eventually take place in May 1995. This came shortly after a statement from the president of the Security Council, issued at the behest of the secretary-general, had made the explicit link between the full deployment of the UN force and such a meeting.[54] Boutros-Ghali and Blondin Beye had also orchestrated a campaign of persuasion by those few African states still regarded as broadly sympathetic to UNITA, most notably Zaïre and Côte d'Ivoire.[55] This project was greatly helped by the fact Blondin Beye had been a senior figure in Francophone African diplomacy before he took on his current responsibility. The meeting between the two leaders when it was finally held in Lusaka on

---

50   UN document S/1995/177, 5 March 1995.
51   Ibid.
52   Letter from secretary-general to president of the Security Council. UN document S/1995/230, 28 March 1995.
53   UN document S/1995/274, 7 April 1995.
54   UN document S/PRST/1995/18, 13 April 1995.
55   UN document S/1995/350, 3 May 1995.

6 May appeared to be reasonably successful. Great significance was attached by some to the initial embrace between the two men and Savimbi's reference to dos Santos as 'my president'.[56] But few who had followed the twists and turns of the Angolan conflict and who were familiar with the behaviour patterns of Jonas Savimbi were willing to give much weight to such gestures. And, it was true, no commitments were made at the meeting to accelerated progress on the implementation of the Lusaka agreement. In the aftermath of the meeting it was very much business as usual, with UNITA resuming its now established policy of delay punctuated by minor movement. Just the fact that the meeting had taken place, however, was sufficient for Boutros-Ghali to authorize the deployment of UNAVEM's main infantry element. By the end of May almost 1200 troops from Britain, India, Portugal, Romania and Uruguay had arrived in the first phase of the operation. They joined about 430 military observers and staff officers as well as more than 200 civilian police who had already been deployed.[57]

UNAVEM's military and political role

In the Lusaka Protocol the UN had been assigned responsibility for the management and verification of the principal military aspects of the peace process. It was to supervise and monitor the cease-fire and verify the disengagement of forces. It was also to control the cantonment and eventual demobilization of most of the UNITA army and supervise the integration of the remainder into the new national force (*Forças Armadas Angolanas* – FAA). The issue of cease-fire implementation confronted the UN with a dilemma. A principal condition attached by the secretary-general to the deployment of UNAVEM III's main infantry element had been the existence of a durable cease-fire. The UN had therefore both to encourage and monitor the cessation of hostilities agreed at Lusaka with inadequate resources. Otherwise, as we have seen, it would have had to sacrifice the little leverage on events it possessed by embarking on the main deployment before the truce was unambiguously in place. Fortunately, after 'last-minute' land-grabs, which carried on for some time after hostilities were supposed to end, the cease-fire began to take hold at the beginning of 1995. The early momentum of the peace process had, it appeared, been sufficient to carry it through initial strains. The monitoring of the cease-fire remained an onerous responsibility on UNAVEM III and violations persisted, but they diminished steadily throughout 1995.

---

56 *The Economist*, 15–21 July 1995.
57 In all, thirty-four states were involved in this early stage of the operation. UN document S/1995/458, annex, 4 June 1995.

Management of the mutual disengagement of opposing forces and the cantonment and demobilization of UNITA forces was even more burdensome for the UN. In many respects this was the most important aspect of the whole process. It was the failure to implement this part of the *Acordos de Paz* that had permitted UNITA to return to war with such relative ease after its electoral defeat in 1992. It was unlikely that any meaningful progress could be made on the political front without clear movement towards the demobilization of fighters. Ominously, the process seemed to go little better after Lusaka than it had after Bicesse. In August 1995, three months after the deployment of UNAVEM III's main infantry units, the Security Council expressed deep concern at the slow pace of disengagement.[58] Only after coordinated pressure backed by the United States did UNAVEM succeed in getting the first UNITA fighters to present themselves at the cantonment centres, and then only a year after the Lusaka Protocols were signed. Boutros-Ghali, reporting to the Security Council, ascribed the problem to both 'political and logistical reasons', but in reality the delay was a deliberate, now habitual, ploy by UNITA which recognized that maintaining forces in preparedness was effectively its only remaining counter.[59]

Even when UNITA elements began to present themselves for cantonment, they did so in scant numbers and with few and rudimentary weapons. The MPLA was not slow to make its frustrations over this 'trick' clear to UNAVEM headquarters in Luanda. Boutros-Ghali himself had a keen sense of the significance of the unsatisfactory pace of demobilization. He was constantly aware of the post-Bicesse experience when UNITA had withheld its most effective fighters and armaments while making minimal gestures of compliance with the cantonment process.[60] In December 1995 the worst fears of both UNAVEM and the MPLA seemed to have been realized when UNITA suspended the process altogether, alleging offensive actions by government forces. It would now, it announced, 're-evaluate the whole application process of the Lusaka protocol'.[61] The Joint Commission, on Blondin Beye's initiative, moved quickly to resolve the crisis. Predictably, though, the price of a resolution was compromise with UNITA's grievances. The consequence of this temporizing was that the timetable for the completion of military issues agreed at Lusaka became meaningless and had to be formally extended in January 1996.[62]

---

58   UN document S/RES/1008, 7 August 1995.
59   UN document S/1995/1012, 7 December 1995.
60   Ibid. By 1 December 1995 only 363 UNITA 'fighters' had registered at quartering centres.
61   *The Financial Times*, 6 December 1995.
62   UN document S/1996/75, 31 January 1996. UNITA was roundly condemned in a
     Security Council resolution as a result – UN document S/RES/1045, 8 February 1996.

By the following April continued lack of movement had led the Luanda government to threaten a boycott of the Joint Commission. Both Boutros-Ghali and the Security Council continued to apply such pressure as they could on UNITA. But their efforts tended merely to expose their limited leverage. The terms of their censure hardened throughout 1996. In May the Security Council expressed its 'profound regret' at the pace of the process.[63] It denounced UNITA's delaying tactics as 'no longer acceptable' in October.[64] But such scolding was just about the limit of the UN's authority. The target number of former UNITA fighters who were to be integrated in the FAA was 26,300, but by October 1995 only 10,000 had come forward. Nor had UNITA's nominated generals for the new force appeared in Luanda. UNITA checkpoints and installations remained in place in the territory it controlled – which included the diamond-rich north-east. UNAVEM and the Luanda government had a particular concern about the large and well-armed personal 'security detachment' of Savimbi himself. This was in reality the elite unit of the UNITA army composed of its most experienced and best-equipped fighters, and there was little prospect of it being demobilized.

Some movement towards compliance with the military aspects of the Protocol were detected towards the end of 1996. Typically, even this was a calculated concession by UNITA in the face of a peak in external pressure. The main regional organization, the twelve-member Southern African Development Community, had been snubbed by Savimbi's non-appearance at a summit in October, which led to the even greater marginalization of UNITA in regional politics. About the same time, the Security Council renewed its threat to implement the sanctions against UNITA, whose application had been suspended in late 1993.[65] The device of deflecting pressure at key points by limited compliance was becoming depressingly familiar to UNITA's interlocutors in the process.

A major question for the secretary-general and the Security Council – one that was central to the entire UN approach in Angola – was whether these UNITA tactics were deliberately designed to sabotage the entire process. This was not necessarily the case. UNITA's temporizing could simply have been a consequence of a genuine uncertainty and sense of vulnerability. It may in fact have been the case that the UNITA leadership, including Savimbi himself, were unsure of their own motives, and unclear themselves as to whether they sought to bring the process down by constant erosion or see it through, however grudgingly. In this psychological landscape it was

---

63   UN document S/RES/1055, 8 May 1996.
64   UN document S/RES/1075, 11 October 1996.
65   UN document S/RES/1075, 11 October 1996.

always possible that external patience and compromise would build the necessary confidence to secure the more positive outcome.

Such patience had to be extended to the political aspects of the Protocol as well as the military ones. There were three fundamental components in the political settlement agreed at Lusaka. Firstly, the process of national reconciliation required the seventy UNITA deputies elected to the National Assembly in 1992 to go to Luanda in preparation for taking their seats. At the same time, UNITA was to nominate the ministers, deputy ministers and governors to fill the posts allocated to it in Lusaka. Secondly, Savimbi's own political role in post-settlement Angola had to be defined. There could only be one president of Angola, but the implication of the Bicesse process had been that the loser would simply fade into the background. Lusaka instead recognized the special 'national' status of the runner-up and sought to tie him into the political process.[66] This was made both essential and hugely difficult by Savimbi's planet-sized ego. Thirdly, central government administration had to be extended to areas that had been controlled by UNITA at the end of hostilities. Movement on these issues proved no easier to achieve than progress on the military aspects of Lusaka.

As we have seen, aware that the Bicesse process had foundered when the political aspects of the *Acordos de Paz* were pushed ahead of the military ones, UNAVEM III placed a prime importance on disengagement and demobilization. But by mid-1996 the UN began to press for political progress as a means of accelerating the sluggish pace of the military process. Central to this was the establishment of the new political architecture that required the participation of UNITA's parliamentary deputies and its nominations to government. The United States, as one of the Observer States as well as UNITA's one-time patron, backed UN efforts. Leading a delegation to Angola in October 1996 President Clinton's secretary of state, Warren Christopher, made clear to UNITA Washington's support for the UN's insistence on the issue. This joint pressure appeared to have worked as the names of UNITA's ministers for the new government were submitted to the UN in Luanda immediately after the Americans' departure. By now, though, there was widespread suspicion that this was simply the familiar response of UNITA to the rise and fall of external pressure. On its own the mere publication of a list of names was not a major concession and such gestures were of diminishing value as negotiating currency. The now battle-hardened UN – in both Luanda and New York – was sceptical. In his last report on Angola Boutros-Ghali (on the eve of his standing down as secretary-general to be replaced by Kofi Annan) warned that the rapid establishment of the unity government

---

66   *The Economist*, 18–24 June 1994.

was essential if the 'willingness of the international community to maintain its extensive involvement in Angola' was to be maintained.[67]

Beyond the inauguration of the new parliament and the establishment of a new administration, the third element of the Lusaka agreement – the formal status of Jonas Savimbi – was also problematic at this stage. Although strictly speaking the election of the national president had yet to be resolved by the completion of the 1992 poll (which had been interrupted by UNITA's return to war), the victory of dos Santos in the long-delayed second round seemed inevitable. Savimbi himself appeared to accept this but he was characteristically uncooperative in the search for an appropriate constitutional role he himself might perform. Early in the post-Lusaka process he had indicated a preference for remaining outside of national government. This, though, would have negated the attempt to bind him into the structures of post-settlement Angola, an important objective at Lusaka, where the parties feared the consequences of him being left to his own, potentially disruptive, devices. In August 1995 Savimbi and dos Santos had another rare face-to-face meeting, this time in Gabon. Here the UNITA leader was offered the post of vice-president of Angola. This was not as big a concession as it appeared. There was to be a second vice-president nominated by the MPLA and the functions associated with the post were not elaborated. Initial reports suggested that Savimbi had accepted the proposal but he soon reverted to the 'default' position of delay and obfuscation.[68] Uncertainty continued for most of the following year until, in mid-1996, Savimbi finally and unequivocally rejected the idea.[69]

The situation remained unresolved into 1997, though the UN continued its efforts to pin Savimbi down. Urgency was injected into the issue as the Security Council had already voted at the end of 1996 to begin the phased withdrawal of UNAVEM III on the basis that its mandate should have been completed.[70] Reporting on Angola for the first time to the Security Council the new secretary-general, Kofi Annan, indicated that Savimbi might now be persuaded to accept a newly defined post as 'principal adviser' to the president with special responsibilities for rural development and national reconciliation. This would also give him effective control over a cluster of ministries.[71] This was not acceptable to the MPLA, however, which could reasonably cite its democratic mandate from 1992. The idea had to be dropped. Concerned lest the issue sabotage the formation of the unity

---

67   UN document S/1996/1000, 2 December 1996.
68   *The Financial Times*, 12 August 1995.
69   *The Economist*, 14–20 September 1996.
70   UN document S/RES/1087, 11 December 1996.
71   UN document S/1997/115, 7 February 1997.

government – which may have been Savimbi's intention – the Luanda government and the UN eventually patched together an almost wholly undefined 'special status' for him.[72] In the absence of any clear function, the designation of this role was both literal and prosaic: Savimbi was to be 'Leader of the Largest Opposition Party'.

The unity government (GURN) prescribed by the Lusaka Protocol was inaugurated on 11 April 1997. The ceremony was attended by almost all the heads of state of Angola's regional neighbours but not by the Leader of the Largest Opposition Party. Savimbi's absence was a source of regret but not of surprise to the secretary-general and his special representative. On the positive side, UNITA nominees had come forward to occupy their assigned positions. The MPLA incumbents remained in the posts of president and prime minister (dos Santos and José da Franca van Dunem, respectively) but with UNITA nominees occupying the four portfolios agreed at Lusaka. These included two key economic ministries, Mines and Trade, as well as Health and Tourism. A UNITA nominee was also appointed to the new post of vice-president originally offered to Savimbi.

The establishment of GURN came at the end of some tense weeks of UNITA brinkmanship. Beyond the now habitual tactic of obstruction by delay there may have been an added element at this time: a testing of the mettle of the new secretary-general. Annan proved a robust operator on the issue, however. His firmness was aided by the strong support of the Security Council. In securing this he had the natural benefits of the new appointee but he also enjoyed a warmth on the part of the permanent members not always extended to Boutros-Ghali in his last phase in office, particularly by the United States. At the end of January the president of the Security Council had demanded that the government of national reconciliation should be formed 'without any linkages and without further delay'. The Security Council would otherwise 'consider appropriate measures . . . against those responsible'.[73] The point was driven home by Annan himself a few days later when he indicated that the future of UNAVEM itself could be in question.[74] Further warnings to UNITA from New York followed in February and March. UNITA's most substantial excuse for delay was that the new government had no agreed programme and that it could not reasonably take power without one. This provoked a visit to Angola by Annan himself in the last week of March for what he described as a 'frank tête-à-tête' with Savimbi at his headquarters in Bailundo. This seems to have provided the final impetus for the formation of the new government. Now, though, no

---

72   UN document S/1997/304, 14 April 1997.
73   UN document S/PRST/1997/3, 30 January 1997.
74   UN document S/1997/115, 7 February 1997.

further room was given for obstruction. After his return to New York Annan sought a bare two weeks extension to UNAVEM III's mandate as a means of maintaining the credibility of the threat of total withdrawal by the UN.[75]

From UNAVEM to MONUA

At the beginning of June 1997, in his final report to the Security Council on the work of UNAVEM III, Annan's assessment was that events had 'generally been moving in a positive direction', despite difficulties in some areas of the country.[76] These were to do in large part with UNITA's determination to retain control of its last significant resource, the diamond fields of the north-east. A further destabilizing factor, however, was the revolution then under-way in Zaïre, where the thirty-three-year rule of Mobutu Sese Seko was in its death throes (see above pp. 86–7). Although by most calculations the departure of Mobutu should have dealt a body blow to UNITA as it meant the loss of its last pillar of regional support, the chaos in the Congo inevitably seeped over the border into northern Angola. This created difficulties for UNAVEM military observers monitoring the cease-fire in the area as well as a smoke-screen under which UNITA forces could be regrouped and redeployed. Both Angolan parties had been involved in the conflict in Zaïre. UNITA troops crossed the border from its northern strongholds to fight on Mobutu's side. As we saw in the previous chapter, the MPLA for its part took the opportunity to speed the disintegration of the old regime in Kinshasa by transporting anti-Mobutu forces (such as the 'Katangan Tigers') into Zaïre in support of Laurent Kabila's rebel movement.[77]

The formation of GURN and the consequent winding down of UNAVEM III therefore disguised the fact that major issues relating to the implementa-tion of the Lusaka Protocol had still to be resolved. As well as the problems on the northern border, the process of integration of UNITA elements into the FAA and a new national police force had made little progress. The future of Savimbi's personal security force remained unresolved. On the political side, the process of extending the control of the (now supposedly power-sharing) central government throughout the national territory was still being stalled by UNITA.

Despite this uncertain environment the Security Council determined in June 1997 to replace UNAVEM III with a more modest operation, the United Nations Observation Mission in Angola. This was known as MONUA, the

---

75   UN document S/1997/248, 25 March 1997.
76   UN document S/1997/438, 5 June 1997.
77   *Africa Confidential*, 38(8), 11 April 1997.

acronym of its Portuguese title (*Missão de Observação das Nações Unidas em Angola*). Annan's justification for the change was that the Lusaka process had taken some significant steps forward in recent months, notably the formation of GURN and the return of UNITA's legislative representatives to Luanda. What the secretary-general did not seem to consider, however, was the danger of allowing the history of UNAVEM II in 1992 to repeat itself. Yes, there had been ostensible advance on the political plane in 1997, just as the scheduled elections had taken place in a free and fair manner in 1992. But the linkage between military disengagement and political restructuring – which was correctly seen as absolutely essential by the drafters of the Lusaka Protocol if it was not to go the same way as the Bicesse agreement – was in danger of being disregarded.

The replacement of UNAVEM III was in part an attempt to make a virtue of necessity. The Security Council had been determined to wind up the operation since the previous year, not least because of its cost (about US$1 million a day). Beyond this, though, in the war of signs and symbols that paralleled the one of bombs and bullets in Angola, there was an argument for replacing UNAVEM, which had been mandated to implement a peace agreement, with a new movement charged with observing the 'completed' process. It was possible that the pace of implementation could actually be accelerated by the public implication that it was to all intents and purposes a 'done deal'. Underlying this calculation was the gamble that UNITA's continued obstructiveness had become mere habit rather than a substantive political strategy designed to sabotage the settlement.

MONUA was created by a Security Council resolution in June 1997 and, utilizing elements already in the field with UNAVEM III, became operational the following day. Its initial strength was 3500 (including troops, military observers and civilian police), an immediate reduction from the 4200-strong UNAVEM III in its final phase.[78] MONUA's strength, however, would decline rapidly over the following year to just over 1000 and then to 500 at the point of its termination at the beginning of 1999. Initially the Security Council looked for an even more rapid draw-down, with the 'expectation of full completion of the mission by 1 February 1998'.[79] But it soon became clear that the gamble underlying the establishment of MONUA, if such it was, had been misplaced. The move did not have any significant impact on the tempo of the peace process. If anything this now lost pace. Annan acknowledged as much in a report to the Security Council in mid-August in

---

78 By March 1997 thirty-two states were contributing to UNAVEM III. This included eleven Africans and a wide range of west and east Europeans and Asians. There were three Portuguese-speaking contributors: Portugal, Guinea-Bissau and Brazil.

79 UN document S/RES/1118, 30 June 1997.

which he noted that the 'peace process in Angola is experiencing some of the most serious difficulties since the signing of the Lusaka Protocol'. The 'international community', he warned, 'expects no less than a credible and unconditional implementation by UNITA of [its] fundamental obligations'.[80] In response, the Security Council voted to apply sanctions against UNITA, including those measures agreed to but held in abeyance since 1993.

The sanctions option

Acting under Chapter VII of the Charter the Council now required all states to refuse entry and transit to senior UNITA officials, to close UNITA offices abroad and to deny landing and over-flight permission to aircraft originating in Angola other than those approved by the Luanda government.[81] These measures were, of course, additional to the arms embargo against UNITA in force since September 1993. UNITA was given a grace period of a month to show a willingness to comply with UN demands before the sanctions would be implemented. No movement was detectable, however, and the restrictions came into force in October 1997. There was no obvious sign that the increased pressure had any effect over the next year. UNITA compliance with its Lusaka obligations virtually ceased, though Blondin Beye continued to press on New York, as he had done since his appointment, a policy of continued negotiation with Savimbi. This approach had long since begun to appear as drift and weakness rather than positive diplomatic engagement, however. Gradually but inexorably fighting restarted, intensified and spread.

Now as in the past Angola's destruction was fed by its wealth. UNITA's continued control of the northern diamond fields both paid for its continuing war and provided it with the resources systematically to evade the sanctions. On the other side, Angola's huge off-shore oil wealth resourced the Luanda regime's war effort. Savimbi's biographer and one-time admirer, Fred Bridgland, wrote of 'South African, Lebanese, Nigerian and Portuguese dealers [flying] regularly into UNITA territory to barter arms for diamonds'. Despite the sanctions, African states, particularly from the Francophone group, still sympathetic to UNITA aided and abetted it efforts. Morocco, Togo and Burkina Faso permitted the trans-shipment of weapons that were acquired now for the most part from former communist states in eastern Europe.[82] UNITA therefore showed itself able not only to maintain its military capability in the face of sanctions, but to surmount the disappearance of the

---

80   UN document S/1997/640, 13 August 1997.
81   UN document S/RES/1127, 28 August 1997.
82   *The Sunday Herald* (Scotland), 1 August 1999.

Mobutu regime in Zaïre as well. By the end of 1998 it was fielding a well-equipped army of about 70,000 despite the 'loss' of some of its fighters to the demobilization process in the immediate post-Lusaka period. On the political level it was also largely unaffected by the defection of a number of its parliamentary deputies who opted to remain in Luanda and who, with the encouragement of the MPLA, broke from Savimbi and formed a new party, UNITA-Renovada ('Renewed UNITA').

In an attempt to cut off the financial basis of UNITA's activities the UN imposed even more draconian sanctions in June 1998, a year after MONUA had been established and four months after its mission was supposed to have been successfully completed. Again referring to Chapter VII of the Charter, the Security Council sought to freeze UNITA's external assets, banned non-authorized travel to UNITA-held territory in Angola and placed a general ban on all diamond imports from Angola not authorized by Luanda.[83] This had no more impact than the earlier measures, however. Market forces and governments unwilling to comply with even mandatory decisions of the Security Council combined to render the new sanctions largely useless. Diamonds continued to be exported, but through intermediate African countries that provided false certificates of origin. By the estimation of Luanda's own state diamond company, only about 10 per cent of Angolan diamonds were being exported legally by the end of the 1990s.[84]

Reaching the inescapable conclusion that the sanctions regime against UNITA had failed up to that point, the Security Council established a Panel of Experts to analyze its shortcomings. The UN issued the report of this group in March 2000. A number of states were named as sources of arms and support. Among UNITA's more prominent Francophone supporters were Burkina Faso, Togo and Côte d'Ivoire. It was implied that Savimbi had deliberately developed relationships with these countries as an alternative to Mobutu's Zaïre, where the old dictator's grip on power had been loosening throughout the 1990s. Less predictably, the cross-currents of central African politics had also led to a new relationship with post-genocide Rwanda which found common cause with UNITA in a shared antagonism to the Kabila regime that replaced that of Mobutu in the renamed Democratic Republic of Congo. The principal sources of UNITA's weapons were identified as Ukraine and Bulgaria. Unsurprisingly, the Panel concluded that the adhesive holding together this sanctions-busting web was diamonds.[85] Whatever the

---

83   UN document S/RES/1173, 12 June 1998.
84   David Cortwright and George A. Lopez, *The Sanctions Decade: Assessing UN Strategies in the 1990s* (London: Lynne Rienner, 2000), pp. 159–60.
85   Report of the Panel of Experts on Violations of Security Council Sanctions against UNITA', UN document S/2000/203, 10 March 2000.

Panel's findings, however, it was clear that the main issue around the failure of sanctions was not the identity of foreign guilty parties, but the UN's inability to act against them, despite their plain contravention of international law. Imposed under Chapter VII of the UN Charter, observation of the sanctions was legally binding on all states, but there was no serious discussion of punitive measures being taken against those breaching them. The Security Council coalition that had driven the peace process in Angola was neither wide enough nor cohesive enough to move in this direction.

In the meantime, the UN's peacekeeping and peacemaking efforts on the ground had unravelled. Blondin Beye's personal efforts to bring Savimbi round by painstaking diplomacy ended in tragedy in June 1998 when he and several members of his staff were killed when their plane crashed in Côte d'Ivoire as they shuttled between meetings of regional leaders. His successor as special representative, another Francophone African, Issa Diallo from Guinea, took up his post in almost impossible circumstances as Angola lurched from crisis to crisis. It is unlikely that Blondin Beye's departure from the scene did anything to accelerate the final collapse of the peacemaking effort. By the end his approach had lost credibility. Fighting between government forces and UNITA in the north of Angola had returned to pre-Lusaka levels by the end of 1998 and it had become increasingly difficult to sustain the notion that any 'peace process' was still in train. Moreover, low-level harassment of MONUA peacekeepers by UNITA forces took a critical turn with the deliberate shooting down of two UN aircraft in December 1998 and January 1999.[86] In his report to the Security Council on 17 January 1999 Annan acknowledged that Angola was now back at war and the peacekeeping effort had become meaningless. Consequently, he recommended that MONUA be rapidly scaled down and withdrawn, with all personnel concentrated in Luanda by mid-February prior to repatriation.[87] By now, the Luanda government itself had turned against the UN, furious at MONUA's failure to prevent UNITA's blatant rearming and redeployment.[88] The peacekeepers had come to be seen by the MPLA as no more than an inconvenience to its own war effort.

The end of the UN's peacekeeping engagement with Angola's troubles came with a speed and finality that utterly belied the glacial pace and equivocation that had characterized the process it had been called into being to oversee. All military personnel were out of Angola by mid-March 1999. The UN's various humanitarian agencies remained, along with a small

---

86 Although denied by UNITA at the time, its culpability was confirmed by the evidence of senior defectors to the panel on sanctions violations.

87 UN document S/1999/49, 17 January 1999.

88 *The Guardian*, 19 January 1999.

political presence, but any sense that an over-arching process was being facilitated by international intervention was absent. Whatever gloss might be put on it, Angola's warring factions had now been left to their own devices.

The dynamics of failure

The United Nations had maintained a peacekeeping presence in Angola for almost exactly ten years by the time of MONUA's withdrawal. This presence had taken various forms and been represented by four separate missions. Success had attended only the first of these. UNAVEM I, as we have seen, easily fulfilled a mandate that was one component of a broader regional accommodation. The linked settlement, which saw Namibian independence and the withdrawal of Cuban forces from Angola, had been negotiated and constructed by world powers who had 'franchised' its management to the United Nations. They nevertheless maintained a firm political control over a process that they perceived as important to their own national interests. The experience of UNAVEM II and III, and finally MONUA, was utterly different.

UNAVEM II was probably destined to fail on the basis of the flaws inherent in the process it had to manage. The Bicesse agreement (in the construction of which the UN had not been involved) required too much too quickly of both the Angolan protagonists and the under-resourced peacekeepers themselves. The Lusaka process, which was designed to correct the flaws of Bicesse, was superior in terms of time-scale, expectations and resources. The causes of its failure, therefore, lay beyond the 'management' shortcomings inherent in the attempt to implement Bicesse.

In Angola itself, the perceptions of the parties remained shaped by a view – initially encouraged by the Bicesse agreement – that saw the process as a contest rather than a mutual accommodation. Progress is not necessarily impossible in such a situation. Fundamental realignments between contending sides can provide a way forward. Indeed in 1997 and 1998 there were indications that this process was underway. The emergence of UNITA-Renovada from among the deputies who had presented themselves in Luanda, along with the defections of a number of UNITA military commanders, raised the possibility that a new Angolan political class was in the course of formation. In the event, critical mass was not achieved and the centre of opposition gravity remained with Savimbi and his generals. This historical cleavage between the MPLA and UNITA was entrenched by the extent of the spoils awaiting the victor. Angola's wealth has been a major cause of its long-drawn-out agony. Oil and diamonds, at the service of the MPLA and UNITA, respectively, have sustained the war both by paying for it and by providing a motivation for it.

Beyond Angola, the interests of the major powers in the Security Council, while obviously engaged at a human level, lacked the drive born of pressing self-interest. As a result, insufficient pressure was brought to bear on UNITA, either directly or indirectly via its foreign backers in Africa and elsewhere. While an adequate level of resources was generally available to UNAVEM III, it was not accompanied with the necessary level of political will. Neither the United States nor Russia retained any core interest in the conflict after the end of the cold war and the withdrawal of the Cubans. Therefore neither they nor, more relevantly perhaps, France, given the extent of Francophone support for UNITA, was willing to exert the necessary leverage against external forces, whether states, companies or individuals, who were content to see the conflict continue for their own reasons.

The withdrawal of MONUA had little discernible impact on the dismal rhythm of Angola's decades-old civil war. The UN's deployment of so-called 'smart sanctions' against UNITA's leaders and its financial resources had little immediate impact as we have seen. In the short term the rebel war machine remained well supplied through the enduring network sympathetic states in Francophone west Africa and the new breed of arms entrepreneurs in the former communist states of eastern Europe. The absence of UN military observers merely facilitated this trade, though in truth their presence had done little to contain it. Even before MONUA's withdrawal the conflict had been exported across Angola's northern border when, in August 1998, government troops were sent into the Democratic Republic of Congo to support the embattled Kabila regime (see above p. 88). UNITA, apparently little fazed by the disappearance of its patron Mobutu, was engaged in attempting to capture its own part of the DRC's lively illegal diamond trade. In Luanda's calculation, Kabila, although far from a reliable ally, was the best block available to these ambitions. In this way the conflicts of southern and central Africa were shown to have their own inter-regional links.[89] The following years saw no meaningful move towards a resolution in Angola itself, where the intensity of the conflict was ameliorated only by the dwindling supply of physical targets for destruction.

In February 2002 Jonas Savimbi met what many would have regarded as an appropriate end. After perpetuating a civil war in which perhaps one million Angolans had died, with countless more maimed and made destitute, the UNITA leader was killed in a skirmish with government troops in the remote east of the country. His death came at a time of weakness in UNITA's strategic position unprecedented since 1995. In the previous year or so the

---

89 For the circumstances of Angola's intervention in the DRC at this time see Norrie MacQueen, 'Angola', in Oliver Furley and Ron May (eds), *African Interventionist States* (Aldershot: Ashgate, 2001), pp. 104–10.

UN sanctions had finally been making an impact on the movement's supply chain, disrupting the inflow of weapons and the export of the gemstones that paid for them. This in turn enabled government forces to challenge UNITA's position in the diamond fields, further debilitating its military capacity. But on previous evidence few would have been confident in claiming that this was more than a back-beat in the natural tempo of the war. The baleful longevity of the Angolan conflict had several times in the past defied predictions of an endgame. Even the demise of Savimbi did not of itself ensure the end of the conflict. Although his personal control of UNITA was in most respects absolute, the movement's tentacles were spread widely across the country, and the danger of a fragmentation of its power into haphazard warlordism was very real. Beyond doubt, however, Savimbi's death changed fundamentally the hitherto static terms of the war.

Coming after the failure of similarly large-scale ventures in Somalia, the Angola experience seemed to confirm a fundamentally negative view of 'big' military involvements by the UN in Africa in the 1990s. Yet this apparent 'rule' was contradicted by an intervention in a situation strikingly similar in a number of ways to that in Angola. Portugal's other territory in southern Africa was Mozambique which, like Angola, became independent in 1975 following a protracted guerrilla war and the collapse of the imperialist regime in Lisbon. As in Angola, the post-independence state in Mozambique followed a Marxist path under the control of the anti-colonial guerrilla movement that had taken power after the departure of Portugal. In both states the rule of these movements came to be fiercely contested. The hugely destructive civil wars that afflicted each country had internal roots in ethnic and regional divisions. In both countries conflict was encouraged and resourced by external interests. But Mozambique's experience of UN involvement and the outcome it supervised was sharply different from that of Angola. As we shall now see, though the expansive, multifunctional peacekeeping venture was discredited by the failure of those in Somalia and Angola, it had already produced positive results in Mozambique.

Success in Mozambique, 1992–94

Mozambique emerged as an independent state in June 1975 with one clear advantage over Angola – an undisputed successor regime. Throughout the war against the Portuguese there was one clearly dominant liberation movement in Mozambique in contrast to the three in Angola. The Front for the Liberation of Mozambique (*Frente para a Libertação de Moçambique* – Frelimo) had been formed in 1962 from a number of smaller movements and was

Mozambique

led initially by Eduardo Mondlane, an American-educated international civil servant. It began its guerrilla campaign in September 1964 in the northern province of Cabo Delgado where it drew a significant part of its fighting force from among the local Makonde people. The war against the Portuguese in Mozambique began with less explosive violence than in Angola

147

in 1961, but subsequently, while the Angolan movements began to fight among and within themselves rather than against the colonialist enemy, the conflict in Mozambique proved much more of a challenge to the Portuguese. By the time of the Lisbon coup Frelimo was active throughout the northern half of Mozambique and was pressing southwards.[90] There was little doubt after the revolutionary events in Portugal in April 1974 that Mozambique would quickly become independent. Nor was there much question that this would involve the transfer of power to Frelimo (now led by Samora Machel after the assassination of Mondlane by the Portuguese in 1969). In Angola the Portuguese evacuated the capital without any formal transfer of power and, effectively, left the three rival movements to fight for it amongst themselves.

The 'front-line' in southern Africa: external destabilization

The post-independence years in Mozambique, although not as traumatic as those in Angola, were nevertheless characterized by great social and economic dislocation and, in certain regions, considerable violence. Angola's civil war began before its independence as a result of internal factionalism. It was then 'absorbed' into broader regional and global rivalries. The sequence in Mozambique was different. There was no significant challenge to Frelimo in 1975 despite attempts by a number of small movements to oppose its assumption of absolute power during the immediate pre-independence period. The civil war that eventually overtook it was, initially at any rate, an almost wholly external contrivance.

Mozambique had the misfortune to come to independence just as the guerrilla struggle against white minority rule in neighbouring Rhodesia was entering its final phase. Under the Portuguese Mozambique had provided a major lifeline for the white rebel regime. The ports of Mozambique, which historically had served the land-locked British territories to the west, helped Rhodesia to survive despite mandatory United Nations sanctions designed to bring it down. Now, the already desperate Rhodesian regime was confronted by a particularly grim prospect. Not only had it lost its neighbour's sanctions-busting service, but the new regime in Mozambique's capital, Maputo, was both African and Marxist. The guerrillas of the Zimbabwe African National Union (ZANU), led by Robert Mugabe, could now operate

---

90 On Frelimo's war against the Portuguese see Norrie MacQueen, *The Decolonization of Portuguese Africa: Metropolitan Revolution and the Dissolution of Empire* (London: Longman, 1997), pp. 43–9.

from bases in central Mozambique, striking deep within Rhodesia before withdrawing eastwards back across the border.

The Rhodesian regime responded to this new threat in two ways. Firstly, it began to launch military raids into Mozambique supposedly aimed at ZANU bases but frequently against purely Mozambican targets. Secondly, and much more destructively for the long term, the Rhodesian Central Intelligence Organization (CIO) set up a proxy force composed of anti-Frelimo Mozambican elements. These included former soldiers in the colonial army, remnants from the small groupings that had opposed the wholesale transfer of power to Frelimo at independence and various ex-Frelimo dissidents who had parted company with the movement for a variety of personal and political reasons before and after independence.[91] This Mozambican National Resistance Movement eventually became known as Renamo (*Resistência Nacional Moçambicana*). It began its operations inside the country in 1976 and over the following four years its destructive impact grew rapidly. Its original functions were to provide local knowledge and guides for Rhodesian infiltration forces and, later, to cause murderous destruction in its own right.[92] Renamo eventually sowed terror throughout a swathe of Mozambique north and south of the central 'Beira corridor', which linked Mozambique's second city by road and rail with eastern Rhodesia. Its efforts were helped by the incompetence of the Mozambican military. Although the armed forces had grown out of a formidable guerrilla movement it had not evolved successfully into a conventional army capable of mounting an effective anti-guerrilla strategy. And, although receiving Soviet bloc aid, Mozambique, unlike Angola, could not call on any significant Cuban combat forces. Frelimo's relations with Moscow (and therefore Havana), although close, were not as intimate as those of Angola. In addition, although Renamo was virtually bereft of any political programme, let alone a guiding ideology beyond a vague rhetorical 'anti-communism', it benefited from a growing disenchantment in the countryside. Frelimo's authoritarian rule, particularly over land-holding and production issues, as well as its perceived failure to deliver on economic promises made at independence, had caused its support in many rural areas to drain away.

In 1980 an agreement reached in London that had been brokered by the Commonwealth paved the way for the end of minority rule in Rhodesia and the coming to power of Mugabe's ZANU in the new Zimbabwe. The government in Maputo had every confidence that the worst was now behind

---

91   Glenda Morgan, 'Violence in Mozambique: towards an understanding of Renamo', *Journal of Modern African Studies* 28(4), 1990, p. 605.
92   Steven Metz, 'The Mozambique National Resistance and South African foreign policy', *African Affairs* 85(341), 1986, p. 493.

the country and that it could focus its efforts on the massive problems of economic reconstruction and development. This was a cruelly misguided expectation. Renamo, although set adrift by its one-time Rhodesian sponsors, was still a 'going concern' in terms of its capacity for murderous destabilization. Now South Africa which, with the settlement in Rhodesia/Zimbabwe, was the last bastion of white rule in Africa and increasingly aware of its vulnerability, simply took over the 'management' of Renamo from the Rhodesian CIO. The movement's new quartermasters were to be found in the murkier regions of the South African military and security forces. Not only did Renamo now have a new and rather more reliable source of foreign sustenance, it also gained from closer contact with the considerable community of right-wing Portuguese in South Africa who had fled Mozambique at the time of independence.[93]

At a formal level South Africa's relations with Mozambique since its independence in 1975 had been ambiguous. Historically the Transvaal, South Africa's economic heartland, had relied on the port of Maputo (Lourenço Marques as it had been called under the Portuguese) for a large part of its trade. Mozambique likewise had depended on South Africa for much of its goods and services as well as a destination for migrant labour. This pragmatic relationship between the two states, white racist and African Marxist, continued after 1975. There was obvious unease on both sides, but nothing approaching the military confrontation that characterized the South Africa–Angola relationship. However, the mounting pressures on South Africa (not least from the conflicts in Namibia and Angola) had turned the South African Defence Force and the shadowy agencies associated with it into something of an autonomous power within the state. The extent to which the 'adoption' of Renamo by South Africa was initiated or even approved by the civilian government itself as opposed to the military therefore remained unclear. This ill-defined distribution of power was to have serious and long-term consequences for Mozambique.

South Africa's specific grievance against Mozambique derived from the Maputo regime's support for the opposition ANC. In fact, mindful of its interdependent relationship with South Africa, Mozambique was not in the first rank of the ANC's supporters. It provided no military training facilities for ANC fighters as Angola did and the movement's political presence in the country was closely monitored. But given its geographical position, Mozambique provided an obvious infiltration route for ANC guerrillas *en route* to South Africa, and this was certainly tolerated by the Frelimo government. Maputo had also become a major haven for high-profile ANC exiles from

---

93 Hilary Andersson, *Mozambique: a War Against the People* (London: Macmillan, 1992), p. 57.

South Africa. While civilian politicians in Pretoria may have accepted that politically Mozambique had little option but to display at least this level of solidarity, the military was less understanding. Consequently, southern Mozambique began to suffer the same two-pronged assault as had the central region during the last years of Rhodesia. ANC premises around Maputo became a target for commando raids by the South African military itself, while Renamo was equipped and encouraged to create bloody havoc in the countryside. South African support, much more extensive than that of Rhodesia, also meant that Renamo could maintain its activities further north which had begun during the phase of Rhodesian sponsorship.

By 1983 its 10,000 or so fighters were active in ten of Mozambique's eleven provinces, with only the Makonde-dominated Frelimo heartland of Cabo Delgado in the extreme north unaffected directly. The entire economic and social life of the country was being destroyed, with food production and transport in utter disorder and health and education services, once the pride of Frelimo's revolution, in ruins. In addition to the man-made misery of Renamo, Mozambique at this time was also beset by a sequence of natural disasters with alternating flood and drought in the very areas most afflicted by the war. These environmental catastrophes cost the lives of perhaps 100,000 people in 1983–84 alone.

At this time, amidst the rapidly deteriorating national situation, Frelimo reluctantly reached the view that the crisis facing the country could be tackled only through a direct agreement with the South African government. It was forced to seek such an accommodation partly by the chronic failure of its own military to make any decisive progress against Renamo. But Maputo was also encouraged to move in this direction by a number of western states, prominent among them the United States, Portugal and Britain. Mozambique took their views seriously because they were offered in the context of a new approach to foreign policy in Maputo designed to lessen Mozambique's dependence on the Soviet bloc. Although these new friends were sympathetic to Mozambique's plight, they made it clear that it had little option but to seek a regional settlement. Accordingly, in March 1984 after several months of negotiations, Mozambican president Samora Machel met South African prime minister P.W. Botha at Nkomati on the common border between the two countries. The accord they signed here was supposed to end South African support for Renamo. This, it was assumed, would mean that the movement would simply wither away. In return Mozambique agreed to expel the ANC (except for a small 'diplomatic mission') from its territory. The agreement also included a number of functional aspects. These, it was hoped in Maputo, would bring the two countries closer together economically and in so doing create a new sense of mutual self-interest in security matters.

Despite a great deal of optimism in Mozambique itself and internationally, it became clear within a few months that the key South African undertaking on Renamo was not being met. The Mozambicans had been scrupulous in meeting their commitments with regard to the ANC, but there was no discernible reduction in Renamo activities. Evidence continued to implicate South Africa in these. The initial and obvious conclusion reached was that the South African government had simply been deceitful in its dealings around Nkomati, achieving its own ends while continuing to orchestrate the infliction of misery on Mozambique. It was more likely that Botha and his cabinet concluded the agreement in good enough faith but were simply disregarded by the military, which was not about to surrender such a powerful weapon as Renamo. In the run-up to the Nkomati agreement, the South African security forces had evidently pre-empted its impact by greatly increasing its supplies to Renamo. This enabled the rebels to accumulate large stockpiles within Mozambique in anticipation of continued violence.

It was unlikely anyway that even if South Africa had stuck to the last letter of Nkomati, Renamo would have quickly and quietly disappeared. Renamo also enjoyed limited but significant support from beyond South Africa. By the early 1990s the long-established but diplomatically eccentric government of Hastings Banda in neighbouring Malawi was also providing it with base areas. Beyond this at the state-to-state level, Renamo consistently failed to win the level of support enjoyed by UNITA in Angola. Even during the presidency of Ronald Reagan – which virtually by reflex supported any group claiming to be motivated by anti-communism – Renamo failed to make any significant inroads in official Washington.[94] But some right-wing elements in Portugal, which had not come to terms with the loss of the African territories – and often personal assets in them – supported both UNITA in Angola and Renamo in Mozambique equally. Other extreme right-wing groupings in western countries provided political support and publicity for the movement, as did certain conservative Islamic interests in the Middle East.

Renamo's continued vigour after Nkomati was also due in part to the fact that it had started to gain some genuine support in the countryside, however passive. The Bicesse process in Angola, it will be recalled, foundered in part because of a misreading of the power base of UNITA. Although the civil war in Angola had been fed and nurtured from outside, internal factors could not be wholly disregarded. There was an internal as well as an external dynamic to the conflict, which was fatally underestimated. To a lesser extent this was the situation in Mozambique as well. Resentment at Frelimo's

---

94 Michael Wesley, *Casualties of the New World Order: the Causes of Failure of UN Missions to Civil Wars* (London: Macmillan, 1997), p. 83.

often brutal centralizing policies along with its patent incapacity to defend its citizens was, as we have seen, an early factor in the situation. There was also an ethnic and regional dimension exploited by Renamo in the absence of a coherent political ideology. Frelimo's guerrilla army and its post-independence military were disproportionately 'northern'. On the other hand, its political leadership before and after independence was dominated by southerners. Renamo was thus able to generate some resentment among the Shona people of central Mozambique over their supposed exclusion from power. Afonso Dhlakama, who emerged as Renamo's political leader in the 1980s after protracted internal wrangles and rivalries, was himself of Ndau ethnicity, a people traditionally allied to the Shona. In this way Renamo eventually, in the words of one observer, 'had gained a momentum of its own which its former paymaster and arms supplier could not reverse'.[95]

The war continued with little respite until the beginning of the 1990s. By this time about a million people had died directly or indirectly as a result of the fighting and about 4.5 million (out of a total population of twelve million) were refugees either internally or in neighbouring countries.[96] The conflict was effectively stalemated, but the deadlock was characterized by continued violence of a horrific level. The writ of the government ran no further than the major cities, which were themselves in a state of apparently terminal decline as infrastructure and services collapsed. Mozambique had now become the poorest country in the world according to standard development indicators. By 1988 foreign aid accounted for 70 per cent of its gross domestic product.[97]

In October 1986 Samora Machel had died in a plane crash (in circumstances which to many suggested South African assassination). He was replaced by Joaquim Chissano, a figure with a less authoritarian style and more diplomatic skills. But this change at the top had no obvious impact on the situation either internally or externally. Frelimo had become increasingly dependent on Zimbabwean troops to provide security along the vital Beira corridor, but even this was patchy and limited. Yet, however feeble politically and militarily Frelimo had become, Renamo was never close to taking power in the country. The cities remained closed to it despite frequent hit-and-run raids on outlying suburbs. The war was increasingly one of pure destruction, with neither side able to contemplate either victory or defeat.

---

95   David Birmingham, *Frontline Nationalism in Angola and Mozambique* (Oxford: James Currey, 1992), p. 87.

96   The dispersal of refugees throughout the region was roughly as follows: Malawi 1,058,500; South Africa 250,000; Zimbabwe 137,900; Zambia 25,400; and Tanzania 20,000. Chris Alden, 'The UN and the resolution of conflict in Mozambique', *Journal of Modern African Studies* 33(1), 1995, p. 111.

97   Joseph Hanlon, *Mozambique: Who Calls the Shots?* (Oxford: James Currey, 1991), p. 6.

Mediation

By the end of the 1980s the Frelimo regime, although in no immediate danger of overthrow by Renamo, was barely functioning and the concept of a 'Mozambican state' had become increasingly notional. The pressures of the apparently endless civil war and the sequence of natural disasters that had harried the country helped accelerate Mozambique's journey on the path taken by the other one-time revolutionary states of Portuguese-speaking Africa towards fundamental constitutional change. The narrow Marxist-Leninist approach to economic management adopted after independence had gradually been abandoned during the 1980s. At the beginning of the 1990s the political system was brought into line with this ideological shift. President Chissano himself presented a proposal to the central committee of Frelimo for far-reaching reform in 1990. After some heated debate between the old and the new guards in the party a new constitution was agreed relatively quickly. Mozambique ceased to be a 'People's Republic' and became a simple 'Republic'. Freedom of the press was proclaimed and the judiciary was made independent of the government. Most significantly for the resolution of the civil war, the Frelimo one-party state was to be replaced by a multi-party democracy.

This radical change in the nature of the Mozambican state effectively removed any fragment of legitimacy that could be claimed by Renamo. There was now in principle no obstacle to it transforming itself into a political party and putting its case to the Mozambican people in a democratic election. Such limited support it had enjoyed from ultra-conservative elements in Europe and North America now drained away. Perhaps more threatening to the future of Renamo as a military force, however, was the increasing pace of change in South Africa initiated at the beginning of 1990 with the release from prison of Nelson Mandela. Much more dependent on the support of the South African military than UNITA was in Angola, Renamo had now to contemplate a fundamental change in its fortunes.

The first direct talks between Frelimo and Renamo took place in July 1990. They were organized and facilitated by a non-governmental organization, the Italian based Sant' Egidio community, which had been involved in development work in the country for some time.[98] The outcome was reasonably encouraging. The parties agreed to a partial cessation of hostilities in the economically important areas of the Beira and Limpopo corridors (linking Mozambique respectively with Zimbabwe and South Africa) and to a protocol for definitive peace negotiations at a later date. The later talks

---

98   Sam Barnes, 'Peacekeeping in Mozambique', in Oliver Furley and Roy May (eds), *Peacekeeping in Africa* (Aldershot: Ashgate, 1998), p. 16.

were given added weight by the appearance of Italian government officials alongside the Sant' Egidio mediators.[99] These negotiations were less immediately successful than the first round but protracted discussions between July 1991 and October 1992 produced an outline agreement. This involved military disengagement and mutual demobilization of forces prior to parliamentary and presidential elections.

The role of the United Nations in the process up to this point had been slight. It had not been formally involved in the Italian efforts. During these negotiations the eventual role of the UN was assumed as a given, however. In the spirit of the time this was almost a matter of course. The standard machinery of conflict resolution in Africa at that time – in operation from Namibia to Angola to Somalia – had the United Nations at its centre. There were, however, differences between the parties over the potential extent and character of the UN's mandate.[100] The Frelimo government was sensitive about the slight to the sovereignty of 'its' state implied by an extensive 'internationalization' of the process. On much the same grounds Renamo favoured a major role for the UN as such internationalization would undermine assumptions of Frelimo's legitimacy. Ultimately, the extent and complexity of the conflict meant that any effective UN commitment would have to be a large one if it was to be successful, whatever the political points to be won or lost as a result. Consequently, the General Peace Agreement (GPA) signed by President Chissano and Afonso Dhlakama in Rome on 4 October 1992 cast the United Nations in the central role in its implementation.

The UN was to chair the Supervision and Control Commission (*Comissão de Supervisão e Controle* – CSC), which would be composed of government and Renamo delegations along with representatives from Italy, Britain, Portugal and the United States, and which was to have overall responsibility for the implementation of the agreement. At the political level the UN was to organize and monitor the electoral process at the centre of the settlement. Its military functions included the supervision of the cease-fire between Frelimo and Renamo as well as the disarmament and cantonment of opposing forces and the control of surrendered arms.[101] The United Nations was also to oversee the withdrawal of foreign troops who had been deployed to protect their own countries' supply lines to the Indian Ocean. Although the majority of these were Zimbabweans in position along the Beira corridor,

---

99   The general role of the church in the peace process is explored by Moses Venâncio, 'Mediation by the Roman Catholic Church in Mozambique, 1988–91', in Chan and Jabri (eds), *Mediation in Southern Africa*, pp. 142–58.

100   Ibid., p. 160.

101   The full terms of the GPA can be found in *The General Peace Agreement 1992* (Amsterdam: African-European Institute, 1992).

Malawian troops were also involved further north following their government's reversal under diplomatic pressure in 1986 of its earlier support for Renamo.

Immediately following the signing of the GPA President Chissano wrote to Boutros Boutros-Ghali appealing to the UN to accept these responsibilities and make the necessary resources available. The following week the Security Council responded by authorizing the secretary-general to appoint a special representative and to despatch a military advance party.[102] The Italian diplomat Aldo Ajello was duly named as special representative, in part in acknowledgement of the Rome government's central role in the process leading up to the signing of the GPA.

The cease-fire agreed under the GPA came into effect on 15 October 1992 and, initially, was frequently violated. The formal establishment of the UN-chaired CSC at the beginning of November helped ease the situation. But the apparent fragility of the peace process at this time moved Boutros-Ghali to warn the Security Council in December of the danger of collapse unless a momentum was created behind the implementation of the GPA. In this report the secretary-general made no attempt to minimize the difficulties that would be faced by the UN in Mozambique. There was utter devastation outside of the capital, with the transport and communications infrastructure more or less destroyed. Against this background the GPA was involved in an inherently complex process and the capacity of the contending parties, the Frelimo government and Renamo, to manage it was highly questionable. '[I]n the light of recent experiences elsewhere,' Boutros-Ghali observed, UN involvement 'may be thought to invite the international community to take a risk. I believe that the risk is worth taking; but I cannot disguise that it exists.'[103]

On 16 December the Council approved the creation of the United Nations Operation in Mozambique, which became known as ONUMOZ, from its Portuguese title, *Operação das Nações Unidas em Moçambique*. The deployment of ONUMOZ was approved until the end of October 1993. By this date the electoral process at the centre of the GPA was originally planned to have taken place and the ONUMOZ role, in theory, to have been completed. The maximum personnel envisaged for the operation was 7000 and its total budgeted cost was US$260 million. It was clear from the authorizing resolution, though, that beyond the political and human risks involved, the permanent members were wary of the operation's impact on already stretched financial resources for peacekeeping. Economies, it indicated,

---

102 UN document S/RES/782, 13 October 1992.
103 UN document S/24892, 3 December 1992.

should be sought through phased deployment and all other available means.[104]

The deployment of ONUMOZ and the demobilization process

The effective deployment of ONUMOZ did not follow its authorization with the speed that was intended by Boutros-Ghali. Military personnel did not begin to arrive in significant numbers in Mozambique until May 1993, six months after the resolution mandating the operation. The force did not come up to its full initial strength of 6000 until July. There were a number of reasons for this. The concerns about costs and budgeting expressed in the authorizing resolution caused real nervousness among potential force contributors. These concerns aggravated considerable anxiety already present among these states about participation in the basic project. By the beginning of 1993 when Boutros-Ghali was soliciting troop contributions, the UN was already heavily involved in Africa and elsewhere. The previous year had seen a peak in UN commitments, with large, difficult missions established in Somalia as well as in Cambodia and the former Yugoslavia. In addition, the UN's major and complex role in the Lebanon continued. Most worryingly, perhaps, UNAVEM II remained in place in Angola after the collapse of the peace process there – a process very similar to that now proposed for Mozambique.

In addition to the wariness and caution of potential troop contributors about the likely risks to be faced on the ground in Mozambique, the financial dimension to the operation became a recurring issue in the Security Council. It was present in the terms of virtually every pronouncement made on the operation. A final budget was not confirmed until well into 1993, and this climate of economic stringency – and potential uncertainty – fed the concerns of troop contributors.

The problems around deployment did not emerge only from this international milieu. The Frelimo government in Maputo was slow and reluctant to conclude the customary status of forces agreement with the UN covering necessary immunities for ONUMOZ personnel and operations. Always a potential source of difficulty, the status of forces issue was particularly sensitive in Mozambique, where government legitimacy and the capacity of the state to control its territory were the central issues that had brought United

---

104   UN document S/RES/797, 16 December 1992.

Nations involvement in this first phase. Despite consistent pressure from New York, the agreement was not finally delivered until May 1993. This accretion of difficulties did not, however, prevent an effective force being put together. Eventually, some thirty-five states would provide troops, military observers or civilian police, with Bangladesh, Italy, Uruguay and Zambia providing the most substantial contingents. Deployment, when it eventually got under way, took place smoothly and efficiently.

Fewer difficulties arose around the purely humanitarian side of the UN's role. This formed a major part of ONUMOZ's overall responsibilities in Mozambique, though it often interlocked with the military role in practice. The main agency established by the Supervision and Control Commission to undertake the manifold humanitarian responsibilities of ONUMOZ was the Office of Humanitarian Aid Co-ordination (UNOHAC). UNOHAC's main work lay in refugee return and resettlement as well as in the reintegration into society of the Frelimo and Renamo fighters demobilized under the terms of the GPA. Its task was enormous, particularly as it had to be carried out against the background of continuing cyclical natural crises of drought and flood that had beset Mozambique since the late 1980s. International donors, though, appeared more forthcoming on this aspect of funding than the Security Council did in respect of the military ones.

Although the cease-fire generally held, with initial violations dwindling after the deployment of ONUMOZ, there were considerable doubts about the prospects for the process of cantonment and demobilization that was central to the GPA process. One obvious reason for this concern was, once again, the recent collapse of the Bicesse process in Angola and the return to war there. The very similar military–political model balancing processes of disengagement and elections had evidently failed disastrously in Angola, and there was nothing in the Mozambican situation to guarantee a different outcome. On the contrary, a major worry for the foreign patrons of the peace process in Mozambique and the UN planners responsible for overseeing its implementation was the lack of control exerted by the Renamo leadership over its forces compared to that of UNITA in Angola. In the event, the very absence of this tight discipline may well have been a factor in the success of the Mozambique process. UNITA had been able to return to war so quickly and so devastatingly after its failure in the elections precisely because of the firm discipline exerted by Jonas Savimbi. But in the latter part of 1993 Dhlakama's evident inability to control his fighters in this manner was seen as a dangerously destabilizing element in the process.

Worryingly, Dhlakama appeared to be compensating for his incomplete authority over his fighters by flaunting his power in other areas of the process. In particular he repeatedly obstructed the work of the Supervision and Control Commission after initially refusing even to participate in it.[105] It is likely that this initial hindering of the peace plan derived from deeper insecurities than just that around his personal control of his own forces, however. Much more than UNITA in Angola (which by the early 1990s had evolved into a formidable 'conventional' army), the dispersed and lightly equipped forces of Renamo ran the danger of a general disintegration amidst the processes of demobilization. Frelimo, Dhlakama reasoned, was poised to exploit this danger, reassert its control over the country and finally extinguish Renamo as both a political and a military force. Here the role of the UN as guarantor of the GPA and monitor of its terms was crucial to the peace process. Dhlakama insisted that 65 per cent of the total UN force must be fully deployed before Renamo would begin to demobilize. This he regarded as an essential safeguard against a Frelimo 'coup'.

The implication of this was that the military aspect of the settlement could fall out of synchronization with the political ones. The secretary-general was determined that the mistakes of Angola – where in 1992 the electoral phase of the settlement was allowed to begin before the process of military disengagement had reached an appropriate stage – would not be repeated in Mozambique. He had made this clear when he recommended to the Security Council that the Mozambique operation should be undertaken. In view 'of the recent experience in Angola', he believed 'it to be of critical importance that the elections should not take place until the military aspects of the agreement have been fully implemented'.[106] It soon became clear, therefore, that the original timetable of the GPA, which marked October 1993 for the legislative and presidential elections, would have to be changed if the delicate – and crucial – relationship between the military and the political aspects of the process was to be maintained. Instead of elections, therefore, Mozambique had a visit from Boutros-Ghali in October 1993 during which he pressed and cajoled both parties, but especially Renamo, to move the process forward. To some extent, the secretary-general was pushing on at least a half-open door. At the beginning of September 1993 Chissano and Dhlakama had held face-to-face talks in Maputo (a level of direct contact the UN had struggled to achieve between the Angolan parties), and had reached a reasonable degree of agreement on outstanding issues. Boutros-Ghali now sought to accelerate the momentum thus created. He rejected outright, however, Dhlakama's suggestion that the elections could be held before demobilization was complete.[107]

Out of Boutros-Ghali's visit came a new timetable, agreed by each side. Now fighters from both forces were to be concentrated in their assembly

---

105   Alden, 'The UN and the resolution of conflict in Mozambique', p. 114.
106   UN document S/24892, 3 December 1992.
107   Parsons, *From Cold War to Hot Peace*, p. 151.

areas in November 1993 and final demobilization was to begin in January 1994, with half the process to be completed by March and the rest by May. A new national army was to be in the field by September. Keeping pace with these military developments, on the political side registration of voters for the elections would take place from April to June 1994, and there would be six weeks of political campaigning in September and October with the polls themselves taking place by the end of October.[108] In conformity with the new timetable, the first assembly points for the cantonment of fighters (located in areas designated by the two parties) opened in November. Before the end of the month twenty of the planned forty-nine camps (twelve Frelimo and eight Renamo) were operational. The process of demobilization was not problem-free. The enforced cantonment of thousands of young men, most of them anxious to return to their homes, was hardly likely to be managed without incident. But no crisis emerged of a scale that could threaten the overall process. Accordingly, by July 1994 (about two months behind the schedule agreed by the Security Council at the end of the previous year) the demobilization of the designated fighters was virtually complete.

Less successful was the simultaneous formation of the new national force to supplant those of Frelimo and Renamo. The Defence Forces of Mozambique (*Forças Armadas de Defesa de Moçambique* – FADM) faced a major recruitment crisis before they came into existence. The force was designed and planned at a meeting in Lisbon in July 1993 between officials from Portugal, Britain and France after the Security Council had made it clear that the UN would not commit itself to either the training or the formation of the FADM.[109] A special course was set up in Zimbabwe where potential officers (about 540 in total from both sides) were trained themselves and equipped to pass on this training to others in Mozambique. Joint commanders were duly designated by Frelimo and Renamo. In Angola there had been major problems in tying UNITA's leadership to its commitment to participate in a new unified force. In Mozambique the difficulty was at grass-roots level. Individual Frelimo and Renamo soldiers sought demobilization rather than a continuing military career. By the end of the war few ordinary soldiers were volunteers and their experiences had been traumatic in the extreme. Demobilization, moreover, brought real material benefits to former fighters. A generous terminal payment along with food benefits and agricultural tools were provided by international agencies keen to ease the reintegration of former fighters into postwar society.[110] As a result, by

---

108 UN document S/26666, 1 November 1993. The Security Council agreed to the new timetable a few days later: S/RES/882, 5 November 1993.
109 UN document S/RES/850, 9 July 1993.
110 Barnes, 'Peacekeeping in Mozambique', p. 173.

September 1994, when the FADM was supposed to be fully operational, there was a considerable shortfall in its proposed strength. Little more than one third of the planned 30,000 soldiers had been recruited, and those who had been were disproportionately of officer and NCO rank.

The electoral process

With the military aspects of the peace process progressing satisfactorily if not flawlessly after the renegotiation of the timetable in October 1993, planning for the electoral process contingent on them and now fixed for October 1994 could begin. The settlement plan included provision for a directly elected president serving for a five-year term. On the legislative side, there was to be a 250-seat National Assembly, also directly elected. As with other aspects of the GPA, the UN had been given a central role in the organization and administration of the polls. Accordingly, ONUMOZ established an 'Electoral Division' composed of 148 international officials. The Electoral Division determined early on that both ONUMOZ resources and Mozambican self-respect would benefit from the maximum amount of administration and planning being left to local agencies. These included the rival parties themselves as well as Mozambique's National Election Commission. This contrasted with recent practice in Cambodia, where the United Nations Transitional Authority (UNTAC) had taken on itself virtually every task associated with the electoral process.[111] In Mozambique the management of voter registration, the campaign and the election itself certainly did not seem to be compromised by this high level of 'localization'. The psychological effect of such self-sufficiency – the more impressive in a polity that had never before been involved in this sort of democratic exercise – had its own importance in bonding the country to the making of its own political future.

The aspect of election management where local resources were least adequate to meet requirements was policing. The Mozambican police's inefficiency, corruption and implicit bias (it was, after all, a 'Frelimo' force) would be likely to generate difficulties during the tense pre-election period. The problem was compounded by the absence of a national military force during much of 1993 and 1994. Accordingly, Boutros-Ghali sought authorization from the Security Council in January 1994 for the attachment of a large force of international civilian police (UNCIVPOL) to ONUMOZ (in addition to the small component already present under the terms of the GPA) to monitor and, where possible, train the local force.[112] The potential

---

111   N.D. White, *Keeping the Peace: the United Nations and the Maintenance of International Peace and Security* (2nd edn, Manchester: Manchester University Press, 1997), p. 275.

112   UN document S/1994/89/Add.1, 28 January 1994.

hazards posed to peacekeeping missions by 'unreliable' local police had already been confronted in Namibia, and the secretary-general could reasonably have expected a positive response from the Security Council. In the event, though, the Council imposed conditions. It agreed to the despatch of 1144 civilian police but this was to be contingent upon the secretary-general reducing the military component of ONUMOZ proportionately to guarantee that the existing budget was not exceeded.

The same Security Council resolution requested the secretary-general to present a firm plan for the final 'draw-down' of ONUMOZ by the target date of the end of November 1994.[113] It was another indication that those bearing the greatest burden of costs were not prepared to offer a bottomless pocket at this high tide of post-cold war peacekeeping. In the circumstances the 'police for troops' trade-off was a reasonable one for ONUMOZ as an operational whole. By this stage the requirement for military personnel was declining as demobilization gained pace and the sensitive transport corridors became more secure. The presence of a significant force of civilian police was now more appropriate than the maintenance of existing troop levels.

The political outcome to the process envisaged by the General Peace Agreement was identical to that of the 1991 Bicesse agreement for Angola in that the elections would end with a winner-take-all result. As we have seen, a great deal of the blame for the collapse of the Angolan peace process in 1992 had been laid at the door of this zero-sum arrangement. The MPLA victory in the legislative elections and Savimbi's defeat in the presidential contest effectively left UNITA with nothing to show for seventeen years of war. As Mozambique had no democratic tradition within which such a defeat could be rationalized, a return to conflict should have been predicted, so argued some with the benefit of hindsight. The Lusaka process on Angola that followed the failure of Bicesse sought to deal with this problem by building in a commitment to coalition government as a key stage in a permanent settlement. Sensitive as always to the Angola precedent, the foreign sponsors of the peace process in Mozambique sought to adjust the GPA to embrace a similar mechanism. From the beginning it was a deeply unattractive prospect for Frelimo which, by virtually all estimates, was certain to win the elections. The United States, Boutros-Ghali and, on his behalf, Nelson Mandela sought to bring pressure to bear on Chissano to accept this change in the political target of the process.[114] Chissano was resolute, however, insisting that the original terms of the peace agreement be adhered to. It was possibly the case that the interests of long-term stability in post-settlement Mozambique were best served by this. Once Dhlakama's agreement to accept

---

113   UN document S/RES/898, 23 February 1994.
114   Alden, 'The UN and the resolution of conflict in Mozambique', p. 125.

the role of opposition leader was secured, government by single party was almost certainly the most efficient and productive way forward into the phase of social and economic reconstruction. Whatever the shortcomings of Frelimo's performance in government since independence, it had acquired almost twenty years of experience. On the basis of its own meagre political history Renamo's contribution to any coalition with Frelimo may have caused more problems than it helped resolve.

Dhlakama's acquiescence in the arrangement was bought relatively cheaply, in political if not financial terms. Early in the process Dhlakama indicated that the transformation of Renamo into a 'political party' would require a large – and largely unaccountable – financial subvention from the donor community. Many observers considered this to be little more than a bribe to Dhlakama and his immediate circle at the top of the movement. At the urgings of Aldo Ajello, who took a characteristically pragmatic view of the situation, the secretary-general agreed that a 'trust fund' be established among the sponsors of the peace process for this purpose. He then included the proposal in a report to the Security Council at the beginning of July 1993.[115] Some US$12 million found its way into Renamo's coffers from this source. A further US$300,000 was paid to Dhlakama as 'election expenses' by the Portuguese government. However questionable this financial 'encourage-ment' might have been in terms of probity, it appeared to have rapid results in terms of the pace of the peace process. Dhlakama moved to Maputo, where he established himself and Renamo as part of the national political fabric. Those who had followed events in Angola could only view this as a major step forward. Savimbi had resolutely refused to move to Luanda or participate in any significant way in day-to-day political activity, which would have been crucial to the credibility of the overall process in Angola. Nevertheless, suspicions about Dhlakama's personal motivation raised by the trust fund issue seemed to be justified when his long list of conditions for his relocation to Maputo seemed to have more to do with personal luxury than either security or political efficiency. At the time, though, Ajello was probably justified in seeing the trust fund as 'a most valuable instrument' in finally weaning Dhlakama from the 'military temptation' at a critical point.[116]

The process of voter registration and the election campaign itself passed with regular angry recriminations between the parties but with little serious incident. This was a considerable achievement. The task of identifying eligible voters had been a hugely difficult one. Few meaningful data were avail-able from previous, post-independence elections in the country, which had been conducted by Frelimo on the basis of a kind of Leninist 'democratic

---

115 UN document S/26034, 2 July 1993.
116 *The Guardian*, 6 August 1994.

centralism' quite alien to a competitive party system. Most damagingly, though, the massive wartime displacement of population, both internally and externally, had created enormous problems. The vote itself became the subject of an elaborate supervision and monitoring operation. The United Nations and other inter-governmental and non-governmental organizations deployed some 2300 election observers. The new political climate – and the security guarantees provided by ONUMOZ – had led to a proliferation of small parties that set out to provide 'third-way' options between Frelimo and Renamo. The political parties themselves fielded some 35,000 poll monitors between them.[117]

On 27 October, the first day of voting, an ominous statement from Renamo shook the cautious optimism that had been building among Mozambicans and foreign observers alike over the previous months. Unspecified 'irregularities' in the election, Dhlakama now announced, had left Renamo with no option but to withdraw entirely from the process. The Angolan experience of 1992, when Savimbi had rejected the elections and took UNITA back to war, had receded from the consciousness of those involved in the peace settlement in Mozambique as the process there moved forward. Now, however, the Angolan spectre returned more vividly than ever. But the international momentum behind the process in Mozambique proved too strong to be deflected by Renamo at this stage, and it had become clear over the previous two years that Renamo was no UNITA and Dhlakama no Savimbi when it came to the capacity and control necessary to reignite the civil war. An immediate and irresistible international response more or less bludgeoned Dhlakama back on to the electoral track. Boutros-Ghali, the president of the Security Council, the countries of the CSC (Britain, Italy, Portugal and the United States), as well as Nelson Mandela and Robert Mugabe, all applied pressure. The following day a chastened Dhlakama announced Renamo's re-engagement with the election, which was now extended for a further day to compensate for the confusion that had been created by his behaviour. The process and its result were endorsed by the Security Council, following certification of its fairness by the observers on the ground.[118]

The turn-out in the vote was 85 per cent nationally (and over 90 per cent in some provinces). As in Angola in 1992, the commitment of the population to political rather than military solutions to conflicts was beyond any doubt. The outcome was the predicted one: victory for Frelimo in the National Assembly elections and for Chissano in the presidential poll. Renamo, however, performed better than many observers expected. Frelimo took 149 of the 250 legislature seats (with 44.3 per cent of the vote) but Renamo secured

117   White, *Keeping the Peace*, p. 275.
118   UN document S/RES/960, 21 November 1994.

a creditable 112 seats (37.8 per cent of the vote). Of the fourteen smaller parties contesting the election, the only one to pass the 5 per cent threshold for representation laid down in the electoral law was the Democratic Union (*União Democrática*), which took nine seats. In the presidential contest Chissano won more convincingly with 53 per cent of the vote against Dhlakama's 33 per cent (none of the other ten candidates making any significant impact). In line with his refusal early in the process to consider coalition government, Chissano immediately formed a new Frelimo administration with Renamo in opposition.

Mozambique and the spectre of Angola

A fundamental question has recurred throughout our exploration of the UN mission in Mozambique. Why did the peace process there (and the United Nations' management of it) succeed while a strikingly similar undertaking failed in Angola? There is no single answer to this. The explanation lies in a complex of interconnected factors, both local and international.

The key element on the ground in Mozambique was, quite simply, the existence of a fundamental desire on the part of both protagonists to extricate themselves from the conflict. While the commitment of the MPLA government in Angola to securing peace through UN intervention was probably as strong as that of Frelimo, the position of UNITA was much more ambiguous than that of Renamo. The war option was always closer to Savimbi's hand than it was to Dhlakama's. In part this reflected the relative positions of UNITA and Renamo. With origins in the anti-colonial struggle of the 1960s UNITA had a continuous history of anti-MPLA struggle since before independence. Thus UNITA was simply a more formidable organization than the artificially created and politically compromised Renamo. UNITA's political strength was bolstered by its military capacity. It had been supplied and trained over the years of a long civil war by a range of western sponsors and had become battle-hardened in conventional warfare. Renamo, in contrast, was brutal and destructive in its tactics but in comparison to UNITA it was poorly supplied by an unreliable and limited range of foreign patrons. Its physical capacity to relaunch its war against Frelimo after the peace process had gained momentum was therefore very doubtful. Once in cantonment, Renamo fighters seemed impatient for rapid demobilization and thought little about maintaining preparedness for a return to battle.

Nor was Renamo's lack of political tradition and military capacity counter-balanced by a clear ethnic or regional identity. Although its support was to some extent clustered in the Shona areas of central Mozambique, this did not constitute anything like the tight power-base of UNITA among the Ovimbundu of Angola's central plateau. There was also a major difference in leadership capacity. The charismatic, enduring and, on occasion, brutally Machiavellian Savimbi enjoyed a largely unchallenged supremacy at the head of UNITA. Dhlakama, in contrast, cut an unimpressive figure and was singularly lacking in soldierly vigour. In short, while Savimbi could be confident that his forces could and would resume fighting on his orders, Dhlakama could not credibly make any such claim.

Finally, regardless of the bases and leadership of the two rebel movements, the economic dimension to the two civil wars was quite different. Angola's wealth, as we have noted, was immense. Mozambique had nothing to compare with these assets. Its wealth was potential rather than actual, and less immediately portable than that of Angola. Mozambique's immediate economic prospects centred on the provision of port and transport facilities to neighbours, on agriculture and on tourism. All of these required stability, long-term development and prudent management. The preference of the 'warlord' between these two classes of wealth is obvious. There was, quite simply, less booty to wrestle over in Mozambique, and consequently less appetite for the fight on the part of Renamo. Electoral 'trust funds' and Maputo villas were, in a sense, as good as it could get for the Renamo leadership, and they willingly paid the required dues for these.

Clearly, then, the United Nations confronted fundamentally different conflict dynamics in Angola and Mozambique. Crucially, it was quick to profit from recognition of these differences and to use this in the interests of the peace process in Mozambique. Most obviously, of course, the UN's engagement with Mozambique began almost simultaneously with the failure of the Bicesse process in Angola in 1992. The lessons of the one could now be learned and mistakes avoided in the other. This helped to guarantee that the Security Council devoted sufficient resources to ONUMOZ. However much the permanent members might cavil at the financial burden of the Mozambique operation, it ensured that the disastrous attempt at shoestring peacekeeping with UNAVEM II was not repeated. ONUMOZ, with more than 7000 troops and civilian police, was twenty times the strength of UNAVEM II at the point of breakdown in the peace process in Angola in 1992.

This relative strength within the overall dynamic – along with the intrinsic weakness of Renamo already discussed – gave the UN an authority it never enjoyed in Angola. It could, as result, flatly reject pressure to allow military demobilization and the electoral process in Mozambique to be knocked out of alignment with each other as they had been in Angola, where this had facilitated UNITA's return to war. Renamo was in general more vulnerable to outside pressure, which the secretary-general and Security Council could, when required, mobilize on their own behalf. The pressure applied by the leaders of South Africa and Zimbabwe as well as the governments of the CSC countries at the time of Dhlakama's abortive attempt to sabotage the elections was just the most dramatic example of this. Other less formal actors exerted influence at this time too, including the Catholic church and the British multinational company Lonhro which had extensive interests in the southern African region. Much more than UNITA, Renamo sought to avoid giving offence to powerful players, whatever their identity.

The enthusiasm and commitment of the secretary-general's representative, Aldo Ajello – and the parties' perceptions of his character and his role – were also factors in the success of the operation. In Angola the special representative during the failed attempt to implement the Bicesse agreement was the British international civil servant Margaret Anstee. While energetic and utterly competent, as a woman required to operate in the profoundly masculine world of African politics and warfare Anstee began formidably handicapped. Loud revolutionary rhetoric about women's equality was offered by both sides in Angola, particularly the nominally Marxist MPLA, but it had little real substance. Similarly, Anstee's replacement by an African, Blondin Beye, was welcomed in principle as an appropriate appointment to an African crisis. In reality, though, the fact that he had been an active African politician meant that inevitably he was seen to bring his own political baggage (that of Francophone Mali) to the Angolan conflict. Ajello, as a European, was self-evidently free of any such association.

Ultimately, though, it was the character of the Mozambique situation itself rather than the United Nations response to it that was of primary importance. It was a conflict that was by its nature resolvable at the particular point at which external intervention took place. That intervention ended formally in January 1995 with the withdrawal of the last ONUMOZ personnel. Its total cost, excluding humanitarian aid, had been approximately US$500 million. In the broad context on UN peacekeeping in Africa it had been money well spent.

CHAPTER FOUR

Controlling the Warlords
West Africa

Since 1993 three United Nations operations have been mounted in two neighbouring countries of west Africa – Liberia and Sierra Leone. The two conflicts, although distinctive in their local origins, afflicted states that had certain historical and sociological similarities. The lines of political division were drawn in both countries between cosmopolitan coastal 'elites' and more traditionally organized tribal societies in the interior. Although this cleavage (more marked in Liberia than in Sierra Leone) did not map precisely on to the tangled conflicts of the 1990s that brought UN intervention, they were central facets of political cultures that had a propensity to division between competing patrimonial poles. Beyond the parallels between the civil conflicts in Liberia and Sierra Leone, each to some extent fed the other. Interests on each side of the common border exploited the disorder on the other side at various times in their own interests, precipitating a complex regional crisis reaching far beyond the two protagonists themselves.

United Nations involvement in each country also shared unique features. First in Liberia and then in Sierra Leone, the UN's intervention was of a limited and secondary character. Its function was to legitimize and supervise a larger 'peacekeeping' presence provided by the regional intergovernmental organization, the Economic Community of West African States (ECOWAS). In both cases, this role was neither articulated nor performed in a satisfactory manner. As a result it did not become the model for subsequent UN interventions in Africa as some had hoped. In the case of Sierra Leone, in fact, after the failure of this limited initial role the UN mounted a large-scale military operation directly under its own auspices.

The experiences of both countries raised fundamental questions about the purposes and impact of multilateral interventions in civil crises in Africa. In Liberia the effect of foreign intervention by the regional body under supposed UN supervision appeared simply to be to delay the victory of the faction that eventually proved dominant – and to extend the conflict and the misery it caused as a result. In Sierra Leone there were fewer voices questioning the advisability of intervention; the implications of leaving the country to its fate were simply horrific. The problem here was less to do with the principle of intervention than the quality and capacity of the UN force that did the intervening. No clear answers to these questions were forthcoming from west Africa.

Supervision and legitimization: Liberia, 1993–97

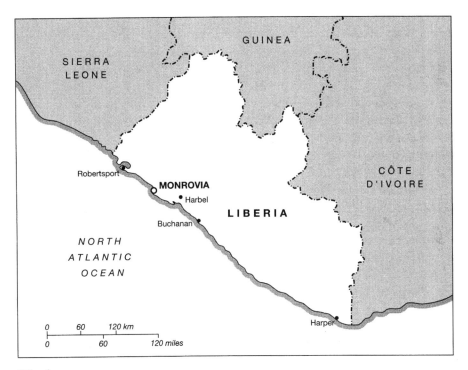

Liberia

The United Nations intervention in Liberia lasted exactly four years from September 1993 to September 1997. With a maximum strength of little over 300 military personnel in its initial phase – and considerably fewer in later stages – it was not a large presence. Nor, in the circumstances it found itself, was it a particularly consequential one. It was a significant undertaking, however, in terms both of its novel mandate and of its possible implications for future patterns of UN involvement in Africa. The mission was not a 'peacekeeping force'; it was not even a conventional military observer mission. Its primary function was to monitor – and in doing so 'legitimize' – the activities of a regional intervention force.

In August 1990 ECOWAS had established its own military operation to intervene in Liberia's civil war which had broken out at the end of the previous year. It was soon clear that the title of this operation, the ECOWAS Military Observation Group (ECOMOG), was, to say the least, a misnomer. Almost immediately on its deployment the 3000-strong west African force had itself become a faction in the civil war, and soon came to occupy a central position in the military balance in Liberia. The war, and ECOMOG's participation in it, continued for the next three years until, in July 1993, a peace agreement was signed between the main parties. It was at this point that the United Nations became involved as the west African force sought to 'reconfigure' its role from one of partisan enforcement to supervision of the peace process. The UN's function was to 'monitor the monitors' in order to build confidence among the parties to the conflict without 'de-Africanizing' the intervention. The relationship between ECOMOG and the UN mission was closely scrutinized over the following four years for any lessons it might provide about future collaborative peacekeeping operations in Africa. Ultimately, however, such indications as were discernible were ambiguous, and proved of only limited relevance beyond the particularities of Liberia itself.

The nature of the Liberian state and its destruction

Liberia is one of the most singular of all sub-Saharan African states. Never colonized in the sense usually understood in the discourse of African 'imperialism', it was an independent republic decades before the European 'scramble' got underway. In 1821 a group of freed slaves arrived from the United States to settle the coast of what would later be named Liberia. The territory became formally independent in 1847 after adopting a constitution modelled on that of the United States. It was soon recognized diplomatically by the main world powers of the period. In this way coastal Liberia at least was generally regarded as 'off-limits' when imperial competition among the European powers intensified in the 1880s and 1890s.

This self-denying ordinance on the part of the European powers did not, however, fully extend to the interior, where the writ of the new state was extremely weak. Eventually it took the diplomatic intervention of the United States in the 1890s to secure Liberia's boundaries. It would be another fifty years before the regime in the capital, Monrovia, could claim effective control of the interior. The weakness of state authority was related to a fundamental cleavage that defined Liberian politics and society up to the convulsions of the 1980s and 1990s that led eventually to United Nations involvement. Originally the new settlement had been established following an agreement between the American Colonization Society (which had been formed to resettle liberated slaves) and native chiefs. Later its 'Americo-Liberian' population would be augmented by other 'outsiders' freed from ships intercepted by anti-slavery patrols on the high seas. Between them these groups came to constitute a tightly knit 'national' elite.

From the beginning the relationship between the settlers and the indigenous peoples of the interior was fraught with difficulties. The new state was, of course, a product of the settlers who dominated its organs of government and were recognized internationally as its rulers. The Americo-Liberian elite, like other colonialists in Africa, created an exploitative relationship with the indigenous people as the 'modern' sector of the economy developed. In the 1920s the American Firestone company established a huge rubber plantation after negotiating a concession from the Monrovia government. Henceforward rubber production would be the dominant element in Liberia's economy. The country now became locked in to the global economic system on the basis initially of this monoculture (and then, from the 1950s, iron ore production). From an early stage international attention was focused on Liberia's labour practices, particularly on the rubber plantations (just as it had on those in King Léopold's Congo half a century previously). Liberia's behaviour – or more specifically that of the Americo-Liberian elite that dominated the economy – was denounced by the League of Nations in the 1930s, which concluded that the exploitation of native labour amounted to slavery. Although the scandal brought reforms (quietly encouraged by the United States), the fundamental division in Liberian society – and the resentments it nurtured – persisted. The indigenous peoples, although forming about 95 per cent of the population, remained disenfranchised and excluded from the economic benefits their labour brought to the country.

For twenty-seven years from 1944 Liberia had one president, William Tubman, who led what was effectively a one-party state. The True Whig Party provided the focus for the political, economic and even social activities of the coastal elite and was effectively coterminous with the state itself. In short, the party occupied the centre of a patrimonial network. Although voting rights were gradually extended to the population of the interior, political power remained firmly in the hands of the Americo-Liberian elite and opposition political activity was discouraged to the point of suppression. Following his death in office in 1971, Tubman was succeeded by his long-time vice-president, William Tolbert. Under Tolbert efforts to develop the interior and integrate its people into national political life gained some pace. But his period in power was beset by the economic consequences of the oil crises of the 1970s. The relative prosperity of the Tubman years now gave way to mounting economic difficulties and consequent social and political tensions as the distributable assets of the patrimonial state dwindled. Finally, in April 1980, a coup led by an army sergeant, Samuel Doe, overthrew the regime. In the violent upheaval surrounding the coup Tolbert and several of his ministers were executed.

Doe, a member of the Krahn tribe, was Liberia's first non-Americo-Liberian leader. Now, at the head of a so-called People's Redemption Council, he suspended the constitution and assumed dictatorial powers. Early expectations on the part of the indigenous majority of a rapid improvement in their condition were not, however, fulfilled. Incompetent, capricious and corrupt, Doe did nothing to reverse the economic and social problems from which his coup had sprung. He made enemies of a large part of the indigenous population as well as the Americo-Liberians by the blatant favour he showed for his own Krahns at the expense of other ethnic groups. His behaviour led to the ending of the American aid on which Liberia had become increasingly dependent in the 1980s, and this, along with his regime's comprehensive mismanagement of the national economy, further reduced the resources for the patrimonialism on which Liberian government had traditionally been based. Doe's response was to pursue personal survival by increasing repression. The result was civil war. In December 1989 a rebel force invaded the north-east of the country from Côte d'Ivoire. This group, the National Patriotic Front of Liberia (NPFL), was led by Charles Taylor. Returning to Liberia after being educated in the United States, Taylor had initially been prominent in the Doe regime before being dismissed in 1984 for embezzlement. Although Taylor was himself an Americo-Liberian, the brutality of Doe's Armed Forces of Liberia (AFL) towards supporters of his rebellion, actual or suspected, guaranteed him the support of a wide swathe of disaffected indigenous Liberians, particularly from the Gio and Mano tribes. The NPFL incursion marked the beginning of eight years of civil war in which some 200,000 people would die and which would create refugees of almost half of the country's 2.5 million population.

From the beginning the balance of forces and interests in Liberia went beyond the country itself. The conflict was touched by a number of regional diplomatic crosscurrents that would complicate future international involvement. However unpopular with just about every faction in Liberia, Doe had nurtured something of a special relationship with the west African regional hegemon, Nigeria. For his part, Taylor had the tacit support of both Côte d'Ivoire and Burkina Faso. The rulers of both of these countries had maintained close personal and political relations with the Tolbert regime and therefore fiercely opposed Doe's coup and were outraged at his brutality

towards those he had overthrown. This regional division mapped on to a
deeper Anglophone–Francophone competition in west Africa. In this way
ECOWAS, and by extension ECOMOG, became the arena for wider international rivalries.

The ECOMOG intervention

Despite – or perhaps because of – the fairly high diplomatic stakes involved
in the conflict, regional attempts to broker a peace agreement in the civil war
began almost immediately. The ECOWAS heads of state quickly established
a Standing Mediation Committee (SMC) to provide good offices.[1] But the
situation continued to deteriorate, with a proliferation of armed factions
beginning to swarm over the corpse of the Liberian state. The NPFL itself
split when one of Taylor's lieutenants, Prince Yormie Johnson, broke away
to form a rival 'independent' faction (the INPFL). In August 1990, with the
war now having reached Monrovia and with no apparent prospect of a settlement in sight, ECOMOG was deployed. Controversially, this west African
force (and in reality it was a 'force') was composed almost entirely of troops
from Anglophone states. By far the largest component was Nigerian and,
after a short initial period under a Ghanaian general, Nigeria provided all
subsequent force commanders.[2] On the political plane, the impossibility of a
negotiated settlement between Taylor and Doe was acknowledged with the
creation – effectively by ECOMOG – of an Interim Government of National
Unity (IGNU) under the presidency of the 'neutral' Dr Amos Sawyer. Samuel
Doe, out of office and now largely irrelevant to the course of events, met a
grisly end at the hands of Johnson's INPFL which captured him during
fighting in Monrovia despite supposed ECOMOG protection.[3]

By the end of 1990 the west African troops had established reasonable
control over the capital. Now a series of agreements was reached between
the NPFL, the INPFL and the AFL, which had mutated from the national

---

1 The sixteen members of ECOWAS consist of five Anglophones: Gambia, Ghana, Liberia,
Nigeria and Sierra Leone; eight Francophones: Benin, Burkina Faso, Guinea, Côte d'Ivoire,
Mali, Niger, Senegal and Togo; and two Portuguese-speaking states: Cape Verde and
Guinea-Bissau. The other member, Mauritania, is officially Arab-speaking but within the
Francophone orbit.

2 Guinea was the only Francophone contributor. Mali and Togo – the Francophone
members of the SMC – had originally agreed to participate but then withdrew their offers.
Eric G. Berman and Katie E. Sams, *Peacekeeping in Africa: Capabilities and Culpabilities* (Geneva:
United Nations Institute for Disarmament Research, 2000), p. 89.

3 A graphic account of conditions in Liberia at this time is provided by Lynda Schuster,
a journalist married to an American diplomat in Monrovia, in 'The final days of Dr Doe',
Granta 48 (Harmondsworth: Penguin, 1994), pp. 41–95.

army into another contending faction. The IGNU under Sawyer was now reinvigorated with the tacit support of these main factions. A UN estimate at this time put the number of dead in the conflict thus far at 150,000, with about half a million people displaced by the fighting. But a sustainable peace was still a distant prospect. The peace process failed to make headway during 1991. In key respects, indeed, it slipped backwards. The conflict in the interior, at Taylor's initiative, spread across Liberia's northern border into the diamond mining region of Sierra Leone. Control of diamond production and trade provided him with the resources needed to continue his pursuit of total victory. In the now-destabilized border region, however, a new faction, the United Liberation Movement of Liberia (ULIMO), emerged from among former AFL and tribal allies of the late Samuel Doe and began to attack NPFL forces. Taylor now found himself in a paradoxical position. Although he led what was probably the most powerful of the Liberian factions in military terms, his prospects of using this strength to capture the state as a whole were frustrated by the presence of a foreign 'peacekeeping' force determined to maintain its grip on the balance of power. In this way ECOMOG became the natural 'enemy' of the strongest faction.

This dynamic became evident in October 1992 when Taylor's NPFL launched a major attack – 'operation Octopus' – on ECOMOG positions in Monrovia from its base at the Firestone rubber plantation at Harbel. The objective was nothing less than the capture of the capital, which was designed to lead on to the expulsion of the regional force and the establishment of a 'national' government. Taylor came very close to success in this when ECOMOG, taken by surprise, initially showed signs of collapse. Hastily reinforced, however, it managed to drive back the NPFL forces. But if the failure of Taylor's plan was a testament to the west Africans' fighting capacity, it was simultaneously the end of any residual claim they had to be performing a 'peacekeeping' role. Moreover, Operation Octopus had been defeated by the (often indiscriminate) use of heavy weaponry in a conventional battle by ECOMOG. This contributed to an existing unease in Liberia and beyond at the conduct of the regional force and increasing questions as to whether the moral plane it occupied was really so much higher than the Liberian factions it confronted.

This crisis of credibility for the regional intervention was particularly damaging because, paradoxically, the setback suffered by the NPFL at the hands of ECOMOG had helped drive on the peace process. Taylor had been forced to accept that, despite controlling about two-thirds of the country, he could not win outright control of the state by force of arms. Consequently, in July 1993 an agreement was signed between Taylor, ULIMO and Amos Sawyer's interim government in Cotonou, the capital of Benin. The United Nations, while not taking a primary role in the Cotonou negotiations, had an important preparatory input. The Security Council's initial position on the Liberian crisis had been implicit support for the regional management of the crisis through ECOWAS/ECOMOG. In 1992, however, it had drawn closer to the issue when it imposed an arms embargo on all parties to the conflict except ECOMOG.[4] At this time secretary-general Boutros-Ghali had appointed a special representative, Trevor Gordon-Somers from Jamaica, who began a series of separate talks with the main factions. This led on to a co-operative effort with the OAU to bring the parties together in Geneva, which in turn cleared the ground for the talks in Benin.

The Cotonou agreement was supposed to initiate a process beginning with a cease-fire followed by demobilization of fighters and, eventually, national elections. Central to its management was the presence of a widely accepted international mission to monitor implementation. An attempt was now made to bridge ECOMOG's growing credibility gap in the crisis. This had two aspects. Firstly, the OAU arranged for the participation of a non-ECOWAS element in the operation in the form of troops from Tanzania and Uganda. Secondly, the imprimatur of the United Nations was sought as a means of underpinning the west African role. The creation of a United Nations monitoring mission was prefigured in the Cotonou agreement itself, and the likelihood of Security Council approval of such an enterprise had probably been signalled at the preliminary talks in Geneva. But while precise functions were assigned to the UN mission, there was no clarification of its underlying purpose. The United Nations Observer Mission in Liberia (UNOMIL), as it was to be called, was to monitor and verify the creation of buffer zones along Liberia's borders to deter the movement of fighters. But the zones themselves would evidently be established and managed by ECOMOG. The west African force was also to be responsible for monitoring and supervising all points of entry to the country. But the UN in turn would 'monitor, verify and report on the implementation' of these activities.[5] Similarly, the belligerent parties were to 'disarm to and under the supervision of ECOMOG, monitored and verified by the United Nations Observer Mission'.[6]

The imprecision of the UN's proposed role and how it was to interlock with that of what the Cotonou agreement styled the 'ECOMOG Peace-Keeping Force' created hostages to fortune that, in the relief at the achievement of any kind of agreement in mid-1993, were readily enough handed over. It was probable that the participation of the UN in the implementation

---

4   UN document S/RES/788, 19 November 1992.
5   Cotonou Agreement, Section C, paragraphs 3–4. Issued as United Nations document S/26372, 9 August 1993.
6   Cotonou Agreement, Section E, paragraph 1.

process had been the minimum essential price for the NPFL's acceptance of the Cotonou agreement, given the state of its relations with ECOMOG. It was not feasible to expect the NPFL to disarm to what had latterly been its enemy on the battlefield. The verification of the process by the UN, it was judged, took just sufficient edge off the sensitivity of the process to give it a chance of success.

Apparently undeterred by the unresolved issues around the mission's mandate, the Security Council gave final authorization to the establishment of UNOMIL in September 1993, two months after the Cotonou agreement, with an authorized strength of just over 300.[7] Over its four years' duration the operation involved military observers from twenty-two states (of which three – Congo, Guinea-Bissau and Kenya – were themselves sub-Saharan Africans). The UN had now embarked on its first military mission in co-operation with one already established by a regional organization. Although this new structure of intervention emerged as no more than a by-product of arrangements specific to the Liberian situation, it soon attracted the attention of military and political analysts of peacekeeping as a potential new model for UN intervention. By assuming a monitoring and legitimizing role, 'UN' peacekeeping, it seemed, could be freed from the major constraints of finance and availability of personnel that had been growing in pace with the growing post-cold war demand for multilateral intervention. Ideally, it would also provide a boost to the basic concept of regionalism and in that way help prevent the emergence of local conflicts before global intervention was required.

UNOMIL, therefore, carried considerable expectations as it was deployed in September and October 1993. However, as it reached its full authorized strength at the beginning of 1994, the Cotonou agreement began to unravel. The deteriorating security situation threw the uncertainty of the UNOMIL– ECOMOG relationship into sharp relief. ECOMOG, as the 'operational force' in the arrangement, was able to set the agenda. It did so with a distinct lack of diplomatic finesse. The UN observers were entirely dependent on the west Africans for their personal security and that of their mission as a whole. UNOMIL vehicles were subject to humiliating stop-and-search tactics at ECOMOG checkpoints, and UN personnel were required to obey night-time curfews imposed by the regional force. The low-level hostility underlying these terms of exchange derived in part from west African resentment at the assumption that 'supervision' was required. In part too it came from a perception that the UN was naïve and insufficiently 'robust' in dealing with

---

7   UN document S/RES/866, 22 September 1993. The despatch of an advance party of military observers had been authorized by the Security Council the previous month (by S/RES/856, 10 August 1993).

the armed factions, particularly the NPFL.[8] At the political level the precise prerogatives of Gordon-Somers, the secretary-general's special representative, were not set out in any inter-agency agreement. Given the balance of military capacity, however, the initiative lay with the (usually Nigerian) commander of ECOMOG. Inevitably, the prestige of the UN presence as a whole in Liberia suffered from this. Local suspicions grew about the intentions of ECOMOG and there was mounting dismay at its behaviour on the ground.[9] The apparent powerlessness of UNOMIL to do anything about these issues did nothing for its standing in an environment in which the standard currency was physical force. This generally low opinion of UNOMIL was, crucially, shared by the armed factions in the conflict. Whether these favoured or opposed the west African presence, they tended to regard ECOMOG as the only significant external actor. It soon became clear that UNOMIL was simply not configured to carry out the fundamental role assigned to it at Cotonou of supervisor and arbiter of ECOMOG strategy, tactics and behaviour.

The vulnerability of UNOMIL and the tight limits of its effectiveness were harshly illustrated in September 1994 when more than forty UN observers were captured, abused and had their transport and equipment expropriated by elements of Taylor's NPFL in a number of locations in the north and east of the country. Reliance on ECOMOG protection was weakness enough, but when this was not forthcoming UNOMIL was effectively redundant. Soon the UN observers began to be withdrawn from areas of risk until they were concentrated just in Monrovia. Henceforward, the UN's role, both on the ground and in the broader search for a sustainable peace, was extremely limited. For better or worse, the crisis was now left largely to regional attention, while the wider international system stood further and further back from it. The United States, which had been reasonably generous in funding the peace process, gradually disengaged itself, citing concerns over ECOMOG's political and military behaviour but in reality probably motivated by its general post-Somalia, post-Rwanda *Weltschmerz*.

The western powers, including the United States, did, however, work to encourage a rapprochement between Taylor's NPFL and the Nigerian government. Overcoming the hostility between these two – respectively the strongest Liberian faction and the dominant regional state – would be the key to the eventual resolution of the civil war. By August 1995 relations

---

8 Christopher Tuck, ' "Every car or moving object gone": the ECOMOG intervention in Liberia', *African Studies Quarterly* 4(1), February 2000. Found at http://web.africa.ufl.edu/asq/v4/v4:1a1.htm.

9 The expression 'every car or moving object gone' was popular among sceptics in Monrovia as an alternative meaning for the acronym 'ECOMOG'. See Gerry Cleaver, 'Liberia: lessons for the future from the experience of ECOMOG', in Oliver Furley and Roy May (eds), *Peacekeeping in Africa* (Aldershot: Ashgate, 1998), p. 232.

had improved to the extent that a new peace plan could be agreed. The ECOWAS heads of state and the Liberian factions met in the Nigerian capital, Abuja. The Abuja accord supposedly augmented the 1993 Cotonou agreement, but in reality it supplanted it. A new cease-fire was agreed and a widely based Council of State was formed under the figurehead of the Liberian writer Wilton Sankawulo. It was the collective vice-chairmanship of the Council that was significant, however. This consisted of Taylor along with two of his most significant rivals. Alhaji Kromah, of the Moslem Mandingo tribe led a faction of the now divided ULIMO. George Boley, a Krahn, was leader of the (startlingly misnamed) Liberian Peace Council, which was made up of elements of the old AFL and other smaller militia and ethnic groups hostile to Taylor.[10] The leaders of other groupings were assigned individual ministries.

The very effectiveness of the new arrangement precipitated a certain degree of violence, however, as the protagonists began to realize that the civil war was moving towards its endgame. Violations of the cease-fire were frequent. The Security Council responded to the new situation by adjusting the mandate of UNOMIL to add the provision of good offices between hostile factions to its responsibilities. Simultaneously, though, its maximum authorized strength was reduced to 160, an acknowledgement of the UN's dwindling military role.[11] In reality, UNOMIL's strength would not approach even this modest maximum during the remaining term of its deployment. In the first months of 1996 Monrovia was beset with factional violence as groups that felt themselves marginalized by the Abuja process sought desperately to make their presence felt before it was too late. In April alone some 1500 people were killed in the capital. At this time the United States evacuated the majority of foreign nationals from the country – including eighty-eight of UNOMIL's total force at the time of ninety-three. For several months thereafter UNOMIL personnel in Liberia could be counted in single figures.[12]

In the wake of this round of fighting the United States resumed a more activist diplomatic role, establishing an International Contact Group for Liberia (ICGL). Subsequently the ECOWAS governments and the ICGL brought the factions back to Abuja, where the peace process was reinvigorated and commitments entered into for elections during 1997. Following this new affirmation ECOMOG resources were increased and, with a general if weary acceptance now prevalent among the factions that the end of the conflict was in sight, the process of disarmament and demobilization of

---

10 Kromah led the Mandingo-dominated ULIMO-K group, while UNLIMO-J was led by 'General' Roosevelt Johnston, a Krahn.
11 UN document S/RES/1020, 10 November 1995.
12 Berman and Sams, *Peacekeeping in Africa*, p. 103.

fighters finally made progress. Between November 1996 and February 1997 the west Africans disarmed and demobilized – on a largely voluntary basis – 23,000 of the 35,000 fighters estimated to make up the Liberian factions. The role of a drastically reduced UNOMIL in this process was minimal.

In the elections of July 1997 Charles Taylor was the decisive victor, a reflection of his faction's control of an overwhelming proportion of the country outside of the capital.[13] Taking this apparent political settlement as a reasonable cue, the Security Council withdrew UNOMIL two months later. While it was questionable whether the translation of a warlord from guerrilla leader to head of state represented a genuine and sustainable achievement for peace and democracy in Liberia, it was sufficient to allow the UN to disengage itself from a less than exemplary intervention. Sure enough, interfactional tensions remained high. Taylor's commitment to reconstruction, reconciliation and development, as opposed to the imposition of yet another system of patrimony in pursuit of personal enrichment, remained highly questionable. While peace of a sort descended on war-weary Liberia, Taylor's regime was subsequently active, for his own acquisitive reasons, in the destabilization of neighbouring Sierra Leone, as we shall shortly see.

Taylor had led the dominant military faction throughout the civil war in Liberia from the time of his first incursion at the end of 1989. Only the intervention of ECOMOG had denied him an early victory. It is a reasonable question therefore whether the west African intervention and the UN one that it brought in its wake were ultimately justified in the sum of the experience of Liberia's afflicted people. It would certainly seem that external intervention merely delayed the inevitable, costing the lives of countless thousands on the way. This is, of course, one of the largest and most difficult questions over external military intervention in general, however well intentioned it may be in conception. Easier answers are available to the more specific questions about the nature of the UN intervention in the 'pioneering' form it took in Liberia. It was not a success and did not provide any viable model for future practice. As we have seen, the failure to set down precise terms at Cotonou or immediately after for the relationship between the 'supervisory' UNOMIL and the 'executive' ECOMOG was in many ways fatal. It allowed the organization with the larger physical presence and the greater local intelligence to become dominant. Along with this, points of friction between the organizations at all levels – from political direction to local command right down to personnel on the ground – created an undercurrent of mistrust and mutual disrespect. There was, in short, no basis on which the

---

13 Taylor's party won some 75 per cent of the popular vote in what international observers agreed were generally fair and free elections. Cleaver, 'Liberia: lessons for the future', p. 235.

UN could carry out its task of supposedly masterful oversight. In consequence, the UN's prestige was considerably eroded in Liberia itself and throughout the west African region at a time, post-Somalia and post-Rwanda, when it could least afford it. Nor did the prospects for the new departure in peace-keeping promised by United Nations supervision and monitoring of local forces have a particularly auspicious introduction in Liberia. Local failure or not, though, the approach remained attractive to an increasingly pressured peacekeeping machinery in New York. Its next African application was to follow quickly on that in Liberia, just across the border in Sierra Leone.

The slippery slope: Sierra Leone, 1998–

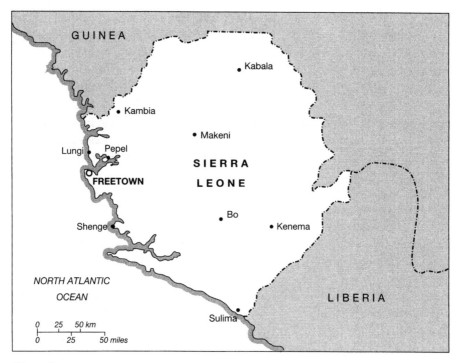

Sierra Leone

Sierra Leone experienced many of the same difficulties as its southern neigh-bour during the 1980s and 1990s. Like Liberia it was destabilized by military coups and it shared the chaotic political consequences. Among these were brutal civil wars in each country that led to intervention by regional peacekeepers and the involvement of the United Nations in a 'supervisory' capacity. In Sierra Leone as in Liberia the intention was that substantive peacekeeping would be undertaken under the auspices of the regional body, ECOWAS, through its 'military observer group', ECOMOG. The UN's role was supposed to be limited to monitoring (and, at the political level, legitimizing) these operations.

This common experience of Liberia and Sierra Leone was not entirely accidental. Although a number of points of similarity were merely fortuitous, there was also interconnection. In the early 1990s these causal elements came from a spilling over of Liberia's security problems into Sierra Leone. There, these imported difficulties encouraged and exacerbated internally generated violence. But while, as we have seen, Liberia eventually found a form of salvation through the 'political' victory of its strongest faction, Taylor's NPFL, no such resolution was available to Sierra Leone where the challenge to the political process proved stronger than the forces of democracy. There was, in other words, no 'warlord' leader in the Taylor mould in Sierra Leone capable of bending the process to his advantage. On the contrary, as the new century began, Sierra Leone's crisis continued, still complicated by the ruinous intervention of its neighbour to the south in pursuit of the relatively easy riches available as a consequence of the collapse of the state.

United Nations involvement in Sierra Leone passed through two distinct phases, the second and more substantial of which began in 1999 with the deployment of a large force mandated to oversee an internal peace agreement. Initially, though, the main 'peacekeeping' initiative lay with ECOMOG, as it had in Liberia, and within it the UN had only a minimal role.

The setting

Beyond the shared characteristics of their respective crises in the 1990s, Sierra Leone and Liberia had a number of historical features in common as well. Although first named by the Portuguese, who had landed in the region in the fifteenth century, Sierra Leone, like its neighbour, could be described as an artefact of the slave trade. Liberia, it will be recalled, had been 'founded' as an African home for freed slaves from the United States. Sierra Leone – specifically the area around its capital, Freetown – was used by Britain as a landing point for freed slaves and those rescued by the Royal Navy patrols after the outlawing of the slave trade. It was designated a crown colony in 1808 and later in the nineteenth century became a component part of Britain's west African empire. Although a lesser jewel in this particular imperial crown in terms of size and population than, for example, Nigeria, Sierra Leone was nevertheless one of the most prosperous and stable colonies in the region. Its wealth was based on bauxite and diamonds, and later the strategic material titanium dioxide (rutile).

The transition to independence in Sierra Leone was remarkably smooth. It flowed from the 'constitutional' nationalist political activity of the 1950s, which had been encouraged and nurtured by the colonial state itself. Independence came in 1961, with the government of the new state led by the veteran nationalist leader, Sir Milton Margai. In many ways typical of the first generation of post-colonial leaders in former British Africa, Margai was seen, depending on the perspective of the observer, as a moderate and cautious politician or as blinkered and constrained by his background in the 'permissible' nationalist politics of the colonial state. At all events, he enjoyed considerable domestic popularity and international respect. His brother, Albert, who succeeded him in 1964, did not. Influenced by the rapidly developing trends in other African states at the time, Albert attempted to place his Sierra Leone People's Party (SLPP) at the centre of a one-party state. The neo-patrimonial nature of this strategy was indicated by the SLPP's distinct ethnic base among the Mende of southern Sierra Leone. Typically, Albert Margai's manoeuvre resulted in the creation of a countervailing regional movement in the north, the All-People's Congress (APC), led by Siaka Stevens, which sought to capture the resources of the state for its own ethnic 'clients'. This the APC appeared to do when in 1968 Stevens came to power after the long period of political uncertainty and instability under Albert Margai. Stevens remained in office for a remarkable seventeen years, but the longevity of his rule was not a reflection of its virtue. Increasingly corrupt and incompetent, his regime squandered the resources of the nation, both material and human. To assist this process, a new constitution was confected by Stevens, which in 1978 turned Sierra Leone formally into a one-party state under the control of his APC.

In 1985 Stevens left office, apparently voluntarily, to be replaced by the army commander Joseph Momoh. Little changed internally in Sierra Leone's fortunes under Momoh who himself now led the APC. Described in one commentary as 'a well-meaning, drunken womaniser with few political skills or leadership qualities', he was not the man to reinvigorate Sierra Leone after the stale years of the Stevens regime.[14] And, critically, events in the broader region were soon beginning to impact on the country. As we have seen, in 1991 Charles Taylor's military campaign to control Liberia was deliberately extended across the border into the southern part of Sierra Leone. His objective in this was control of the region's diamond resources, which he sought to finance his rebellion. This irruption would have shaken even the most stable and cohesive of African states; for one as insecure and

---

14 *Africa Confidential*, Special Reports, 'Chronology of Sierra Leone: how diamonds fuelled the conflict'. Found at http://www.africa-confidential.com/special.htm.

fractious as Sierra Leone it proved devastating. The Sierra Leone Army (SLA) had some initial success in containing the incursions and pushing the Liberians back across the border but it proved ultimately inadequate.

Amidst this chaos a new and profoundly destructive force appeared in Sierra Leone politics. The so-called Revolutionary United Front (RUF) led by a former army corporal, Foday Sankoh, emerged to challenge Momoh's government. The precise political colour of the RUF and the nature of its support base remained obscure. Its populist revolutionary rhetoric was not supported by any comprehensible political programme. It appeared to represent (and seemed to be largely manned by) the large and disaffected population of over- and under-educated youth that had grown up during the stagnant years of the Stevens regime. These young men could find no obvious place in Sierra Leone's economy and society in the early 1990s and were vulnerable to the heady mixture of revolutionary slogans and violence associated with the RUF. At the same time, the RUF made a claim to represent the people of the rural interior against the coastal urban 'elite', which it claimed had dominated national politics in its own interests since independence. The brutal tactics of the RUF did not point to a genuine popular movement, however. Seizing and ruling its territory through apparently arbitrary intimidation and violence, the RUF soon became a paradigm of Africa's new, almost 'apolitical' terrorism.[15]

While far from a disciplined force, the RUF was sufficiently effective to hold down the national army. Badly trained, paid, equipped and led, the SLA was deeply demoralized and soon showed an alarming proclivity for fraternization and even co-operation with the supposed enemy. Soon the term 'sobel' (soldier/rebel) was coined to describe SLA troops who were happy to kill, maim and loot either independently or along with the RUF as the mood took them. In this dire scenario, in April 1992, a group of junior officers confronted the ineffectual Momoh. Interpreting their representations over the state of the army as an attempted coup, the president fled. Power now passed to the twenty-six-year-old Captain Valentine Strasser. The new president initially drew (and revelled in) comparisons with the charismatic Flight Lieutenant Jerry Rawlings, who had seized and then effectively exploited power in neighbouring Ghana in 1981. There were now some battlefield successes for the momentarily reinvigorated SLA. By the end of 1992, in

---

15 For a detailed and comprehensive exploration of the RUF see Ibrahim Abdullah and Patrick Muana, 'The Revolutionary United Front of Sierra Leone: a revolt of the lumpenproletariat', in Christopher Clapham (ed.), *African Guerrillas* (Oxford: James Currey, 1998), pp. 173–93. See also Ibrahim Abdullah, 'Bush path to destruction: the origin and character of the Revolutionary United Front/Sierra Leone', *Journal of Modern African Studies* 36(2), 1998, pp. 203–35.

fact, the RUF appeared to have been pushed across the border into Liberia again to seek refuge with its sponsors. But early in the following year they were back.

The reappearance of the RUF in Sierra Leone was, unsurprisingly, connected with events in Liberia. Charles Taylor now had a further motive in supporting the RUF in addition to the access this had given him to Sierra Leone's diamonds. As we have already described it, the main obstacle to his control of Liberia was the Nigerian-dominated ECOMOG 'peacekeeping' force deployed there. By orchestrating Sierra Leone's collapse into chaos Taylor sought, successfully, to ease Nigerian/ECOMOG pressure on his own forces. During 1993 two ECOMOG battalions and a considerable proportion of its air power were transferred to Sierra Leone to support the SLA. Eventually, ECOMOG's role expanded far beyond that of mere backing for Sierra Leone's own increasingly feeble national forces. The SLA had been hugely increased in strength under Strasser (from about 5000 to 15,000) but the new recruits were often little more than children and were barely trained and poorly equipped. Soon, almost by default, ECOMOG had assumed the effective leadership of the anti-RUF campaign.

The war dragged on over the following years with mounting brutality but no clear destination. For a time in the first half of 1995 it looked as if the RUF might actually take control of Freetown. It was prevented from doing so almost exclusively by foreign forces. In addition to the 2000-strong ECOMOG contingent of Nigerians and Ghanaians there was also, by this time, another military player. In March 1995, with the RUF at the edge of the capital, the increasingly desperate Strasser had bought in a mercenary force from the South African 'security' company, Executive Outcomes (EO). The ECOMOG–EO 'double-act' seized the military initiative, pushing the rebels back from Freetown and pursuing them into the interior, seizing their economic resources as they did so. In the case of EO at least, the capture of mineral production centres and the 'business opportunities' that ensued were evidently part of the deal with the Sierra Leone state.[16] By the beginning of 1996 Foday Sankoh was forced to negotiate with the government in Freetown while, simultaneously, outside pressure (notably from Britain) was applied for national elections.[17] Thirteen parties fought these elections in February 1996 with none achieving sufficient support for an outright win in the first

---

16 See Abiodun Alao, 'Sierra Leone: tracing the genesis of a controversy', Royal Institute of International Affairs Briefing No. 50, June 1998. Found at http://www.riia.org/briefingpapers/bp50.html.

17 Strasser was ousted from power in a palace coup among the military in the run-up to the elections. His successor, Brigadier Julius Maada-Bio, evidently had some thoughts of postponing the elections in the customary manner of those who make military coups, but these were quickly abandoned in the face of implacable national and international pressure.

round. The second round in mid-March saw Ahmad Tejan Kabbah of the southern-based SLPP (originally the Margai brothers' party) elected president.

From the beginning it was far from clear whether Kabbah, a low-profile former United Nations bureaucrat, had the determination and the leadership qualities necessary to rebuild the country. At the head of a party historically regarded as regionally based, his 'national' appeal was limited. This problem was aggravated by his enthusiasm for the Kamajor militia. This had been formed from among traditional Mende hunters from the southern part of the country where the SLPP had its power base. The Kamajor had fought ferociously and effectively alongside ECOMOG and EO against the RUF. Kabbah was now suspected of grooming them as a kind of praetorian guard to counter-balance a still unreliable SLA. The army itself was now effectively divided between pro- and anti-presidential factions, the latter of which seemed to be moving ever closer to the rebels.

In November 1996 an agreement was reached between the government and the now debilitated RUF at Abidjan in Côte d'Ivoire. By this, a multiparty government was to be formed with RUF participation. Fatally, as it would turn out, part of the arrangement insisted upon by the RUF involved the withdrawal of Executive Outcomes. Had Kabbah moved ahead decisively and driven on the formation of the new administration there may have been some prospect of a longer-term settlement. But delay and vacillation – and the unexpected detention of Foday in Nigeria while on a visit there in February 1997 – saw the Abidjan agreement run into the sands. The UN, the OAU and the Commonwealth – which had pronounced themselves joint 'moral guarantors' of the agreement when it was signed – expended little energy to sustain it.

At the end of May 1997, amidst this political drift, Kabbah was overthrown in a coup mounted by an army major, Johnny Paul Koroma, and fled to Guinea. Koroma cut an even poorer figure as a coup leader than Strasser had five years previously. However, his SLA faction, invigorated by the prospect of plunder, proved a match for the Nigerians who continued to back the elected government. ECOMOG was forced out of Freetown while Executive Outcomes had already left the country under the terms of the now-irrelevant Abidjan agreement. Almost immediately, the unpredictable Koroma announced his affinity with the 'ideology' of the RUF, invited them to join him in 'government' and inaugurated a reign of chaos and terror in the parts of the country over which he could claim control.

UN involvement

The Security Council had first become involved in the Sierra Leone crisis in November 1994 at the time when the Strasser regime was under pressure from the RUF as it advanced towards Freetown. The then secretary-general, Boutros Boutros-Ghali, appointed a special envoy to work with the parties with a view to a negotiated settlement. As we have seen, this was overtaken by events, and the immediate crisis was resolved by military action mainly by ECOMOG and Executive Outcomes. The UN did have a background role in the Abidjan process in November 1996, but this was restricted essentially to a watching brief. Its next major intervention came with a Security Council oil and arms embargo in October 1997.[18] These measures were not effective among the permeable borders and easily negotiable natural resources of the region, however, and the embargo was widely breached.

More successful than any embargo was the continuing military campaign against the junta and its RUF allies from three separate but frequently interdependent directions. The Nigerian-led west African force remained in the north of the country and proved increasingly effective against the catastrophically disorganized and undisciplined SLA and RUF troops. In the meantime, the Kamajor militia had become a formidable fighting force in the interior. Finally, from exile in Guinea, Kabbah had entered into an agreement with a group of businessmen to re-engage mercenary forces against the junta. The pay-off for this would be access to Sierra Leone's diamond fields after they had been wrested from the RUF. The mercenaries were supplied this time by Sandline, a London-based sister company of Executive Outcomes.[19] During the first months of 1998 this combined effort succeeded in driving Koroma's junta out of power and dispersing its forces. In March, Kabbah returned to office in Freetown. But it was soon evident that his grip on power was no stronger than it had been on the eve of the Koroma coup.

One considerable asset Kabbah did command was broad support from an international community sickened by the excesses of the Koroma–RUF regime, and keen to back an electorally validated alternative. Reflecting this, the Security Council moved to shore up Kabbah's position. In the short term it was urgent that his continued dependence on the Nigerian-dominated ECOMOG force should be given some broader legitimization. To this end – encouraged by Boutros-Ghali's successor as secretary-general, Kofi Annan, who was himself west African – the Security Council followed the model it had first constructed for Liberia. It established an observer mission to 'shadow' ECOMOG's operations. In July 1998 the United Nations Observer Mission in Sierra Leone (UNOMSIL) was established. This was to consist initially of

---

18   UN document S/RES/1132, 8 October 1997.
19   The 1997 arms embargo was directed at the Koroma–RUF junta, but the resolution was drafted (probably by oversight) in such a way that the Kabbah government was also subject to its prohibition. The British government thus came under some domestic criticism when it emerged that it had been party to the Sandline arrangement.

up to seventy military observers with support staff. It was, firstly, to monitor 'the role of ECOMOG in the provision of security and in the collection and destruction of arms'. Secondly, it was to observe the west Africans' 'respect for international humanitarian law'.[20] Within six months the first of these roles would be irrelevant and the second impossible.

The relative calm in Sierra Leone in which UNOMSIL had been established – and which its presence was intended to bolster – was not to persist. While elements of Koroma's junta force did demobilize and disarm, others fled to the bush, styled themselves the Armed Forces Revolutionary Council (AFRC) and joined up with the RUF. Foday Sankoh was still detained in Nigeria, from where he made a series of contradictory pro-nouncements about the direction that the RUF should take. But the extent of his authority as well as his intentions was unclear by this stage. In October 1998 the Kabbah government, emboldened by the evident neutralization of Sankoh and the presence of ECOMOG and the UN, began a series of trials leading to the execution of captured junta soldiers and a death sentence *in absentia* on Sankoh himself. This proved to be a typical miscalculation on the inexperienced Kabbah's part. Rebel activity intensified, attaining levels that took ECOMOG and the government's forces by surprise. In December 1998 the RUF was once again on the outskirts of Freetown. Fighting in and around the capital at this time cost several thousand lives and was accom-panied by the most atrocious abuse of the civilian population by the rebel forces.[21] The rebels' onslaught was aided by their old friends in Liberia, though Charles Taylor himself claimed, unconvincingly, to be trying to stop cross-border movement.[22] By the time that the west African and Kamajor forces eventually pushed the RUF back from Freetown in January 1999, the UNOMSIL presence in the country had been reduced to a residue of a mere eight military observers. This virtual evaporation of the UN presence was strikingly similar to the situation in Liberia during the fighting there in April 1996 (see above p. 178).

The central paradox of the United Nations mission was now harshly illus-trated in Freetown as it had been earlier in Monrovia. In the intensity of battle – just where effective monitoring of ECOMOG behaviour and human rights observance was most necessary – UNOMSIL was largely useless. Only

---

20   UN document S/RES/1181, 13 July 1998.
21   Calculations of casualties varied widely in the confusion of the events. Anything between 2000 and 8000 people, mostly civilians, were killed at this time according to *Africa Confidential* 40(2), 22 January 1999. The UN later put the figure at between 3000 and 5000. Security Council press release SC/6653, 11 March 1999.
22   Report of the Secretary-General, UN document S/1999/237, 4 March 1949. Help for the RUF was also reportedly provided by Burkina Faso, an ally of the Taylor regime. BBC World Service (Africa) report, 12 January 1999.

forty of the planned seventy military observers had been deployed before the peace process disintegrated with the RUF offensive at the beginning of 1999, when even this small presence was quickly run-down. Therefore, the wide-spread abuses perpetrated by the west African troops during the fighting, later deplored by the secretary-general, were not reported by UNOMSIL; it was not present to witness them.[23] UNOMSIL's other function, it will be recalled, had been to oversee the collection and destruction of arms by ECOMOG. But this had been made irrelevant even before the fighting around Freetown. The general deterioration of the situation, which preceded this key battle, had effectively ended the process of the voluntary disarmament of forces on both sides. With its supposed peacekeeping function now made impossible, ECOMOG reverted to a battle-fighting posture. At this point it was simply unclear what UNOMSIL was supposed to be doing in Sierra Leone.

The Lomé agreement and the establishment of UNAMSIL

As well as exposing the inadequacies of the UN presence, the events of early 1999 underlined what should always have been evident: that the Kabbah government had neither the resources nor the support base necessary to assert its control of the country. Moreover, the presence of the ECOMOG intervention force, while tipping the balance in the government's favour on a crisis-by-crisis basis, could provide no remedy to the continuing chaos. The response of the United Nations to this reality – along with individual countries of influence like Britain and the United States – was to press Kabbah into a deal with Sankoh and the RUF. On 7 July 1999 an agreement, brokered in large part by President Clinton's envoy Jesse Jackson, was signed in the Togo capital, Lomé. The proposed settlement would bring the RUF/AFRC into a new national government and this would be followed by the demobilization and disarming of the various military forces that had plagued the country over the previous years.

It was in many respects a shabby deal, but ultimately a necessary one. Neither ECOMOG nor the UN was in a position to mount the all-out enforcement action required to inflict final defeat on the RUF/AFRC. 'Peace' in the circumstances of Sierra Leone at the time, it seemed, could only come at the price of allowing the RUF into government. Even after this price had

---

23   In a report to the Security Council in January 1999, secretary-general Kofi Annan reported the arbitrary execution of suspected rebels and their supporters as well as the indiscriminate use of air power by ECOMOG. UN document S/1999/20, 7 January 1999.

been paid, it was clear that a major multilateral peacekeeping effort would be needed to produce the return. The impact of UNOMSIL on the course of events up to now had been almost wholly negligible. The short-lived and ineffectual attempt at giving UN 'legitimacy' to the regional intervention on the Liberian pattern (which itself had been largely a failure) gave way to a more familiar peacekeeping model. The Lomé agreement reversed in key respects the 'model' for such accommodations already familiar in UN interventions in Africa. In Angola and Mozambique, for example, demobilization and disarmament were supposed to precede political 'normalization'. The impossibility of this in Sierra Leone had, it seemed, been acknowledged by the brokers of the deal when the RUF's place in government was secured before demilitarization had taken place. A large-scale international presence was clearly going to be necessary if this fragile and dangerous sequence was going to be carried through. To this end the United Nations Observer Mission in Sierra Leone was now to be supplanted by the United Nations Mission in Sierra Leone (UNAMSIL).

UNAMSIL was established by the Security Council in October 1999, three months after the Lomé agreement was signed. The new force was to have a strength of 6000 infantry troops and military observers. It was mandated to co-operate with the Freetown government and the RUF (though, whether through tact or embarrassment, this was rendered in the resolution as 'other parties' to Lomé) in implementing the agreement. It was to organize the programme of disarmament, demobilization and reintegration central to Lomé and to this end establish and control cantonment centres in various parts of the country. It was also to maintain freedom of movement for UN personnel and provide security for aid distribution. ECOMOG was to remain, at least in the short term, and would continue to control the areas it held and also act as a protection force for the government. In other words, continuing 'enforcement' as opposed to 'peacekeeping' activities would remain the prerogative of the regional force. UNOMSIL would cease to exist immediately UNAMSIL was established, and its resources were to be absorbed by the new operation.[24]

The tasks confronting UNAMSIL were formidable. There were an estimated 45,000 fighters to be persuaded into cantonment and then disarmed and reintegrated into an already devastated society. There were few grounds for confidence that the political and security environment necessary for this to take place would be established. The Kabbah government did not enjoy wide support outside of Freetown and even in the capital it was perceived as weak and ineffectual. The Lomé agreement itself had a mixed impact on

---

24   UN document S/RES/1270, 22 October 1999.

Kabbah's prestige. On the one hand it was seen as at least offering a prospect of an end to the horrors of the past years. On the other, however, the legitimacy it extended to Sankoh's RUF and Koroma's AFRC was deeply offensive to people whose lives had been destroyed by their brutality. From this perspective Lomé was confirmation of Kabbah's weakness and subordination to the foreign powers that had encouraged the agreement.

The omens for the success of the process were mixed. The notoriously unpredictable Foday Sankoh and his anarchic band of rebels could not be said to offer reliable interlocutors for Kabbah or for the UN. More positively, though, the continued presence of the ECOMOG force provided a 'sharp-end' to the multilateral intervention. It at least posed some kind of deterrent to a resurgence of rebel violence which the untested UNAMSIL on its own could not. At the diplomatic level the United States and Britain, the principal powers behind the new peacekeeping venture, seemed committed to seeing the process through, rather than treating the Lomé agreement as a 'fire-and-forget' initiative. Neither power had been willing to commit significant forces to UNAMSIL beyond a handful of British military observers, however. The initial UNAMSIL force came principally from five states. Three of these – Gambia, Ghana and Nigeria – were also members of ECOWAS. Kenya supplied another African element. The fifth was India, which also provided the first force commander. However, the United States (somewhat in disregard of the restrictions laid down in PDD 25 in 1994) undertook to pay a quarter of the total costs of UNAMSIL. Britain also took on an enlarged financial commitment. And, even as the Security Council was debating the establishment of UNAMSIL, US secretary of state Madeleine Albright was in Sierra Leone emphasizing to all the major parties American determination to see a durable peace established.[25] Sierra Leone's government of national unity was formed simultaneously with the deployment of UNAMSIL in October 1999. The RUF/AFRC was given four of its twenty ministries, with Sankoh (now freed by the Nigerians) becoming vice-president as well as minister for mines. This portfolio, specifically requested by the RUF leader, gave him control of the diamond industry that had financed his terror campaign.

There were soon serious questions about whether the injuries and insults inherent in the Lomé process were producing the results that supposedly justified them. In December 1999 Annan reported to the Security Council that the previous two months had seen a deterioration in the security situation rather than the improvement that the formation of the new government and the deployment of UNAMSIL was supposed to guarantee. The

---

25 BBC World Service (Africa) report, 18 October 1999.

response to the demobilization programme had been 'very poor'. The RUF and the AFRC had, to no one's great surprise, turned against each other and were fighting out their quarrel in the interior, with the RUF emerging as the victor. More worryingly from a strictly peacekeeping perspective, the RUF was refusing to permit the deployment of UNAMSIL in its eastern heart-lands where it maintained its brutal domination. In this worrying climate, ECOMOG, the secretary-general admitted rather plaintively, continued 'to play a critical role'.[26]

The withdrawal of ECOMOG and the crisis of May 2000

Critical or not, it was a role that Nigeria – and therefore ECOWAS as a whole – was already planning to lay down. Despite repeated pleas from the secretary-general for financial support for the ECOMOG contributors, Nigeria had been left with the mounting bill for the operation, and during 1999 it had undergone a considerable domestic economic crisis. Its own return to civilian rule under President Obasanjo had entailed a series of expensive elections. There had also been a damaging fall in world oil prices that had hit Nigeria, as major producer, particularly hard.[27] Accordingly, at the end of December 1999 Kofi Annan was informed that the west African force would be withdrawn, although the large Nigerian detachment in UNAMSIL (paid for by the UN) would remain.

The impact of ECOMOG's withdrawal – which began immediately and was to be completed by the beginning of May 2000 – was considerable, both in the short and the longer term. At Annan's urging the Security Council revised UNAMSIL's mandate to allow its troops to take over the functions originally assigned to the west Africans. It also agreed to almost double the strength of UNAMSIL to 11,000.[28] In the transition period, during which ECOMOG forces withdrew from key positions around Freetown and were replaced by unfamiliarized UNAMSIL troops, there was a general heightening of tension and an increase in incidents of lawlessness and banditry as miscellaneous armed elements sought to exploit the situation. More substantially the departure of ECOMOG ended the tacitly accepted terms of the security relationship between the RUF and the intervention forces. Hitherto the former rebels had maintained a healthy respect for the robustness of the west Africans' rules of engagement and this had imposed limits on

---

26   UN document S/1999/1223, 6 December 1999.
27   *Africa Confidential* 40(8), 16 April 1999.
28   UN document S/RES/1289, 7 February 2000.

their behaviour. Now the RUF sought to probe and test the resolve of the UNAMSIL forces that had replaced ECOMOG. As initial provocations went largely unchallenged the level of RUF aggression towards (and evident contempt for) the UN force grew. UNAMSIL detachments were denied freedom of movement in rebel areas, harassed and robbed of weapons and equipment. All this took place without any real resistance from the UN, despite the force's post-ECOMOG mandate having assigned it Chapter VII enforcement powers. The morale of the force declined as its shortcomings became more and more obvious in the first half of 2000.

The provocations against UNAMSIL reached a climax at the beginning of May – coinciding exactly with the departure of the last ECOMOG detachments. Cantonment centres in RUF areas were destroyed and UNAMSIL troops attacked and abducted.[29] By the middle of the month 350 Indian, Kenyan and Zambian UN troops were being held by the RUF. In the mounting chaos it became evident that another attack on Freetown was in the offing with every prospect that it would result in the same mayhem and horror as that at the beginning of the previous year. There was no confidence locally that the demoralized and humiliated UNAMSIL forces could effectively resist such an onslaught. Only the appearance of a new, non-UN intervention force reversed the slide into anarchy when Britain accepted its responsibility as a major force behind the Lomé agreement. On 7 May a rapid reaction force of 800 paratroops and marine commandos landed in Freetown supported by a powerful naval presence off-shore. Although the ostensible task of this force was the evacuation of British nationals, it was soon clear that this was largely a pretext for a more substantial intervention. The British occupied key strategic positions around the city and the high visibility of their presence effectively deterred the RUF from moving on the capital. Then, on 17 May, Foday Sankoh (who was thought to have been out of the country during the crisis) was captured near his official government residence in Freetown, leaving the RUF without a political leader.[30]

The predicament that the hapless UN force had found itself in, and the more general failure of the organization to drive forward the peace process in Sierra Leone against RUF obstruction, had led to perhaps the greatest crisis for United Nations peacekeeping in Africa since the Rwanda genocide of 1994. Nor was the UN's position helped by the fairly rapid stabilization of

---

29 The secretary-general suggested that the anti-UN upsurge might also have been connected with the fact that UNAMSIL was then preparing to move into the RUF's diamond mining areas. UN document S/2000/455, 19 May 2000.

30 Sankoh was captured by the forces of his former supporter, Koroma's AFRC, which had allied itself with Kabbah after the Lomé agreement and the subsequent violent breach with the RUF. Somewhat against the odds, he was handed over to the custody of the government in one piece.

the crisis after the British intervention. On the contrary, the apparent ease with which a small non-UN force had been able to turn the situation round merely highlighted UNAMSIL's inadequacy.

A range of basic questions about the UN engagement with Africa as a whole were now raised. Its earlier apparent failures from Angola to Somalia to Rwanda were picked over once more. In Sierra Leone the issues were not around the adequacy of the mission's resources or mandate. UNAMSIL was a large force by peacekeeping standards and was equipped with strong Chapter VII powers. The questions here were about general processes and particular practices. Why had the United Nations failed to learn the lessons of Angola in 1991 and Rwanda in 1993 by committing itself to the implementation of a flawed peace settlement into which it had little institutional input? On more sensitive ground, how could such a large force allow itself to be humiliated by the RUF? Specifically, how were several hundred well-armed UN troops kidnapped and held prisoner with such evident ease by gangs of thugs and boy-soldiers? What did this say about the training and motivation of contemporary UN peacekeeping contingents? Was the otherwise laudable idea that predominantly African contingents should undertake African peacekeeping duties putting political priorities above operational efficiency? These were important questions, but no easy answers were available and in the event none was attempted by the UN.

To a degree they could be evaded because the crisis that had provoked them receded relatively quickly and the situation throughout the country gradually stabilized over the following year. There were a number of reasons for this, few having anything to do with UN efforts, even though UNAMSIL was enlarged by stages after the May crisis to 16,000 by September 2001.[31] British troops remained as a separate but complementary military mission. They served as a standing deterrent against more rebel adventures as well as undertaking an extensive training programme for the nascent national army. British special forces were also involved directly in anti-RUF operations. This commitment was one of the few tangible components of the 'ethical dimension' to British foreign policy much vaunted by the post-1997 Labour administration.

If the British intervention subdued the RUF as a military threat, Sankoh's imprisonment in Freetown (along with other rebel leaders within reach of the government in May 1999) impaired its capacity to re-establish itself as

---

31 Nigeria was now no longer the largest contributor to the force, though its contingent of 3328 was considerable. Bangladesh provided, 4363 men and Pakistan 4277. Other major contributors were Kenya (1081), Ghana (928), Zambia (818), Guinea (790) and Ukraine (638). In all, thirty-one states were contributing military personnel to UNAMSIL. UN document S/2001/857/Add.1, 10 September 2001.

a political force. In November 2000 the government and the RUF in the Nigerian capital, Abuja, signed a new agreement sponsored by ECOWAS and the UN. As well as putting a cease-fire in place, an undertaking was given by Sankoh's successor, Issa Sessay, that the RUF would accept the deployment of UNAMSIL forces in all parts of the country, return equipment taken from the UN during the May crisis and co-operate in the resumption of the demobilization and disarmament process.[32] After some initial confusion on the ground and characteristic delay by the RUF, the terms of the Abuja agreement were generally complied with. By March 2001 UNAMSIL personnel were deployed throughout the country, including the diamond mining areas. Heavy weapons and vehicles stolen from the UN the previous May had been returned. A few months later demobilization of RUF and other militias was taking place at an unprecedented pace. Presidential and parliamentary elections, which the UN would help administer, had been agreed for the first half of 2002.[33] At the beginning of 2002 the civil war was formally declared to have ended with the completion of the disarmament process.[34]

Beyond the British intervention, the leadership vacuum in the RUF and general exhaustion on all sides, other factors had contributed to the new climate. The same regional dynamics that had first helped to inflict Sierra Leone's agony now helped ease it. In Liberia Charles Taylor's grip on power, once apparently secure, was coming under challenge from new armed factions. Now Taylor's energies were increasingly occupied in protecting his own position rather than in projecting his baleful influence into Sierra Leone.[35] In addition to his internal problems, Taylor was also under powerful international pressure to distance himself from the rebels across the border. In March 2001 the Security Council passed a resolution designed to punish Taylor for his support of the RUF. The measures took the form of so-called 'smart sanctions' aimed personally at Taylor and his associates (preventing foreign travel and financial transactions). They were, however, suspended for two months to allow him to mend his ways.[36] This he was determined to do, and Sierra Leone gained respite accordingly. In this at least the United Nations had proved that it was capable of exerting some control over events.

The broader issues about the UN's peacekeeping role in Africa raised by the crisis of May 2000 were not immediately addressed in the improving

---

32   UN document S/2000/1199, 15 December 2000.
33   UN document S/2001/857, 7 September 2001.
34   UN document S/RES/1389, 16 January 2002.
35   *Africa Confidential* 42(3), 29 June 2001.
36   UN document S/RES/1344, 7 March 2001.

situation. In June 2000 just weeks after UNAMSIL was poised on the edge of collapse in Sierra Leone, a new UN operation in Africa had been authorized. Its early success served to distract institutional attention from the recent failures. The Mission in Eritrea and Ethiopia, however, was 'African peacekeeping' only in a geographical sense. As we will see, the nature of the crisis that gave rise to it and the mandate given to it looked back to the classic, 'Hammarskjöldian' model of interposition between two states with an interim peace already in place. The harder questions remained.

CHAPTER FIVE

Reconstructing and Defining the
Post-Cold War State
The Horn of Africa

The two interventions of the United Nations in the Horn of Africa occupy opposite ends of the 'peacekeeping' spectrum in terms of techniques and objectives. The crises that precipitated them, however, had similar roots in the vicissitudes of global politics in the cold war and after. The Horn of Africa, bounded by the Indian Ocean to the east and the Arabian Sea to the north, occupied a position of special strategic importance in the 'second' cold war of the later 1970s and 1980s. More even than southern Africa, it became a cockpit of superpower rivalry. With the end of the cold war this external, quasi-'imperial' presence was suddenly withdrawn. What had become a major part of the structure of regional politics and diplomacy thus disappeared, with far-reaching effects on the states involved.

In Somalia the consequence was state collapse, the emergence of a political vacuum within the national territory and a fierce multi-sided contest for control of the wreckage. The results of this, in terms both of human misery and of instability within an international system constructed from territorial states, provoked a major multilateral response. This sought, through various configurations, to impose order on the chaos that underlay the humanitarian disaster, and, for the longer term stability of the nation and region, to reconstruct the Somali state. The effort, despite abundant resources and powerful motivation on the part of the external actors involved, failed comprehensively.

The impact of the end of bipolar rivalries on Ethiopia was rather different, as was the character of the UN's intervention there, five years after the end of its peacekeeping efforts in Somalia. In Ethiopia the state, with much deeper cultural roots than that in Somalia, did not disintegrate. It did, however, divide along an obvious historical fracture line. Initially this division, which brought into being the new sovereign state of Eritrea, appeared to be entirely positive in both execution and consequences. An amicable separation of two post-revolutionary regimes of very similar ideological stamp was followed by the development of what seemed to be a model bilateral relationship catering for the different requirements of each side. The collapse of this relationship, while obviously disastrous in its immediate consequences, nevertheless presented the United Nations with a much 'easier' responsibility than that in Somalia. It was one that derived from circumstances that were extremely unusual in sub-Saharan Africa. The requirement in the aftermath of the Ethiopia–Eritrea war was for a 'classic' peacekeeping force. Two armies of still stable and responsible regimes had disengaged from an inter-state conflict over territory and required an interpositionary presence to occupy the space between them.

The two peacekeeping experiences in the Horn, more than anywhere else perhaps, illustrated the essentially contingent nature of UN interventions in Africa. Success or failure turned on the dynamics of the conflicts themselves rather than the UN's impact upon events. In Somalia, as in Angola, it was unlikely that the complex internal components of the conflict could permit a successful multilateral intervention, however configured, mandated or equipped. In the Ethiopian–Eritrean situation a wholly 'international' conflict had reached a point where the simple presence of a 'legitimate' external force was more or less sufficient to meet the needs of the peace process.

Making bad worse? Somalia, 1992–95

If the Congo intervention in the early 1960s had been emblematic of the ambitions of United Nations peacekeeping in the midst of global bipolarity, the operations in Somalia thirty years later occupied a similar place in the organization's post-cold war agenda. Both were large-scale undertakings that passed through various phases of activity in deeply uncertain political environments. In both countries the UN found itself occupying the political vacuum left by the effective disappearance of the state. While in the case of the Congo this vacuum appeared after the UN's initial intervention and was not long term, in Somalia the UN arrived in a territory where the state had already disappeared, and which it was beyond the capacity of the organization to reconstitute. As Boutros Boutros-Ghali later wrote: 'For the past half century it had been assumed that nations emerging from colonialism and gaining entry to the United Nations would achieve "statehood" as a permanent condition: it was never envisioned that statehood could be

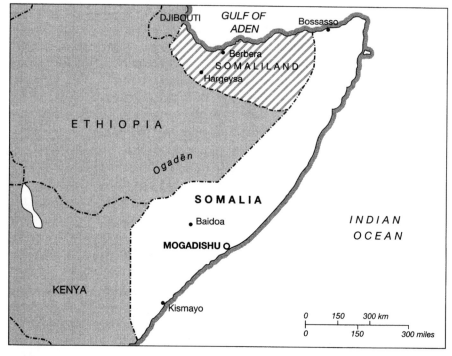

Somalia

lost.'[1] In hindsight the notion of a viable 'Somali state' was perhaps always a tenuous one. There had been no cohesive political structure extending throughout the territory in the pre-colonial period. Later, the peculiarities of its imperial history meant that there was no single, enduring colonial state and therefore no sense even of a second-hand unity via the metropole.[2] After independence succeeding periods of parliamentary democracy and centralized authoritarianism did little to disguise the persistence of clan and regional identities, which took precedence over any notion of a national state. With the collapse of the last vestige of central government at the beginning of 1991 this underlying patrimonial culture immediately reasserted itself. It did so unconstrained by even the pretence of a 'national' political structure.

The United Nations entered this unpromising political landscape ostensibly in what was supposed to be an entirely new type of intervention. Its function was not to keep the peace, or, initially, to make peace on the basis of a reconstructed state, but to secure the distribution of emergency relief. 'Armed

---

1 Boutros Boutros-Ghali, *Unvanquished: a US–UN Saga* (New York: Random House, 1999), p. 53.
2 Peter Woodward, 'Somalia', in Oliver Furley and Roy May (eds), *Peacekeeping in Africa* (Aldershot: Ashgate, 1998), p. 143.

humanitarianism', as this new approach came to be called, begged a range
of complex questions, however. In the attempt to find answers to these, the
United Nations wandered into what would come to be regarded as one of
the most spectacular failures of peacekeeping. The larger failure was constructed on the basis of a series of smaller ones that derived essentially from
the UN's relationships with other actors. Prominent here, of course, were
relationships with the local political and military forces, the fragmented and
competing factions that were the closest approximation available to a 'host
state'. Beyond this, however, the UN as an institution had to manage a
particularly complex web of relations with its own peacekeeping contributors.
The most difficult of these was obviously with the United States, dependence
on which left the UN and its activities in Somalia at the mercy of shifting
American domestic politics and bureaucratic rivalries. But there were other
difficulties as well, in particular with the post-colonial agenda of the Italian
involvement. Finally, there were serious problems to do with internal UN
relations, in particular that between the secretary-general and his own special
representative at one stage. The consequences for the larger peacekeeping
project in Africa and beyond were profound and shaped fundamentally the
UN's approach to conflict resolution in subsequent years. This was most
immediately evident in Rwanda in 1994, when the Security Council appeared
virtually paralysed by the then recent experience in Somalia.

The rise and fall of the Somali state

European interest in the area that eventually formed modern-day Somalia
began in the early nineteenth century. Initially it was merely a 'secondary'
interest, in that Britain sought a presence in the Arabian Gulf–Horn of
Africa region in order to consolidate its sea routes to India. This concern was
sharpened with the opening of the Suez Canal in 1869, and in 1887 Britain
established a formal protectorate over the northern part of the territory of
the future Somali state, which became known as British Somaliland. In the
meantime, as the 'scramble' for Africa gained pace, Italy had begun to show
an interest in the region and negotiated the creation of a colony along the
coast to the south of the British territory. From the beginning both British and
Italian imperialists were confronted by a vigorous series of local revolts and
the region was not effectively 'pacified' until the 1920s. This tradition of
rebellion illustrated the willingness of the local Muslim population to confront
external imposition – but also a matching incapacity to unify its efforts in a
'national' endeavour.

After the Second World War, during which Italy was stripped of its
African territories, there was no agreement about (or pressing interest in)

what should become of its Somali colony. Eventually, at the end of 1949, the United Nations General Assembly determined that it should return to Italian administration but with the status of a UN Trust Territory and with a plan in place to bring it to independence within ten years. In the run-up to decolonization Rome and London co-ordinated their policies in their respective parts of the region in order to bring the two former colonies to independence as a single unified state. On 1 July 1960 the new state of Somalia came into existence with a long eastern seaboard on the Indian Ocean where its capital, Mogadishu, was located. Its northern coast, around the 'Horn', looked across the Arabian Gulf to the Middle East. It was bordered on the west and north by the independent state of Ethiopia, to the south and east by the then British colony of Kenya, and at the northern extreme of its coastline by the tiny French territory of Djibouti.

Somalia's independence day was, coincidentally, that of the Congo as well. Initially, though, the new Somalia appeared to enjoy a far greater degree of stability. For the UN, Somalia was at this time a cause of self-congratulation while the Congo was a crisis that was soon to test it to its limits. For the following nine years Somalia was governed by a reasonably stable constitutional democracy. Its first president, Aden Abdullah Osman Daar, stood down after electoral defeat in 1967. But the apparent democratic stability to which this seemed to point was belied two years later when his successor, Abdi Rashid Ali Shirmarke, was assassinated in a factional power struggle. This was followed by a military coup led by General Muhammad Siad Barre. Once established in power, Siad Barre announced that Somalia would pursue the revolutionary socialist route to development then becoming fashionable in Africa. The depth of his commitment to 'Afro-Marxism' was, though, always questionable.

Territorial acquisitiveness certainly took precedence over socialist solidarity when, in 1977, Siad Barre attempted to exploit the instability of the revolutionary regime in neighbouring Ethiopia to annex the disputed territory of the Ogaden. With extensive Soviet and Cuban support, Ethiopia repulsed the Somali attack and precipitated a major crisis for the Mogadishu regime. A flood of ethnic Somali refugees from the Ogaden aggravated already serious food shortages and the country was faced with widespread famine. Siad Barre – and the Somali state – survived this crisis with American support. Siad Barre's socialist fervour was now in abeyance as he pulled Somalia through a 180-degree shift in its global political affinities. Washington was not wholly enthusiastic about its new client, but at this critical point in the unravelling of superpower détente it was willing to take its 'friends' where it could find them. And, in the strategic priorities of the moment, the Horn of Africa, with its outlets on the northern Indian Ocean and the Gulf of Aden, was a particularly attractive place to find one.

This new American concern for the continuation of Siad Barre's regime might have rescued it from the immediate consequences of the Ogaden débâcle, but it could have little impact on the growing internal opposition. Clan rivalry lay at the root of this, as it did with virtually all conflicts in Somali politics, past and future. Siad Barre, conforming to the requirements of Somalia's highly patrimonial political culture, was seen to be favouring his own Marehan clan at the expense of other powerful groups. These now sought to capture the state in their turn. Despite belated attempts by Siad Barre to reach a compromise with his rivals, the civil war continued until, by the end of the 1980s, the government's effective control of the state had shrunk to a fraction of the national territory. In the meantime, the end of the cold war meant a rapid dwindling in American interest in the country. Its support for the corrupt and dictatorial regime that nominally ruled it declined accordingly. An alliance – though a temporary and uncomfortable one – was eventually forged between Siad Barre's clan enemies, and this provided the final impetus for his overthrow in January 1991.

Any hopes that the removal of Siad Barre would lead to a new coalition politics among the clan factions were short-lived. With the removal of the common enemy the loose rebel alliance quickly disintegrated as each faction attempted to capture power for itself and to exclude the others. Now, as one writer put it, 'bad government was replaced by no government.'[3] Heavily armed by virtue of the militarization of the country during the conflict with Ethiopia and through widespread gun-running, the factions continued with the civil war much as before, though now without even the fiction of a central state. The competing forces involved in the fighting polarized into two factions of the powerful Hawiye clan, which dominated the United Somali Congress (USC) party. The leaders of these factions were Ali Mahdi Mohammed and Mohamed Farah Aideed.[4] Ali Mahdi had the stronger claim to political legitimacy, having been nominated in a rare interval of consensus as interim president by the competing groups after the fall of Said Barre. The Aideed faction, which formed the Somali National Alliance (SNA) breakaway within the USC, was the more effective militarily, however (Aideed himself had been a professional soldier). By the last weeks of 1991 the two factions were locked in all-out war in Mogadishu, with fighting spreading to other centres. Meanwhile, in the territory of the old British Somaliland, the fighting brought mounting clamour for separation from the

---

3 William Shawcross, *Deliver Us from Evil: Warlords and Peacekeepers in a World of Endless Conflict* (London: Bloomsbury, 2000), p. 67.
4 For a detailed examination of clan politics and factional rivalry in Somalia at this time see Daniel Compagnon, 'Somali armed movements', in Christopher Clapham (ed.), *African Guerrillas* (Oxford: James Currey, 1999), pp. 73–89.

conflict-ridden south. As world attention focused on the violence of the rest of Somalia over the coming months, 'Somaliland' quietly seceded from the already collapsed Somali state.[5]

Between the beginning of 1991 and the end of 1992 about 50,000 people were killed directly in the war. Perhaps six times that number starved to death as the continued fighting allowed Somalia's ever-present shortage of food to develop into a full-blown famine. The fighting then confounded attempts by humanitarian agencies to bring relief. Eventually about 4.5 million people – or half the country's population – were at risk from famine. Aid increasingly became a weapon of the war, with the factions vying to control its distribution. Looting of supplies and attacks on convoys became commonplace. Even with the best of intentions, the non-governmental organizations involved in the relief effort could not avoid becoming unwilling accomplices to the disgraceful and macabre exploitation of hunger for political ends. Famine itself became a policy pursued by the factions in the manoeuvring for advantage against each other. While the war obstructed and distorted the deployment of large-scale humanitarian efforts, it did not prevent the various media from reporting in harrowing detail the consequences of this obstruction. The 'CNN-effect' began to operate on western politicians, as public opinion demanded that something must be done. In the face of this, national politicians in the west leaned instinctively towards the 'multilateralization' of the issue rather than unilateral responses. The obvious agency for this was, of course, the UN and the obvious response was military intervention of some sort.

The United Nations intervenes – UNOSOM I

Independently of the western powers, the UN as an institution was also focusing its attention on Somalia by the end of 1991. In January 1992 the United Nations under secretary-general for humanitarian affairs, James Jonah, went to Mogadishu to attempt to improve the machinery for aid distribution. He had been sent by Javier Pérez de Cuéllar, who, in the last weeks of his term as secretary-general, had determined that the UN should offer a lead in the attempt to restore peace to Somalia. By the time Jonah's mission had arrived in the country, however, Boutros Boutros-Ghali had come to office, and the UN's involvement in Somalia would come to be associated with his leadership. At the end of January the Security Council discussed the

---

5   On the position of the north-west at this time see Ioan Lewis and James Mayall, 'Somalia', in James Mayall (ed.), *The New Interventionism 1991–1994: United Nations Experience in Cambodia, Former Yugoslavia and Somalia* (Cambridge: Cambridge University Press, 1996), pp. 106–7.

crisis at some length and produced a resolution imposing an arms embargo on the territory and urging the secretary-general to seek a cease-fire between the factions.[6] In pursuit of this, Aideed and Ali Mahdi were invited to send representatives to negotiations at UN headquarters in New York at the end of February that would also involve the OAU, the Arab League and the Conference of Islamic States. These talks produced an agreement by the rival factions to hold substantive talks in Somalia itself that would be facilitated by Jonah. Held soon afterwards in Mogadishu, these negotiations produced a cease-fire agreement. It proved to be a far from perfect truce, however, and humanitarian agencies remained prey to banditry and extortion driven to greater or lesser degrees by political motives. Included in the Mogadishu agreement between the factions had been an acceptance of a vaguely defined UN security presence to help secure the delivery of relief supplies. This permitted the Security Council at last to contemplate a 'peacekeeping' intervention.

Initially there was considerable wariness about military intervention, particularly on the part of the United States. The absence of even a nominal central government raised unique problems, legal as well as operational, for any peacekeeping venture. There could, for example, be no possibility of a formal 'status of forces' agreement when there was no 'host state' with which to negotiate one. More importantly, however, there was no great confidence in the durability of any inter-factional cease-fire. As a first step, therefore, a fifty-strong military observer group was sent to Mogadishu to monitor the truce.[7] In the interim the Security Council merely agreed 'in principle also to establish . . . a United Nations security force to be deployed as soon as possible'.[8] The new mission was to be called the United Nations Operation in Somalia (UNOSOM). At the same time, Boutros-Ghali appointed the Algerian diplomat and former assistant secretary-general of the OAU, Mohammed Sahnoun, as his special representative in Somalia. Sahnoun worked energetically with the main factions. He also sought to involve the older traditional clan leaders and the few element of 'civil society' (such as religious leaders and women's groups) that existed in Somalia.[9] Aware that the problems of Somalia did not stop at the city boundaries of Mogadishu, Sahnoun also attempted to put aid distribution on a more organized and equitable geographic basis. In July the Security Council approved the

---

6 United Nations document S/RES/733, 23 January 1992.
7 The observers were to be uniformed but unarmed. The group was made up of personnel from Austria, Bangladesh, Czechoslovakia, Egypt, Fiji, Finland, Indonesia, Jordan, Morocco and Zimbabwe under the command of a Pakistani brigadier-general.
8 The despatch of fifty observers was authorized by resolution S/RES/751, 24 April 1992.
9 Woodward, 'Somalia', pp. 145–6.

designation of operational areas around the four centres of Mogadishu, Kismayo, Berbera and Bossasso.[10]

Despite this energy and commitment Sahnoun was unable to make any fundamental impact on the problems of aid distribution. Accordingly, in the summer of 1992 Boutros-Ghali began to press for the despatch of the 'security force' agreed in principle the previous April. At this point he made what would later be a much quoted intervention touching on the whole issue of the UN's activities in Africa. As he recalled in his later memoir: 'I tried to goad the Security Council into a sense of urgency. I contrasted their indifference to the horrors of the Horn of Africa with their preoccupation with the "rich man's war" in the former Yugoslavia. . . . I said that this double standard must stop.'[11] On this occasion the Security Council responded. 'Gravely alarmed by the deterioration of the humanitarian situation', it was prepared to approve a force of 4200 troops in addition to the existing fifty observers. Their primary role was to ensure the delivery of humanitarian aid and they were to be deployed in strength in each of the four zones that had earlier been designated by Sahnoun.[12]

From the beginning the operation was dogged by problems, both organizational and strategic. The first elements of the new force did not arrive in Somalia until mid-September. This gap of three weeks between approval and deployment contrasted sharply with the virtually instantaneous response to the Congo crisis all of thirty-two years previously. It was an inauspicious start to what would, it was clear, be an immensely difficult intervention. It reflected a new wariness on the part of contributing states that had developed particularly in the post cold-war period, when the 'rules' of UN intervention had become less predictable.

The slow start to the peacekeeping response was also partly a function of the new pattern of contribution to peacekeeping. In the cold war period, as we have seen, the main burden of peacekeeping on the ground was borne by a familiar group of western 'middle powers'. Now the net was cast more widely. In the case of UNOSOM at this stage the principal contributor was Pakistan, which, although hardly a newcomer to peacekeeping, nevertheless did not maintain as high a level of 'preparedness' as did, say, Sweden, Ireland or Canada in the 1960s and 1970s. Beyond this, though, there were fundamental issues besetting the mandate of the mission. As Lewis and Mayall have observed: '[t]here were simply no precedents for deploying UN forces on a humanitarian rather than a peacekeeping mission when there was no

---

10   United Nations document S/RES/767, 27 July 1992.
11   Boutros-Ghali, *Unvanquished*, pp. 54–5.
12   United Nations document S/RES/775, 28 August 1992. Units of up to 750 UNOSOM troops were to be deployed to each of the four designated zones.

government with which to negotiate and where the practical decision . . . was always going to be whether to appease those with the power on the ground or oppose them by force.'[13] These unresolved ambiguities continued into the deployment of the new force. Resistance from the factions prevented UN deployment throughout Sahnoun's four operational zones. Concentrated in Mogadishu, UNOSOM forces were subject to constant harassment at their base at the airport by Aideed's SNA fighters, while delivery of aid to the port area was obstructed by the Ali Mahdi faction.

In October the operation suffered a major blow with the resignation of Sahnoun as special representative. Although originally on good personal terms, relations between Boutros-Ghali and Sahnoun had deteriorated since the latter's arrival in Somalia. Sahnoun complained of the rigidity and sluggishness of UN agencies in the field – and of the contrasting pressure for a 'quick-fix' solution from headquarters in New York.[14] On the other side there were criticisms of the concessions Sahnoun seemed willing to make to the armed factions in return for limited co-operation. Boutros-Ghali himself later wrote that Sahnoun's approach 'did, indeed, make it possible to deliver food and aid, but it perpetuated the criminal establishment that had taken over the country'. Too much of the aid flow was still being diverted to the warlords as 'tax' and, ultimately, 'Sahnoun's UN operation had fallen victim to a Somali protection racket.'[15]

At the beginning of November a new special representative, Ismat Kittani, was appointed. A former Kurdish Iraqi diplomat who had at one time been president of the UN General Assembly, Kittani was more 'conventional' in his approach to the job. When, immediately after his appointment, Aideed tested his limits by insisting that UNOSOM's Pakistani troops leave their positions at the airport, the special representative refused to comply and the UN troops came under attack. Other UN units that had now managed to begin operations outside of Mogadishu were also subject to continuous harassment. Clearly, the overall strength and tactical configuration of UNOSOM at this stage were inappropriate to its mandate. Meanwhile, public opinion in the west – informed by relentless media images – brought mounting pressure to bear on national politicians for decisive action. The secretary-general himself left the Security Council in no doubt about the

---

13 Lewis and Mayall, 'Somalia', p. 109.
14 Ibid., p. 108; Christopher Clapham, *The United Nations and Peacekeeping in Africa* (South Africa Institute of Strategic Studies Monograph – no date). Found at http//www.iss.co.za/pubs/monographs/mg%2036/unitednations.html.
15 Boutros-Ghali, *Unvanquished*, pp. 56–7. According to Boutros-Ghali it was his questioning of an expensive and unnecessary conference that Sahnoun had convened without permission in the Seychelles that was the immediate reason for the special representative's resignation.

gravity of the political and humanitarian crisis. At the end of November he wrote to the president of the Council describing the situation in almost apocalyptic terms:

> Looting and banditry are rife. Amidst this chaos, the international aid provided by the United Nations and voluntary agencies has become a major (and in some areas the only) source of income and as such is the target of all the 'authorities', who may sometimes be no more than two or three bandits with guns. In essence, humanitarian supplies have become the source of an otherwise non-existent Somali economy.[16]

In response the Council asked Boutros-Ghali for specific proposals. These he provided in the form of a set of alternatives in a further letter on 29 November. The first of these would be a redoubling of efforts to carry out the current mandate under existing conditions. Secondly, that mandate, by which UN troops were supposed to protect relief supplies, could be abandoned altogether as a lost cause and the humanitarian agencies involved left to make their own arrangements. However, neither of these should be acceptable, in Boutros-Ghali's view. There were three other options that offered a hope of long-term success for the UN in Somalia. Firstly, UNOSOM could present a show of overwhelming military force in Mogadishu to overawe the factions there – though this might not have the desired effect nationwide. Next, an extensive enforcement-type operation could be mounted by a group of UN member states that could be 'legitimized' by the Security Council but that would not constitute a 'UN' operation as such. The final option was for this type of operation to be undertaken by the UN itself. In the light of current resources, however, this would not, in the secretary-general's view, be feasible. The favoured option, therefore, was for action by 'willing parties' with UN approval. And, as it happened, Boutros-Ghali was able to report on a meeting with the acting American secretary of state, Lawrence Eagleburger, a few days previously at which a commitment had been given that the United States would provide the leadership and resources for such an endeavour.[17] The model favoured by the Bush administration in Washington, now in its last weeks before the inauguration of Bill Clinton, was that of Operation Desert Storm in the Gulf in 1991. The designation would be 'Operation Restore Hope' and it would be carried out by a 'Unified Task Force' (UNITAF).

---

16   United Nations document S/24859, 24 November 1992.
17   United Nations document S/24868, 29 November 1992.

The 'coalition of the willing': UNITAF

On 3 December 1992, following Boutros-Ghali's recommendation and with the American commitment confirmed, the Security Council passed a new resolution on Somalia.[18] This began with a frank admission of failure up to that point that was unusual in such resolutions. It was 'necessary to review the basic premises and principles of the United Nations effort in Somalia'. UNOSOM as currently constituted was not 'an adequate response to the tragedy in Somalia'. Enforcement action under Chapter VII of the Charter should now be taken to 'establish a secure environment for humanitarian relief operations'. The American offer to lead this was acknowledged and accepted. Now 'all necessary means' were to be used in pursuit of the humanitarian objective. There was palpable relief in the Security Council and the secretariat at the American intervention. What had been developing into an apparently intractable problem for the organization – and for the credibility of peacekeeping as a means of conflict management – seemed now to be on the way to resolution. The concept of a 'legitimized coalition' had been rescued from its cold war taint in Korea by the evident success of the Gulf operation the previous year. The end of the cold war had also removed the implicit bar on direct big-power participation in peacekeeping. Now it seemed that the Somali 'peacekeeping' intervention would be novel not merely in its objectives but in its composition and command structure as well.

The sense of release from an insoluble crisis inevitably distracted attention from some important issues. For one thing, American 'policy' on the issue had emerged out of 'bureaucratic politics' between different parts of the Washington administration. These sectoral interests did not necessarily share the same vision of the task in hand. The pace seemed to have been set by George Bush himself as a last executive action before enforced retirement. Such an extensive commitment to humanitarian multilateralism would normally be unexpected from a conservative American president, the temptation to relive the golden moments of Operation Desert Storm notwithstanding. But Bush would not be the first (or the last) inhabitant of the White House to seek to be remembered for his 'world statesmanship' by launching a bout of international activism in the dying days of his term. On the other hand, it has also been suggested that a supposedly 'safe' fast-in-fast-out operation in Somalia was a means of distracting criticism of his administration's consistent refusal to commit ground forces in Bosnia.[19]

Another interpretation suggests an even less creditable basis for the motives of the Bush White House at this time. The transfer of power between the

18   United Nations document S/RES/794, 3 December 1992.
19   Shawcross, *Deliver Us from Evil*, p. 66.

207

Bush and Clinton administrations over the winter of 1992–93 was marked by a heightened degree of personal animus between the two men themselves and their 'people'. It was certainly conceivable that the Somalia commitment was a carefully poisoned chalice being passed from a president whose electoral defeat had been both unexpected and deeply resented to a successor for whom he had little warmth or respect. In this way it might be possible to gain the historical kudos for the initiative while projecting the blame for its eventual failure to a disliked successor. Having said this, though, there was nothing inevitable about the ghastly denouement of America's involvement with Somalia. This, when it came, was the result of a wilful disregard of the established lines of command in the international force and bad operational decisions taken on the basis of bad political and military intelligence.

Whatever the attitude of the White House, there was more caution among the military command in the Pentagon. The military establishment would remain largely intact between administrations and therefore had a keen appreciation of inherited risks. General Colin Powell, then chairman of the US joint chiefs-of-staff (and later secretary of state to the second President Bush), reluctantly came round to supporting an American-led operation, but only after imposing some important conditions. The mission was to be restricted in its objectives, its geographical range and its time-scale. It would be concerned only with the distribution of relief aid. It would operate only in the worst famine-hit areas and every effort should be made to restrict its duration to weeks rather than months.[20] This, according to Boutros-Ghali, contradicted an understanding that he had with President Bush that UNITAF 'should take effective action to ensure that the heavy weapons of the factions are neutralized and brought under international control, and that the irregular forces and groups are disarmed [before it] withdraws'.

President Bush was either unwilling or unable to over-rule his military command.[21] It seemed that he had placed his faith in Powell's assumption that the mere presence of thousands of highly visible, heavily armed American troops would be sufficient to intimidate the various militia factions into compliance with the will of the United Nations. This was an example of what might be described as the 'whiff of grapeshot' fallacy regularly deployed and just as regularly discredited in African conflicts. It is based on the assumption that armed groups in Africa, whatever their training, arms and motivation, will tend to disintegrate at the first encounter with disciplined military units. It has distorted United Nations reactions not only in Somalia but in Rwanda and Sierra Leone as well. Whatever the politics of the matter

---

20 Lewis and Mayall, 'Somalia', pp. 110–11. Ideally, Powell wanted UNITAF to complete its mission before the inauguration of the new president (Clinton) in January 1993.
21 Boutros-Ghali, *Unvanquished*, pp. 59–60.

in New York and Washington, the failure of UNITAF to grasp the nettle and disarm the militia factions was to prove a fatal miscalculation. Another – connected – problem raised by the UNITAF concept was the nature of the relationship between the American-led force and UNOSOM. The original UN force remained in station during the UNITAF 'interlude'. More importantly, the plan was for this force, appropriately reconfigured, to take over again after the end of the American mission. Yet no clear picture of inter-force relations was ever offered by either the UN in New York or the administration in Washington.[22] Again, this would have important negative consequences as events unfolded.

These difficulties, if thought about at all at the highest levels, were put to one side when at dawn on 9 December 1992 the first elements of a force that would eventually reach a strength of 37,000 began to disembark from landing craft on the beaches of Mogadishu. Staged deliberately in front of a battery of television cameras, the event was designed to transmit a variety of messages. To the armed factions it was an unequivocal warning of the force's potential ('overawing') fire-power. To the wider CNN-informed world it could signify either the capacity of the 'international community' to respond to humanitarian disaster or the potency and continued 'necessity' of the world's last super-power. In fact, the initial efforts of UNITAF to provide security for aid distribution were quite successful. An effective military presence was soon established in the main centres of aid supply throughout the country by UNITAF while UNOSOM remained in its positions in Mogadishu. The more lurid manifestations of factional aggression – attacks on UN personnel, open displays of military hardware and acts of banditry – declined sharply. In the new and relatively stable environment more UN member states were persuaded to provide contingents to UNOSOM – and what would in due course become UNOSOM II after the departure of UNITAF. Well-trained and equipped units from western states like Australia, Canada, Belgium, France and New Zealand were particularly welcomed by the Department of Peacekeeping Operations in New York. An Italian contingent was, according to Boutros-Ghali's later account, accepted with more reservations because of the former colonial relationship with Somalia. It was, however, agreed to as the price of Italian participation in the contemporaneous operation in Mozambique.[23]

This concern over Italian involvement reflected the larger issue of the control and command of peacekeeping contingents, and the danger of national objectives superseding those of the UN. It was not a problem unique to Somalia. It was one that would later be highlighted, as we have already seen,

---

22   The establishing resolution for UNITAF (S/RES/794) referred only to the attachment of
      'a small UNOSOM liaison staff to the Field Headquarters of the unified command'.
23   Boutros-Ghali, *Unvanquished*, p. 96.

by the UN's own inquiry into the failures of peacekeeping in Rwanda. The situation in Somalia was, however, complicated by the particular provenance of UNITAF. By its conception and nature UNITAF was not a 'UN' force. It was, though, carrying out a UN mandate and doing so by means familiar to (though in the case of Somalia beyond the capacity of) United Nations forces. In this sense comparisons with Operation Desert Storm in the Gulf or even the Unified Command in Korea, while 'constitutionally' valid, were politically and strategically misleading. In both of these earlier undertakings the UN essentially offered a multilateral respectability to what were in reality American politico-military objectives. This was a truth widely recognized if not publicly acknowledged by governments and the UN alike. In Somalia the United States appeared, genuinely, to be an agent of the United Nations. The issues of overall direction and the location of authority were therefore of particular importance. The UNITAF military commander was, of course, an American. But the American presence now became increasingly obvious at all the higher levels of the international effort in Somalia. The head of UNITAF's civilian operations was the former United States ambassador to Mogadishu, Robert Oakley. At the beginning of March 1993, apparently at the request of the United States National Security Adviser, Anthony Lake, Ismat Kittani was replaced as UN special representative by the retired American admiral Jonathon Howe, who was a former security adviser to the Bush administration.[24] Inevitably, it seemed, he who paid the piper was now calling the operational tune.

Initially, the impact of UNITAF was seemingly a positive one on the political as well as the humanitarian planes. In early January an apparently successful sequence of meetings between the rival factions was held under UN auspices in Addis Ababa. These concluded with a supposedly permanent inter-factional peace agreement. They also produced agreed structures for national reconciliation talks that would, it was hoped, lead to the re-establishment of a central state. There were, however, countervailing forces beginning to operate. While the initial 'shock' of UNITAF's deployment had these beneficial effects, there was an inevitable erosion of its impact as familiarity began to breed contempt on the part of the factions. This gained pace when it became clear that, however provoked, the intervention force would not undertake the disarmament of the various warlords' militias. A probing of the limits of UNITAF's determination, hitherto assumed to be absolute, gradually intensified in Mogadishu and other centres.

Mohamed Aideed's SNA caused the greatest problems in this respect. Soon the vicissitudes of American domestic politics and the vulnerability of

---

24 Ibid., p. 92.

the mission in the face of them began to be revealed. UNITAF had not completed the task it set itself in January as General Powell had hoped. Instead,
it appeared to have become bogged down in an increasingly dangerous
situation. The consequences of the high command's refusal to sanction the
effective disarmament of the factions at the outset were now becoming
worryingly evident. American domestic opinion had been happy to support
the idea of UNITAF when the images of death and despair had been high
in its consciousness at the end of 1992 and then to celebrate its theatrical
arrival on the beaches. But the threat of a protracted involvement in a
dangerous Third World conflict had bad resonances in the post-Vietnam
American consciousness. In the meantime, American officials and, with
their encouragement, the media began to focus on Aideed as the clear and
identifiable author of Somalia's problems.

At the beginning of March 1993 Boutros-Ghali presented a plan to the
Security Council for the transition from UNITAF 'back' to UNOSOM. The
new UN operation should, according to the secretary-general, follow four
phases. The first of these would involve the transfer of operational control
from UNITAF. 'UNOSOM II' would then extend its operational control
throughout the country including the border areas. Thereafter the UN force
would reduce its direct responsibility for security, gradually moving into a
support role as local authorities expanded their responsibilities. Finally, the
UN mission would be progressively reduced and eventually withdrawn.[25]
The operational mandate proposed by the secretary-general for the new,
expanded UN force was in most respects a continuation of that of UNITAF.
It would, though, have the important additional responsibility of, finally,
disarming the factions. To this end the operation would be equipped with
enforcement powers under Chapter VII of the Charter. There was, however,
to be a significant reduction in the size of the force. This was set by the
Security Council at 28,000 – 9000 less than UNITAF at its peak. It would
still be a formidable force, however, some 8000 stronger than that in the
Congo at the height of the operation there in the early 1960s.

The Security Council formally adopted the plans for the new force at the
end of March 1993. Its detailed mandate involved *inter alia* the prevention
of violence by 'appropriate action' as well as the control of heavy weapons
and the seizing of small arms from 'unauthorized armed elements'. It would
also continue to secure transport and communication routes for the distribution of humanitarian assistance.[26] Although the responsibilities laid on
UNOSOM II by the Security Council were onerous, just as it was being

---

25 United Nations document S/25354, 3 March 1993.
26 United Nations document S/RES/814, 26 March 1993.

established there were signs that some real political progress might at last be underway. Consequently, there was a prospect that the UN's military activities might not be as dangerous as initially feared. On 27 March, the day following the Security Council vote establishing UNOSOM II, two weeks of intensive negotiations at a UN-sponsored Conference of National Conciliation in Addis Ababa between fifteen separate political groupings ended with an outline agreement. The Conference represented the follow-up to the earlier Addis talks held at the beginning of the year and it produced a blueprint for the re-establishment of a Somali state. A Transitional National Council (TNC) was to be established that would be the interim constitutional locus of Somalia's 'sovereignty'. The seventy-four members of the TNC were to be appointed on the basis of representation among the regions and the political movements. A sub-structure of regional and local councils would be formed below the 'national' TNC.

As with the deployment of UNITAF a few months previously, the relief that followed this apparent breakthrough rather blinded international observers to its imperfections and potential dangers. Not least of these was the less than emphatic commitment to the new process of Aideed's SNA. Aideed had been suspicious of each phase of the multilateral intervention in Somalia. As probably the strongest faction leader in military terms, he had cause to fear a strong foreign input into the physical security and political reconstruction of the country. Such a presence obviously threatened to alter a balance of power that hitherto had favoured his SNA. In this his situation was similar to that of Charles Taylor in Liberia at this time, who, as the strongest factional leader there, stood to lose most by the countervailing ECOMOG intervention and thus came to be seen as its natural enemy (see above p. 174). The UN (at least after the departure of Sahnoun) and the United States regarded Aideed with particular hostility and were not always even-handed in their dealings with him. Within the complex tangle of Somali politics in 1992 and 1993 Aideed provided a convenient villain around which the intervention could be mediated.[27]

The project disintegrates: UNOSOM II

The formal transfer of operational control from UNITAF to UNOSOM II took place on 4 May 1993. The transition did not, however, involve a whole-sale American withdrawal from Somalia. Although UNOSOM II included

---

27 See Debarati G. Sapir and Hedwig Deconinck, 'The paradox of humanitarian assistance and military intervention in Somalia', in Thomas G. Weiss (ed.), *The United Nations and Civil Wars* (London: Lynne Rienner, 1995), pp. 164–6.

contingents from thirty states broadly representative of the UN membership as a whole and drawn from all regions of the world, the United States still had a dominant place in it.[28] Boutros-Ghali chose a Turkish general, Çevik Bir, as force commander, but his deputy was an American, General Thomas Montgomery. Moreover, Admiral Howe remained in post as the secretary-general's special representative. Some 4000 American troops now donned blue helmets and were incorporated in UNOSOM in support and logistics roles. But the main American element in Somalia – 17,000-strong – was now styled the 'United States Joint Task Force in Somalia' and remained under direct American control. The mix-and-match structure of the international intervention was now dangerously loose and its muddy command structure would soon have disastrous consequences for the Americans themselves. More broadly, it set an operational tone for UNOSOM, which encouraged other contingents, most notably the Italians, to disregard the UN chain of command and to take their direction from their home governments.

The first month of UNOSOM's term of overall control in Somalia was marked by mounting tensions. Things were particularly bad in Mogadishu and Kismayo, where Aideed felt himself increasingly marginalized by the UN. UNOSOM, he believed, was now actively favouring the Ali Mahdi faction, which had recently grown in strength through tactical alliances with other clan factions.[29] On 5 June the situation came to head with a major outbreak of violence. In pursuit of UNOSOM II's mandate to effect the disarming of the factions, members of the Pakistani contingent began an inspection of a suspected SNA arms dump in Aideed's south Mogadishu stronghold. They were attacked by his militia and suffered heavy casualties. Simultaneously, SNA fighters also attacked another group of Pakistani troops that was engaged in aid distribution. By the end of the day twenty-six Pakistanis and at least as many Somalis had been killed. Ten more UN troops were reported missing and several others had been wounded. The way in which the UN–US axis reacted to this incident was to prove fatal for the mission in Somalia as a whole. It would also illustrate the deeply unsatisfactory situation of command and control divided between global organization and global superpower. The assumption that had become widespread in the early 1990s that the end of the cold war, and therefore of global bipolarity, would remove the

---

28 The states providing elements of UNOSOM II were: Australia, Bangladesh, Belgium, Botswana, Canada, Egypt, France, Germany, Greece, India, Indonesia, Ireland, Italy, Kuwait, Malaysia, Morocco, Nepal, New Zealand, Nigeria, Norway, Pakistan, South Korea, Romania, Saudi Arabia, Sweden, Tunisia, Turkey, the United Arab Emirates, the United States and Zimbabwe.

29 Michael Wesley, *Casualties of the New World Order: the Causes of Failure of UN Missions to Civil Wars* (London: Macmillan, 1997), p. 73.

bar on superpower participation in peacekeeping was, in Somalia at any rate, quite premature.

The events of 5 June confirmed the demonization of Aideed and the SNA by the intervention forces. However interpretations of ensuing developments may later have differed in the interests of self-justification, the state department in Washington and the UN secretary-general were at one on this in the immediate aftermath. The attack on UNOSOM troops was not to be 'absorbed' as a tragic but inevitable part of such a complex mission. Blame would be apportioned and all energies expended in pursuing the guilty party. On 6 June the Security Council unanimously passed a resolution that, under Chapter VII of the Charter, called for 'all necessary measures against those responsible for the armed attacks . . . including against those responsible for publicly inciting such attacks', leading to 'their arrest and detention for prosecution, trial and punishment'.[30] This was followed by the posting of a reward for information on the attacks, although there was no doubt about the identity of the perpetrators. Three days after the fighting eleven of the most significant Somali factions (though not, of course, Aideed's) denounced the killings unconditionally. This might have been an opportunity for UNOSOM to capitalize politically on what looked very much like a disastrous own-goal by the SNA. Armed with the Security Council resolution, however, Boutros-Ghali and Howe pressed on with the military option. On 12 June a systematic assault began on SNA 'assets', including Radio Mogadishu which was forcibly removed from Aideed's control. SNA weapons dumps were destroyed, an action justified by reference to the disarmament clause of the March resolution. Five days later Howe, acting under the terms of the Security Council's directive of 6 June, called on Aideed to surrender to the UN and directed General Çevik Bir to arrest him if he failed to comply.

In the meantime UNOSOM, and in particular the American forces associated with it, continued its attacks on supposed SNA installations in south Mogadishu. Frequently based on faulty intelligence, and carried out with indiscriminate force, these tactics proved counter-productive. Increasingly, Aideed was able to represent himself as a pan-Somali nationalist confronting the neo-imperialist might of the world's last superpower. He also proved adept at diplomatic gamesmanship. He persuaded former American president Jimmy Carter, who in retirement had become prominent in a number of conflict-resolution processes in various parts of the world, that the UN's pursuit of him was misguided. Additionally, Aideed had, according to Boutros-Ghali's later account, benefited from bilateral contacts with the

---

30   United Nations document S/RES/837, 5 June 1993.

Italian UNOSOM contingent. This was allegedly working, on orders from Rome, to advance the interests of the former colonial power in gaining influence in a post-conflict Somalia at the expense of the UN mission.[31]

Undeterred by its lack of tangible success and accumulating political difficulties, Admiral Howe, with Boutros-Ghali's support, maintained the campaign against the SNA, justifying it on the basis of the June Security Council resolution. In July Howe sought the deployment of the elite US Delta Force of army rangers and commandos, which, with some reluctance, Powell agreed to field at the end of August.[32] By now the reservations of the military command in the Pentagon were coming to be shared by the state department. After a number of American personnel had been killed in landmine incidents in and around Mogadishu in August there were clear signs of a shift in American public – and indeed Congressional – opinion away from its initial support for the Somali undertaking. The secretary-general, by his own account, was now informed by the American permanent representative to the UN, Madeleine Albright (who had hitherto been a supporter of the military option against Aideed), that she was concerned at the closeness of the identification of UNOSOM with American forces and that the mission should have a greater international identity. This was followed up by a suggestion by Albright's superior, the US secretary of state, Warren Christopher, that the pursuit of Aideed should be quietly abandoned, and a greater public emphasis given to the humanitarian side of the UNOSOM mission. For his part, Boutros-Ghali suggested that the current crisis would not have existed had the Americans done what was necessary at the beginning and forcibly disarmed the factions.[33]

Despite the growing concern in Washington, the aggressive interpretation of the Security Council mandate favoured by Boutros-Ghali and Jonathan Howe prevailed into October. It was at this point that one chaotic event effectively sealed the fate of the UN's engagement with Somalia. On 3 October two American assault helicopters were shot down while attacking SNA positions in south Mogadishu. The operation had been authorized and planned by the United States special forces command in Florida, and neither the UN in New York nor mission commanders on the ground (including Admiral Howe) were informed of it until the last moment. Delta Force troops who were deployed to rescue the helicopter crews soon found themselves trapped in the maze of alleys that made up Aideed's domain and had

---

31 According to the secretary-general there were suspicions that the Italians under General Bruno Loi had been providing Aideed with advance intelligence about UN operations. Boutros-Ghali, *Unvanquished*, pp. 96–7.

32 Shawcross, *Deliver Us from Evil*, p. 100.

33 Boutros-Ghali, *Unvanquished*, pp. 97–100.

themselves to be extricated by UNOSOM troops. Perhaps as many as 1000 Somalis died in the original attacks by the Americans and in the ensuing gun battles, many having simply been caught in the cross-fire.[34] It was the death of eighteen Americans that would prove crucial to the future of the UN operation in Somalia, however. Public opinion in the United States, already wavering over the commitment, now turned decisively against it. The body bag count – and the graphic filmed images of the Americans' humiliation – had become unacceptable.

Four days after the calamity in south Mogadishu President Clinton addressed the American people, undertaking that all American personnel would be out of Somalia within six months (by the end of March 1994). In the meantime, however, he would increase the American force numbers by 1700 and reinforce them with tanks and armoured vehicles. Additionally, an aircraft carrier would be stationed off-shore. He also announced that American forces would be placed under 'national' command, thus implying – quite disingenuously – that recent events were somehow the fault of the United Nations. In the later, admittedly self-serving, words of Boutros-Ghali, '[t]he 'United States had ended the United Nations' effort to restore Somalia to nationhood. There was nothing to do but try to help the United States depart with as little lasting harm as possible.'[35] Without a continuing American presence in force, UNOSOM had no real prospect of fulfilling the mandate set out in the Security Council resolution of the previous March. There was no likelihood that other national contingents could be recruited to enter the violent chaos for which the Americans were in part responsible and from which they were now disengaging. Before the end of 1993 the other principal western contributors to UNOSOM II – Belgium, France and Italy – had announced their intention to withdraw as well.[36] In November pursuit of individuals in the SNA suspected of complicity in attacks on UN personnel was formally suspended and those already detained were released. The United Nations had, in effect, been forced into a surrender. However questionable its original objectives, their abandonment was inevitably greatly damaging to UN prestige in Africa and beyond.

The course of events from October 1993 until the end of the year signalled as effectively as any formal statement could that the enforcement phase of the United Nations presence was effectively ended. The factions remained

---

34 UNOSOM and eventually the Security Council itself denounced the SNA's evidently deliberate tactic of using unarmed civilians as shields when engaging UN forces. *The United Nations and the Situation in Somalia*, United Nations Department of Public Information Reference Paper, April 1995.
35 Boutros-Ghali, *Unvanquished*, p. 122.
36 Lewis and Mayall, 'Somalia', p. 119.

as well armed and as aggressive as ever. Always the strongest militarily, the SNA's position – both in its own estimation and that of other actors at home and abroad – had been hugely enhanced by its apparent humbling of the UN and the United States. In January 1994 Boutros-Ghali presented a report to the Security Council that urged a new, 'non-enforcement' mandate for the residue of UNOSOM II following the imminent withdrawal of the Americans and west Europeans.[37] Now UNOSOM was merely to encourage 'the Somali parties . . . in their co-operative efforts to achieve disarmament'. It would also continue with its broader humanitarian activities such as aid delivery and refugee resettlement. In short, it was supposed to revert to the type of 'peacekeeping' activities undertaken with no great success by UNOSOM I before the first American intervention in the form of UNITAF. The Security Council resolution endorsing the change of mandate paid lip-service to the continued relevance of Chapter VII, but gave little impression of any continuing commitment to invoke it. The mission would be gradually reduced in size and would end March 1995, that is to say, one year after the American withdrawal.[38] Simultaneously with the adoption of the new mandate, Admiral Howe resigned as special representative, to be replaced by his Guinean deputy, Lansana Kouyate.

The 'failure' of the intervention: an unfeasible mandate?

The effective collapse of UNSOM II had a number of consequences in Somalia, none of them good. The damage done to the credibility of the UN was such that it now lacked the necessary respect required of a mediator. It could do little, therefore, to reverse the unravelling of the always tenuous Addis Ababa agreement on which UNOSOM II's role had been predicated. The prospect of the UN's military withdrawal, first by the western participants and then by the residual Third World contingents, created heightened inter-factional tensions. Aideed's military superiority was pitched against the wider support base of the Ali Mahdi coalition with no moderating influence capable of intervening. Violence grew as the factions stockpiled arms with renewed urgency. Yet there seemed little prospect that simply 'letting events take their course' would move the situation on in any way. The balance of forces in Somalia in 1994 was such that no one faction could hope to dominate the others in order to control (or, more correctly, create) a central state. Three months after the UN withdrawal Aideed pronounced himself

---

37   United Nations document S/1994/12, 6 January 1994.
38   United Nations document S/RES/897, 4 February 1994.

president of Somalia, but it was a largely empty gesture as none of the other faction leaders acknowledged him as such. Additionally, the northern part of the country – the former British Somaliland – maintained its secession. Then, in July 1996 Aideed was killed in one of Mogadishu's routine gun battles. He was succeeded by his son, Hussein Mohammad Aideed, as leader of the SNA, and no fundamental change was wrought in the political situation. Repeated attempts, facilitated by UN mediators, to construct the basis of a new state among clan leaders met with little success.

In the meantime the reduced – and increasingly beleaguered – UNOSOM II gradually withdrew from its positions and projects during 1994 to concentrate in Mogadishu prior to withdrawal. By the end of January 1995 its numbers were down to less than 8000. The evacuation of the last elements took place on schedule in March 1995 (with a deterrent military shield provided by the United States and Britain). By this point its presence had become largely irrelevant to the violent realities of Somalia's factional politics. During its two-year duration UNOSOM II had cost the United Nations more than US$1.6 billion. About 150 of its personnel had been killed and it had been responsible directly or indirectly for the deaths of many times this number of Somalis, both guilty and innocent. It must of course be acknowledged that UNOSOM II – and perhaps more so UNITAF before it – also helped save many lives. The humanitarian role of the international military intervention, however imperfect, rescued many thousands of Somalis from famine. This was done, moreover, while the victims' compatriots sought to perpetuate their plight for their own political purposes.

Inescapably, though, the United Nations 'failed' in Somalia if the judgement is made in terms of its own mandates to secure peace and restore national government. Frequently, discussion of the UN's performance, across the spectrum of its activities but perhaps most particularly in peacekeeping, begins with the assumption that all problems have a solution and, by corollary, that all failures could have been avoided. This optimistic starting point is understandable but not always rational. Over Somalia it is perhaps reasonable to pose the prior question as to whether any intervention of any character would have achieved the objectives the UN was set by its leading members in the Security Council. It should not perhaps be taken as a counsel of despair to suggest that Somalia's problems were so multifarious, so deep-rooted and so intractable as to be simply beyond solution in the early 1990s.

Whether or not this proposition is accepted, it is still possible to identify shortcomings in the UN's response to Somalia – even if their impact on the final outcome was not decisive. As we suggested at the outset, the over-arching problem was constructed from smaller ones of relationships between key actors.

There was a fundamental lack of empathy throughout the intervention in Somalia between the international soldiers and the protagonists in the crisis. The contrast between the apparently insouciant, often drug-fuelled violence of the militias, on the one hand, and the human misery that this created, on the other, was a major cause of angry bewilderment for the peacekeepers. What has been described as the 'political instrumentalization of disorder' by the factions, that is to say, the calculated exploitation of others' desperation, was uniquely shocking to those engaged in an operation designed both to manage security and alleviate humanitarian disaster.[39] Perhaps tellingly in this regard, Somalia was the first operation in which peacekeepers themselves were guilty of widespread abuse of prisoners. The fundamental inability to 'understand' the attitudes and motivations of local actors was a major factor in the demoralization of peacekeeping contingents and clearly affected their performance on the ground. At a less visceral level, the labyrinthine complexity of factional politics, incomprehensible to most outsiders, was also a cause of both mystification and miscalculation higher up the decision-making ladder. A source of generalized frustration, this ignorance at certain points did tangible damage when commitments were not honoured and intelligence misinterpreted. Even those with a supposed 'feel' for the situation, like the secretary-general's first special representative, Mohammed Sahnoun, could themselves reasonably be criticized when the price of their 'sensitivity' to local conditions was the appeasement and legitimization of warlords and warlordism.

Beyond relations between peacekeepers and those whose peace was supposedly being kept, there were obvious difficulties in 'internal' relationships in the interventionist coalition. The primary problem here, of course, concerned those between the United Nations and the United States. From the end of 1992 the tactical direction of the intervention in Somalia was provided by the United States, whether in its 'own' UNITAF operation or in UNOSOM II which was wholly dependent on American resources. This meant that the United Nations 'culture' of military intervention, whether in classical peacekeeping or in more robust actions, was supplanted by an American national one. A certain tendency to identify, demonize and pursue villains, therefore, took precedence over the more nuanced assessment of events normally associated with UN direction. It may be, of course, that this apparent prudence has more to do with a traditional lack of resources rather than evolved policy on the part of the UN. Certainly Boutros-Ghali was quite happy with the American efforts to pursue and neutralize Aideed

---

39   The term is used by Patrick Chabal and Jean-Pascal Daloz in *Africa Works: Disorder as Political Instrument* (Oxford: James Currey, 1999).

after June 1993 when the necessary resources for this were available courtesy of the United States army. But whatever the cause of traditional UN circumspection, it has tended to make for more successful peacekeeping, a key tenet of which, it will be recalled, was to avoid identifying 'aggressors' and focus on the management of the crisis instead. Secondly, the availability of advanced weapons and transport systems, along with the domestic imperative of avoiding American casualties, tended to result in the use of inappropriate means by UNOSOM II. The deployment of air-to-ground missiles and helicopter gun-ships in crowded urban areas, while perhaps helping to safeguard international personnel, inevitably resulted in large-scale civilian casualties. This had a disastrous effect locally on the prestige and credibility of the international force and its mission. Thirdly, the ambiguous position of the American Joint Task Force, which remained parallel to but separate from UNOSOM II, inevitably impacted on the efficiency and morale of the multilateral intervention as a whole. This was particularly well illustrated when even the American UN special representative, appointed at Washington's insistence, was kept in the dark about special forces operations planned in the United States.

Finally, outside of Somalia itself, relationships between decision-makers at the top of the intervention, which had been quite positive in the beginning, rapidly deteriorated. Boutros Boutros-Ghali, as a former Egyptian minister, had served his political apprenticeship in the culture of non-alignment and 'Third Worldism'. Like others from such a background, he also maintained a highly developed sense of his own dignity and prerogatives. He was not therefore best suited to maintaining a dependent relationship with a United States administration ever-mindful of the domestic impact of its actions and divided within its own bureaucratic factions. American discontent with Boutros-Ghali (which resulted in an unprecedented refusal to permit him a second term as secretary-general) was widely ascribed to disagreements over the Middle East and the management of the Arab–Israeli conflict. By his own account, however, relations with the state department, and particularly the then UN representative – and later secretary of state – Madeleine Albright, soured as the United States disengaged itself from Somalia. As we have seen, they declined further the following year over the proper response of the UN to the genocide in Rwanda.

Yet, again we have to consider that it may simply be wrong to assume that all problems have a solution if only the UN as an institution, the states that comprise it and its officers on the ground 'get it right'. For years after the withdrawal of the UN from Somalia the territory remained as far as ever from the re-establishment of a viable state and a return to political stability. Intriguingly for those who assumed that chaos would follow the removal of even one brick of territorial statehood from the superstructure of the

Westphalian system, the nightmare of Somalia appeared initially to have little impact on the texture of international relations as a whole. As one writer remarked, 'borders mean little when the state no longer exists: the borders of Somalia are intact, but they enclose a vacuum.'[40] Perceptions of the threat posed to the broader international system by such a vacuum intensified, however, in the aftermath of the attacks on the United States in September 2001. For the more hawkish strategists of the subsequent military action, Muslim Somalia, bereft of an internationally responsible state, provided just as viable an environment as Afghanistan had for networks of international terrorists to thrive in. This belief, perhaps combined with a residual bitterness over the events of October 1993 in south Mogadishu, put Somalia high on many lists of suitable fronts for the continuing 'war against terrorism'. 'Peacekeeping' was not a term widely used in discussions of such an intervention.

Textbook peacekeeping? Ethiopia and Eritrea, 2000–

If the United Nations intervention in Somalia at times appeared to be a catalogue of what peacekeeping should not be, the subsequent experience in the Horn of Africa following the 1998–2000 war between Ethiopia and Eritrea was in contrast a model of traditional 'Hammarskjöldian' interposition. The United Nations Mission in Ethiopia and Eritrea (UNMEE) was established by the Security Council in June 2000 to monitor the ceasefire between the two belligerents and to supervise troop withdrawals agreed as part of a comprehensive peace settlement. The successive configurations of the Somalia involvement wrestled with a hugely complex set of internal conflicts within a vacuum where the 'host state' should have been. UNMEE in contrast was charged with the supervision of a peace agreement between two sovereign state members of the United Nations. The forces to be monitored were national armies under firm command and the issues at stake were the relatively precise ones of territorial distribution. The character of the operation was, therefore, very close indeed to that of the United Nation Emergency Force established after the Suez crisis of 1956, widely seen as the starting point and 'classic' model of the UN's peacekeeping project.

---

40   Marina Ottaway, 'Post-imperial Africa at war', *Current History*, May 1999, p. 206.

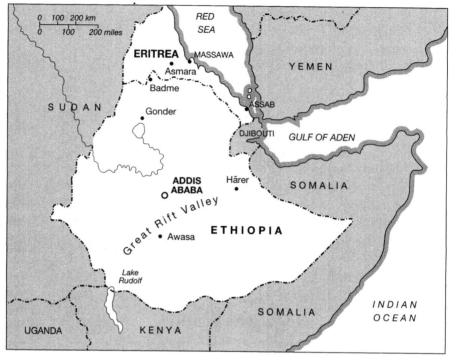

Ethiopia – Eritrea

The conflict: Ethiopia and Eritrea in historical context

Eritrea lies to the north of Ethiopia in the Horn of Africa with a panhandle of territory extending south-east along the Red Sea coast. This strip of Eritrea, an inheritance of colonial history, denies Ethiopia a direct outlet to the sea. South of Eritrea, Ethiopia is blocked from the coast by Djibouti, a small territory that had been a French protectorate until 1977. Beyond this to the south and east Ethiopia is separated from the Red Sea and Indian Ocean by Somalia. This landlocked condition was obviously a major preoccupation for a country of the considerable size of Ethiopia and a major factor in its relations with Eritrea.

Ethiopia is one of the longest established 'sovereignties' in the international system, with origins that can be traced to biblical times. Although its borders changed over the centuries, a central territorial identity always persisted. The country was impinged upon to varying degrees by European imperial powers – at different times Portugal, Italy and Britain had all shown interest – but it was never 'colonized' in any significant sense. As we have already seen in our discussion of Somalia, Italy developed a particular interest in the Horn of Africa during the 'scramble' of the later nineteenth century. The Red Sea coast was especially attractive as its economic potential was transformed with the opening of the Suez Canal in 1869. In the 1870s and 1880s Italian military expeditions seized various points of the coast adjacent to Ethiopia. This territory, which Italy would eventually colonize formally in 1890, was Eritrea. It had historically been under the loose jurisdiction of the Ethiopian emperor but had functioned as a largely independent entity before the Italian irruption. In 1889 the territorial issue was supposedly formalized by an Italo-Ethiopian treaty. However, Rome's own liberal interpretation of this agreement was that it gave Italy a protectorate over all of Ethiopia rather than merely a commitment to co-operation in the region. The result was war and the rout of the Italian army at Adowa in 1896.

It would have been humiliation enough for any would-be imperial power in the nineteenth century to be seen off in this way by the supposed lesser race that it sought to 'protect'. For Italy, a noisy newcomer to the imperial game and itself only recently a unified state, it was particularly so. From this perspective it was not surprising when, with the rise of fascism in the 1920s with its ideology of extreme nationalism, Italy resurrected this national dream of territorial expansion. Turning its expansionist instincts against Ethiopia had the added spice of an opportunity to settle old military scores. In 1935 Mussolini's forces launched an attack on Ethiopia from Eritrea, which had remained an Italian colony after the war of 1896. In an extremely brutal campaign the Italians succeeded in occupying the capital, Addis Ababa. The Ethiopian emperor, Haile Selassie, was forced into exile. Italy was able to act in this way with apparent impunity because the major powers in the League of Nations failed to invoke effectively the principles of collective security against international aggression upon which the organization had been founded. This abandonment of Abyssinia (as Ethiopia was commonly called at the time) was a key milepost in the accelerating disintegration of the League's authority.[41] Italy now reintegrated Ethiopia and Eritrea along with Italian Somaliland in a new imperial entity, 'Italian East Africa'.

Italy's new place in the sun was short-lived. The Second World War in Africa brought its expulsion from both Ethiopia and Eritrea in 1941 by British and Ethiopian forces. While Ethiopia was restored to the emperor's rule shortly afterwards, Eritrea as a recognized colonial territory remained under British administration until 1952. As we saw in the previous section, when the UN considered the future of the former Italian Somaliland in 1949 it determined that it should be returned to Italian administration pending

---

41   A detailed account of the League of Nations response to the Italian invasion of Abyssinia is given by F.P. Walters, *A History of the League of Nations* (Oxford: Oxford University Press, 1969), pp. 623–91.

decolonization. The case of Eritrea was more complicated, however, because of proximity to and historical association with Ethiopia. A sense that Eritrea had been forcefully torn from the Ethiopian 'motherland' by Italy in 1890 contributed to a feeling that its future should lie in some form of unification with its larger neighbour. This view may also have been encouraged by a certain inherited guilt complex in the UN over the League's failure to protect Ethiopia in 1935. The General Assembly stopped short of acceding to Ethiopian demands for outright annexation, but neither was it willing to entertain Eritrean nationalist claims for full independence. Instead it voted for the creation of a federation between the two countries to be established by 1952.[42]

Clearly, this was not a partnership of equals. Ethiopia's population was about fifteen times that of Eritrea. It also had the established machinery of an independent state, including a large army. It did not, however, have access to the sea and Eritrea did. But this was a dubious advantage in such a relationship, representing a threat to Eritrean autonomy rather than a guarantee of it. Once the federation was established its political domination by the Ethiopian emperor and his government meant that it was soon transformed into an annexation. This was formalized in 1962 when Eritrea was reduced to the status of a province of Ethiopia. The nationalist Eritrean Liberation Front (ELF), which had been formed in 1958, now mobilized armed resistance to Addis Ababa and a long civil war ensued. This war eventually became woven into broader conflicts between other separatist groups and the central government and between Ethiopia and its neighbours. The most destructive of the latter was the conflict with Somalia over the disputed Ogaden region, which was exacerbated by recurring famine and social dislocation afflicting both countries over the next three decades. The Eritrean struggle therefore became a motif running through a series of convulsions affecting Ethiopia as a whole.

In 1974 Haile Selassie was overthrown in a military coup driven, supposedly, by revolutionary Marxist objectives. No ground was given to Eritrean nationalism, however, despite its struggle now being dominated by the Eritrean People's Liberation Front (EPLF), which had originally been a leftist faction of the ELF. The EPLF had split from the 'parent' movement in 1970 under the leadership of Isayas Afwerki. The new regime in Addis Ababa – the so-called Derg – enjoyed considerable Soviet and Cuban military support as it took Ethiopia across from the western to the eastern pole in the cold war. This momentarily slowed the momentum of the EPLF, but throughout the 1980s it extended its control of Eritrea, expelling Ethiopian forces from one centre after another. In 1990 it captured the key Red Sea port of

---

42   See H.S. Wilson, *African Decolonization* (London: Edward Arnold, 1994), p. 122.

Massawa, crucial to the supply of the beleaguered forces of the Derg. Then, in 1991, it took control of Asmara, the inland capital of Eritrea.

In the meantime, internal opposition to the Ethiopian regime had been growing. The Derg's relentless violence towards perceived opponents, its comprehensive mismanagement of the economy and its failure to tackle the recurring food crises that afflicted the country had deprived it of the support of everyone except a narrow 'revolutionary' client group. It had, it was true, 'won' the war in the Ogaden against Somalia but only at horrific cost in lives and resources. Foremost in a loose alliance of resistance was the Ethiopian People's Revolutionary Democratic Front (EPRDF) led by Meles Zenawi. The parallel struggles of the EPLF in Eritrea and the EPRDF in Ethiopia, although strictly speaking unrelated, were mutually supporting. Almost simultaneously with the EPLF's capture of Asmara, the EPRDF had encircled Addis Ababa. The Derg – without friends at home or, with the end of the cold war, abroad either – simply crumbled away. There was no question on the part of the new regime in Addis Ababa about the future of Eritrea: it would become an independent state. Following the collapse of the Derg the ELPF established a provisional government in Asmara and indicated its intention to legitimize Eritrean statehood by a referendum. This was held in April 1993 and, after a virtually unanimous vote for independence, Eritrea was admitted to the United Nations as a fully sovereign member state the following month.

The initial phase of the post-separation relationship appeared to be almost wholly amicable. This seemed to be underlined at the personal level by the relationship between Meles Zenawi and Isayas Afwerki, who became the heads of government (respectively, prime minister and president) in Ethiopia and Eritrea. Both men, in fact, had their family origins in the same ethnic group from Tigray in northern Ethiopia. Extensive bilateral consultation was maintained in order to manage what was inevitably a special diplomatic relationship.[43] The two economies remained closely connected. Eritrea retained the Ethiopian currency in the years after independence and the now landlocked Ethiopia had special rights in the Eritrean port of Assab. At a more fundamental level, however, the two countries were diverging in their political styles and cultures. Eritrea under Isayas Afwerki began to display the sometimes prickly nationalist sensitivities that frequently characterize small, newly emergent (or re-emergent) states, particularly those born of protracted armed struggle. During the first few years of its statehood it acquired something of a reputation as a difficult neighbour after appearing

---

43   On the complex ethnic-regional background to the conflict see Ruth Iyob, 'The Ethiopian–Eritrean conflict: diasporic vs. hegemonic states in the Horn of Africa, 1991–2000', *Journal of Modern African Studies* 38(4), 2000, pp. 659–82.

to provoke conflicts with both Sudan and Yemen. Ethiopian politics, on the other hand, played out in a country exhausted after decades of futile conflict and facing continuing problems, tended to be more inwardly focused.

To much of the outside world the settlement of the early 1990s and the evident closeness of the bilateral relationship between Ethiopia and Eritrea constituted an African good news story just at the time when hopes and expectations of an African 'renaissance' were beginning to fade among the blood and chaos of Angola, Somalia, Liberia and Rwanda. Moreover, both countries frequently expressed their commitment to sustainable and self-reliant development and showed clear signs of practising what they preached. This provided badly needed relief to Afro-optimists, who had, by the end of the 1980s, been forced to accept that their previous enthusiasm for the Marxist projects of the Portuguese-speaking states had been misplaced. There was, therefore, considerable surprise and disillusion internationally when fighting between Eritrea and Ethiopia erupted in May 1998.

The outbreak of war and attempts at mediation

The *casus belli* was a long-standing territorial dispute over part of the northern Ethiopian region of Tigray affecting about 400 square kilometres. The issue was complicated by the absence of definitive cartographic evidence of where the border between the two countries actually ran in legal terms. The area had been demarcated during the time of Italian colonial rule, but inconsistently. The potential for future difficulties over the shared border had not been given great prominence amidst the tumult of the separation of the two countries in 1991. By the late 1990s, however, the issue seemed to become a growing preoccupation for the Eritrean government. Mindful of the precedents of the other regional conflicts the Afwerki government had provoked, Ethiopia could only see this a potential threat.

There were other factors in the mounting tension between the two states as well. In 1997 Eritrea, motivated as much by national *amour propre* as by economics, introduced it own national currency. It did so on the assumption that the new *birr*, as it was called, would maintain parity with the Ethiopian *nafka*, which Eritrea had now abandoned. Ethiopia would not go along with this, however, and insisted that transactions between the two countries would have to be conducted in fully convertible currency. Ethiopia had, of course, a pressing cause for concern amidst the growing – and from its point of view quite gratuitous – hostility from Eritrea. The breakdown of the partnership between the two countries posed a threat to its sea outlet. To pre-empt the loss of port facilities, Ethiopia began to redirect its trade through Djibouti – which in turn further deepened Eritrean resentment.

Each side accused the other of initiating the fighting that broke out on 6 May 1998 around the town of Badme, 170 kilometres south-east of Asmara. In June new fronts opened up even closer to the Eritrean capital and near the port of Assab. Air power was deployed by both sides, resulting in considerable civilian casualties. By July fighting had subsided, but Eritrean forces continued to occupy disputed territory in Ethiopia and both countries had engaged in the mass expulsion of the other's citizens. An increasingly bitter propaganda war seemed to indicate that this was a lull rather than a truce.

The identity of the antagonists – both well regarded throughout Africa and in the broader world – brought a wave of mediation efforts from different international actors. The character of their conflict also encouraged this. This was a 'classic' inter-state dispute over specific territory. Italy, the former colonial power, as well as the United States attempted to negotiate a peace agreement. The Organization of African Unity (itself founded at a meeting in Ethiopia in 1964 with that country as a major driving force) was involved from the beginning of the conflict. At the end of June the issue came before the UN Security Council, which, in a strongly worded resolution, demanded an end to the hostilities, proposed the good offices of the secretary-general, Kofi Annan, and offered UN technical resources to help the parties arrive at an agreed border demarcation.[44] OAU efforts also continued throughout 1998, but its proposed 'Framework Agreement' for a military disengagement leading to a negotiated settlement was rejected by Eritrea. The starting point of the Framework was withdrawal from occupied territory prior to substantive settlement negotiations, and Eritrea had more to lose on the ground by this than had Ethiopia.[45] In the event, the deadlock was broken on the battlefield. At the beginning of February 1999, just a week after a second Security Council resolution calling for the acceptance of the OAU Framework, a major Ethiopian offensive drove the Eritrean occupation forces out of Badme.[46] On 28 February, after finally acknowledging Ethiopia's success in an extremely bloody campaign, Eritrea announced its acceptance of the Framework Agreement.

Significant movement towards a permanent settlement was not forthcoming, however. Frequent eruptions of fighting continued over the next year, and it seemed that without an increase in its momentum the nascent peace process was in danger of running into the sand. At the end of 1998 Kofi Annan had despatched his 'Special Envoy for Africa' to the region to give UN support to the efforts of the OAU. This was Mohamed Sahnoun of Algeria

---

44   UN document S/RES/1177, 26 June 1998.

45   The full terms of the Framework Agreement can be found at www.primenet.com~ephrem2/eritreanoau/oau_peace_proposal.html.

46   UN document S/RES/1226, 29 January 1999.

– whom we have already encountered as the controversial UN representative in Somalia during 1992. Although his relations with Boutros-Ghali had broken down at that time, Annan recognized his energy and flair, and sought to exploit them against Africa's manifold conflicts after he came to office in 1997. Sahnoun worked throughout 1999 to overcome supposed technical obstacles to the implementation of the full terms of the Framework Agreement. Pressure was maintained on both parties in 2000 when, at the beginning of May on the second anniversary of the outbreak of the war, a high-ranking Security Council delegation visited the region. This was led by the United States representative Richard Holbrooke and visited both Addis Ababa and Asmara for direct talks with Meles Zenawi and Isayas Afwerki.[47] The visit appeared to have no immediate effect on the behaviour of the two countries, however, as fresh fighting broke out soon after its departure. In response the Security Council invoked Chapter VII of the Charter to impose a mandatory arms embargo on both sides.[48]

The establishment of UNMEE

At this point a combination of international pressure and a growing awareness on both sides of the futility of further military action finally brought movement. Fought with trench warfare tactics more familiar in 1916 than in 2000, the conflict had already cost tens of thousands of lives and threatened to subside into a stalemate.[49] Additionally, there were signs that the war was undermining Isayas Afwerki's grip on what had hitherto been a highly centralized Eritrean state. Opposition groups were filling the administrative vacuums created by the fighting in the affected parts of Eritrea.[50] A ceasefire agreement was consequently reached at proximity talks in the Algerian capital organized by the OAU. The way now seemed open for the implementation of the Framework Agreement. The last section of this had committed the OAU 'in close co-operation with the United Nations [to] be the guarantor for the scrupulous implementation of all the provisions of the . . . Agreement, in the shortest possible time'. This clause was now invoked, and the Security Council was called upon to authorize the requisite operation.

---

47   UN press release SC/6861, 12 May 2000. The delegation also included, in addition to Holbrooke, the French and British representatives to the Security Council. The non-permanent members were represented by the delegates of the Netherlands, Mali, Namibia and Tunisia.

48   UN document S/RES/1298, 17 May 2000.

49   The principal front consisted of 'a zig-zagging line of trenches 1000 km (620 miles) long'. *The Economist*, 30 September–6 October 2000.

50   BBC World Service (Africa) report, 23 May 2000.

The initial phase of this involved the establishment of a military observer group of 100 officers to be located in Addis Ababa and Asmara. Their task was to establish a Military Co-ordination Commission under the Algiers agreement, which would act as a liaison body between the parties. This was duly agreed by the Security Council at the end of June.[51] It was understood that this was intended to be a preliminary to the formation of a much more substantial interpositionary force.

The Algiers agreement had already spelled out a fairly extensive provisional mandate for the peacekeepers. The UN would act 'under the auspices of the OAU'. It would monitor the cease-fire and the redeployment of national forces while overseeing a Temporary Security Zone between the sides. It would also take responsibility for fixing definitively the position of the border, and would remain in place until this process had been completed.[52] In the light of recent experience in Africa in general – and more immediately the protracted efforts necessary to wring a truce agreement out of Ethiopia and Eritrea – the Security Council was wary of moving more than one step at a time. Annan, who was himself fully committed to a major UN role, was in the meantime given the task of preparing a plan for the larger interpositionary commitment.[53] Six weeks later he presented this to the Security Council. It called for a total force of 4200 made up of 220 military observers and three infantry battalions.[54] The Council adopted the plan unanimously the following month and the United Nations Mission in Ethiopia and Eritrea began to build up to full strength.[55]

Interposition and disengagement

A year after the Security Council first discussed the nature and extent of the intervention the work on UNMEE was far from complete. It had moved more quickly to the fulfilment of its mandate than in many other UN operations in Africa established in the previous ten years. Unusually, its strength had exceeded that authorized by the Security Council, rising to 5600. The main force contingents were from India, the Netherlands, Canada and Kenya. In total, twenty-four states had contributed personnel in the first year of the operation.[56] The Temporary Security Zone – the buffer area on

---

51   UN document S/RES/1312, 30 June 2000.
52   The full terms of the Algiers peace plan can be found at http://news.bbc.co.uk/hi/english/worl/africa/newsid_787000/787602.stm.
53   UN document S/RES/1312, 30 June 2000.
54   UN document S/2000/785, 9 August 2000.
55   UN document S/RES/1320, 15 September 2000.
56   UN document S/2001/608, 19 June 2001, Annex III.

the disputed border in which UNMEE troops were to position themselves – had been formally declared in mid-April 2001. Both sides had complaints about its precise delimitation, however, and they maintained some military and paramilitary forces within it. The UN was also still to complete negotiations on a comprehensive status of forces agreement, though this had not materially affected the work of UNMEE and was not regarded as a major issue. The mood in New York remained one of cautious optimism. Kofi Annan, although acknowledging that serious difficulties remained, nevertheless commended both sides for their commitment to the process.[57]

The particular character of the conflict between Eritrea and Ethiopia and the nature of its proposed settlement were crucial in eliciting the commitment necessary from the Security Council. At times of evident difficulty in the process UN spokespersons reiterated the clarity of UNMEE's role between formal and responsible international actors.[58] The structure and planned sequence of the UN's intervention was strikingly similar to the simultaneous 'peacekeeping' engagement with the Democratic Republic of Congo. In both places a preliminary deployment of military observers in a liaison capacity was intended to prefigure a large-scale force commitment. In the DRC, however, there was no movement beyond the initial stage. Into the violent tangle of national, regional, inter-ethnic and international interests that constituted the crisis in the DRC, the Security Council was not willing to venture in any force. Consequently, the plan for the United Nations Mission to the Congo (MONUC) to expand into an infantry force over 5000-strong remained on the drawing board (see above pp. 91–6). The infinitely 'cleaner' lines of the conflict in the Horn, and its requirement for relatively straightforward interposition to maintain an already established international peace, provided a much more acceptable risk.

The Eritrea–Ethiopia conflict also provided the occasion of one of the more successful joint ventures between the UN and a regional organization – in this case the OAU. The reasons for this success are likewise to be found in the nature of the crisis as a conventional inter-state dispute. The joint approach to the peace process by the two organizations was nevertheless carefully managed. The overall settlement negotiations were the province of the OAU, which conducted them in an appropriate regional context. It fell to the UN, however, to provide the peacekeeping input. The UN, unlike

---

57   UN document S/2001/608, 19 June 2001.
58   Explaining delays in the peace process in March 2000, for example, the secretary-general's special representative, Joseph Legwaila, insisted that there was no fundamental problem as the 'UN Mission was negotiating with two disciplined leaders, two disciplined nations and two disciplined armies'. Press Briefing, UNMEE/PR/40, UNMEE Public Information Office, 14 March 2001.

the OAU, could call on a range of effective non-African contingents that could provide high operational efficiency without raising concerns about the pursuit of any national interests of their own, as, say, the ECOMOG interventions in Liberia and Sierra Leone did.[59]

Propitious as the particular circumstances of the Eritrea–Ethiopia conflict were for peacekeeping, the inescapable reality is that they were not typical. Not only was its relatively straightforward inter-state character unusual in sub-Saharan Africa, by the end of the twentieth century it had become a rare type of conflict anywhere in the world.

---

59   Eritrea was reported to favour a dominant role for the UN against Ethiopia's preference for the OAU as lead mediator. The eventual distribution of roles probably went some way to meet this potentially difficult situation. BBC World Service (Africa) report, 18 June 2000.

CHAPTER SIX

Making Borders
Trans-Saharan Africa

The region we have described as trans-Saharan Africa (that is to say, the area of the continent composed of states on the interface between the 'Arab' north and the 'Bantu' south) saw two United Nations operations launched in the 1990s. The first was a major undertaking in the territory of Western Sahara and the second a very small-scale observation mission in northern Chad. The contrast between these two quite different involvements highlighted, as had the contrasting missions in both southern Africa and the Horn, the centrality of local dynamics to the 'success' or 'failure' of UN peacekeeping operations.

In Western Sahara a crisis of 'decolonization' similar in many ways to that in Namibia brought in a United Nations mission with the task of organizing and supervising what should have been a straightforward referendum on the territory's future. Both local parties to the issue saw UN intervention as an instrument that would enable them to achieve their diametrically opposed objectives and accordingly found a range of 'legitimate' means of encouraging and deterring particular courses of action. While the task of 'physical' peacekeeping in Western Sahara was easily enough carried out, there was no corresponding commitment to a 'political' peace, and the UN simply did not have the capacity to effect one. In contrast, both parties to the dispute in northern Chad (Chad itself and its neighbour Libya) were fully committed to an agreed outcome, and success was, accordingly, assured to the foreign mission invited to verify it.

Supervising intransigence:
Western Sahara, 1991–

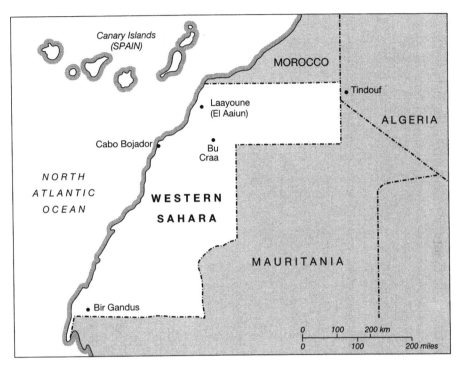

Western Sahara

Up to now we have asserted a general rule of UN peacekeeping endeavours in Africa: they have been most successful when concerned with the implementation of agreements between established international actors. The independence of Namibia and the Cuban withdrawal from Angola are the clearest illustrations of this perhaps, but it has also been evident in the interposition between Ethiopia and Eritrea, which we have just explored. There is, though, one significant exception to this general principle: the stalled settlement process in Western Sahara. Since 1988 the United Nations has struggled to manage and implement what initially appeared to be a straightforward process involving a plebiscite on self-determination and statehood that had been fully agreed in advance by recognized international entities. Its efforts have been unavailing, and may only be reinvigorated by an abandonment of fundamental principle.

The background to the conflict

The territory of Western Sahara occupies 267,000 square kilometres of desert and Atlantic coastline in north-west Africa. It is bounded in the north by Morocco and Algeria, and to the south and east by Mauritania. Its sparse population of Arab and Berber livestock herders has traditionally lived nomadically, the desert conditions being unsuitable to settled agriculture. From the late nineteenth century until 1976 the territory formed part of Spain's small and scattered African 'empire'. The first Europeans to land in the area of present-day Western Sahara were the Portuguese as early as the mid-fourteenth century. No attempt was made to establish any settled European presence, however, until Spain began to show an interest in the area at the beginning of the seventeenth century. Although the territory offered no primary economic advantage, it provided a landing point for Spanish ships at a time when contacts with the Americas were rapidly intensifying. However, Spain was displaced after a few years by Morocco, which imposed a limited and haphazard rule. When Morocco itself began to attract the attention of the European imperialists in the nineteenth century, Spain reinvigorated its old claim to the Western Sahara. At the Berlin Conference in 1884 Madrid's residual claim was recognized and it declared protectorates over the two regions of Saguia el Hamra, which composed the northern third of the territory, and Río de Oro, which covered the southern two-thirds. 'Spanish Sahara', however, was effectively contained along the coastal strip. The extent of Spanish control was constrained both by French claims to Mauritania in the south and east and by the resistance of the indigenous population of the interior. Effective occupation of the territory as it exists today was not achieved by Spain until the mid-1930s.

The years following this were largely uneventful, but in the mid-1950s the territory began to attract some international attention. Morocco regained its independence from France in 1956 and the following year its government, an assertive monarchy, laid claim to 'its' lost colony. Following France's decolonization of Morocco, Spain had agreed to withdraw from a number of enclaves it held in the region as its position in them became untenable. Madrid, however, regarded the more substantial and contiguous territories of Saguia el Hamra and Río de Oro as a separate issue, to the dismay of the Moroccan king, who considered them to be component parts of a 'greater Morocco'.[1] To underline its determination to stay put, Spain ended the

---

1 Spain retained two northern enclaves of Ceuta and Melilla. It has been suggested that Madrid's willingness to withdraw from its other possessions in Morocco was motivated in part by the calculation that adopting an 'anti-colonial' stance there would mean that African support could be mobilized behind Spain's claim against Britain for Gibraltar. J.D. Hargreaves, *Decolonization in Africa* (London: Longman, 1988), p. 204.

administrative division between the two territories of Western Sahara in 1958, bringing them together as an 'overseas province' of the metropole. This device was also designed to deflect unwelcome pressure from the United Nations for concrete moves towards the decolonization of non-self-governing territories. (Spain's neighbour Portugal had used this sleight of hand to preserve its own African territories some years earlier.) Pressure for Spanish withdrawal grew rather than diminished, however, especially when in 1960 Mauritania, which was itself newly independent of France, laid claim to the southern part of the territory. Beyond the natural territorial assertiveness of a new state, Mauritania's claim was motivated by suspicion of the 'greater Morocco' project. For its part, Morocco saw an advantage in acknowledging Mauritania's claim as a means of increasing its own diplomatic leverage against Spain. Morocco's claim, itself originally rooted in this nationalist *amour propre* of the newly decolonized state, gained a strong economic impetus in 1963 when extensive phosphate deposits were discovered at Bu Craa in the northern portion of the territory.

Western Sahara had passed through the most intense period of anti-colonial agitation in Africa as a whole largely untouched by the advancing tide of nationalism. This was in large part due to the nomadic, clan-focused character of the region's political culture. But by the later 1960s the first signs of a 'modern' nationalist movement were beginning to emerge among the Saharan people (or the 'Sahrawi' as they were known). Spain, which had been ruled by the authoritarian right-wing dictatorship of General Franco since the end of its civil war in 1939, responded instinctively with repression. This merely had the effect of entrenching indigenous resistance rather than suppressing it. In 1973 the Popular Front for the Liberation of Saguia el Hamra and Río de Oro was formed. The movement became known as 'Polisario' (the acronym of its Spanish name, *Frente Popular para a Liberación de Saguia el-Hamra y Río de Oro*). The Polisario embarked on a guerrilla campaign against the Spanish presence. As it became evident that Madrid had become less than enthusiastic about retaining the territory, Morocco under King Hassan II redoubled its own diplomatic campaign for possession. Hassan's interest was more than just acquisitive. The issue was also seen as providing an opportunity to outflank a growing nationalist challenge to his rule inside Morocco itself. Mauritania, anxious lest its own claims be shunted aside in the intensifying contest, now reasserted its own ambitions for a share of the territory.

The two neighbouring countries originally pursued their claim to the territory on twin fronts. As well as the diplomatic route involving Spain, a legal opinion was sought through the UN General Assembly from the International Court of Justice. Morocco and Mauritania claimed jointly that, at the time of its colonization by Spain, Western Sahara had not been, in legal terms, *terra nullius* (land belonging to no one) but that sovereignty had lain with them. In an Advisory Opinion issued in October 1975 the Court accepted that certain relationships had existed but found that there was no evidence of 'any tie of territorial sovereignty between the territory of Western Sahara and the Kingdom of Morocco or the Mauritanian entity'. Therefore, the General Assembly would be right in pursuing 'the decolonization of Western Sahara [based on] the principle of self-determination through free and genuine expression of the will of the peoples of the territory'.[2] This was a major legal setback for the claimant states, and one which would have a considerable impact on future developments.

At the time the Opinion was given, however, the two countries were making major diplomatic advances. Spain had now become determined to relieve itself of its increasingly difficult colonial presence in the territory. This was a position made more easily adoptable by the death of General Franco in the autumn of 1975 and the ensuing expectation of political liberalization in Spain. In the interests of national dignity and international prestige, however, Madrid sought to avoid the creation of a political vacuum on its departure. Having done nothing to prepare the indigenous people for self-government, and having been dissuaded by Morocco from moving ahead with a vague plan for a plebiscite on the territory's future, Spain's options were extremely limited. It chose the easiest of these, which was to accede to Moroccan–Mauritanian demands for power to be transferred to them jointly after 'decolonization'. The intense pressure applied by Morocco after its legal defeat quickly overcame any objections to this approach in Madrid. Ignoring UN Security Council appeals, King Hassan personally led a 'non-violent' demonstration of some 350,000 Moroccans (the so-called 'Green March') across the northern border of Western Sahara.[3] The numbers involved were sufficient to alter the demographic character of the sparsely populated territory. The 'marchers', as Moroccan citizens, Hassan's logic ran, had every right to move across and settle in 'Moroccan' territory.

'Decolonization' and partition

In this tense climate the territory was jointly administered by Morocco and Mauritania with Spain until February 1976, when the colonial power formally withdrew. This arrangement had been secretly and hastily agreed in a set of accords signed by the three states in Madrid in November 1975 and

---

2   International Court of Justice Case Summaries: Western Sahara, Advisory Opinion of
    16 October 1975. Found at www:icj-cij/icjwww/idecisons/isummaries/isummary751016.htm.
3   UN document S/RES/379, 2 November 1975.

immediately implemented. During this transitional period Spain acquiesced in the rapid extension of military control of the territory by the other two. In principle Western Sahara ceased to exist when the last Spanish administrators left. The Madrid accords passed the northern two-thirds of the territory (along with its phosphate deposits) into Moroccan sovereignty while the southern third went to Mauritania. Spain was to be compensated by a 35 per cent stake in the phosphate venture and fishing concessions off the Saharan coast. The secret agreement was given a gloss of international formality by a bilateral treaty between Morocco and Mauritania, the Rabat Agreement, signed in the Moroccan capital in April 1976.[4] Needless to say, the Polisario had other ideas and the 'occupying' forces became subject to guerrilla attack.

The Polisario's key ally in its campaign was Algeria in the north-east. Algeria had itself made a historical claim to the territory during Spanish rule but had not pressed it against the demands for self-determination on the part of Polisario. In the mid-1970s Algeria regarded itself as a leading Third World 'radical' and could hardly be seen to oppose an anti-colonial liberation movement in pursuit of its own territorial aggrandizement. Algeria's interests, its government calculated, were better served by acting as mentor to the Polisario. In this way it could accrue a number of advantages. It could sustain its radical credentials internationally by supporting African liberation and self-determination. Its support for the guerrillas would also discomfort its regional and ideological rival, the pro-western and conservative Morocco. And, if the Polisario's campaign were to be successful and an independent Western Sahara did emerge, Algeria would benefit from the gratitude of the new state both diplomatically and – in view of the phosphates – materially as well. Consequently, Algeria began to provide both military supplies and bases for the fighters of the Polisario.

Increasingly, as the guerrilla conflict intensified, the harsh desert terrain of the Tindouf region of south-west Algeria also became a haven for a swelling number of Sahrawi refugees. The population of their camps quickly grew to around 60,000. The Polisario established its headquarters in the area, where it effectively created a 'state-within-a-state' extending across the network of camps. Equipped with emblems of sovereignty (such as its own 'national' anthem and flag), the Polisario provided an efficient administration for the camps as well as a broad range of social services within them. The camps also became a recruiting ground for new political and military cadres. The pattern was similar to that established by the Palestine Liberation

---

4   William Durch, 'United Nations Mission for the Referendum in Western Sahara', in William Durch (ed.), *The Evolution of UN Peacekeeping: Case Studies and Comparative Analysis* (New York: St Martin's Press, 1993), p. 407.

Organization in camps in Jordan and Lebanon in the 1960s and 1970s, though the less cosmopolitan, more tightly knit culture of the Sahrawi provided the Polisario with an even firmer political hold on its people.

Another similarity with the Palestinian experience was that the distinction between refugee and activist became difficult to draw. The refugee camps that grew in the Tindouf region of Algeria became, in effect, the political base of the Polisario. Specifically, this was the location of the government in exile it had created at the time of the Spanish withdrawal in 1976 when it declared the 'Saharan Arab Democratic Republic' (SADR). Its quasi-state functions extended beyond the provision of order and services in the camps to widespread international and 'diplomatic' activities. Soon the SADR – with the help of Algeria's diplomatic influence – had won the formal recognition of some seventy states. These supporters came from the Soviet bloc, including Moscow's main proxy in African affairs, Cuba. Diplomatic backing also came from another important regional actor, Libya, and from among the more radical states of the Third World as a whole. On the other side Morocco and Mauritania, long perceived as 'friendly' to the interests of the west in North Africa, drew support from the United States and its allies. In this instance anyway this included France, which had strong historical links with the region (having been the imperial power in both Morocco and Mauritania) and which still exerted considerable influence. In this way the Western Sahara conflict, like that being played out simultaneously in Angola, was drawn into the bipolar contest of the cold war, which in the later 1970s was deepening once again.

Initially, the Polisario performed well in the guerrilla war against both occupying forces. Its strength lay in its intimate familiarity with the singular and difficult terrain of Western Sahara, the support of the sparse and scattered population and the capacity to strike rapidly with light arms over a geographically wide area of operations. It was most successful against the Mauritanians in the south. Mauritania had less economic incentive in the territory, more limited military resources and weaker political will than Morocco and therefore proved the easier opponent to overcome. As a result, in 1979 a diplomatic rapprochement with Algeria provided the vehicle for Mauritanian withdrawal from Western Sahara. It now declared its neutrality in the continuing conflict against its erstwhile ally, Morocco.

The effective defeat of one of its enemies might have been expected to position the Polisario much closer to an ultimate victory. Certainly it provided a huge boost to the morale of the Polisario fighters as well as to its diplomatic position. But Morocco, while strained by the conflict, was proving increasingly effective militarily against the guerrillas' tactics. In particular it refined its use of air power, to which the Sahrawi had no effective reply. The conflict thus slowly ground towards stalemate. This found physical embodiment in 1980 when Morocco began the bold initiative of building a sand wall – or 'berm' – more or less encircling the territory. The three metre-high berm, which would take seven years to complete, eventually ran for 3000 kilometres south-west from the Morocco–Western Sahara–Algeria frontier round 90 per cent of the territory to the sea just north of its border with Mauritania. It was perhaps the first such example of military engineering since Roman times. In addition to being 'traditionally' defended by thousands of troops, the berm was also equipped with more modern 'assets' such as minefields and electronic surveillance devices. The effect of the berm was physically to exclude the Polisario guerrillas from almost the entire territory, now bounded by the sea in the west, Morocco in the north and the sand wall in the east and south.

Towards a 'settlement'

The cumulative effect of improved Moroccan military tactics and the construction of the berm was to slow the war down almost to a standstill. The conflict remained a major drain on the Moroccan economy, however. Moreover, no matter how well contained, the Polisario could not be totally extinguished as a military threat and its hold on the now 120,000-strong refugee population in the Algerian camps was absolute. The SADR also continued to enjoy considerable diplomatic support. Aware of the potential for internal division among its membership, the Organization of African Unity had maintained a low profile on the issue at the time of Spain's 'decolonization'. Following Mauritania's withdrawal from the territory, however, it took on a more activist role. Firstly, the Polisario was recognized by the OAU as the legitimate government of the SADR. Then, at the urgings of the more radical states (notably the former Portuguese colonies and the 'front-line states' confronting South Africa), the SADR was admitted as a full member of the organization. This decision was taken in the run-up to the 1982 summit, which – significantly – was held in Libya. It led to Morocco and a significant group of its conservative supporters suspending their membership of the OAU.[5] The issue now threatened to polarize the international relations of the African continent as a whole, and the OAU, concerned for its own institutional future in such an environment, began to press for the United Nations to become involved in the search for a permanent settlement.

The UN secretariat was not initially enthusiastic about assuming this more active role in the conflict. The constraints of cold war bipolarity still

---

5   Ibid., p. 408.

circumscribed the UN's possibilities in the mid-1980s. The secretary-general, Javier Pérez de Cuéllar, was reluctant to inherit a 'regional' problem from the OAU that could prove both intractable and divisive in New York. With the conflict close to deadlock, however, both the Polisario and the Moroccan government began to show more flexibility on the question of a long-term settlement. This was accompanied by a general lessening in cold war tensions in the broader international system. There was consequently less reason to fear that active engagement by the UN in Western Sahara might draw in wider hostilities. In other words, the 'Congo scenario', present in the institutional memory of the UN since the 1960s, seemed less of an immediate threat. Within the UN too, the General Assembly, in conformity with its historical responsibility for issues of decolonization and self-determination, began pressing the secretary-general to engage more closely with the issue.[6] With both the internal and international dynamics of the conflict apparently changing for the better, therefore, a new phase of UN activism began. In 1985 the secretary-general established a 'good offices' mission in co-operation with the OAU to negotiate separately with Morocco and the Polisario. These 'proximity' talks were necessary because Morocco consistently rejected the Polisario's calls for direct negotiations as this would imply recognition of the SADR's legitimacy. Then, in 1988, after a period of shuttle diplomacy between Rabat, Algiers and the Polisario headquarters in Tindouf by Pérez de Cuéllar himself, a general settlement plan was produced.

Central to this was to be an act of self-determination in the form of a referendum. The population of the Western Sahara would, it was intended, finally decide whether the territory was to be a sovereign independent African state or to be incorporated in 'greater Morocco'. The proposal was apparently straightforward and should have been easily implemented. In the event it proved anything but this. From the beginning a key, evidently unresolvable, 'technical' question prevented significant movement: who was to be eligible to vote in the referendum? The original plan, whose UN architects were well aware of the dangers of ambiguity, set out to be as specific as possible.[7] As a general principle the demographic shift created by Morocco's Green March in 1975 and its aftermath was to be discounted. The right to vote was to be restricted to those with clear roots in the territory before the Spanish

---

6 General Assembly resolution 40/50, 2 December 1985. The Assembly had first engaged with the issue in 1966 when it passed a resolution critical of continued Spanish presence and calling for self-determination for the territory. Between 1967 and 1973, before passing the issue to the International Court of Justice, the Assembly passed a further six such resolutions.

7 The full terms of the settlement proposal are set out in a report from the secretary-general to the Security Council in mid-1990. UN document S/21360, 18 June 1990. The plan was adopted by a Security Council resolution – UN document S/RES/658, 27 June 1990.

withdrawal. The colonial authorities had undertaken a census in 1974, less than two years before the transfer of power. This had recorded a remarkably low population figure of only 74,000 and was to form the basis of voter identification for the referendum. Those Sahrawi counted in the census and who would be at least eighteen years old at the time of the referendum would constitute the core of eligible voters.

However, because of the uniqueness of Saharan culture and society – notably the large proportion of nomadic tribespeople within the general population – there were significant exceptions to this census criterion.[8] These included Saharans whose seasonal movements meant that they could not be counted in the 1974 census. The immediate family (parents and children) of both those included in the census and those resident but unable to be so included would also be permitted to vote. So would the children of a father born in the territory, whether they themselves were resident or not. Additionally, members of a Saharan tribe who had lived in the territory for six consecutive years (or for twelve years intermittently before December 1974) would also be included. The management of this labyrinthine registration task was to be given to an Identification Commission.[9] Both Morocco and the Polisario agreed to this formula and seemed confident that the outcome would vindicate their contending positions. This in itself should have been an intimation of how complex, potentially uncertain and politically fraught the undertaking was to prove.

Beyond the central issue of the management of the referendum, the settlement plan involved a number of preparatory and confidence-building measures that were to take place in the six months leading up to the vote. This period was determined, wildly optimistically as it would turn out, as sufficient for the Identification Commission to complete its work and draw up an electoral roll. In the meantime there was to be a formal cease-fire. The number of Moroccan troops in the territory was to be reduced (initially from 100,000 to 65,000) and they were to be confined to agreed locations. The UN was to take control of key administrative activities in the territory and, crucially, facilitate the return of some 120,000 refugees (a figure that dramatically undermined the findings of Spain's 1974 census) from Algeria and Mauritania prior to the vote. The poll itself would take place after a

---

8 The complex issue of territorial identity and the concept of a Western Saharan 'population' is explored in Joshua Castellino, 'Territory and identity in international law: the struggle for self-determination in the Western Sahara', *Millennium: Journal of International Studies* 28(3), 1999, pp. 523–51.

9 Foreign and Commonwealth Office (UK), 'Focus International' paper, *Western Sahara: Moving the Peace Process Forward* (December 2000). Found at http://files.fco.gov.uk/info/briefs/wsahara/pdf.

three-week campaign. Depending on the outcome of the vote, one side would immediately withdraw its forces from the territory, which would then adopt its chosen constitutional identity.

The establishment of MINURSO

The initial agreement by both sides to the settlement proposals was treated with optimism by the Security Council rather than the scepticism that hindsight suggests would have been appropriate. The plan was formally accepted by Morocco and the Polisario on 30 August 1988. Three weeks later the Security Council passed a unanimous resolution authorizing the appointment of a special representative to Western Sahara and urging the secretary-general to move ahead with planning for the referendum in co-operation with the OAU.[10] Although fighting on the ground virtually ended after the joint agreement, a formal cease-fire between the two sides was not finally declared until early 1991. It came at that time as an essential preliminary to the establishment of the military mission charged with managing the referendum and the transitional period. With the situation on the ground thus formalized, at the end of April 1991 the Security Council established the United Nations Mission for the Referendum in Western Sahara.[11]

The operation was called MINURSO from its French name, *Mission des Nations Unies pour l'Organisation d'un Référendum au Sahara Occidental*. Coming before the main onrush of the post-cold war demand for peacekeeping operations, the mission was able to draw on a relatively large pool of contributors. The apparently stable and controlled environment in which the peacekeepers were to operate – there was a 'peace' to keep – also helped secure offers of contingents. The initial deployment of 200 military observers under the initial command of Major General Armand Roy of Canada took place at the beginning of September 1991 as the cease-fire came into effect. The operation's headquarters were established in the territory's 'capital', Laayoune. It was never to be a large-scale undertaking in terms of manpower. In the following ten years the total military personnel in place at any one time would never exceed 300.

MINURSO's mandate was comprehensive. It was to monitor the Moroccan–Polisario cease-fire and verify the agreed reduction of Moroccan troop levels. It was to supervise the confinement of both sides' remaining forces to agreed cantonment areas and to ensure the release of Sahrawi detainees held by Morocco and supervise the exchange of prisoners of war

---

10   UN document S/RES/621, 20 September 1988.
11   UN document S/RES/690, 29 April 1991.

between the sides. Onerous though these responsibilities were, they were secondary to MINURSO's role in preparing for, administering and supervising the referendum. To this end, in co-operation with the UN High Commission for Refugees (UNHCR), it would put in place a repatriation programme to bring back the refugees from Algeria and Mauritania prior to the vote. Through the Identification Commission, MINURSO would also verify and register eligible voters. Finally, it would organize and police the referendum and certify its result.

Problems would attend all the components of this mandate, but from the beginning it was clear that voter identification would be the most difficult and the most contested by the parties. The fundamental problem for MINURSO was that each side saw the settlement plan as a route to victory. By the terms of the plan, that victory would be absolute. It would mean either the exclusion of Morocco from the territory or Moroccan control of it. Each side had made its own calculations and concluded that it would win this zero-sum game. Neither would have agreed to the plan and the consequent creation of MINURSO on any other basis.

Prevarication and stasis

From the outset it was clear that the twenty weeks initially allocated for voter identification and registration would be wholly inadequate. There would certainly be no referendum in January 1992 as originally envisaged by the secretary-general. With both sides determined to win and expecting to do so, the process could never be quick or simple. The model of the Transition Assistance Group in Namibia was, naturally enough, in the forefront of planning assumptions for MINURSO. In terms of previous UN experience it was the closest available precedent. But the political differences between the two undertakings at different ends of the continent were in reality enormous. The independence of Namibia was to all intents and purposes a foregone conclusion. South Africa, although capable of limited spoiling gestures, had made its calculations and opted for withdrawal from Namibia as a reasonable trade-off for disentanglement from Angola. Morocco had no such strategy; it intended to 'win' Western Sahara and would take whatever steps necessary to ensure it did.[12]

Voter eligibility was the inevitable battleground, which should have been predictable when the original settlement plan was worked out. At the time, though, the determination of the UN to reach an agreement, and its relief when one seemed to present itself, tended to suppress critical judgements.

---

12 Durch, 'United Nations Mission for the Referendum in Western Sahara', p. 418.

In a report to the Security Council in December 1991, three months after the cease-fire was established and MINURSO military observers deployed, Pérez de Cuéllar pointed to the problems inherent in the process. He noted that

> because of their nomadic way of life, the people of the Territory move easily across the borders to the neighbouring countries. . . . [This] ebb and flow of people . . . makes it difficult to take a complete census of the inhabitants of the Spanish Sahara and also poses the complex problem of the identification of the Saharans of the Territory and makes it even more difficult to take a satisfactory census of refugees.[13]

The Polisario, for its part, was determined that only the 74,000 inhabitants recorded in Spain's 1974 census should be eligible for registration. Morocco, fully aware that if this position prevailed it would lose the referendum outright, sought a much wider electorate. Firstly, it claimed that the 1974 census itself had been incomplete and that thousands of other Sahrawi present in the territory at the time should be located and registered. Secondly, it insisted that a significant proportion of the territory's population had fled to Morocco as refugees during the fighting between the Polisario and the Spanish colonial forces, and that these individuals, now Moroccan residents, should also be eligible to vote. Finally, Morocco noted that Spain had ceded to it parts of the north of the territory in the 1950s and 1960s. The original inhabitants of these areas, now part of southern Morocco, should, the Rabat government insisted, also be entitled to vote.[14] In this way Morocco sought eligibility for some 120,000 'new' (and almost entirely pro-Moroccan) voters. This was not much less than twice the number counted in the 1974 census – and equal to the population of the Polisario-controlled refugee camps in Algeria.

The process of 'Moroccanization' was, moreover, ongoing. Effectively unopposed by the UN, tens of thousands of poor peasants from southern Morocco were enticed by their government into tented shanty towns around Laayoune. Various financial incentives were provided, along with the promise of land in the territory when it passed definitively to Moroccan control after the referendum. As the voter identification process became increasingly protracted, the centrality of the 1974 census to the process was progressively undermined as more and more Sahrawi who had not been born at the time reached the age of eighteen and thus became eligible for registration.

The work of the Identification Commission would have been difficult enough in its technical aspects even if there had been consensus on the

---

13   UN document S/23299, 19 December 1991.
14   UN document S/2000/131, 17 February 2000.

criteria for eligibility. Against the background of intense mutual hostility and irreconcilable views on the basis of voter registration, however, its work more or less ground to a halt. By the beginning of 1996 there had been no significant movement in the settlement process. Beyond the issue of voter identification, there had been no progress on the repatriation of the refugees or the release of prisoners of war and political detainees. The only positive aspect of the process was the maintenance of the cease-fire. Even this had been achieved as a result less of MINURSO pressure than of the political calculation of the rival forces that vied with each other for international prestige and support.

Morocco, although holding to the original truce, was not fully co-operative with MINURSO. Frequently elements of its 120,000-strong force in the territory and along the berm actively impeded the freedom of movement and operational efficiency of the UN mission. It was often unclear, however, whether this was a result of calculated policy emanating from Rabat or simply mischief on the part of local commanders. Certainly, the absence of a formal status of forces agreement complicated the conduct of the operation. Without a legally recognized 'host state', however, such an agreement proved difficult to conclude. Negotiations, which focused on MINURSO military observation activities on the largely uncontested international borders of the territory, continued throughout the 1990s. An understanding in principle was reached with Algeria and Mauritania for a status of forces agreement in the border areas, but Morocco remained obstructive, provoking sharp criticism from the secretary-general.[15] Morocco did not reach such an agreement with the UN until the beginning of 1999, and then only because the renewal of MINURSO's mandate by the Security Council was in doubt unless it did so.[16] It was not in Morocco's interest to draw international criticism of its day-to-day behaviour towards the UN military operation while it pursued victory in the political process. But more particularly, any threat to the continuation of MINURSO would have undermined Morocco's larger strategy of prevarication in pursuit of conditions that would guarantee its victory in the referendum. A similar judgement guided the Polisario's attitude to MINURSO's observers, at least in the first years of the operation. With its 8000 or so fighters restricted to the outside of the berm, though, there was less opportunity for friction between the Polisario and the UN anyway.

The central raison d'être of MINURSO was, as its name indicated, the preparation of the referendum, not routine cease-fire monitoring. With progress on this effectively having ceased by the end of 1995, the UN's credibility

---

15   UN document S/1998/634, 10 July 1998.
16   BBC World Service (Africa) report, 12 February 1999.

was diminishing fast. In response Boutros Boutros-Ghali, who was by now secretary-general, recommended that the Security Council formally suspend the voter identification process and scale down MINURSO's other activities. The military component was accordingly reduced by 20 per cent and the UN's political presence was maintained only by a single office in Laayoune. Boutros-Ghali's frustration was clear in his report to the Council:

> I am compelled to conclude that the required willingness does not exist to give MINURSO the co-operation needed for it to resume and complete the identification process within a reasonable period of time. In these circumstances, I feel obliged to recommend that the identification process be suspended until such time as both parties provide convincing evidence that they are committed to resuming and completing it without further obstacles. . . .[17]

Another push: James Baker and the Houston Accord

At the beginning of 1997 Boutros-Ghali, having incurred the hostility of the Clinton administration in Washington, was replaced as secretary-general by Kofi Annan. The new secretary-general set about attempting to get the process back on track and to accelerate its pace. In March 1997, within a few weeks of his taking office, Annan appointed a 'Personal Envoy' to the area. This new post was distinct from that of secretary-general's special representative on the ground. Its purpose was essentially diplomatic rather than operational, and this was reflected in the identity of the appointee. James Baker had been US secretary of state under President George Bush. He had been in office during the Gulf crisis of 1990–91 and had later led one of the periodic efforts to find an agreement between Israel and the Palestinians. Although associated with the conservative rather than liberal strand of American foreign policy, Baker was nevertheless widely regarded as an independent and open-minded diplomatic operator. His particular experience seemed to equip him for the delicate role of intermediary and facilitator between Morocco and the Polisario. Perhaps most importantly, though, he was an American, and therefore could exert real leverage on Rabat, source of the main obstruction to the overall process. He immediately brought pressure to bear on both sides to agree to direct talks with each other. A series of meetings followed that began with more indirect proximity negotiations in London before moving on to face-to-face meetings between Moroccan and Polisario delegates in Lisbon in June 1997.[18] The final round of talks

---

17   UN document S/1996/343, 8 May 1996.
18   *Africa Confidential* 38(13), 20 June 1997.

took place in Houston, Texas, in September, where a new agreement was reached dealing with the specific issues causing the deadlock in the process.[19] The 'Houston Accord' in principle resolved the conflicts around the voter identification process and set out a code of conduct for the referendum campaign.[20] Commitment to movement on the other stalled aspects of the settlement plan – the repatriation of refugees, the release of prisoners of war and political detainees – was also given by the parties.

Yet the success of Baker's efforts proved largely illusory. The Houston Accord did not relaunch the settlement process in any meaningful sense. Mutual recriminations quickly crowded out the apparent new bases of co-operation. In a sense, perhaps, the very qualities that appeared to make Baker the perfect choice for the job proved ultimately counter-productive. He was undoubtedly a figure with an authority unusual among United Nations officials, one capable of exerting considerable leverage in the negotiations. But the danger in this situation was that the parties would be subdued into an 'agreement' that they had insufficient political will to make stick in the longer term. The Identification Commission did resume its work at the end of 1997, but it was dogged by renewed complaints and recriminations from both sides and it was soon clear that a new target date for the referendum in December 1998 would not be met.

Perversely, it seemed, the UN was determined to maintain an optimistic front even in the face of this. Hopes that the referendum might really be on the horizon seemed high by the end of 1998, and a visit by Kofi Annan to the region, including the Tindouf camps, produced outwardly encouraging responses from both sides and their regional neighbours. Another American, Charles Dunbar, a widely experienced former diplomat, was appointed special representative of the secretary-general. His task would be to speed preparations for the referendum on the ground, notably by arranging the process of refugee repatriation. For the first time since 1992 there seemed to be real expectations in the United Nations that a referendum was actually feasible and a provisional date was fixed for December 1999.

It was not to be, however. Institutional optimism could not disguise the continuing problems in the identification process. Although both sides had accepted a new set of protocols to speed the work of the Commission, they had done so without enthusiasm and with evidently separate and incompatible agendas. A request from Morocco in March 1999 for the December date to be put back into 2000 may have been motivated by political calculation, but it was not an unrealistic proposal given the state of MINURSO's

---

19 *Western Sahara: Moving the Peace Process Forward*, p. 10.
20 The Houston Accord is outlined in UN document S/1997/742, 24 September 1997.

preparations. The secretary-general now set 31 July 2000 as the new referendum date, but he did so in an atmosphere of fading expectations.[21] By the end of 1999 the identification process was supposedly 'complete'. A total of 147,000 applications had been processed by the Identification Commission from which 86,381 were approved for registration. Morocco, aware that this arithmetic pointed to an overwhelming victory for the Polisario, raised 130,000 appeals.[22] As Kofi Annan remarked ruefully: 'Judging from the Mission's past experience with both parties, whose concerns and attempts at controlling the identification process have been the principal cause of the difficulties and delays encountered, the appeals process could be even lengthier and more cumbersome and contentious than the identification itself.'[23] The identification process had, of course, taken more than eight years by that stage.

New leadership in Morocco: plus ça change?

The sudden death of King Hassan of Morocco in July 1999 had momentarily raised expectations of a less intransigent approach from Rabat, but it became clear that his son, who succeeded him as King Mohammed VI, would be just as obdurate. Worryingly from the Polisario point of view, Mohammed seemed set on improving relations with Algeria, thus potentially jeopardizing its position with its own chief ally.[24] Worse still, any hope that a Morocco–Algeria rapprochement might lead to more flexibility on the part of the new king were dispelled in January 2000 when Rabat declared itself dissatisfied with the voter registration process in its entirety and finally and formally set itself against a referendum. Throughout 2000 intensive efforts by James Baker to resurrect the process were unavailing. Increasingly acrimonious talks held in London and Geneva in June and July simply confirmed the breakdown of even the limited agreement wrung out of the parties in Houston three years earlier.

Faced by this now virtually complete absence of common ground between the parties, Annan and Baker were left to search for the 'third way' absent from the original winner-takes-all settlement proposals. The new plan, presented to the Security Council at the end of June 2001, represented nothing less than the reversal of the United Nations' thirty-five-year commitment to self-determination for the territory. Baker proposed that Moroccan sovereignty

21   BBC World Service (Africa), report, 18 May 1999.
22   *Africa Confidential* 42(10), 18 May 2001.
23   UN document S/2001/613, 20 June 2001.
24   *Africa Confidential* 40(16), 6 August 1999.

over the territory be recognized subject to a constitutional arrangement guaranteeing a degree of regional political and fiscal autonomy. Unsurprisingly, the Polisario reacted with outrage to what it saw as an act of betrayal by the United Nations. It might not have done so, paradoxically, had a similar plan been proposed before the 1988 settlement proposals. But by adopting the 1988 scheme the UN had undertaken to guarantee an act of free choice. Now it seemed simply to have capitulated to Moroccan intransigence. For its part, Morocco greeted the proposals cautiously but with understandable satisfaction.[25] Baker sought a period of months to win over the Polisario.

It was unclear how he could expect to be successful in this, but it was equally unclear what cards the Polisario had to play against the new plan if the Security Council sought to present it as a *fait accompli*. While a considerable well of international sympathy still existed for the Polisario and its aspirations, the diplomatic leverage that it could deploy was limited. The post-cold war international system was not as receptive to the 'Third World lobby' as it had been in the era of bipolarity. More specifically, Algeria's continued support for the Polisario was far from assured. Increasingly preoccupied with its own internal political and security problems, Algeria was keen to build new international relationships, locally with Morocco and globally with the west. Its historical commitment to self-determination for Western Sahara might now be qualified.

The end of bipolarity also altered fundamentally the reception of the Baker plan by the Security Council. During the cold war a Soviet veto of such a proposal would have been certain. It was far from clear that Russia – or China – would now regard the issue as sufficiently significant to resist pressure from the western powers on the Security Council. Moreover, the support of the western permanent members for the new plan looked solid. Beyond historical affinities with pro-western Morocco another consideration encouraged support for the plan. There was diminishing justification for continued expenditure on what had become a redundant 'peacekeeping' operation, and by 2000 MINURSO was costing about US$4.5 million each month.

The 'immorality' of the UN's threatened abandonment of its key principle of self-determination over Western Sahara seemed clear to many. But the shifting architecture of the regional and global structures within which this apparent denouement arrived had an inescapable logic. From the beginning of the conflict Morocco had the implicit support of its western patrons. While the end of the cold war may have threatened automatic support for client regimes in other parts of Africa (Zaïre and Somalia come most readily to mind), the Moroccan regime was not so outrageously odious as to provoke

---

25   *The Guardian*, 22 June 2001.

abandonment. On the contrary, it retained considerable geo-strategic importance to the west even after the end of the cold war because of various perceived threats in and around North Africa. As well as enjoying this continued favour in the west, Morocco remained in effective occupation of Western Sahara (particularly after the construction of the berm). In short, therefore, self-determination for the territory remained dependent on Morocco. Morocco remained of value to, and therefore in favour with, the western powers – which in turn set the terms of debate within the Security Council. This was a reality, however unpalatable to many. Rabat had simply to play the long game – which it did with considerable cynicism and some skill – in order to deny victory to its rivals if not secure it unconditionally for itself. The frequent complaints at the UN's failure to stand up to Morocco's 'bullying' during the settlement process were understandable, but it was not clear how the organization could have done this in practical terms.

There were only two conceivable means by which this Moroccan control of events could have been broken: one would have been meaningful diplomatic and economic pressure from the west; the other would have been through enforcement action under Chapter VII of the Charter. The first was unlikely; the second simply unthinkable. The Security Council had expressed only limited criticism of Morocco throughout the years of its intransigence. Boutros-Ghali's suspension of the identification process in 1996 was the high point of the UN's 'punitive' action. William Durch summed up MINURSO's central dilemma in these terms: '[s]eeing what it was supposed to do, and comparing that with what it has been able to do, suggests the degree to which the operation was carried forward by a kind of collective wishful thinking on the part of an organization unwilling to admit the limits of international moral authority in a confrontation with nationalism.'[26] Taking the recent experience in Namibia as its compass in the early 1990s, the UN inevitably lost direction when Morocco proved to have none of the broader motives of South Africa to see the process of self-determination succeed. The hope that Morocco, driven by a historical nationalism and fuelled by economic self-interest, would eventually come behind the process was ultimately futile.

A perfect miniature: Chad, 1994

The protracted and repeatedly frustrated efforts of MINURSO contrasts sharply with the experience of UN intervention in a situation in another

---

26 Durch, 'United Nations Mission for the Referendum in Western Sahara', p. 413.

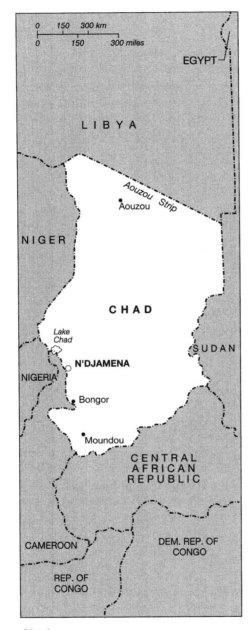

Chad

part of trans-Saharan Africa which, although on a wholly different scale, nevertheless bore similarities to that in Western Sahara. During 1994 a small group of MINURSO military observers was seconded to northern Chad. The United Nations established an Observer Group (UNASOG) in May of that year to oversee the withdrawal of Libyan forces who had occupied part of the border area between Chad and Libya, the Aouzou Strip. As in Western Sahara, the UN's involvement in Chad derived from a settlement process between international protagonists over an issue of contested sovereignty. In both cases the original conflict had its legal roots in uncertain colonial frontier agreements. In each case too the proposed settlement was derived from a judgment of the International Court of Justice. There, however, the similarities ended. In Chad the outcome had been mutually agreed and was fundamentally acceptable to both sides. There was no question of a referendum, let alone one for which the UN itself would have to be responsible. UNASOG's role was a purely verificatory one. To this end, its personnel consisted of a mere fifteen people – nine military observers and six civilian officials. A major complicating factor in this otherwise straightforward process, however, was a larger picture of long-term political chaos in Chad, in which Libya and other foreign actors were deeply involved. But despite this threatening context, the UN mission was completed in a matter of weeks, an unalloyed success – albeit one on a very modest scale.

The Republic of Chad is at the nexus of a number of distinct regions of Africa. To the west its neighbours are Nigeria, Niger and Cameroon, to the south, the Central African Republic, and to the east, Sudan. The northern half of Chad, however, forms part of the Sahara, where its neighbour is Libya. The European colonization of Chad dates from 1891 when France supplanted the loose control of Sudan that had been exerted earlier in the nineteenth century. In 1910 the territory became part of the French Equatorial African Federation. In reality, though, the colonial state had only limited political and economic impact. Long-established indigenous structures of authority and production (predominantly subsistence agriculture) remained little changed until independence in 1960, which came as part of France's simultaneous decolonization of its sub-Saharan territories.

The pressures of independent statehood very quickly sharpened underlying regional and ethnic cleavages in Chad. Reflecting the country's location on a key cultural crossroads in Africa, Chad's seven million people could be divided broadly into two regional groups. The north was predominantly Muslim in religion with strong Arab cultural influences. The south consisted largely of non-Muslim black Africans who were either Christians or followed traditional religions. The southerners constituted the greater part of the population, but their majority was not a large one.[27] At independence power

---

27 Muslims made up about 40 per cent of the population. About 35 per cent was Christian and 25 per cent followed indigenous beliefs, and this combined majority inhabited the 'Bantu' south.

was transferred by the French to a southern president, François Tombalbaye, in conformity with the colonial power's long-standing policy of favouring the 'African' south against the 'Arab' north. Muslim resentment now deepened. The northern population felt excluded not just from political power but also from the patrimonial favour that determined the distribution of economic benefits in a desperately poor and ill-resourced country. Tensions grew until, in the late 1960s, an anti-government guerrilla campaign began in the north and east. The outbreak of fighting coincided with Colonel Gaddafi's seizure of power after the overthrow of the Libyan monarchy. There was a connection between the uprising in northern Chad and the radicalization of Libyan politics and foreign policy that followed Gaddafi's coup. The new regime in Tripoli encouraged and supplied the Chadian insurgents – who fought under the umbrella of the Chad National Liberation Front (*Front de Libération Nationale Tchadien* – Frolinat) against the French-supported regime in the capital, N'Djamena.

Gaddafi's Libya had a range of motives for supporting Frolinat. There was a broad, international dimension to the issue in that the southern-dominated regime in N'Djamena was seen by some of the more radical Third World states (a group with which Gaddafi strongly identified) as a puppet of the French and therefore as an agent of neo-colonialism. More immediately, however, Libya had obvious cultural affinities with the northern people as well as a specific territorial claim in the region that in fact long pre-dated Gaddafi's assumption of power. The 114,000 square kilometre Aouzou Strip is a largely inhospitable desert area between the two states but a treaty had been signed in 1935 by the two colonial powers of the period – France for Chad and Italy for Libya – which had assigned the Strip to Libya, though the treaty was never formally ratified. After the Second World War Italy was required to renounce its claim to Libya (which had been a battlefield during the conflict) and its administration was taken over by the allied powers. This was never intended to be more than an interim arrangement, however, and in December 1951 Libya became independent and assumed responsibility for its own borders. A treaty was then signed between Libya and France at the instigation of the government in Paris in 1955 in order formally to settle all its colonial borders in the region.

It was on the interpretation of this complex and lengthy agreement that the territorial dispute with Chad turned. Libya argued that this treaty had not finalized the border in the Aouzou Strip and that, effectively, there was no border and that one should now be fixed. The Tripoli regime did so in the confidence that the inhabitants of the area would favour government from oil-rich, Islamic Libya rather than impoverished, 'African' N'Djamena. Chad, on the other hand, argued that the 1955 Franco-Libyan treaty had in fact fixed the Aouzou Strip border, including it in French – now Chadian – territory.[28]

The issue was brought to a head by the apparently irremediable political anarchy that beset post-independence Chad. In all practical terms Libya already exerted control over the disputed area and had done from the late 1960s through its patronage of a Frolinat faction, Goukouli Oueddei's Toubou rebels. The state of apparently permanent civil war in Chad during the 1970s and 1980s also periodically brought direct occupation of the Aouzou and other parts of Chad by Libyan forces as Gaddafi backed his *protégés* against the southern factions supported by France.

In 1975 President Tombalbaye was assassinated and replaced by another southerner, an army general, Félix Malloum, as Frolinat was progressively widening the area of the war. The protracted, violent chaos that was rapidly becoming the status quo of Chadian politics elicited a series of 'peacekeeping' responses, though not initially on the part of the United Nations. In 1979 the Malloum regime fell to the forces of the north. This did not bring any sort of stability as by this stage Frolinat itself had become factionalized. The years of fighting had caused a descent into warlord politics in the north with two rivals contesting control of the insurgency and thus, ultimately, national power. The pro-Libyan Oueddei was opposed by the more nationalist-oriented Hissène Habré. Consequently, although the southern-dominated government in N'Djamena had been brought down, there was no cohesive and united political movement to replace it. A Nigerian force of about 800 men intervened after the fall of the Malloum regime in 1979 in an ill-prepared and confused operation intended to impose order.[29] The following year the crisis deepened when Libya sent troops in support of Oueddei, who was now nominally president of Chad. Tripoli was driven in this by a determination to defeat the continuing challenge of Hissène Habré, which it saw as the major threat to its regional interests. This brought another 'peacekeeping' intervention, this time by Congo-Brazzaville. Despite Congo's Francophone identity this was no more effective than the Anglophone Nigerian force had been. Subsequently, the Organization of African Unity undertook to mount a multilateral intervention in 1981–82 to 'replace' the 15,000-strong Libyan force, which was by then the main source of security in Chad. It did so with little evident enthusiasm. A limited consensus among the membership of the OAU itself, acute problems over financing and a

---

28   The ICJ judgment provides the details of this extremely complex dispute. 'Case Concerning the Territorial Dispute (Libyan Arab Jamahiriya/Chad)', 3 February 1994. Found at www.icj-cij/icjwww/icases/idt/idt_ijudgments_19940203.pdf.

29   Eric G. Berman and Katie E. Sams, *Peacekeeping in Africa: Capabilities and Culpabilities* (Geneva: United Nations Institute for Disarmament Research, 2000), pp. 220–1.

fundamental vagueness as to objectives beyond keeping a peace that in reality did not exist meant that this operation was no more successful than the previous interventions.[30] The Libyan forces withdrew from most of Chad in November 1981 but retained forces in the Aouzou Strip.

Civil war continued throughout the 1980s, with Habré ousting Oueddei in 1983 and, with French and (less directly) American support, fighting on against Oueddei and his Libyan backers in the north. In reality, formal 'possession' of the state was increasingly meaningless as the country succumbed to the centrifugal forces of regional factionalism and local rule by warlords. At the same time, though, the conflict had become progressively internationalized, and it was unlikely that the west – in the late 1980s close to 'winning' the cold war – would allow its client to be defeated, however fragmentary the rewards of 'victory'. In the north at least Habré's army was able to assert itself and by 1988 it had driven Libyan forces from Chad, though they remained in the Aouzou Strip.

Paradoxically, this Libyan defeat led directly to an improvement in relations. Habré's evident victory gave him as close to 'national' control as any regime in Chad had enjoyed for some time. This meant that the two countries could now regard each other as regional neighbours rather than antagonists in an endless civil war. In August 1989 representatives of the two states met in Algiers and produced a 'framework agreement' for the settlement of the Aouzou problem. This set a period of one year for the parties to resolve the issue by 'political means'. If, at the end of this, a settlement had not been agreed, the matter would be passed to the International Court of Justice for arbitration on the historical legal merits. The protagonists would accept the Court's judgment as binding. A bilateral accommodation was not reached and accordingly, at the end of August 1990, the issue was passed to the ICJ.[31] The Court delivered its judgment in February 1994. This rejected Libya's claim that the border had never been defined and accepted Chad's counter-argument that it had been fixed by the 1955 Franco-Libyan treaty.[32] In short, the Aouzou Strip was in Chad, and Libya was now committed to renounce its claim and withdraw its occupation forces.

Displaying less grace than when it was confident of success at the Hague, Libya initially sought to delay the implementation of the judgment. By the beginning of April 1994, however, Tripoli had agreed to the full

---

30 Ibid., pp. 47–56.
31 The 'framework agreement' was laid out in the two states' joint submission to the ICJ. 'Special Agreement', 31 August/3 September 1990. Found at www.icj-cij.org/icjwww/icases/idt/idtframe/htm.
32 'Case Concerning the Territorial Dispute (Libyan Arab Jamahiriya/Chad)', 3 February 1994. Found at www.icj-cij.org/icjwww/icases/idt/idt_ijudgments_19940203.pdf.

implementation of the Court's decision, and by the end of that month a plan had been agreed for the withdrawal. The process, which was to be completed by the end of May, would be observed by officers from each country as well as the United Nations. Both governments now wrote to the secretary-general seeking the necessary personnel, and Boutros Boutros-Ghali urged the Security Council to approve the operation.[33] This the Security Council did on 4 May, authorizing the deployment of military observers 'for a single period of up to forty days'.[34] The operation proved to be entirely trouble-free and all Libyan forces were withdrawn on schedule by 30 May. As if to validate Libya's claim on the basis of the self-determination principle if not treaty disposition, the secretary-general's final report noted that predicted humanitarian problems following on the Libyan withdrawal had failed to materialize 'since most of the inhabitants had moved to [Libya]'.[35]

On the basis of the experience and lessons of the UN's various interventions in Africa the success of UNASOG was largely predictable. The chaotic national political environment in which it took place, as well as the historical tensions at the heart of the relationship between Chad and Libya, might have suggested otherwise, of course. But the crucial element in the process was a prior recognition of mutual self-interest on the part of the protagonists. Once this was established and a genuine commitment to the efficient management of the withdrawal was evident, the UN's verificatory role became merely symbolic, almost in fact ceremonial. The experience of UNASOG was in this sense in sharpest contrast to that of MINURSO in Western Sahara, where self-interest was anything but mutual and control of the United Nations intervention was a prize to be fought for between the protagonists. An awareness of this contrast was present in Boutros-Ghali's final report. 'The accomplishment of the mandate of UNASOG', he remarked, 'amply demonstrates the useful role, as envisaged by the Charter, which the United Nations can play in the peaceful settlement of disputes when the parties co-operate fully with the Organization.'[36] It was an observation that could have served as an epitaph for United Nations peacekeeping in Africa since its beginnings thirty-four years earlier.

---

33   UN document S/1994/512, 27 April 1994.
34   UN document S/RES/915, 4 May 1994. This resolution had to include a specific exemption to the terms of a previous one (S/RES/748, 31 March 1992) that had applied sanctions against air travel to Libya in punishment for its alleged involvement in terrorism.
35   UN document S/1994/672, 6 June 1994.
36   Ibid.

CHAPTER SEVEN

Conclusions

'Firing into a Continent' – or Making a Difference?

We began with a quotation from the work of a non-African, Philip Gourevitch, writing about Africa in the late twentieth century. That extract represented a certain liberal, interventionist approach to Africa's problems. Gourevitch's book on the Rwandan genocide of 1994 was an excoriating attack on what he saw as the immoral disregard of that tragedy by the international community, including the United Nations. Joseph Conrad in his novella *Heart of Darkness*, published in 1902, perhaps illuminates the assumptions and prejudices of early twentieth-century western 'liberalism' just as clearly as Gourevitch did for the end of that century.

Conrad's book opens with a description of a voyage from England to the Congo Free State. As the narrator, Marlow, sails down the west African coast to the dark of Léopold II's domain, his ship passes a French gunboat bombarding the interior. Conrad's description has become one of the most striking European literary images of Africa:

> In the empty immensity of earth, sky and water, there she was, incomprehensible, firing into a continent. Pop, would go one of the six-inch guns; a small flame would dart and vanish, a little white smoke would disappear, a tiny projectile would give a feeble screech – and nothing happened. Nothing could happen. There was a touch of insanity in the proceeding, a sense of lugubrious drollery in the sight. . . .[1]

Conrad's racial assumptions and his suggestion that Africa occupied its own black, intangible moral space are dated and unacceptable today. But his implicitly non-interventionist view of Africa and his dismissal of the folly of

---

1   Joseph Conrad, *Heart of Darkness* (Harmondsworth: Penguin, 1999), p. 20.

those who strove to impact upon the continent has an enduring relevance. What has United Nations peacekeeping 'done' for Africa? Have UN efforts justified the resources devoted to them? Has intervention actually perpetuated problems that would otherwise have been resolved locally either by the antagonists themselves or by regional intervention? Should the United Nations perhaps be prepared, as one writer put it, simply to 'give war a chance' as a technique of conflict resolution?[2] In short, has it all been worth it – or has the United Nations merely been 'firing into a continent' like Conrad's gunboat?

Weighing outcomes

There can be no such thing as a straightforward 'balance sheet' of UN peacekeeping in Africa. Assessments of the success or failure of individual operations are only meaningful up to a point. They can do little to answer the 'what if' questions about the alternative means and objectives that might have been used and pursued, or the possible outcomes of intervention by other bodies. Most fundamentally, there is no way of arriving at any reasonable idea of how conflicts would have played out without any intervention. Nevertheless, some general conclusions can be reached without straying too far into conjecture. In general, the peacekeeping undertakings that we have explored can be considered in one of three categories of 'impact'. Some operations appeared to have been wholly positive in their outcomes and to have made a clear difference for the better. The outcomes of other interventions have been either so slender or so conditional as to be largely neutral in their impact. Finally, some operations were simply and unequivocally unsuccessful, and raised the uncomfortable but legitimate question as to whether they may have actually had a negative impact on local conflicts.

The first – and perhaps most unambiguous – of the UN's successes was in Namibia. There, admittedly after some shaky moments at the outset, the United Nations intervention was completely successful in achieving its objectives both as a peacekeeping force and as an agent of political change. Moreover, it is difficult to see how any other actor, either state or institutional, could have carried through the operation. The less spectacular and complex – but nevertheless very important – linked operation that supervised the withdrawal of Cuban forces from Angola was another clear success for UN peacekeeping. In a slightly different sense it was also a job that could only have been carried through effectively by the United Nations. Certainly other actors could have done the job in the sense that they had the necessary

---

2   Edward N. Luttwak, 'Give war a chance', *Foreign Affairs* 78(4), 1999, pp. 36–51.

resources. African regional institutions, most obviously the OAU, could in principle have provided the limited manpower and organization necessary, but it is unlikely that it would have been acceptable to one of the key protagonists, South Africa. Similarly a joint US–Soviet observer mission could have carried out the task in technical terms, but one or other would have been unacceptable to each of the Angolan parties.

For similar reasons, it is difficult to see how the end of the civil war and transition to democracy in Mozambique could have been managed by any other agency than the United Nations. The conflict there was a long-standing one that over the years had provoked strong responses in Africa. It was therefore unlikely that regional organizations that had already taken emphatic positions would have been acceptable to Renamo. For similar reasons it is difficult to see what sort of intervention other than that by the United Nations could have provided the interposition force between Ethiopia and Eritrea. No state actor would have been either able or willing to do so, and even if such a task were within the technical capacities of the OAU, Eritrean perceptions of its partiality towards Ethiopia would have ruled out such an intervention. The case of the Libyan withdrawal from Chad is less clear. The limited resources required and the clarity and solidity of the settlement between the two states involved suggests that other actors could easily have performed the task. The terms of the agreement had, however, emerged from a United Nations agency, the International Court of Justice, and there was a certain appropriateness in the UN verifying its implementation.

The most significant operation to be placed in the second category on the scale of success – interventions with limited or questionable outcomes – is the UN's first in Africa, that in the Congo. It was certainly the case that in July 1960 foreign intervention in the Congo was essential if the disorder that had begun almost immediately after the Belgian flag had been lowered was not to plunge the entire country into bloody chaos. It was also clear that the intervention by Belgian troops, which the UN force was initially established to 'replace', was unsustainable. But less clear, four years later when the UN withdrew, was what enduring contribution the enormous and expensive intervention had made to the country. Yes, the secession of Katanga had been finally ended by the use of force by the UN. But that is not to say that it would not have ended anyway when confronted by a more organized and determined central government and amidst the hostility of independent African neighbours. Beyond the issue of Katanga the impact of the UN appeared small indeed. With or without the UN presence it is likely that Mobutu, exploiting the self-interest of the west, would still have come to power and maintained his grip as he did into the late 1990s. In short, UN efforts did nothing to improve the future lot of the Congolese people. Nor, given the anger and tensions generated in New York, did the intervention serve any larger institutional good. A similar conclusion can be reached about the small UN presence in Liberia. There, an international force (formed largely by the regional organization rather than the UN itself) appeared simply to delay rather than prevent the victory of a particular party.

This second, 'conditional' category would also include the mission for the referendum in Western Sahara, which, ten years after being established, oversaw a situation in which the referendum appeared further away than ever. Yet it is at least arguable that the peacekeeping function of the operation, narrowly defined, had been successful. There was little violence in the territory after the deployment of UN personnel to supervise the cease-fire between Morocco and the Polisario. Here too it is unlikely that any agency other than the UN could have done the job. Certainly, the OAU would have been unacceptable to Morocco given the wrangles in the organization over the issue in the 1980s.

In the Central African Republic multilateral intervention had some success for as long as foreign forces were in position. Developments after their withdrawal, however, when the underlying conflicts in local politics and society re-emerged as strongly as ever, indicate that the impact was not enduring. In this case it is not clear that the UN brought any unique qualities to the situation. The intervention had originally been one by a group of Francophone states mobilized by France itself. The shift to UN control did not even involve any fundamental change in personnel as the contingents remained overwhelmingly French-speaking. In the CAR the purpose of the United Nations appeared to be mainly to provide convenient and timely relief to France as reservations grew in Paris about the national commitment.

The third category is more simple to construct than the others if for no other reason than measurement of failure against stated objectives is easier than success. Throughout the 1990s the war in Angola proved beyond the capacities of the United Nations to resolve. What turned out to be a misleading cue from the supervised withdrawal of Cuban forces at the time of the Namibia settlement led to repeated political and military failures in Angola in the 1990s. Initially, insufficient resourcing by New York was blamed, but it eventually became clear that the crisis was in a real sense simply unresolvable by outside forces until its internal dynamics changed. Kofi Annan's belated recognition of this in 1999 and his consequent urging of UN withdrawal was, in a strange sense, a 'victory' for peacekeeping in that it recognized that it was simply not an appropriate activity in the Angolan situation.

The failure in Somalia was of a different order. In contrast to the Angolan situation, the operations there – both United Nations- and United States-led – involved direct, armed confrontation with the local protagonists. Intervention in Somalia was an attempt to enforce peace rather than nurture an existing peace process. Failure in this was due to a fundamental, though, in the horrific circumstances of the time and place, an understandable, miscalculation of what could be achieved. Ironically, perhaps, it is possible that a more conventional, Angolan-style peacekeeping posture in Somalia, while no doubt maddening to the sensibilities of those who had to follow the deepening misery of the civilian population, might have produced better results, though they would always have been limited. As it was, once the intervention force had focused on an 'enemy' and had determined to pursue him by all-out military means, the 'peacekeepers' became merely another protagonist in Somalia's multi-sided civil war.

In the Rwanda operation, which came in the wake of Somalia and was shaped accordingly, the failings of the UN presence were due to an insufficiently aggressive posture. A more combative approach was simply not an option as long as the members of the Security Council refused to authorize and the members of the General Assembly refused to provide the necessary forces. To this extent the failure to prevent the genocide in Rwanda was not a deficiency on the part of the 'UN' in an institutional sense. The presence of a UN force, although inadequate to intervene in any meaningful way, in fact provided an alibi for states that were being pressed by public opinion to respond but that were determined to avoid embroilment in an area of no discernible national interest to them. As long as blue berets were present, in however reduced numbers, then the world's failure could be represented as the UN's failure.

African solutions to African problems?

We have already pointed to a number of situations in which, for various political and diplomatic reasons, a United Nations presence was the only external one feasible. In other African conflicts, other actors have mounted more or less multilateral interventions. Although the OAU attempted limited interventions in, for example, Chad and Rwanda, the main activity came from a more narrow regional organization. In Liberia and Sierra Leone the Economic Community of West African States took the lead. Later, in 1998, ECOWAS was also involved in the civil war in Guinea-Bissau, in this case without UN 'legitimization'. In 2001 a South African force was deployed in Burundi, which was grappling with political and ethnic difficulties very similar to those of its neighbour, Rwanda. In general, however, these 'African solutions to African problems' have come with a number of difficulties.

In west Africa there was a persistent question about the extent to which the actor intervening in Liberia and Sierra Leone was Nigeria, the regional hegemon, or ECOWAS, the regional organization. Francophone members of ECOWAS in particular were unhappy with the provenance of these interventions, which they saw as serving Nigerian national interests. In Guinea-Bissau, in contrast, French-speaking states were suspected of using the cover of ECOWAS to secure the former Portuguese colony for the 'Francophone space' in the region.[3] The use of an institutional veil to legitimize the pursuit of national aims was also evident, though in a less emphatic way, when Zimbabwe, Angola and Namibia intervened to prop up Laurent Kabila in the Congo in 1998. At the time some half-hearted claims were made that the intervention had been sanctioned by the Southern African Development Community – to which, conveniently, Rwanda and Uganda, which intervened against Kabila, did not belong.[4]

In addition to questions of motivation, there are others touching on military capacity, discipline and respect for human rights that have also dogged African interventions. United Nations operations in Africa have had their failures in all of these areas too. Subject to question has been the UN force's capacity in Sierra Leone, its discipline in Rwanda and its human rights record in Somalia. But in general, host populations appear to be better served by forces under direct United Nations command. Whatever their operational failures, UN forces do appear to retain greater confidence from local populations than do their regional counterparts.

Success and failure in African peacekeeping

Throughout our account of the history of United Nations peacekeeping in Africa we have emphasized the limited capacity of external forces to shape the outcomes of local conflicts. Peacekeeping is, in principle, an entirely different activity from 'peacemaking', though on the ground and in the perception of those who make judgements about success and failure the distinction is rarely clearly drawn. It is possible for a UN mission to succeed as a peacekeeping operation while simultaneously failing in broader peacemaking objectives. The clearest example of this is a European rather than an African one. The United Nations operation in Cyprus that was established in 1964 was virtually

---

3   The Security Council established a 'Peace-Building Support Office' in Guinea-Bissau, but there was no suggestion of a UN military presence. The Francophone/ECOWAS response followed a failed attempt by Portugal to organize an intervention by Portuguese-speaking states.

4   In addition to the three interventionist states, Angola, Namibia and Zimbabwe, and the then recently admitted DRC itself, the Southern African Development Community was made up of Botswana, Lesotho, Malawi, Mauritius, Mozambique, Seychelles, South Africa, Swaziland, Tanzania and Zambia.

a textbook case of successful interpositionary peacekeeping. But the basic conflict that it was created to manage remained unresolved decades later. Peacemaking, in short, lagged behind peacekeeping, and the UN's involvement in Cyprus tended consequently to be characterized as a 'failure'. In Africa similar situations could be seen in both Western Sahara and the Central African Republic, where UN forces 'kept' an interim peace quite effectively but larger efforts to 'make' a durable peace were unsuccessful. Even in Somalia, which has come to epitomize peacekeeping failure in Africa, the performance of the multilateral intervention in its various phases had its successes at certain levels, for example in securing aid delivery and distribution. The intervention as a whole, however, failed because sufficient peace could not be 'made' to create conditions for it later to be 'kept'.

In general terms, at least one of three often interconnected conditions had to be present for a peacekeeping intervention to have a chance of success. The capacity of the peacekeepers themselves – or even the UN as an institution to create these conditions – was very limited in Africa.

Firstly, the experiences in Namibia, Angola during the Cuban withdrawal and Mozambique underline the importance of having external powers fully behind a pre-determined peace process. When this support is not present – or not sufficiently emphatic – the odds against the success of a peacekeeping intervention are high. In the Congo in the 1960s, for example, the eastern and western blocs frequently pulled in diametrically opposite directions, with grave consequences for both the peacekeepers on the ground and the United Nations as an institution. In Western Sahara and in Rwanda big powers attempted to exert pressure, certainly, but with insufficient commitment. In the case of Rwanda the lack of commitment concerned the provision of necessary resources. In Western Sahara there was a holding back of political pressure, for reasons of national self-interest, on the part of western states with influence over Morocco.

Yet, powerful commitment on the part of significant external actors was not in itself a guarantee of success. If it were, the problems of civil war in Angola and state collapse in Somalia would have been resolved. A second crucial factor was absent in these crises: protagonists who were both willing and able to act as responsible and effective interlocutors. UNITA in Angola and the warlord factions in Somalia simply did not meet the bill in this respect. In Namibia, in contrast, the South African, Angolan and Cuban governments were certainly under strong external pressure to reach an agreement and implement it. But for the peace process to succeed it was essential that the protagonists should respond appropriately to this pressure. Similarly, UN interposition between Ethiopia and Eritrea, and its observation task between Chad and Libya, were immeasurably eased by the fact that the parties were established and responsible states, whether under external pressure or not.

The 'responsible' interlocutors that we have just identified were, of course, all sovereign states, though this is not a necessary requirement. The success of the Mozambican peace process required the commitment of Renamo as well as that of the Frelimo state, and, encouraged when necessary by pressure from external powers, this commitment was forthcoming. In general, however, the most reliable partners in peacekeeping were indeed established states. Moreover, this reliability was most in evidence in inter-state disputes over common borders. This is not, as we have seen, the characteristic type of conflict that has led to peacekeeping in Africa. Of the thirteen main conflicts into which UN military personnel were deployed in the continent between 1960 and 2000, only four were of a substantive inter-state character. While some of the others may have had distinct international dimensions, they were essentially civil conflicts.

In these, the third – and by far the most important – general condition of peacekeeping success is uppermost. The stage reached in a conflict and its general character (what we have described as its 'dynamics') must be such as to maximize the benefits of external intervention. The contrasting examples of Mozambique and Angola have already been discussed in this respect, with the first having been identified as 'amenable' to successful intervention and the second immune to the benefits of peacekeeping. Similar judgements could be made about Somalia. While the intervention there could have been scaled differently and pursued more modest and narrow objectives, it is unlikely that a general 'solution' to the country's problems was ever within reach. In the Central African Republic a multinational presence helped stabilize the situation, but the fundamental dynamics of the crisis there were such that violent conflict resurfaced when the international force was withdrawn. Once again, the peacekeepers could do little about a situation in which fundamental peacemaking had yet to take place.

The fact that the success of United Nations peacekeeping in Africa since 1960 has been so contingent on other actors and local circumstances should not detract from its fundamental importance. Even if UN intervention has been largely secondary to conflict resolution, the role has frequently been indispensable. Even in the least successful missions the presence of the United Nations probably saved lives, in some cases in large numbers. This was achieved either through the fact of military personnel on the ground or through the political message their presence delivered to the protagonists. It is unlikely that even the most unsympathetic hypothesis could credibly suggest that fewer lives would have been lost and less misery caused if the UN had not intervened in a particular crisis. While the impact of United Nations intervention may appear relatively limited in the scheme of African suffering since the 1960s, it has assuredly been greater than the haphazard and futile engagement of Conrad's early twentieth-century metaphor.

Chronology

1944

August

- Dumbarton Oaks conference – American, Soviet, British and Chinese representatives agree outline for a new international organization based on the principle of collective security.

1945

February

- Yalta conference – plan for the UN is discussed by Roosevelt, Stalin and Churchill.

April

- San Francisco conference to finalize preparations for the new organization. Attended by the 'big five' (US, USSR, UK, France and China) and fifty other anti-Axis states.

May

- Germany surrenders.

August

- Japan surrenders.

1948

May

- British Mandate ends in Palestine – State of Israel declared and war breaks out.

June

- United Nations Truce Supervision Organization (UNTSO) established for Palestine.

1949

January

- United Nations Military Observer Group in India and Pakistan (UNMOGIP) established.

1950

June

- North Korea invades the South across 38th parallel. Security Council demands its withdrawal. Korean War begins.

1953

April

- Dag Hammarskjöld of Sweden succeeds Trygve Lie as UN secretary-general.

July

- Armistice signed in Korea.

1956

July

- Egypt nationalizes Suez Canal.

November

- Anglo-French forces invade Suez.
- General Assembly resolution establishes United Nations Emergency Force (UNEF) for Suez.

1958

October

- Hammarskjöld produces 'Summary Study' on lessons of Suez.

1960

June

- Independence of Congo from Belgium.

July

- Congolese army mutinies – Belgian troops intervene.
- Congolese prime minister (Lumumba) and president (Kasavubu) seek UN assistance.
- Katanga announces secession from Congo.
- Security Council resolution (S/RES/143) establishes United Nations Operation in the Congo (ONUC).
- Independence of Somalia from Italy and union with former British Somaliland.

August
- Independence of Central African Republic from France.
- Independence of Chad from France.

September
- Congolese government crisis – Kasavubu dismisses Lumumba and vice versa. UN orders closure of airports and radio station.
- Congolese army commander Mobutu announces coup and allies himself with Kasavubu. Lumumba under UN protection.
- Khrushchev denounces 'pro-western' stance of UN force in Security Council – calls for troika to replace office of secretary-general.

November
- General Assembly recognizes Kasavubu–Mobutu faction as legitimate government of Congo.
- Lumumba leaves UN protection and is captured by Mobutu's forces.

1961

January
- Lumumba murdered after being transferred by his captors to Katanga.
- John F. Kennedy succeeds Dwight D. Eisenhower as US president.

February
- Security Council resolution authorizes UN troops to use force if necessary to prevent civil war in Congo.

April
- Independence of Sierra Leone from Britain.

August–September
- Unsuccessful UN military operations against Katanga.

September
- Death of Hammarskjöld *en route* to meet Katangese leaders in Northern Rhodesia. Succeeded as secretary-general by U Thant of Burma.

November
- New Security Council resolution on Congo denounces secession of Katanga.

1962

July
- Independence of Rwanda from Belgium.

December
- Following mounting provocations UN troops move against mercenaries in Katanga.

1963

January

- Katangese secession formally ended.

1964

March

- United Nations Force in Cyprus established in response to widespread inter-communal violence.

May

- Establishment of Organization of African Unity (OAU).

June

- Withdrawal of UN force from Congo.

1965

December

- Joseph Mobutu takes power in Congo.

1967

May

- UNEF withdrawn from Suez at request of Egypt on eve of 'Six Day War'.

1969

January

- Richard Nixon sworn in as US president.

1970

January

- Security Council formally terminates South African trusteeship over South West Africa (Namibia).

1972

January

- Kurt Waldheim of Austria succeeds U Thant as UN secretary-general.

1973

October

- War in the Middle East. Second United Nations Emergency Force (UNEF II) deployed between Israeli and Egyptian armies in Sinai.

1974

June

- United Nations Disengagement Observer Force deployed between Israeli and Syrian armies in Golan Heights.

1975

April
- Saigon falls to North Vietnamese forces.

June
- Independence of Mozambique from Portugal.

October
- International Court of Justice rejects Moroccan and Mauritanian claims to Western Sahara.

November
- Portugal withdraws from Angola amidst civil war between US- and Soviet-backed factions. Cuban troops intervene in support of Marxist government.
- Spain agrees to division of Western Sahara between Morocco and Mauritania after decolonization (Madrid agreement).

1978

March
- Israeli invasion of Lebanon. Establishment of United Nations Interim Force in Lebanon (UNIFIL).

September
- Security Council agrees to establish a 'transition assistance group' for Namibia.

1979

January
- Fall of Siad Barre in Somalia. Disintegration of central state.

December
- Soviet invasion of Afghanistan.

1980

March
- End of white minority rule in Rhodesia/Zimbabwe. Robert Mugabe elected prime minister.

1982

January
- Javier Pérez de Cuéllar of Peru succeeds Kurt Waldheim as UN secretary-general.

1984

March
- Nkomati Accord between Mozambique and South Africa.

1985

March

• Mikhail Gorbachev becomes leader of Soviet Union.

1986

October

• Death in plane crash of Mozambican president Samora Machel.

1989

January

• George Bush sr sworn-in as US president.
• First United Nations Angola Verification Mission (UNAVEM I) formed.

April

• United Nations Transition Assistance Group (UNTAG) for Namibia established.

August

• Framework plan agreed by Chad and Libya for future of Aouzou Strip.

November

• Berlin Wall comes down.

December

• Rebel invasion of Liberia precipitates civil war.

1990

March

• UNTAG completes mission in Namibia. Independence of Namibia.

August

• Iraq invades Kuwait.
• West Africa (ECOMOG) force intervenes in Liberia.

October

• Tutsi-dominated RPF rebel movement launches attacks on Rwanda from bases in Uganda.

November

• Security Council authorizes military coalition against Iraq.

1991

January

• US-led and Security Council-approved Operation Desert Storm begins against Iraq.

April

• United Nations Mission for the Referendum in Western Sahara (MINURSO) established by the Security Council.

May
- UNAVEM I completes mission in Angola ahead of schedule.
- Bicesse agreement between the sides in the Angolan civil war and the establishment of the Second Angola Verification Mission (UNAVEM II).

August
- Mengistu regime ('Derg') overthrown in Ethiopia.

September
- Soviet Union formally dissolved.

1992

January
- Boutros Boutros-Ghali of Egypt succeeds Pérez de Cuéllar as UN secretary-general.

March
- United Nations Protection Force (UNPROFOR) for former Yugoslavia established.
- United Nations Transitional Authority in Cambodia (UNTAC) established.

April
- United Nations Operation in Somalia (UNOSOM) established.
- Coup in Sierra Leone. Strasser in power.

June
- Boutros-Ghali publishes *An Agenda for Peace*.

October
- 'General Peace Agreement' signed by Mozambican government and Renamo.
- Abortive elections in Angola – return to civil war.

December
- United Nations Operation in Mozambique (ONUMOZ) established.
- American-led Unified Task Force in Somalia (UNITAF) undertakes 'Operation Restore Hope'.

1993

January
- Bill Clinton succeeds George Bush sr as US president.

May
- UNITAF withdrawn from Somalia. Replaced by UNOSOM II.
- Independence of Eritrea from Ethiopia.

June
- United Nations Observer Mission Uganda–Rwanda (UNOMUR) established.
- Pakistani UNOSOM II troops suffer high casualties in Mogadishu fighting.

July
- Cotonou agreement between Liberian factions.

August
- Arusha agreement between Rwandan government and RPF rebels.

September
- United Nations Observer Mission in Liberia (UNOMIL) established.

October
- United Nations Assistance Mission for Rwanda (UNAMIR) established.
- Eighteen US special forces troops killed in Mogadishu fighting.

1994

February
- International Court of Justice opinion that Aouzou Strip belongs to Chad.

April
- Genocide begins in Rwanda following assassination of presidents of Rwanda and Burundi.

May
- President Clinton signs 'PDD 25' restricting the terms of American support for peacekeeping.
- End of white minority rule in South Africa. Nelson Mandela elected president.
- UNAMIR in Rwanda given more extensive mandate by Security Council.
- Security Council establishes observer mission to oversee Libyan withdrawal from Aouzou Strip (Chad). Completes mission within month.

June
- Security Council authorizes French-led 'Operation Turquoise' for Rwanda.

July
- RPF takes power in Rwanda. Exodus of Hutu refugees to eastern Zaïre.

September
- UNOMUR withdrawn from Uganda–Rwanda border.

October
- ONUMOZ supervises elections in Mozambique. Frelimo victory.

November
- Signing of Lusaka agreement on Angola.

December
- ONUMOZ completes mission in Mozambique.

1995

February
- UNAVEM II wound up in Angola. Third United Nations Angola Verification Mission (UNAVEM III) formed.

March
- UNOSOM II withdraws from Somalia.

August
- Abuja agreement on Liberia.

1996

March
- Withdrawal of UNAMIR from Rwanda.
- Elections in Sierra Leone. Kabbah becomes president.

October
- Rwandan (RPF) invasion of eastern Zaïre.

November
- Abidjan agreement between the Sierra Leone factions.

1997

January
- Kofi Annan of Ghana succeeds Boutros-Ghali as UN secretary-general.

February
- Francophone peacekeeping force (MISAB) deployed in Central African Republic.

April
- Mobutu overthrown in Zaïre (former Congo). Replaced by Laurent Desiré Kabila. Zaïre renamed 'Democratic Republic of Congo'.
- 'Unity' government formed in Angola.

May
- Coup in Sierra Leone – pro-RUF Koroma ousts Kabbah.

June
- UNAVEM III wound up in Angola. Replaced by United Nations Angola Observation Mission (MONUA).

July
- Elections in Liberia. Charles Taylor becomes president.

September
- Houston Accord on Western Sahara.

1998

March
- Security Council establishes mission in Central African Republic (MINURCA) to replace Francophone force.

May
- War breaks out between Ethiopia and Eritrea.

July
- Security Council establishes observer mission for Sierra Leone (UNOMSIL).

August
- Outbreak of civil war (with foreign involvement) in Democratic Republic of Congo.

November–December
- Reversion to civil war in Angola.

1999

January
- Fierce fighting in Sierra Leone brings war to Freetown.

July
- Lusaka agreement on Democratic Republic of Congo.
- Lomé agreement on Sierra Leone.
- Death of Hassan II of Morocco. Succeeded by his son, Mohammed VI.

March
- Withdrawal of MONUA from Angola.

August
- Security Council authorizes peacekeeping mission for Democratic Republic of Congo (MONUC).

October
- Security Council establishes new large-scale mission for Sierra Leone (UNAMSIL).
- UN Transitional Administration for East Timor (UNTAET) established.

December
- UN's Independent Report on Rwandan genocide published.

2000

February
- MINURCA withdrawn from Central African Republic.

May
- Withdrawal of ECOMOG from Sierra Leone. Intensification of fighting and British military intervention.

July
- UN mission for Ethiopia and Eritrea (UNMEE) established.

2001

January
- George Bush jr succeeeds Bill Clinton as US president.
- Laurent Kabila assassinated in Democratic Republic of Congo. Succeeded as president by his son, Joseph.

June
- Fresh crisis in Central African Republic.
- New pro-Moroccan plan on Western Sahara proposed to Security Council.

September
- Terrorist attacks in the United States.

2002
January
- Formal declaration of end of civil war in Sierra Leone.

February
- Death of UNITA leader Jonas Savimbi in Angola.

UN Peacekeeping Operations in Africa

United Nations Operation in the Congo (ONUC)
Original Authorization: Security Council resolution 143, 14 July 1960
Duration: July 1960–June 1964
Maximum strength: 20,000
Function: Initially to supervise the withdrawal of Belgian forces; later to provide stability in, and ensure the territorial integrity of, the new state.

First United Nations Angola Verification Mission (UNAVEM I)
Original Authorization: Security Council resolution 626, 20 December 1988
Duration: January 1989–May 1991
Maximum strength: 70
Function: To supervise withdrawal of Cuban forces from Angola. Mission successfully completed ahead of schedule. Part of linked agreement for decolonization of Namibia

United Nations Transition Assistance Group (UNTAG)
Original Authorization: Security Council resolutions 435, 29 September 1978; 629, 16 January 1989
Duration: April 1989–March 1990
Maximum strength: 8000
Function: To provide security and administrative support during Namibia's transition to independence from South Africa. Mission successfully completed within a year. (Process linked with UNAVEM I activities in Angola.)

United Nations Mission for the Referendum in Western Sahara (MINURSO)
Original Authorization: Security Council resolution 690, 29 April 1991
Duration: April 1991–
Maximum strength: 2500
Function: Following agreement between Morocco and Polisario Front, to supervise disengagement of both sides' forces and to prepare vote on the future of the territory.

Second United Nations Angola Verification Mission (UNAVEM II)
Original Authorization: Security Council resolution 696, 30 May 1991
Duration: May 1991–February 1995
Maximum strength: 350
Function: To verify cease-fire between Angolan government and UNITA guerrillas, and to monitor national elections.

United Nations Operations in Somalia (UNOSOM I/II)
Original Authorization: Security Council resolutions 775, 28 August 1992; 814, 26 March 1993
Duration: April1992/May 1993–March 1995
Maximum strength: 28,000
Function: To restore peace and stability by ending factional fighting in Somalia and to secure the distribution of humanitarian aid. United States-led Unified Task Force (UNITAF) deployed in period between UNOSOM I and UNOSOM II.

United Nations Operation in Mozambique (ONUMOZ)
Original Authorization: Security Council resolution 797, 16 December 1992
Duration: December 1992–December 1994
Maximum strength: 7000
Function: To assist in the implementation of the peace agreement between Mozambican government and Renamo guerrillas; to administer and supervise national elections.

United Nations Observer Mission Uganda–Rwanda (UNOMUR)
Original Authorization: Security Council resolution 846, 22 June 1993
Duration: June 1993–September 1994
Maximum strength: 80
Function: To ensure no military forces or material permitted to cross Uganda–Rwanda border.

United Nations Observer Mission in Liberia (UNOMIL)
Original Authorization: Security Council resolution 866, 22 September 1993
Duration: September 1993–September 1997
Maximum strength: 160
Function: To support and monitor the peacekeeping efforts of the Economic Community of West African States Military Observer Group (ECOMOG) in Liberia after the end of the civil war in 1993.

United Nations Assistance Mission for Rwanda (UNAMIR)
Original Authorization: Security Council resolution 872, 5 October 1993
Duration: October 1993–March 1996
Maximum strength: 5500
Function: Originally, to implement peace agreement between Rwanda government and rebel forces. Overtaken by genocide and subsequent revolution in Rwanda in mid-1994. Given a renewed humanitarian mandate in aftermath of this.

United Nations Aouzou Strip Observer Group (UNASOG)
Original Authorization: Security Council resolution 915, 4 May 1994
Duration: May–June 1994
Maximum strength: 15
Function: To supervise the withdrawal of Libyan administration and military forces from the Aouzou Strip following an International Court of Justice opinion that it formed part of the territory of Chad.

Third United Nations Angola Verification Mission (UNAVEM III) and United Nations Observation Mission in Angola (MONUA)
Original Authorization: Security Council resolutions 976, 8 February 1995; 1118, 30 June 1997
Duration: February 1995/July 1997–March 1999
Maximum strength: 7000
Function: To supervise implementation of Lusaka peace agreement of 1994 after resumption of civil war between government forces and UNITA in 1992. UNAVEM III replaced by smaller MONUA in July 1997.

United Nations Mission in the Central African Republic (MINURCA)
Original Authorization: Security Council resolution 1159, 27 March 1998
Duration: April 1998–February 2000

Maximum strength: 1400
Function: To provide (in succession to French-led Francophone force) security in the Bangui (national capital) area and to supervise the storage of arms surrendered following the negotiated end of army mutinies.

United Nations Mission Observer Mission in Sierra Leone (UNOMSIL)
Original Authorization: Security Council resolution 1181, 13 July 1998
Duration: July 1998–October 1999
Maximum strength: 70
Function: To monitor, in co-operation with the Economic Community of West African States Military Observer Group (ECOMOG), the security situation in Sierra Leone and assist in the disarmament and demobilization of former fighters in the civil war.

United Nations Mission in the Democratic Republic of Congo (MONUC)
Original Authorization: Security Council resolution 1258, 6 August 1999
Duration: November 1999–
Maximum strength: 2400
Function: To liaise with the government of the DRC, rebel groups and foreign intervention forces to assist in the implementation of the Lusaka agreement to resolve the civil war.

United Nations Mission in Sierra Leone (UNAMSIL)
Original Authorization: Security Council resolution 1270, 22 October 1999
Duration: October 1999–
Maximum strength: 17,500
Function: To provide security for Sierra Leone while supervising the implementation of the Lomé agreement between the government and the Revolutionary United Front supposedly ending the country's civil war.

United Nations Mission in Ethiopia and Eritrea (UNMEE)
Original Authorization: Security Council resolution 1320, 15 September 2000
Duration: July 2000–
Maximum strength: 3870
Function: To supervise the cease-fire and provide an interposition force in disputed territory between Ethiopia and Eritrea following the end of the two-year war between the countries.

BIBLIOGRAPHY AND FURTHER READING

A. Secondary sources and memoirs

Abdullah, Ibrahim, 'Bush path to destruction: the origin and character of the Revolutionary United Front/Sierra Leone', *Journal of Modern African Studies* 36(2), 1998, pp. 203–35.

Abdullah, Ibrahim and Muana, Patrick, 'The Revolutionary United Front of Sierra Leone: a revolt of the lumpenproletariat', in Christopher Clapham (ed.), *African Guerrillas* (Oxford: James Currey, 1998), pp. 173–93.

Abi-Saab, George, *The United Nations Operation in the Congo, 1960–1964* (Oxford: Oxford University Press, 1978).

Alao, Abiodun, 'Sierra Leone: tracing the genesis of a controversy', Royal Institute of International Affairs Briefing No. 50, June 1998. Found at http://www.riia.org/briefingpapers/bp50.html.

Alden, Chris, 'The UN and the resolution of conflict in Mozambique', *Journal of Modern African Studies* 33(1), 1995, pp. 103–28.

Andersson, Hilary, *Mozambique: a War Against the People* (London: Macmillan, 1992).

Anstee, Margaret, 'Angola: a tragedy not to be forgotten', *The World Today* 52(7), July 1996, pp. 190–1.

Anstee, Margaret, *Orphan of the Cold War: the Inside Story of the Collapse of the Angola Peace Process, 1992–93* (London: Macmillan, 1996).

Ascherson, Neal, *The King Incorporated: Leopold the Second and the Congo* (London: Granta, 1999).

Barnes, Sam, 'Peacekeeping in Mozambique', in Oliver Furley and Roy May (eds), *Peacekeeping in Africa* (Aldershot: Ashgate, 1998), pp. 159–77.

Bayart, Jean-François, *The State in Africa: the Politics of the Belly* (London: Longman, 1993).

Berdal, Mats, 'Peacekeeping in Africa, 1990–1996: the role of the United States, France and Britain', in Oliver Furley and Roy May (eds), *Peacekeeping in Africa* (Aldershot: Ashgate, 1998), pp. 49–79.

Berman, Eric G. and Sams, Katie E., *Peacekeeping in Africa: Capabilities and Culpabilities* (Geneva: United Nations Institute for Disarmament Research, 2000).

Berridge, G.R., 'Diplomacy and the Angola–Namibia accords', *International Affairs* 65(3), 1989, pp. 463–79.

Berridge, G.R., *Return to the UN: UN Diplomacy in Regional Conflicts* (London: Macmillan, 1990).

Birmingham, David, *Frontline Nationalism in Angola and Mozambique* (Oxford: James Currey, 1992).

Boutros-Ghali, Boutros, *Unvanquished: a US–UN Saga* (New York: Random House, 1999).

Bratton, Michael and van de Walle, Nicholas, *Democratic Experiments in Africa* (Cambridge: Cambridge University Press, 1997).

Bridgland, Fred, *Jonas Savimbi, a Key to Africa* (Edinburgh: Mainstream, 1986).

Burns, Arthur Lee and Heathcote, Nina, *Peacekeeping by UN Forces from Suez to the Congo* (London: Pall Mall, 1963).

Castellino, Joshua, 'Territory and identity in international law: the struggle for self-determination in the Western Sahara', *Millennium: Journal of International Studies* 28(3), 1999, pp. 523–51.

Chabal, Patrick and Daloz, Jean-Pascal, *Africa Works: Disorder as Political Instrument* (Oxford: James Currey, 1999).

Clapham, Christopher, *Africa in the International System* (Cambridge: Cambridge University Press, 1996).

Clapham, Christopher, 'Rwanda: the perils of peacemaking', *Journal of Peace Research* 35(2), 1998, pp. 75–92.

Clapham, Christopher, *The United Nations and Peacekeeping in Africa* (South African Institute of Strategic Studies Monograph – no date). Found at http//www.iss.co.za/pubs/monographs/mg%2036/unitednations.html.

Cleaver, Gerry, 'Liberia: lessons for the future from the experience of ECOMOG', in Oliver Furley and Roy May (eds), *Peacekeeping in Africa* (Aldershot: Ashgate, 1998), pp. 223–37.

Compagnon, Daniel, 'Somali armed movements', in Christopher Clapham (ed.), *African Guerrillas* (Oxford: James Currey, 1999), pp. 73–89.

Cortwright, David and Lopez, George A., *The Sanctions Decade: Assessing UN Strategies in the 1990s* (London: Lynne Rienner, 2000).

Crockatt, Richard, *The Fifty Years War: the United States and the Soviet Union in World Politics 1941–1991* (London: Routledge, 1994).

Crocker, Chester, *High Noon in South Africa: Making Peace in a Rough Neighborhood* (New York: Norton, 1993).

Durch, William, 'United Nations Mission for the Referendum in Western Sahara', in William Durch (ed.), *The Evolution of UN Peacekeeping: Case Studies and Comparative Analysis* (New York: St Martin's Press, 1993).

Foreign and Commonwealth Office (UK), 'Focus International' paper, *Western Sahara: Moving the Peace Process Forward* (December 2000). Found at http://files.fco.gov.uk/info/briefs/wsahara/pdf.

Furley, Oliver, 'Rwanda and Burundi: peacekeeping amidst massacres', in Oliver Furley and Ron May (eds), *Peacekeeping in Africa* (Aldershot: Ashgate, 1998), pp. 239–86.

Gourevitch, Philip, *We Wish to Inform You That Tomorrow We Will be Killed with Our Families* (London: Picador, 1999).

Guevara, Ernesto, *The African Dream: the Diaries of the Revolutionary War in the Congo* (London: Harvill, 2000).

Hallet, Robin, 'The South African intervention in Angola, 1975–76', *African Affairs* 77(308), 1978, pp. 347–86.

Hammarskjöld, Dag (trans. Leif Sjöberg and W.H. Auden), *Markings* (London: Faber & Faber, 1964).

Hanlon, Joseph, *Mozambique: Who Calls the Shots?* (Oxford: James Currey, 1991).

Harbottle, Michael, *The Blue Berets* (London: Leo Cooper, 1975).

Hargreaves, J.D., *Decolonization in Africa* (London: Longman, 1988).

Heimer, Franz-Wilhelm, *The Decolonization Conflict in Angola: an Essay in Political Sociology* (Geneva: Institut Universitaire de Hautes Études Internationales, 1979).

Iyob, Ruth, 'The Ethiopian–Eritrean conflict: diasporic vs. hegemonic states in the Horn of Africa, 1991–2000', *Journal of Modern African Studies* 38(4), 2000, pp. 659–82.

Jackson, R.H., *Quasi-States: Sovereignty, International Relations and the Third World* (Cambridge: Cambridge University Press, 1993).

James, Alan, *The Politics of Peacekeeping* (London: Chatto & Windus, 1969).

James, Alan, *Peacekeeping in International Politics* (London: Macmillan, 1990).

Khrushchev, Nikita (ed. Strobe Talbott), *Khrushchev Remembers: The Last Testament* (London: André Deutsch, 1974).

Kyle, Keith, 'The UN in the Congo', Initiative on Conflict Resolution and Ethnicity (INCORE) occasional paper. Found at www.incore.ulst.ac.uk/home/publication/occasional/kyle.html.

Lash, Joseph P., *Dag Hammarskjold: a Biography* (London: Cassell, 1962).

Lefever, E.W., *Crisis in the Congo: a United Nations Force in Action* (Washington, DC: Brookings Institute, 1965).

Lewis, Ioan and Mayall, James, 'Somalia', in James Mayall (ed.), *The New Interventionism 1991–1994: United Nations Experience in Cambodia, Former Yugoslavia and Somalia* (Cambridge: Cambridge University Press, 1996), pp. 94–124.

Luard, Evan, *A History of the United Nations: Vol. II. The Age of Decolonization, 1955–65* (London: Macmillan, 1989).

Luttwak, Edward N., 'Give war a chance', *Foreign Affairs* 78(4), 1999, pp. 36–51.

MacKinnon, Michael G., *The Evolution of UN Peacekeeping Policy under Clinton: a Fairweather Friend?* (London: Frank Cass, 1999).

MacQueen, Norrie, *The Decolonization of Portuguese Africa: Metropolitan Revolution and the Dissolution of Empire* (London: Longman, 1997).

MacQueen, Norrie, 'Angola', in Oliver Furley and Ron May (eds), *African Interventionist States* (Aldershot: Ashgate, 2001), pp. 104–10.

Maier, Karl, *Angola: Promises and Lies* (Rivonia: William Waterman, 1996).

Melvern, Linda, *A People Betrayed: the Role of the West in Rwanda's Genocide* (London: Zed, 2000).

Metz, Steven, 'The Mozambique National Resistance and South African foreign policy', *African Affairs* 85(341), 1986, pp. 491–507.

Morgan, Glenda, 'Violence in Mozambique: towards an understanding of Renamo', *Journal of Modern African Studies* 28(4), 1990, pp. 603–19.

O'Brien, Conor Cruise, *To Katanga and Back* (London: Hutchinson, 1962).

Ottaway, Marina, 'Post-imperial Africa at war', *Current History*, May 1999, pp. 202–7.

Page Fortna, Virginia, 'The United Nations Angola Verification Mission I', in William Durch (ed.), *The Evolution of UN Peacekeeping: Case Studies and Comparative Analysis* (New York: St Martin's Press, 1993), pp. 376–405.

Page Fortna, Virginia, 'United Nations Transition Assistance Group', in William Durch (ed.), *The Evolution of UN Peacekeeping: Case Studies and Comparative Analysis* (New York: St Martin's Press, 1993), pp. 353–75.

Parsons, Anthony, *From Cold War to Hot Peace: UN Interventions 1975–1995* (Harmondsworth: Penguin, 1995).

Pereira, Anthony W., 'The neglected tragedy: the return to war in Angola, 1992–3', *Journal of Modern African Studies* 32(1), 1994, pp. 1–28.

Prunier, Gérard, *The Rwanda Crisis, 1954–94* (London: Hurst & Co., 1995).

Prunier, Gérard, 'The Rwandan Patriotic Front', in Christopher Clapham (ed.), *African Guerrillas* (Oxford: James Currey, 1998).

Prunier, Gérard, *Rwanda in Zaïre: From Genocide to Continental War* (London: Hurst & Co., 2000).

Reno, William, *Warlord Politics and African States* (London: Lynne Rienner, 1998).

Sapir, Debarati G. and Deconinck, Hedwig, 'The paradox of humanitarian assistance and military intervention in Somalia', in Thomas G. Weiss (ed.), *The United Nations and Civil Wars* (London: Lynne Rienner, 1995), pp. 151–72.

Schuster, Lynda, 'The final days of Dr Doe', *Granta* 48 (Harmondsworth: Penguin, 1994), pp. 41–95.

Shawcross, William, *Deliver Us from Evil: Warlords and Peacekeepers in a World of Endless Conflict* (London: Bloomsbury, 2000).

Sommerville, Keith, 'Africa after the cold war: frozen out or frozen in time?', in Louise Fawcett and Yezid Sayigh (eds), *The Third World After the Cold War: Community and Change* (Oxford: Oxford University Press, 2000).

Tuck, Christopher, ' "Every car or moving object gone": The ECOMOG intervention in Liberia', *African Studies Quarterly* 4(1), February 2000. Found at http://web.africa.ufl.edu/asq/v4/v4:1a1.htm.

Urquhart, Brian, *Hammarskjold* (London: Bodley Head, 1973).

Venâncio, Moses, 'Mediation by the Roman Catholic Church in Mozambique, 1988–91', in Stephen Chan and Vivienne Jabri (eds), *Mediation in Southern Africa* (London: Macmillan, 1993), pp. 142–58.

Venâncio, Moses, 'Portuguese mediation on the Angolan Conflict in 1990–1', in Stephen Chan and Vivian Jabri (eds), *Mediation in Southern Africa* (London: Macmillan, 1993), pp. 100–15.

Verrier, Anthony, *International Peacekeeping: United Nations Forces in a Troubled World* (Harmondsworth: Penguin, 1981).

Walters, F.P., *A History of the League of Nations* (Oxford: Oxford University Press, 1969).

Wesley, Michael, *Casualties of the New World Order: the Causes of Failure of UN Missions to Civil Wars* (London: Macmillan, 1997).

White, N.D., *Keeping the Peace: the United Nations and the Maintenance of International Peace and Security* (2nd edn, Manchester: Manchester University Press, 1997).

Wilson, H.S., *African Decolonization* (London: Edward Arnold, 1994).

Woodward, Peter, 'Somalia', in Oliver Furley and Roy May (eds), *Peacekeeping in Africa* (Aldershot: Ashgate, 1998), pp. 143–58.

Wright, George, *The Destruction of a Nation: United States Policy Towards Angola since 1945* (London: Pluto Press, 1997).

B. United Nations and related documents

1. Principal United Nations documents consulted

General Assembly and main Committee resolutions.
Secretary-General's Reports to the Security Council.
Security Council press releases.
Security Council resolutions.
Statements by the President of the Security Council.
Verbatim records of General Assembly plenary sessions.
Verbatim records of Security Council meetings.

2. Other key United Nations documents

The Charter of the United Nations (1945).

Hammarskjöld's 'Summary Study' of peacekeeping – United Nations (General Assembly) document A/3943, 9 October 1958.

Boutros-Ghali's *An Agenda for Peace: Preventive Diplomacy, Peacemaking and Peacekeeping* – United Nations (Security Council) document S/22111, 17 July 1992.

The Report of the Independent Inquiry into the Actions of the United Nations during the 1994 Genocide in Rwanda (December 1999). Found at http//www.un.org/News/ossg/ rwanda_report.htm.

'Report of the Panel of Experts on Violations of Security Council Sanctions against UNITA', United Nations (Security Council) document S/2000/203, 10 March 2000.

3. Peace agreements

The 1990 settlement plan for Western Sahara – United Nations (Security Council) document S/21360, 18 June 1990.

The 1991 Bicesse agreement (*Acordos de Paz*) on Angola – United Nations (Security Council) document S/22609, 17 May 1991.

The General Peace Agreement 1992 [Mozambique] (Amsterdam: African-European Institute, 1992).

The 1993 Cotonou Agreement on Liberia – United Nations (Security Council) document S/26372, 9 August 1993.

The 1994 Lusaka Protocol on Angola – United Nations (Security Council) document S/1994/1441, 22 December 1994.

The United Nations and the Situation in Somalia, United Nations Department of Public Information Reference Paper, April 1995.

The Bangui Accords on the Central African Republic (1997) – United Nations (Security Council) document S/1997/561, Appendices III–VI, 4 July 1997.

The 1997 Houston Accord on Western Sahara – United Nations (Security Council) document S/1997/742, 24 September 1997.

The 1998 Organization of African Unity Framework Agreement on Ethiopia-Eritrea. Found at www.primenet.com~ephrem2/eritreanoau/oau_peace_proposal.html.

The Lusaka agreement on the Democratic Republic of Congo (1999) – United Nations (Security Council) document S/1999/815, 23 July 1999.

The Algiers peace plan for Ethiopia–Eritrea (2000) – http://news.bbc.co.uk/hi/english/worl/africa/newsid_787000/787602.stm.

4. International Court of Justice findings etc.

The 1966 International Court of Justice finding on the Ethiopian and Liberian claim of illegality of South African actions in Namibia. Found at http://www.icj-cij.org/icjwww/idecisions/isummaries/ilsaesasummary660718.htm.

The 1971 International Court of Justice Advisory Opinion on the 'Legal Consequences for States of the Continued Presence of South Africa in Namibia (South West Africa)'. Found at http://www.icj-cij.org/icjwww/idecisions/isummaries/inamsummary710261.htm.

The 1975 International Court of Justice Advisory Opinion on Western Sahara. Found at www:icj-cij/icjwww/idecisons/isummaries/isummary751016.htm.

The 1990 joint 'framework agreement' between Chad and Libya on the Aouzou Strip submitted to the International Court of Justice. Found at www.icj-cij.org/icjwww/icases/idt/idtframe/htm.

The 1994 International Court of Justice finding on the Chad–Libya dispute of the Aouzou Strip. Found at www.icj-cij/icjwww/icases/idt/idt-_ijudgments_19940203.pdf.

C. Press and other media

Africa Confidential Vols 38 (1997)–42 (2001).
BBC World Service (Africa) reports.
The Economist.
The Financial Times.
The Guardian.
The Sunday Herald.

D. Further reading

1. General

Adebajo, A. and Landsberg, C., 'Back to the future: UN peacekeeping in Africa', *International Peacekeeping* 7(4), 2000.

Akinrinade, S. and Sesay, A. (eds), *Africa in the Post-Cold War International System* (London: Pinter, 1998).

Ali, T.M. and Mathews, R.O., *Civil Wars in Africa* (Montreal: McGill-Queen's University Press, 1999).

Allan, J.H. and English, J.A., *Peacekeeping* (New York: Praeger, 1996).

Arend, A.C. and Beck, R.J., *International Law and the Use of Force: Beyond the UN Charter Paradigm* (London: Routledge, 1993).

Baehr, P.R. and Gordenker, L., *The United Nations in the 1990s* (New York: St Martin's Press, 1994).

Barnett, M., 'Partners in peace? The UN, regional organizations and peace-keeping', *Review of International Studies* 21(4), 1995.

Bayart, J.-F., Ellis, S.D.K. and Hibou, B., *The Criminalization of the State in Africa* (Oxford: James Currey, 1999).

Bennett, A.L., *International Organization: Principles and Issues* (5th edn, Englewood Cliffs, NJ: Prentice Hall, 1991).

Berdal, M., *Whither Peacekeeping?* (London: International Institute for Strategic Studies) Adelphi Paper 81, 1993.

Berdal, M., 'Fateful encounter: the United States and UN peacekeeping', *Survival* 36(1), 1994.

Beschloss, M., *Kennedy and Khrushchev: the Crisis Years, 1960–1963* (London: Faber & Faber, 1991).

Bourantonis, D. (ed.), *The United Nations in the New World Order: The World Organization at Fifty* (London: Macmillan, 1995).

Bowett, D., *United Nations Forces* (London: Stevens & Sons, 1964).

Boyd, A., *Fifteen Men on a Powder Keg: a History of the UN Security Council* (London: Methuen, 1971).

Calvocoressi, P., *World Politics, 1945–2000* (London: Longman, 2001).

Chabal, P., *Power in Africa: an Essay in Political Interpretation* (London: Macmillan, 1992).

Chabal, P., 'Prospects for democracy in Africa', *International Affairs* 74(2), 1998.

Chafer, A., 'French African policy: towards change', *African Affairs* 91(362), 1992.

Chazan, N., Mortimer, R., Lewis, P., Rothchild, D. and Stedman, S., *Politics and Society in Contemporary Africa* (3rd edn, London: Lynne Rienner, 1999).

Clapham, C., 'New Africa, new agendas', *International Affairs* 74(2), 1998.

Cohen, H.J., *Intervening in Africa: Superpower Peacemaking in a Troubled Continent* (London: Macmillan, 2000).

Coulson, J., *Soldiers of Diplomacy: the United Nations, Peacekeeping and the New World Order* (Toronto: University of Toronto Press, 1998).

Daniel, D.C.F. and Hayes, B.C. (eds), *Beyond Traditional Peacekeeping* (London: Macmillan, 1995).

Deng, F.M. and Zartman, I.W., Conflict Resolution in Africa (Washington, DC: Brookings Institute, 1991).

Diehl, P.F., *International Peacekeeping* (Baltimore: Johns Hopkins University Press, 1993).

Durch, W. (ed.), *UN Peacekeeping, American Politics and the Uncivil Wars of the 1990s* (New York: St Martin's Press, 1996).

Falk, R., 'The new interventionism and the Third World', *Current History*, November 1999.

Fetherston, A.B., *Towards a Theory of United Nations Peacekeeping* (London: Macmillan, 1994).

Furley, O. (ed.), *Conflict in Africa* (London: I.B. Tauris, 1995).

Goodrich, L.M., Hambro, E. and Simons, A., *Charter of the United Nations: Commentary and Documents* (New York: Columbia University Press, 1969).

Gordon, A.A. and Gordon, D.L., *Understanding Contemporary Africa* (3rd edn, London: Lynne Rienner, 2001).

Goulding, M., 'The United Nations and conflict in Africa since the cold war', *African Affairs* 98(39), 1999.

Halliday, F., *The Making of the Second Cold War* (London: Verso, 1987).

Harbeson, J.W. and Rothchild, D., *Africa in World Politics: Globalization and the Changing State System* (3rd edn, Boulder, CO: Westview, 1999).

Harbottle, M. and Rikhye, I.J., *The Thin Blue Line: International Peacekeeping and its Future* (New Haven, CT: Yale University Press, 1974).

Harrelson, M., *Fires all Around the Horizon: The UN's Uphill Battle to Preserve the Peace* (New York: Praeger, 1989).

Harris, G., *Recovering from Armed Conflicts in Developing Countries* (London: Routeledge, 1998).

Higgins, R., *United Nations Peacekeeping 1946–67: Documents and Commentary: Vol. 3. Africa* (Oxford: Oxford University Press, 1980).

Hill, S.M. and Malik, S.P., *Peacekeeping and the United Nations* (Aldershot: Dartmouth, 1996).

Hillen, J., *Blue Helmets: the Strategy of UN Military Operations* (London: Brassey's, 1998).

Horn, C. von, *Soldiering for Peace* (London: Cassell, 1966).

Howe, H.M., 'Private security firms and African stability: the case of Executive Outcomes', *Journal of Modern African Studies* 36(2), 1998.

Howe, H.M., Ambiguous Order: Military Forces in African States (London: Lynne Rienner, 2001).

Hughes, A. (ed.), *Marxism's Retreat from Africa* (London: Frank Cass, 1992).

James, A., 'The United Nations', in D. Armstrong and E. Goldstein (eds), *The End of the Cold War* (London: Frank Cass, 1990).

Jett, D.C., *Why Peacekeeping Fails* (London: Macmillan, 2000).

Joseph, R. (ed.), *State, Conflict and Democracy in Africa* (London: Lynne Rienner, 1999).

Keller, E.J. and Rothchild, D. (eds), *Africa in the New International Order: Rethinking State Sovereignty and Regional Security* (London: Lynne Rienner, 1996).

Khadiagala, G.M. and Lyons, T. (eds), *African Foreign Policies: Power and Process* (London: Lynne Rienner, 2001).

Kumar, K. (ed.), *Postconflict Elections, Democratization and International Assistance* (London: Lynne Rienner, 1998).

Lodge, T., *Towards an Understanding of Contemporary Armed Conflicts in Africa* (South African Institute of Strategic Studies Monograph – no date). Found at http://www.iss.co.za/Pubs/MONOGRAPHS/MG%2036/Armed%20conflict.html.

Luard, E., *A History of the United Nations: Vol. I. The Years of Western Domination, 1945– 55* (London: Macmillan, 1982).

McCoubrey, H. and White, N.D., *International Organizations and Civil Wars* (Aldershot: Dartmouth, 1995).

Mackinley, J., *The Peacekeepers* (London: Unwin Hyman, 1989).

MacKinnon, M.G., *The Evolution of US Peacekeeping Policy under Clinton* (London: Frank Cass, 1999).

MacQueen, N., *The United Nations since 1945: Peacekeeping and the Cold War* (London: Longman, 1999).

McWilliams, W.C and Piotrowski, H., *The World since 1945: A History of International Relations* (London: Lynne Rienner, 1997).

Malan, M., *Peacekeeping in Africa: Trends and Responses* (South African Institute of Strategic Studies Occasional Paper No. 31, June 1998). Found at http://www.iss.co.za/Pubs/PAPERS/31/Paper31.html.

May, R. and Cleaver, G., 'African peacekeeping: still dependent?', *International Peacekeeping* 4(2), 1997.

Mayall, J., 'Introduction', in J. Mayall (ed.), *The New Interventionism 1991–1994: United Nations Experience in Cambodia, Former Yugoslavia and Somalia* (Cambridge: Cambridge University Press, 1996).

Moxon-Browne, E. (ed.), *A Future for Peacekeeping?* (London: St Martin's Press, 1998).

Murphy, J.F., *The United Nations and the Control of International Violence* (Manchester: Manchester University Press, 1983).

O'Brien, K.A., 'Military-advisory groups and African security: privatized peace-keeping?', *International Peacekeeping* 5(3), 1998.

Olonisakin, F., '"Home-made" African peacekeeping initiatives', *Armed Forces and Society* 23(3), 1997.

Ottaway, M. (ed.), *Democracy in Africa: the Hard Road Ahead* (London: Lynne Rienner, 1997).

Ottaway, M., 'Post-imperial Africa at war', *Current History*, May 1999.

Prendergast, J., *Frontline Diplomacy: Humanitarian Aid and Conflict in Africa* (London: Lynne Rienner, 1996).

Pugh, M. (ed.), *The UN, Peace and Force* (London: Frank Cass, 1997).

Ratner, S.R., *The New UN Peacekeeping: Building Peace in Lands of Conflict after the Cold War* (London: Macmillan, 1995).

Rich, P.B. (ed.), *Warlords in International Relations* (London: Macmillan, 1999).

Rikyhe, I.J., *The Theory and Practice of Peacekeeping* (London: Hurst & Co., 1984).

Roberts, A., 'The crisis in UN peacekeeping', *Survival* 36(3), 1994.

Roberts, A., 'The United Nations: variants of collective security', in N. Woods (ed.), *Explaining International Relations since 1945* (Oxford: Oxford University Press, 1996).

Roberts, A. and Kingsbury, B. (eds), *United Nations, Divided World: the UN's Role in International Relations* (2nd edn, Oxford: Clarendon Press, 1993).

Roper, J., Nishihara, M. and Otunnu, O.A., *Keeping the Peace in the Post-Cold War Era: Strengthening Multilateral Peacekeeping* (Washington, DC: Brookings Institute, 1994).

Rosner, G., *The United Nations Emergency Force* (New York: Columbia University Press, 1963).

Shearer, D., 'Africa's great war', *Survival* 41(2), 1999.

Simons, G., *The United Nations: a Chronology of Conflict* (London: Macmillan, 1994).

Simons, G., *UN Malaise: Power, Problems and Realpolitik* (London: Macmillan, 1995).

Smock, D.R. (ed.), *Making War and Waging Peace: Foreign Intervention in Africa* (Washington, DC: US Institute of Peace Press, 1993).

Snow, D.M., *Uncivil Wars: International Security and the New Internal Conflicts* (London: Lynne Rienner, 1996).

Somerville, K., *Foreign Military Intervention in Africa* (London: Pinter, 1990).

Tasier, A. and Mathews, R.O. (eds), *Civil Wars in Africa: Roots and Resolution* (London: McGill-Queen's University Press, 1999).

Thakur, R.C. and Thayer, C.A. (eds), *A Crisis of Expectations: UN Peacekeeping in the 1990s* (Boulder, CO: Westview, 1995).

Thomas, C. and Wilkin, P. (eds), *Globalization, Human Security and the African Experience* (London: Lynne Rienner, 1999).

Thomson, A., *An Introduction to African Politics* (London: Routledge, 2000).

Thornberry, C., *Development of International Peacekeeping* (London: LSE, 1995).

Tordoff, W., *Government and Politics in Africa* (3rd edn, London: Macmillan, 1997).

Tow, W.T., *Subregional Security Co-operation in the Third World* (London: Lynne Rienner, 1990).

United Nations, *The Blue Helmets: A Review of UN Peacekeeping* (3rd edn, New York: United Nations, 1996).

Urquhart, B., *A Life in Peace and War* (London: Weidenfeld & Nicolson, 1987).

Villalón, L.A. and Huxtable, P.A. (eds), *The African State at a Critical Juncture: Between Disintegration and Reconfiguration* (London: Lynne Rienner, 1997).

Vogt, M.A., *Co-operation between the UN and the OAU in the Management of African Conflicts* (South African Institute of Strategic Studies Monograph – no date) Found at http://www.iss.co.za/Pubs/MONOGRAPHS/MG%2036/OAU.html.

Wainhouse, D.W., with Bohannon, F.P., Knott, J.E. and Simons, A.P., *International Peacekeeping at the Crossroads* (Baltimore: Johns Hopkins University Press, 1973).

Walker, M., *The Cold War and the Making of the Modern World* (London: Fourth Estate, 1993).

Walters, B.F. and Snyder, J., *Civil Wars, Insecurity and Intervention* (New York: Columbia University Press, 1999).

Warner, D., *New Dimensions of Peacekeeping* (The Hague: Nijhoff, 1995).

Weiss, T.G., *Collective Security in a Changing World* (London: Lynne Rienner, 1994).

Weiss, T.G. (ed.), *The United Nations and Civil Wars* (London: Lynne Rienner, 1995).

Weiss, T.G. and Blight, J.G. (eds), *The Suffering Grass: Superpowers and Regional Conflict in Southern Africa and the Caribbean* (London: Lynne Rienner, 1992).

White, N.D., 'The UN Charter and peacekeeping forces: constitutional issues', *International Peacekeeping* 3(4), 1996.

Whitman, J., *Peacekeeping and the UN Agencies* (London: Frank Cass, 1999).

Williams, M., *Civil–Military Relations and Peacekeeping* (Oxford: Oxford Universily Press, 1998).

Woodhouse, T. (ed.), *Peacekeeping and Peacemaking: Towards Effective Intervention in Post-Cold War Conflicts* (London: Macmillan, 1998).

Wright, S. (ed.), *African Foreign Policies* (Boulder, CO: Westview, 1998).

Yoder, A., *The Evolution of the United Nations System* (London: Taylor & Francis, 1997).

Zacarias, A. and Chissano, J.A., *The United Nations and International Peacekeeping* (London: I.B. Tauris, 1996).

Zacher, M.W., *International Conflict and Collective Security 1946–77: The United Nations, the Organization of American States, the Organization of African Unity and the Arab League* (New York: Praeger, 1979).

Zartman, W.I. (ed.), *Collapsed States: The Disintegration and Restoration of Legitimate Authority* (London: Lynne Rienner, 1995).

2. Central Africa

Adelman, H. and Suhrke, A. (eds), *The Path of Genocide: the Rwanda Crisis from Uganda to Zaïre* (Somerset, NJ: Transaction, 1999).

Bobb, F.S., *Historical Dictionary of Democratic Republic of Congo (Zaïre)* (2nd edn, Lanham, MD: Scarecrow Press, 1999).

Brabant, K. van, 'Security and protection in peacekeeping: a critical reading of the Belgian enquiry into events in Rwanda in 1994', *International Peacekeeping* 6(1), 1999.

Dayal, R., *Mission for Hammarskjöld: The Congo Crisis* (Oxford: Oxford University Press, 1976).

Destexhe, A. and Shawcross, W., *Rwanda and Genocide in the Twentieth Century* (London: Pluto, 1995).

Dorn, A.W. and Bell, D.J.H., 'Intelligence and peacekeeping: the UN operation in the Congo, 1960–64', *International Peacekeeping* 2(1), 1995.

Dorsey, L., *Historical Dictionary of Rwanda* (Metuchen, NJ: Scarecrow Press, 1994).

Durch, W., 'The UN operation in the Congo, 1960–1964', in W. Durch (ed.), *The Evolution of UN Peacekeeping: Case Studies and Comparative Analysis* (New York: St Martin's Press, 1993).

Evans, G., *Responding to Crises in the African Great Lakes* (Oxford: Oxford University Press, 1997).

Gibbs, D.N., 'Dag Hammarskjöld, the United Nations and the Congo crisis of 1960: a reinterpretation', *Journal of Modern African Studies* 31(2), 1993.

Gibbs, D.N., 'The United Nations, international peacekeeping and the question of "impartiality": revisiting the Congo operation of 1960', *Journal of Modern African Studies* 38(3), 2000.

Hoskyns, C., *The Congo since Independence, January 1960–December 1961* (Oxford: Oxford University Press, 1965).

International Crisis Group Report, *Africa's Seven-Nation War*, May 1999. Found at http://www.crisisweb.org/projectsshowreport.cfm?reportid=38.

International Crisis Group Report, *Scramble for the Congo: Anatomy of an Ugly War*, December 2000. Found at http://www.crisisweb.org/projectsshowreport.cfm?reportid=130.

James, A., *Britain and the Congo Crisis, 1960–63* (London: Macmillan, 1996).

Keane, F., *Season of Blood: a Rwandan Journey* (Harmondsworth: Penguin, 1996).

Klinghoffer, A.J., *The International Dimensions of Genocide in Rwanda* (London: Macmillan, 1998).

Kuperman, A.J., 'Rwanda in retrospect', *Foreign Affairs* 79(1), 2000.

Lefever, E.W., *Uncertain Mandate: the Politics of the UN Congo Operation* (Baltimore: Johns Hopkins University Press, 1967).

Lemarchand, R., 'Patterns of state collapse and reconstruction in central Africa: reflections on the crisis in the Great Lakes', *African Studies Quarterly* 1(3), 1997. Found at http://web.africa.ufl.edu/asq/v1/3/2.htm.

McNulty, M., 'A double discrediting: France, Rwanda and military intervention', *International Peacekeeping* 4(3), 1997.

MacQueen, N., 'National politics and the peacekeeping role: Ireland and the United Nations operations in the Congo', *War & Society* 6(1), 1988.

Manahl, C.R., 'From genocide to regional war: the breakdown of international order in central Africa', *African Studies Quarterly* 4(1), 2000. Found at http://web.africa.ufl.edu/asqv4i1a2.htm.

Martin, I., *After Genocide: the United Nations Human Rights Field Operation in Rwanda* (University of Essex Human Rights Centre, 1998).

Mbadinga, M.I., 'The Inter-African Mission to Monitor the Implementation of the Bangui Agreements (MISAB)', *International Peacekeeping* 8(4), 2001.

O'Ballance, E., *The Congo–Zaïre Experience, 1960–1998* (London: Macmillan, 1999).

O'Toole, T., *The Central African Republic: the Continent's Hidden Heart* (Boulder, CO: Westview, 1986).

Rikyhe, I.J., *Military Advisor to the Secretary-General: UN Peacekeeping and the Congo Crisis* (London: Hurst & Co., 1993).

Simmonds, R., *Legal Problems Arising from the United Nations Military Operations in the Congo* (The Hague: Nijhoff, 1968).

United Nations, *The United Nations and Rwanda 1993–96* (United Nations Blue Book Series vol. 10) (New York: United Nations, 1996).

Weissman, S.R., *American Foreign Policy in the Congo, 1960–64* (Ithaca, NY: Cornell University Press, 1974).

Whitman, J. and Pocock, D., *After Rwanda* (London: Macmillan, 1996).

Willum, B., 'Legitimizing inaction towards genocide in Rwanda: a matter of misperception?', *International Peacekeeping* 6(3), 1999.

3. Southern Africa

Alden, C., 'Swords into ploughshares? The United Nations and demilitarization in Mozambique', *International Peacekeeping* 2(2), 1995.

Alden, C., 'The issue of the military: UN demobilization, disarmament and reintegration in southern Africa', *International Peacekeeping* 3(2), 1996.

Alden, C. and Simpson, M., 'Mozambique: a delicate peace', *Journal of Modern African Studies* 31(1), 1993.

Berman, E., *Managing Arms in Peace Processes: Mozambique* (Geneva: United Nations Institute for Disarmament Research, 1996).

Brittain, V., *Death of Dignity* (London: Pluto, 1998).

Broadhead, S.H., *Historical Dictionary of Angola* (Metuchen, NJ: Scarecrow Press, 1992).

Chan, S. and Venâncio, M. (eds), *War and Peace in Mozambique* (London: St Martin's Press, 1998).

Ciment, J., *Angola and Mozambique: Postcolonial Wars in Southern Africa* (New York: Facts on File, 1997).

Cleaver, T. and Wallace, M., *Namibia* (London: Zed, 1990).

Cliffe, L., *The Transition to Independence in Namibia* (London: Lynne Reinner, 1994).

Cline, S.W., *Renamo* (Lanham, MD: University Press of America, 1989).

Finnegan, W., *A Complicated War: the Harrowing of Mozambique* (Berkeley: University of California Press, 1993).

Freeman, C.W., 'The Angola/Namibia Accords', *Foreign Affairs* 68(3), 1989.

Guimarões, F.A., *The Origins of the Angolan Civil War: International Politics and Domestic Political Conflict, 1961–76* (London: Macmillan, 1998).

Gutteridge, W. and Spence, J.E. (eds), *Violence in Southern Africa* (London: Frank Cass, 1997).

Hall, M. and Young, T., *Confronting Leviathan: Mozambique since Independence* (London: Hurst & Co., 1997).

Hamill, J., 'Angola's road from under the rubble', *The World Today* 50(1), January 1994.

Hanlon, J., *Mozambique* (London: Zed, 1990).

Hanlon, J., *Peace without Profit* (Oxford: James Currey, 1996).

Hart, K. and Lewis, J., *Why Angola Matters* (Oxford: James Currey, 1995).

Human Rights Watch, *Angola Unravels: the Rise and Fall of the Lusaka Peace Process* (New York: HRW, 1999).

Leys, C. and Saul, J. (eds), *Namibia's Liberation Struggle: the Two-Edged Sword* (Oxford: James Currey, 1995).

MacQueen, N., 'Peacekeeping by attrition: the UN in Angola', *Journal of Modern African Studies* 36(3), 1998.

Maier, K., *Angola: Promises and Lies* (London: Serif, 1995).

Malaquias, A., 'The UN in Mozambique and Angola: lessons learned', *International Peacekeeping* 3(2), 1996.

Minter, W., *Apartheid's Contras: an Enquiry into the Roots of War in Angola and Mozambique* (London: Zed, 1994).

O'Brien, K.A., 'Regional security in southern Africa: South Africa's national perspective', *International Peacekeeping* 3(3), 1996.

Pazzanita, A.G., 'The conflict resolution process in Angola', *Journal of Modern African Studies* 29(1), 1991.

Somerville, K., 'Angola: reaping a deadly harvest', *The World Today* 51(8–9), 1995.

Sparks, Donald L., *Namibia* (Boulder, CO: Westview, 1992).

Spikes, D., *Angola and the Politics of Intervention* (McFarland & Co., 1994).

Synge, R., *Mozambique: UN Peacekeeping in Action, 1992–94* (Washington, DC: US Institute of Peace, 1997).

Tvedten, I., *Angola: Struggle for Peace and Reconstruction* (Boulder, CO: Westview, 1997).

United Nations, *The United Nations and Mozambique 1992–95* (United Nations Blue Book vol. 5) (New York: United Nations, 1995).

Vines, A., *Renamo: From Terrorism to Democracy* (Oxford: James Currey, 1996).

Vines, A., 'Disarmament in Mozambique', *Journal of Southern African Studies* 24(1), 1998.

Young, T., 'The MNR/Renamo: external and internal dynamics', *African Affairs* 89(357), 1990.

4. West Africa

Clarke, M., 'Troubleshooting for peace', *The World Today*, 56(6), June 2000.

Dunn, D.E. and Holsoe, S.E., *Historical Dictionary of Liberia* (Metuchen, NJ: Scarecrow Press, 1986).

Ellis, S., *The Mask of Anarchy: the Destruction of Liberia and the Religious Dimension of an African Civil War* (London: Hurst & Co., 1999).

Francis, D.J., 'Mercenary intervention in Sierra Leone: providing national security or international exploitation?', *Third World Quarterly* 20(2), 1999.

Howe, H., 'Lessons of Liberia: ECOMOG and regional peacekeeping', *International Security* 21(3), 1996/97.

Huband, M., *The Liberian Civil War* (London: Frank Cass, 1998).

Hutchful, E., *The ECOMOG Experience with Peacekeeping in West Africa* (South African Institute of Strategic Studies Monograph – no date). Found at http://www.iss.co.za/Pubs/MONOGRAPHS/MG%2036/ECOMOG.html.

Mackinlay, J. and Alao, A., *Liberia 1994: ECOMOG and UNOMIL Response to a Complex Emergency* (United Nations University Occasional Paper Series 2 – no date). Found at http://www.unu.edu/unupress/ops.html.

Magyar, K.P. and Conteh-Morgan, E. (eds), *Peacekeeping in Africa: ECOMOG in Liberia* (London: St Martin's Press, 1998).

Mortimer, R.A., 'Senegal's role in ECOMOG: the Francophone dimension in the Liberian crisis', *Journal of Modern African Studies* 34(2), 1996.

Ofuatey-Kodjoe, W., 'Regional organizations and the resolution of internal conflict: the ECOWAS intervention in Liberia', *International Peacekeeping* 1(3), 1994.

Olonisakin, F., 'UN co-operation with regional organizations in peacekeeping: the experience of ECOMOG and UNOMIL in Liberia', *International Peacekeeping* 3(3), 1996.

Reno, W., *Corruption and State Politics in Sierra Leone* (Cambridge: Cambridge University Press, 1995).

Reno, W., 'Privatizing the war in Sierra Leone', *Current History*, May 1997.

Weller, M. and Lauterpacht, E. (eds), *Regional Peacekeeping and International Enforcement: the Liberian Crisis* (Cambridge: Cambridge University Press, 1994).

5. The Horn of Africa

Bolton, J.R., 'Wrong turn in Somalia', *Foreign Affairs* 73(1), 1994.

Clapham, C., 'Ethiopia and Eritrea: the politics of post-insurgency', in J. Wiseman (ed.), *Democracy and Political Change in Sub-Saharan Africa* (London: Routledge, 1995).

Clarke, W. and Herbst, J., 'Somalia and the future of humanitarian intervention', *Foreign Affairs* 75(2), 1996.

Clarke, W. and Herbst, J., *Learning from Somalia: the Lessons of Armed Humanitarian Intervention* (Boulder, CO: Westview, 1997).

Davidson, B., *The Black Man's Burden: Africa and the Curse of the Nation-State* (Oxford: James Currey, 1992).

Ehrlich, H., *Ethiopia and the Challenge of Independence* (London: Lynne Rienner, 1986).

Farrell, T., 'Sliding into war: the Somalia imbroglio and US army peace operations doctrine', *International Peacekeeping* 2(2), 1995.

Halim, O., 'A peacekeeper's perspective of peacebuilding in Somalia', *International Peacekeeping* 3(2), 1996.

Hirsch, J.L. and Oakley, R.B., *Somalia and Operation Restore Hope: Reflections on Peacemaking and Peacekeeping* (Washington, DC: United States Institute for Peace, 1995).

Iyob, R., 'Regional hegemony: domination and resistance in the Horn of Africa', *Journal of Modern African Studies* 31(2), 1993.

Katz, S., *Operation Restore Hope and UNOSOM* (Hong Kong: Concordia Publications, 1995).

Patman, R.G., *The Soviet Union on the Horn of Africa: the Diplomacy of Intervention and Disengagement* (Cambridge: Cambridge University Press, 1990).

Tripodi, P., *The Colonial Legacy in Somalia – Rome and Mogadishu: from Colonial Administration to Operation Restore Hope* (London: Macmillan, 1999).

6. Trans-Saharan Africa

Azevedo, Mario J. and Nnadozie, Emmanuel U., *Chad: a Nation in Search of its Future* (Boulder, CO: Westview, 1997).

Burr, J.M. and Collins, R.O., *Africa's Thirty Years War: Chad, Libya and the Sudan, 1963–1993* (Boulder, CO: Westview, 1999).

Durch, W., 'Building on sand: UN peacekeeping in the Western Sahara', *International Security* 17(4), 1993.

Foreign and Commonwealth Office (UK), Background Brief: *Western Sahara: Towards the Referendum* (March/November 1998). Found at http://files.fco.gov.uk/info/briefs/westsahara/pdf.

Gardner, A-M., 'Self-determination in the Western Sahara: legal opportunities and political roadblocks', *International Peacekeeping* 7(2), 2000.

May, R. and Massey, S., 'The OAU interventions in Chad: mission impossible or mission evaded?', *International Peacekeeping* 5(1), 1997.

Pazzanita, A.G., *Western Sahara* (Oxford: ABC-Clio, 1996).

Pazzanita, A.G. and Hodges, T., *Historical Dictionary of Western Sahara* (Metuchen, NJ: Scarecrow Press, 1994).

Wright, J., *Libya, Chad and the Central Sahara* (New York: Barnes and Noble, 1989).

Zoubir, Y.H. and Volman, D., *International Dimensions of the Western Sahara Conflict* (New York: Praeger, 1993).

INDEX